Disgrace

Disgrace
Global Reflections on Sexual Violence

Joanna Bourke

REAKTION BOOKS

Published by
Reaktion Books Ltd
Unit 32, Waterside
44–48 Wharf Road
London N1 7UX, UK

www.reaktionbooks.co.uk

First published 2022
Copyright © Joanna Bourke 2022

Printed and bound in Great Britain
by TJ Books Ltd, Padstow, Cornwall

A catalogue record for this book is available from the British Library

ISBN 978 1 78914 599 1

CONTENTS

Introduction:
The Global Crisis

Wanda Coleman is one of my favourite poets. In 1983, she published 'Rape', which centres on a survivor of multiple sexual assaults. The poem addresses a crucial problem in societal attitudes towards rape: *victims* rather than those who *perpetrate* such egregious harms are deemed disgraced. In Coleman's poem, a woman is raped. Her boyfriend blames her for not fighting to her death. He then rapes her as well. Two armed assailants who break into her home demand that she acts as if they are her lovers. They even kiss her goodbye afterwards, saying, 'when you get lonely, call.' The poem ends with the heartbreaking lines:

> she waited
> until she was sure they wouldn't
> come back and kill
>
> she picked up the phone
>
> and made the mistake of thinking the world
> would understand.[1]

Coleman's poem echoes the experience of many survivors of rape. It rekindled my frustration and fury. It is a disgrace that victim-survivors of sexual violence still discover that it is a 'mistake' to think the 'world/ would understand'. It is a disgrace that, globally, one in five girls and women will be sexually abused. It is a disgrace that some people minimize the sexual harms inflicted on people of different genders, sexualities, races, ethnicities, classes, castes, religions, ages, generations, body-types, (dis)-abilities and so on. Shame on boyfriends, lovers and husbands for their casual sense of sexual entitlement. Shame on law enforcement officers who routinely disbelieve people who report having been abused. Shame on powerful people who use their authority to inflict sexual harms. The way rape survivors are treated in 'justice' systems worldwide is a disgrace. It is a disgrace that, in 1970s Britain, only one in three cases of rape that were reported to the police ended in a conviction. Today it is fewer than one in twenty. After forty years of feminist activism and legal reform, this is a disgrace. It is also outrageous that we still haven't devised effective non-carceral ways of dealing with sexually violent people. The failure of so many 'good people' to listen to those who have suffered abuse is something to lament. So, too, is the reluctance of many of us to join movements aimed at eradicating sexual violence.

This book, therefore, is a call for action. Rape and sexual abuse are not inevitable in human cultures. Although the extent of sexual cruelty in the past and the present is often overwhelming, this form of violence can be contested and eradicated. As I hope to show, rape is culturally constructed. It varies widely across time and place. These differences provide clues for forging more harmonious, just and equal worlds. In this book, I will be delving into the factors that facilitate sexual abuse, including institutional, cultural and ideological ones, as well as exploring patterns and practices. But I will also be looking at the various meanings that victims and perpetrators give to violent acts. Only knowledge of the diverse forms of cruelty, coupled with respectful attention paid to the lives of other people, will edge us towards a feminism that can eradicate the scourge of sexual violence throughout the world.

Transnational Tensions

This can only ever be a partial account of sexual violence (both physical and psychological) around the world. After all, forms of abuse are legion. Nineteenth-century peasant women in Ireland who were abducted as a way of forcing marriage have little in common with date-raped high-school students in twentieth-century America. The girls and women violated by Red Army soldiers in 1945 cannot realistically be compared to Dalit women raped by men of 'higher' castes today. The options available to sexually abused women in the occupied territories of Palestine, Rio's favelas or Cité Soleil in Port-au-Prince (Haiti) are different to the protections open to German citizens. French wives who acquiesce to sexual intercourse with their husbands as the 'easier option' bear no resemblance to 'bush wives' in Sierra Leone. It matters if you are a boy, man or non-binary person. It makes a difference if the attacker wields a machete or raises the threat of an unsigned employment contract. There is always a risk of emphasizing similarities over differences. Any assumption that sexual violence is a universal experience insults the specificities of individual histories. Terror is always local.

Terror is also unevenly distributed. One major school of second-wave feminism that developed in the West between the 1970s and 1990s contended that 'rape is indigenous, not exceptional, to women's social condition';[2] 'every female from nine months to ninety years is at risk';[3] and rape is a form of 'global terrorism'.[4] The most influential exposition of this view is Susan Brownmiller's insistence, in her classic *Against Our Will* (1975), that 'From prehistoric times to the present . . . rape has played a critical function. It is nothing more or less than a conscious process of intimidation by which *all* men keep *all* women in a state of fear.'[5] Brownmiller's book changed the way people throughout the world think about sexual violence, but this generalization is not tenable. Some people are more vulnerable than others. Girls and women are at higher risk, as are people who are BME (Black and Minority Ethnic), refugees, asylum seekers, undocumented migrants, LGBTQ and non-binary, and those with physical or learning disabilities.

Crucially, these identities are not discrete badges of vulnerability. Their effects are cumulative. This is the point that Kimberlé Crenshaw made most forcefully in her influential article 'Demarginalizing the Intersection of Race and Sex' (1989).[6] Crenshaw is a legal academic and one of the founders of Critical Race Theory. Her essay introduced a crucial concept for this book: intersectionality. Crenshaw points out that the focus of white feminists in the West 'on the most privileged group members' (that is, other white women) 'marginalizes those who are multiply-burdened'. It is not enough to simply add Black women to 'an already established analytical structure'. This is because 'the intersectional experience is greater than the sum of racism and sexism,' so 'any analysis that does not take intersectionality into account cannot sufficiently address the particular manner in which Black women are subordinated.'[7] In other words, to understand sexual violence in global contexts, attention must be paid not simply to sex discrimination or racial prejudices, but to the *compounding* effects of race, sex, gender, class, caste, religion, (dis)ability, age, generation and so on.

It's Complicated

Crenshaw's intersectional approach requires us to be attentive to the complexities of people's lives. This complexity is one of many complicating features when exploring sexual violence transnationally. Many of these difficulties are discussed in later chapters but, in this introduction, I want to focus on four problems. These are: defining what is meant by 'sexual violence', quantifying it, ensuring that survivors are not only heard but also safeguarded, and paying attention to language.

The first question that must be addressed is: what is meant by 'sexual violence'? We can agree that it includes rape, sexual assault, sexualized abuse and non-consensual sexual activity. But what about consensual sexual activity between people under the legal age of consent? Or female genital cutting? Or the circumcision of boys? Sex trafficking is a form of violence, but is voluntary sex work by adult women worried about how to feed their children also abusive? When a male stranger brandishes a knife, it is easy to assume that a violent act is being perpetrated, but what about when a husband gradually wears down a 'no'? What if a girl or woman hastily marries a man solely in the hope that he will protect her from armed violence from other men?

For the purposes of this book, I will adopt the definition that I used in *Rape: A History from the 1860s to the Present* (2007). In that book, sexual violence was defined as any act identified as such by a participant, victim or third party (the suffering of infants, very young children and those with severe learning disabilities can only be described by third parties). So long as someone says that an act is 'rape', 'sexually abusive' or 'sexually violent', that claim is accepted. The definition also allows for multiple definitions of what is 'sexual'. After all, what is regarded as 'sexual' has changed over time and by geographical region. It allows for culturally distinctive and time-specific definitions of non-consensual, unwanted or coerced, all of which vary widely. The definition enables us to problematize and historicize every component of the complex interactions between sexed bodies.

This definition is also sceptical about legal dogmas. Throughout the world, the law is parsimonious about what it designates as violent sexual behaviour: it fears the criminalization of 'ordinary' male misbehaviour. Vast differences exist between jurisdictions. Is rape an act 'against the will' of a victim or 'without her consent'? Does it require emission of semen? Can a man be violated? The evidence required to prove that a rape occurs fluctuates. Is proof of violence necessary? Does there need to be a witness? Can the victim's sexual history be submitted as evidence? Punishments range from a verbal reprimand, fine or whipping to imprisonment, castration or death. Furthermore, laws around sexual violence can be dramatically transformed within short periods of time. For example, one day, marital rape is legally impossible; the next, it is a heinous crime. An adult who has sex with a person under the age of consent is, by law, engaging in a criminal act, but the legally binding age changes by a simple legislative vote, which can differ considerably when an offender steps across a state line. In the USA at the end of the nineteenth century, for example, the difference between the ages at which a girl's 'yes' was legally deemed to be meaningful could be as young as ten in Mississippi and Alabama and as high as eighteen in Kansas and Wyoming.[8] Throughout the globe, variations in the age of consent were linked to ideas about the onset of puberty, different expectations of childhood, shifting views about the innocence or culpability of infants and youth, and the strength of feminist and other activist movements.[9] As we will see in the next chapter, in many legal domains, victims of sexual violence are either voiceless or silenced.

If the first difficulty is definitional, the second is quantitative. There are a host of impediments to assessing the extent of sexual violence. We don't know how many people perpetrated rape; we don't know how many people they victimized. Various statistics will be mentioned in this book. They don't reflect the true incidence of crime; they don't even reflect police knowledge of crime.[10] The only thing that is certain is that the statistics are substantial underestimates.

Under-reportage is rife due to the reluctance of victims to publicly complain. When they do report abuse, their protests are routinely not 'heard', let alone responded to. The statistics are usually based on the willingness of survivors to speak out. Or they are extrapolated from the number of victims who seek medical treatment or legal redress. As a result, these victims are probably not 'typical' ones. Even when statistics are painstakingly collected, comparisons are often impossible. For example, sometimes the number of people convicted of sexual offences is recorded, while more recently there has been a shift to counting *victims* instead of perpetrators. Innumerable factors can cause sudden and dramatic shifts in reportage. Changes in the number of police available to apprehend criminals, the willingness of people to refer crimes to the police and the relative ranking of crimes (which means that some are pursued more vigorously than others) all distort the numbers.

The statistical inadequacies should not daunt us, however. Sexual violence is a problem; the fact that you are reading this book is proof that you are as determined as I am to understand and eradicate this scourge within our communities.

Safeguarding Survivors

The third challenge for a transnational history of sexual violence is ensuring that survivors are placed centre stage. For centuries, male-biased legal and penal systems have adjudicated on what is sexually abusive: these authoritative voices claim an exclusive privilege to dictate responses to it. Equally, the speech of perpetrators of rape has echoed loudly through time, insisting that they have a right to define what constitutes sexual aggression. The claims of abused people, by contrast, have been routinely questioned, if not disparaged, suppressed and silenced. Paying attention to their voices is important if we are to understand not only the struggles of people in the past but, in addition, the meaning of violence itself.

However, 'paying attention' to the voices of victims is complicated – and in very pragmatic as well as philosophical ways. There is the risk of stripping victims of agency. This point was made most eloquently by African and Caribbean literary scholar Régine Michelle Jean-Charles. She reminds scholars about the need to present 'African women as advocates, survivors, and agitators rather than only as victims and vessels of violation'. These women

> were not the passive female victims who had been subject to countless violations in 'Africa's World War'. These were not submissive receptacles of violence, left for dead on the side of the road. These were not brutalized and victimized women in need of a Western vehicle to make their voice audible.[11]

They are 'subjects rather than objects' in their own lives. There is a great deal at stake in her argument, including anti-racism, anti-colonialism and anti-essentialism.

Writing and speaking about sexual abuse can also reviolate people who have already suffered harms. One way this might happen is through the intrusion of voyeuristic impulses. Mary Hames, Director of the Gender Equity Unit at the University of the Western Cape, warned against this during a roundtable on violence against lesbians in South

Africa. After admitting that 'the most difficult thing to share in a public audience is your own life experience,' she cautioned participants to 'be careful, sensitive about issues like this, because I believe even [in] an audience like this, there's a lot of voyeurs just looking into other people's pain.'[12] The conveners of the workshop – Nonhlanhla Mkhize, Jane Bennett, Vasu Reddy and Relebohile Moletsane – concurred, adding that

> In a context in which part of homophobia involves the overt sexu-
> alisation of lesbians for heterosexual men's consumption, and one
> in which violence is both glorified and exoticised by vast swathes
> of media discourse (including music television, advertisements,
> 'soft' pornography, and sensation-driven daily newspapers), public
> discourse on the violence meted out against black lesbians runs
> the risk of being simply 'the scandal of the day'.

Victims' speech ends up eliciting 'voyeurism rather than outrage'.[13]

Such ethical fissures were starkly exposed in reportage of mass rapes during the conflict in the former Yugoslavia in the early 1990s. Hundreds of journalists and Western NGOs appeared, demanding to interview rape victims and even entering maternity hospitals in Sarajevo and Zagreb, seeking out women who had become pregnant through rape.[14] They rarely provided financial or psychological assistance to victims who shared their experiences. Some were remarkably lax in maintaining confidentiality, naming victims or publishing photographs of their homes. Others interviewed girls and women in front of their families or members of their community.[15] Was it any wonder that activists such as Jovanka Stojsavljevic fumed against the publication of articles and books containing 'gratuitous details of women's experiences of rape', stripping rape victims of their ability 'to voice their [own] trauma'?[16]

If one way to silence victim-survivors was by failing to respect either their privacy or their strategies for coping, another involved appropriating their trauma to serve an agenda not shared by the victims themselves. This was the problem identified by gender scholar Wendy Hesford in her critique of Catharine A. MacKinnon's often-quoted article 'Turning Rape into Pornography' (1993).[17] MacKinnon's article had been published in the American, liberal-feminist *Ms.* magazine and it situated mass rapes in Yugoslavia within a very North American discourse about pornography. MacKinnon claimed that pornography was both a 'motivator and instruction manual' for the rape atrocities in Yugoslavia.[18]

Hesford disagreed. She castigated MacKinnon for constructing 'a fairly simplistic cause-and-effect relationship between the consumption of pornography and the sexualisation of torture'.[19] Hesford maintained that MacKinnon not only 'reproduces a model of spectacular uniqueness and individuality that leads only to repeated trauma', but 'employs the particularities of rape warfare in Bosnia, as conveyed through anonymous women's testimonies, to support a "universal" claim about pornography'. In other words, rather than paying attention to the specificities of the atrocities in the former Yugoslavia, MacKinnon co-opted the testimonies of rape survivors in a way that 'privilege[s] the rhetorical gaze of North American feminism as beyond nation or nationalism'. In a trenchant statement, Hesford accused MacKinnon of being

> more interested in linking human rights violations (in this case, rape warfare) to her anti-pornography stance than she is in exploring these women's testimonials for what they say about the complexities of women's victimisation and agency and the politics of nationalism and transnational feminism.[20]

In this way, MacKinnon created a 'universalized misogyny (as pornography) at work worldwide, with no distinction among sites'.[21] What happened in Bosnia was rendered identical to what happens to women in brothels or pornographic film sets throughout the world. The specificities of the victims' lives were erased.

The appropriation of other people's trauma to serve the political interests of journalists and academic researchers is especially pertinent where there are vast disparities in power between the protagonists. In such contexts, are victim-survivors even *capable* of giving meaningful consent? Guitele J. Rahill, Manisha Joshi and Whitney Shadowens addressed this question during their research with victims of sexual violence in Haiti's Cité Soleil. The lack of privacy in this densely populated and extremely poor shanty town meant that both victims and their assailants were well known within their communities.[22] Survivors were therefore highly apprehensive about being seen talking to researchers. Might it result in further violence if perpetrators believed that the women were planning joint action against them?[23] Power differentials between rape victims and interviewers also intruded. These highly vulnerable women regarded the three researchers as 'authorities', which made informed consent impossible. Rahill, Joshi and Shadowens observed that victims of *kadejak* [rape] and their neighbors are often quick to provide consent before they fully understand the purpose of the proposed research or the benefits and risks associated with it. The victims are eager to tell their stories and when we are time-pressed and resource-limited, the temptation is to advance rapidly, especially since many of the victims have completed less than six years of formal education and reading the consent form aloud to each one individually is taxing.[24]

Destitute, semi-literate survivors of rape had already been stripped of human dignity; were academic researchers going to compound this by interviewing them for the purposes of academic research (and the rewards that accompany subsequent publication) without obtaining their meaningful consent as well?

Harm might not only be done to survivors. Publicly exposing sexual violence can also have devastating effects for others, especially when the perpetrators belong to the victims' own minoritized community. This was recognized by early researchers exploring sexual abuse within gay male communities. By revealing sexual abuse within this beleaguered community, researchers risked tarnishing *all* homosexuals as perverted. It was a problem that feminists and social workers faced when they began disseminating evidence that underaged, white, working-class girls in Rochdale in Greater Manchester were being 'groomed' for sex by 'Asian men'. Newspapers sensationalized the abuse, leading to the vilification of the South Asian community. These same newspapers routinely failed to identify other perpetrators of sexual violence as a problem of 'white Protestants', for example.

Exposés can cement damaging stereotypes, such as those concerning rapacious 'Black men'. Jean-Charles expresses this problem succinctly, complaining that Western commentators exploring the war in the Congo slipped 'too quickly' into 'a problematic Conradian landscape of primordial violence imaging the primitive "heart of darkness"'.[25] As we will see throughout this book, this naturalization of the violence of Black men is not uncommon. It was what infuriated Haitian researchers, who objected to being regularly contacted by American scholars and asked to comment on the way unbridled levels of sexual violence in Haiti were responsible for spreading HIV and AIDS. Such requests fuelled further racism against Haitian boys and men. It was no wonder they turned to the Haitian proverb *Rad sal, se nan fanmi yo lave yo* (Dirty laundry is done in the context of the family).[26]

The naturalization of colonialist views about 'violent Black men' can be illustrated by looking at international responses to what has become known as the New Delhi gang-rape case of 2012, when Jyoti Singh and her male friend were tortured; after being raped, Singh was killed. The incident resulted in massive protests within India and elsewhere in the world, leading to significant legal reforms. However, Indian feminists were dismayed by much of the commentary from the West. First, they noted that it exposed a colonialist mindset within First World feminism that disregarded the anti-rape activism conducted by Black men and women. Second, it revealed ignorance about the extent of the rape crisis in the West, projecting it instead onto 'darker continents'. These problems were bitterly lampooned by Nivedita Menon in a 2013 article published in *Kafila*. She was responding to the announcement that, 'in a bold move', a group of feminists at the Harvard University Women's Center had established a Policy Task Force to 'offer recommendations to India and other South Asian countries in the wake of the New Delhi gang rape and murder'. This was 'good news for embattled and weary Indian feminists', Menon sighed. She sarcastically exclaimed that, after

> All those endless submissions to the Verma Committee [to reform rape law in India] prepared and submitted, all those critiques of the Ordinance written and disseminated, all those street protests, all those meetings with students and the public, all those delegations to government officials, ministers . . . not to mention decades of efforts to amend the rape laws . . . it's a great relief that the Harvard Law School has stepped in to take this burden off our shoulders.

Menon satirically noted that it was

> so good to know that there are Harvard Professors to make all the 'bold moves' that Indian feminists have never made. Attack the impunity of security forces? Now that's a bold move indeed – would any of us shy Indian women be so bold as all that?[27]

The orientalizing of sexual violence is not unique to American feminists. In 2015, white biochemist Annette G. Beck-Sickinger of Leipzig University denied an internship to a male Indian student on the grounds that 'we hear a lot about the rape problem in India.' She contended that it was 'unbelievable that Indian society' was 'not able to solve this problem for many years now'.[28] Her statement ignored the fact that sexual violence has not been 'solved' in the West either. Indeed, India has a population of 1.2 billion and, in 2011, just over 24,000 rapes were reported. In contrast, the USA's population of 300 million saw around 83,400 rapes.[29] Suruchi Thapar-Björkert and Madina Tlostanova complained that

> Constructing Indian culture as the source of the problem also masks the problematic – within the Euro-American academy – notion of insufficient masculinity, which needs to restrain itself or be restrained (through non-entry into 'their' academy) as it poses a threat to white 'female students'.[30]

Blaming 'Indian men' also did not do justice to the fact that all over India, men were active in protesting against the rape. Thapar-Björkert and Tlostanova welcomed the interest being taken by feminists globally in their problem, but they warned that these gestures remained 'largely symbolic' if the Western sisterhood refused to acknowledge their complicity in imperialist domination and the reinstatement of colonial ways of thinking.[31]

These critiques of white feminists' complicity and active involvement in racist projects do not provide an excuse for failing to critique blind spots within certain Black feminist movements. One example is the unique response of Samburu women in Kenya to being cast out from their families and communities on account of having been raped by British soldiers. Rather than accepting their isolation, and therefore the inevitability of poverty, they joined forces and built a village called 'Umoja', which is Kiswahili for 'Unity'. No men are allowed into the village and when their sons reach the age of seventeen, they too have to leave. This radical project was the focus of a documentary directed by Elizabeth Tadic and called *Umoja: No Men Allowed*. Feminists like Kelly Ashew, however, have accused Umoja and the film of endorsing 'age-old stereotypes about African patriarchy, painting Samburu men in uniformly and exclusively negative strokes'. Rebecca Lolosoli, the driving force behind Umoja, was quoted as complaining that Samburu men spend their time 'just sleeping under the trees, from morning until evening, doing nothing'.[32] Ashew points out that the assumption that women do all the heavy labour is incorrect since male work roles are equally tough and include herding livestock across vast distances during the dry season. She notes that Tadic's critique is levelled at Samburu men rather than the British soldiers who were responsible for the rapes. As Ashew explained, 'We are inundated with media misrepresentations of and feminist attacks on traditional societies and how they reputedly disempower Third World women, who consequently require gender uplift by enlightened First World sisters.'[33] In other words, the film ignores fifty years of sexual abuse of Kenyan women by British soldiers stationed and training in the region and focuses instead on stereotypes about 'spear-wielding', Maa-speaking, male pastoral farmers.

Language

All these challenges draw attention to the need to be careful in the use of language. Mis-speak is often subtle: two examples are the use of terms such as 'marital rape' (which implies that wives are as prone to raping their husbands as the opposite) and 'hazing rites' (that is, 'rites of passage' or 'initiation ceremonies' in the military, which are as much about the sexualized abuse of power as about the rituals of 'male bonding').

The language used to refer to sexual violence is often problematic. In Kinyarwanda (a language spoken by around 10 million people in Rwanda, Democratic Republic of the Congo (DRC) and southern Uganda), for example, sexual violence is called *kubohoza*, meaning 'to help liberate'. The term had initially referred to the act of coercing Rwandans to change political parties but was applied during the 1994 genocide to the rape of girls and women.[34] In Rwandan courts, the Kinyarwanda phrase *gufata ku ngufu*, meaning 'to take by force, to rape', was obscure to most witnesses, who consequently preferred using indirect language and metaphors, including 'we got married.' As an unidentified Rwandan court interpreter explained,

> In my culture you don't say the words for genitalia. But in court you have to. It is a shock for interpreters, as well as witnesses. And graphic descriptions of rape are an ordeal for a woman. And the interpreter may be a woman too.[35]

Such sensibilities make it difficult for victims to access a language for reporting assault.

What this unnamed Rwandan court interpreter did not mention was the problem of translation itself: victims and those seeking to provide redress might literally be talking past each other. For example, in the rural Andean highlands, Quechua-speaking people speak about *burlaron de mi* (made fun of) or they allude to 'my condition as a woman' and 'my dignity', rather than referencing sexual violations directly.[36] In contrast to such euphemistic terms, Haitians were more likely to use highly emotive words. After the 2010 Haitian earthquake, between 50 and 72 per cent of women living in Cité Soleil were raped. The health care providers who ministered to them spoke French, a language that three-quarters of the residents did not understand. As a result, the French-speaking professionals would describe a rape victim as a *survivante* and the perpetrator as an *aggresseur*. But to Kreyòl speakers, these words were unfamiliar: they insisted that they were victims (not survivors) who had been *dappiyanmp* ('strangled like a chicken') or 'flooded' (gang-raped). Perpetrators boasted of *kraze matsis* ('crushing the womb') while victims used highly emotional terms such as *asasen*, *bandi* and *malfwa* ('evildoer') to describe their attackers. French and Kreyòl speakers struggled to understand what the other was saying.[37]

In Japan, many of the words used to describe sexualized violence are English ones, such as 'rape', 'survivor' and 'domestic violence' (often abbreviated to 'DV'). As two scholars explained, 'in having a foreign name, there is the implication that the phenomena of DV and rape are foreign imports.' This has 'enabled apologists to claim that DV is not a natural part of Japanese culture and has entered as a result of exposure to other cultures'.[38] When Japanese-language words are employed, they can sound dismissive. In newspapers and other media, the most common word for rape is *itazura*, which means 'cheekiness' or 'mischievous'. The word used to refer to sexual aggressors is *chikan*, or 'a stupid person, especially a man who plays corrupt and naughty tricks on a woman'. Chapter Seven starts by exploring the experiences of so-called 'comfort women' and the 'comfort station', or *ianfu* and *ianjo*, extremely problematic phrases in English as well as Japanese. The phrases come from *ian*, meaning love or sympathy.[39] In English, the Japanese *jūgunianfu* is translated into 'military comfort women'. But *jūgun* has the connotation of following (*jū*) the military (*gun*). In other words, it gives the impression of voluntary camp followers, such as nurses.[40] It was Radhika Coomaraswamy, Sri Lanka activist, UN Special Rapporteur on violence against women and author of a 1996 report about the system of 'comfort women', who insisted on employing the term 'military sex slavery'. She also argued that 'Comfort Stations' should be called 'rape centres'.[41] Crucially, this represents a change in language from 'prostitution' to 'sexual slavery' and 'crimes against humanity'.

Coomaraswamy's demand that researchers and other commentators on sexual violence reflect on language is apposite. In the context of this book, it requires careful thought about concepts such as 'victim' and 'survivor'. In recent decades, a certain strand of feminist thought prefers to call people who have suffered sexual violence 'survivors'. I am ambivalent about this survivor vocabulary. Labels such as 'survivor' serve to construct an identity based on a 'before' and an 'after' to attack, thus forcing victims of sexual violence to (yet again) define themselves in terms of the actions of their assailants. It is also a concept that comes freighted with American ideologies of autonomy, individual freedom and self-determination. The strict dichotomy between (good) 'survivors' and (bad) 'perpetrators' fails to recognize that many 'perpetrators' are 'survivors' of sexual abuse. This is not to deny that the 'victim' label can also bring its own dangers. It might not elicit sympathy but rather the opposite: 'victims' are feminized, upbraided for being morally weak and (according to a u.s. neoliberal discourse) blamed for making the 'wrong choice' or 'lifestyle mistake'.

In this book, then, I will be alternating between 'victim' and 'survivor' terms (and sometimes complicating matters further by referring to victim-survivors). I hope to apply these terms in context-specific ways. In other words, I will employ the terms most appropriate or familiar to the people I am writing about. Thus the word 'survivor' is often preferred by Americans, drawing as it does on discourses based on 'individual choice'. In contrast, the word 'victim' is commonly used by Haitians and other impoverished peoples. Indeed, the term 'survivor' can be wholly inappropriate in the context of women scraping a living in Cité Soleil or girls and women during civil wars. Many 'victims' do not survive, and many 'survivors' insist that they are 'victims', however much they repudiate the passivity that is often attached to that term. To be labelled a 'victim' is not to be stripped of agency. But it does draw attention to worlds of hurt.

As we will see throughout this book, intersectionality is crucial to thinking about sexual violence. It is impossible to understand oppression without it. An intersectional approach draws attention to the fact that gender violence may not be the most egregious harm done to women. It encourages a wariness of hegemonic theories, on the grounds that they risk exchanging diversity for specific, 'Western' paradigms.[42] The book also pays attention to shared vulnerability, interconnectivity and relationality. As opposed to assumptions of autonomy (a particularly

'Western' obsession, which often results in victim-blaming), this book affirms the dependency of each and every one of us on Others in our lives. We become human through relationships with other people, places and things. By embracing a transnational, intersectional approach, this book seeks to contribute to the political task of decolonizing knowledge.

ONE

Shame

There is a cop who is both prowler and father:
he comes from your block, grew up with your brothers,
had certain ideals . . .

And so, when the time comes, you have to turn to him,
the maniac's sperm still greasing your thighs,
your mind whirling like crazy. You have to confess
to him, you are guilty of the crime
of having been forced.

Adrienne Cecile Rich, 'Rape', 1972[1]

Rich's poem alludes to the difficulties in speaking about rape, including fears of not being believed or being judged blameworthy, as well as the sense of shame incumbent on the status of 'victim'. The poem draws attention to stigma attached to being a survivor of sexual abuse and having to 'confess' to being 'guilty of the crime of having been forced'. This chapter explores some of these processes. It shows that even the *fear* of being shamed damages structures of conviviality and other forms of human interaction. Actual and imagined abuse disrupts a person's sense of identity and the way they interact with others. I will also be contending that *perpetrators* of sexual violence are themselves suffering subjects. Indeed, because individual subjectivity is constituted through interactions with other people, acts of violence don't harm only those people who are attacked but those who perpetrate them. In other words, perpetrators are victims of their own monstrous agency. This does not in any way mitigate their responsibility, but it does contend that sexual violence is never exclusively private. As a social interaction, sexual harms destroy worlds of sociability.

#MeToo

Activist Tarana Burke recognized the power of shame when, as part of her work with 'Just Be' (an organization that she founded in 2003 to improve the health and well-being of Girls of Colour), a young girl made a 'confession'. She told Burke that she had been 'guilty of the crime/ of having been forced' to have sex by her mother's boyfriend. Initially, Burke was speechless – until she conceived of 'Me Too' as a way of expressing empathy. The slogan was to change the world.

Who was Tarana Burke? She was born in the Bronx in 1973 and grew up in a housing project. As a girl and a young woman, she was raped and sexually assaulted. With the support of her mother, Burke channelled her pain into community projects, including working with the 21st Century Youth Leadership Movement, the National Voting and Rights Museum and Institute, and the Black Belt Arts and Cultural Center in Selma, Alabama.[2]

Her political work helping girls, women of colour and 'queer folk' overcome their trauma and thrive in their everyday lives escalated after she coined 'MeToo' in 2006. 'MeToo' was a way of creating solidarity between girls and women of colour who had survived intimate partner violence and sexual abuse. Burke's chief message was that the pain and shame of sexual abuse need not consume the lives of survivors. 'All of us aren't walking around constantly in pain and suffering,' she insisted. Victimhood was not a permanent identity, indelibly staining a person's life. Rather, survivors could take comfort from the fact that 'they're not alone'. Burke observed that 'healing happens best in community, and there's a lot of community out there that's waiting and ready and available to support them.'[3]

Burke's civil rights activism and local leadership was well known within her community. But wider recognition came on 24 October 2017 when, in the aftermath of revelations about the persistent sexual abuse perpetrated by Hollywood mogul Harvey Weinstein, white actor Alyssa Milano tweeted #MeToo. She asked her followers to retweet the hashtag if any of them had also been sexually harassed or assaulted. Within a day, #MeToo had been retweeted 12 million times on Twitter and had generated 12 million posts or comments on Facebook.[4] Forty-five per cent of

Facebook users in America had friends who had posted or commented on #MeToo.[5]

Subsequently, #MeToo has trended in at least 85 countries, with the USA, Europe, Australia and India leading the way.[6] National translations quickly emerged. In France, the equivalent is #BalanceTonPorc ('expose your pig'), while in Latin America and Spain #YoTambien ('MeToo') has been adopted. In Spain, feminists and their supporters were outraged in April 2018 by the light sentences given out to the La Manada ('The Wolf Pack') assailants who had gang-raped a woman during the San Fermín festival in Pamplona. The court had judged the violence to be 'assault' rather than 'rape', which would have mandated harsher sentences. Activists popularized hashtags such as #Cuéntalo ('Talk about It'), #NoEsAbusoEsViolación ('It Is Not Abuse It Is Rape'), #YoSiTeCreo ('Yes, I Believe You'), #NoEstásSola ('You Are Not Alone') and #JusticiaPatriarcal ('Patriarchal Justice'). Chinese feminists were equally resourceful. Luo Xixi was the first person to disseminate #MeTooInChina. On the Chinese social media platform Weibo, she published a 3,000-word post describing being sexually harassed by Chen Xiaowu, her PhD supervisor and prominent professor at Beihang University in Beijing.[7] Although Chen Xiaowu was sacked from his job, the authorities were so alarmed by the millions of posts that Luo received documenting their own experiences of sexual abuse that they blocked the hashtag. To circumvent this censorship, the hashtag 'RiceBunny' (米兔 and pronounced 'mi tu') was born. Accompanied by emojis of rice bowls and bunny heads, RiceBunny announced that 'the only thing I want for the coming Lunar New Year is anti-sexual harassment rulings . . . You can take my plate away, but you cannot shut my mouth.'[8] In South Africa, the hashtag was an alarming #AmINext.

For Burke, the global furore created by #MeToo was gratifying – but also worrying. She had dedicated her adult life to improving the lives of girls and women who were 'multiply burdened' in terms of ethnicity, gender, sexuality and social status. Might #MeToo be co-opted by white, middle-class women and celebrities? Although Milano swiftly acknowledged Burke's role in creating #MeToo, the gender studies scholar Leigh Gilmore observed that 'the initial displacement' of Burke by Milano was 'a glaring reminder that for girls and women of color, the site of testimony is also a site of erasure'.[9] Some feminists of colour took this insight even further, issuing the hashtag #SolidarityIsForWhiteWomen. It was a reminder that gender biases are compounded by colour blindness.[10]

The #MeToo movement has been slow to acknowledge the aggravating effects of racism for girls and women of colour who have experienced sexual abuse. In North America, for example, racial conflict has tended to be written out of the history of white feminism. White feminists were thrilled when #MeToo revived interest in the history of women testifying publicly about being subjected to sexual abuse and harassment. Being reminded of feminist pioneers who spoke boldly and shamelessly about rape was empowering.

However, their histories typically began with the activism of 'second-wave' feminists in the 1970s. Iconic activists of that period include Robin Morgan, the author of *Sisterhood Is Powerful* (1970), and Florence Rush, who focused attention on child sexual abuse during her speech at the New York Radical Feminists' Rape Conference in April 1971. In 1975 alone, classics such as Susan Brownmiller's *Against Our Will* and Diana Russell's *The Politics of Rape* were published, drawing extensively on survivors' stories. These influential anti-rape activists were white and middle-class. So, too, were many of the activists attending 'Take Back the Night' events in the 1980s. Indeed, seeing white feminists parading through predominantly Black and Latino neighbourhoods remonstrating against 'rapists' distressed women of colour who were all too conscious of the history of white women making false accusations against their brothers, lovers, husbands and sons. Despite the occasional footnote to sexual violence perpetrated against Black women (one notable instance being Oprah Winfrey's mention of Recy Taylor's 1944 rape during her speech accepting the Golden Globe Cecil B. DeMille Award in 2018), the suffering and the activism of women of colour has been sidelined in mainstream American debates.

This has frustrated some Black activists. As long ago as 1975, Angela Davis observed that women of colour had long used the testimonials of rape survivors in their fight against both racism and sexism. Davis published an article in *Ms.* magazine entitled 'Joan Little: The Dialectics of Rape'. In it, she pointed out that many decades before white feminists began urging women to use their own experiences of sexual abuse to condemn rape cultures, Black women had been doing precisely that. Anti-slavery activists and civil rights protesters had always recognized that it was impossible to separate racial oppression from gendered exploitation. In a powerful statement, Davis contended that

> The rape of the black woman and its ideological justification are
> integrally linked to the portrayal of the black man as a bestial

rapist of white women – and, of course, the castration and lynching of black men on the basis of such accusations.

This has meant that any 'struggle against the sexual abuse of black women' requires activists to simultaneously 'struggle against the cruel manipulation of sexual accusations against black men'. For this reason, Black women 'have played a vanguard role, not only in the fight against rape, but also in the movement to end lynching'. The rape of Black women by white men and the denigration of Black men as rapists are the vicious, mutually reinforcing 'paraphernalia of racism'.[11]

Davis's arguments are powerful. While the history of anti-rape activism in the USA has been dominated by discourses privileging occidental feminism, its roots are based in the struggles of Black women for basic rights to life, liberty and respect. One of the earliest examples of women of colour publicly protesting against sexual abuse perpetrated by white men occurred during the Congressional hearings into the May 1866 race riots in Memphis, Tennessee. Five free Black women gave accounts of being raped by white men during the riots. These courageous women who refused to be shamed were Frances Thompson (a former enslaved person), Lucy Smith (a sixteen-year-old girl who was described as 'of modest demeanour and highly respectable in appearance'), Lucy Tibbs ('intelligent and well-appearing'), Rebecca Ann Bloom and Harriet Amor. For these women of colour, sexual violation was intimately related to racial abuse. The Congressional report accepted their characterizations. 'The mob' were 'breathing vengeance against the negroes and shooting them down like dogs', it reported, adding that 'when they found unprotected colored women they at once "conquered their prejudices" and proceeded to violate them under circumstances of the most licentious brutality.' For the victims, their white assailants' 'feelings of the most deadly hatred of the colored race' were inseparable from the 'brutal and revolting ravishings' of them as 'defenceless and terror-stricken' Black women.[12]

This inseparable relationship between racism and rapism has not diminished in the century and a half since the Memphis riots. It is a theme that continues to animate the activism of women like Burke in the USA and Marai Larasi in the UK. Larasi was the Executive Director of Imkaan, which is dedicated to preventing and responding to violence against Black and Minority Ethnic (BME) girls and women in Britain and globally. She calls for broader 'recognition that different women are subject to harm in different ways'. After all, she points out, 'Young

BME women being harassed on the streets of London are harassed as BME women – they're not black today and then women tomorrow.'[13]

Although explicitly drawing on the intersectional politics of Kimberlé Crenshaw, discussed in the introduction, these activists were very much aware of the longer history of Black feminist action against sexual abuse. The most notable was the Boston-based Combahee River Collective, a Black feminist lesbian group established in 1974. Their defining statement insisted on the need to oppose *all* forms of oppression. They declared themselves

> actively committed to struggling against racial, sexual, hetero-sexual, and class oppression, and see as our particular task the development of integrated analysis and practice based upon the fact that the major systems of oppression are interlocking. The synthesis of these oppressions creates the conditions of our lives. As Black women we see Black feminism as the logical political movement to combat the manifold and simultaneous oppressions that all women of color face.

Furthermore, they contended that

> We know that there is such a thing as racial-sexual oppression which is neither solely racial nor solely sexual, e.g., the history of rape of Black women by white men as a weapon of political repression.[14]

It was a political proclamation that acknowledged that interlocking oppressions are harmful, not because any of the vectors of difference are *in themselves* subordinate. They are *made* inferior by more privileged people. In other words, victims of sexual abuse are ashamed and humiliated by their own violation because *other* people fail to recognize the harm done to them. Central to the 'politics of recognition' is the idea that people are constituted *as individuals and as agents* through interactions with other people and institutions. In other words, the judgements and moral worlds of people we interact with define who we are, including how we see ourselves. They can also lead to lack of recognition or misrecognition. This is not an equal process: some have more power to bestow or block recognition.

This is why one of the main barriers to publicly testifying to being a survivor of sexual violence is shame. It is worth pausing, therefore, to ask: what is shame? Studies exploring the politics of recognition often reflect on shaming practices. Shame is understood as an inter-relational response to societal values and practices. It is not about what a person has done (which is more like guilt), but about how victim-survivors believe *other* people think about them. Accordingly, shame is not a personal attribute but a social emotion that is deeply rooted in historical time, geographical place and a myriad of institutional regimes of power. It is refracted through people's multiple, intersectional selves, including a wide range of genders, races, ethnicities, religions, sexual orientations, ages, generations and so on. Shame is inequitable in its distribution, since it is inculcated through relations of domination, including sexism, racism, colonialism and economic inequalities. As Ann Cvetkovich explains in *An Archive of Feelings* (2004), 'sexual trauma seeps into other categories' of oppression.[15] This is why shame is a particularly strong emotion among socially minoritized groups.[16] There is another way to express this: shame is part and parcel of the process of constituting women and other denigrated people *as* subordinate and disrespected. This is why a feminist politics of recognition must emphasize community, shared experiences and solidarity.

The emotion of shame has been tackled head-on by activists such as Burke, Milano and Larasi. They believe that digital feminism can provide survivors with support, in part by forging connections between people. Retweeting, clicking on 'favourites' and direct messaging are not only symbolic signs of support but active ways of showing solidarity and providing emotional sustenance. Such actions draw attention to the fact that victim-survivors are not alone. The abuse they suffer is systemic, not singular. Online feminism provides cultures of support.

In fact, in many regions of the world, online activism might be the *primary* way to draw attention to sexual abuse, achieve recognition and shrug off the mantle of shame. Although it is indisputable that there are vast inequalities in access to mobile phones, computers, the Internet and electricity to charge devices, online activism can be crucial in the anti-rape fight. This is Nanjala Nyabola's argument in her article 'Kenyan Feminisms in the Digital Age' (2018). She discusses the public neglect of victims of abuse in Kenya, especially in the more remote areas of the country where traditional media is lacking, journalists are largely male and formal justice systems are weak. In these contexts, hashtags are especially empowering. Social media gives Kenyan women permission to be 'combative, opinionated, and uncompromising as is needed in order to create a more just society'.[17] In communities where 'age is sacrosanct', it allows young women to gain a safe public platform. #JusticeforLiz, for example, was a campaign that emerged after the gang members who raped a young girl on 26 June 2013 were simply given community service. Without that hashtag, the case would not have incited community rage.[18] In other words, not only can hashtags reduce the feelings of shame experienced by victim-survivors but they can be a powerful weapon in shaming the authorities and public institutions into responding.

The Politics of Shame

Shame is a profoundly political emotion – and one that has far-reaching effects. The *fear* of the shame that sexual violation will bring on oneself and one's community *precedes* any actual attack. This makes sexual violence a particularly effective tool of oppression – it even terrorizes individuals, families and communities that have not directly been molested. This was well understood under slavery. The fear of sexual violence was pervasive among enslaved peoples, whether or not 'their master' was an abuser himself. The terror of being sold to an even more sadistic 'master' was an important factor in ensuring that enslaved women complied with abusive demands.[19]

In other circumstances, victims of sexual violence are *not even present* at the moment of violation. Children born of rape can be stamped with a shameful stigma, often for life. After the First World War, children born of rape by German troops in France were branded *enfants du barbare* ('children of the barbarians').[20] In 1915, one French commentator even suggested that sexual violation caused an 'indelible mark' to be 'imprinted on the feminine organism . . . the effects of which make themselves felt as long as the reproducing function exists'. In other words, the raped woman's 'internal, physiological environment' would be permanently altered by her experience of sexual violation: children born years later would possess the 'Teutonic heredity' of the rapist.[21] The shame of rape was passed along multiple generations.

More commonly, shame affected the victims themselves and children born as a direct consequence. During the Greek Civil War (1944–9) for example, an unknown number of female political prisoners were raped and forced to give birth. The children, a visible proof of their shame, created a huge sense of ambivalence, with mothers alternating between vehement rejection of them followed by guilt-infused paroxysms of affection.[22] After the conflict in Vietnam, infants born as the result of rape by American soldiers were called 'children of the dust'.[23] In Bosnia, they were 'children of hate';[24] in Kosovo, 'children of shame'.[25] Rwandan 'children of bad memories' were given names such as 'Little Killers', 'The Intruder' and 'I Am at a Loss'.[26] In Darfur, children born as a result of violence perpetrated by government-backed militias were *janjaweed* or 'devils on horseback'.[27] Infants born of rape in the Andean highlands of Peru might be named 'militia' or the soldiers' nickname *puma* ('cougar').[28]

Many foetuses conceived through rape or forced maternity were aborted in attempts to destroy evidence of humiliation. Those who survived to full term had a high death rate. For instance, an estimated 5,000 'bad memory babies' were killed or abandoned during the war (1991–2001) in the former Yugoslavia.[29] As one rape victim explained, 'When people kill your family and then rape you, you cannot love the child.'[30] Forced maternity could be a deliberate destructive strategy by perpetrators. This was seen during the 1971 mass rapes of Bengali women by members of the West Pakistani Army, the 1994 genocide in Rwanda and the 1992–5 conflict in Bosnia-Herzegovina and Croatia. After Bangladesh's (1971) war of independence from Pakistan, large numbers of women who had been impregnated as a result of rape were forced to have abortions to 'cleanse the nation'.[31] Ironically, although the mothers and infants bore the mark of shame, the infants suffered the added harm of being branded with the ethnic identity of the rapists. As one girl who had been conceived because of rape during the war in Bosnia and Herzegovina recognized, she was

> a target that everyone uses . . . The schoolmates exclude me on a regular basis, they shout at me 'you dirty Chetnik', they beat me up, throw stones . . . [cry] . . . They all attack me . . . Every day, over and over, I have to fight.[32]

The rejection of the offspring by their community – often on the grounds that the child was a member of the *paternal* ethnic group – meant that they lacked an identity and, in some places (including Croatia), could be refused citizenship.[33] A similar injury was inflicted on infants born of rape in the Andean highlands of Peru: by not being given a paternal last name, they were denied full membership of the community.[34] For infants, the impact of being rejected by their mothers and communities is similar to the harms all infants face when emotional attention and affection is missing: developmental difficulties are common.[35]

What could be done with infants born of rape? In Bosnia, Croatia and Rwanda, military conflicts killed so many citizens that governments refused to allow children born of rape to be adopted by foreigners. In the words of Aloisea Inyumba, Rwandan Minister of Women's Affairs, 'Adoption to the outside means you are looting an entire population. The solution has to be from inside Rwanda,'[36] even if such policies prolonged women's pain and potentially exacerbated the harm done to the children as well. As one commentator warned, 'housing the children of rape together in a separate institution . . . will mark them in the community and expose them to potential danger from other war victims sick with vengeance or grief.'[37] Post-conflict governments faced formidable challenges in minimizing the harms done to the children of rape victims. Rape, and the shame it produces for mothers and offspring, has been used as a major political weapon. Rape shame is an indication of the politics of sexuality and dignity. The political class has a major responsibility to protect victims from shame.

Medical Harms

For the immediate victims, sexual violence causes suffering for years or decades to come. The psychological harms are not only formidable but are themselves shameful. They include sleep disturbances, eating disorders, flashbacks, headaches, blackouts, difficulties walking and hyper-vigilance. Being present when others are assaulted conveys a powerful feeling of vulnerability; for many, it also incites guilt for having been spared.[38] The historically variable and culturally distinctive psychological harms are so important to any discussion of sexualized violence that I will be devoting an entire chapter to them later.

The difficulties that victims experience when speaking publicly about their ordeals are exacerbated by serious physical injuries, not only to their sexual organs but over their entire bodies. Victims are beaten, bitten and burned. They are attacked with fists and feet as well as penises. In armed conflicts, rape is frequently accompanied by other kinds of torture. Girls and women are penetrated with guns, machetes, bottles, rocks and sticks. Breasts are amputated; sexual organs mutilated. Foetuses are cut from the bellies of pregnant women. Infertility is a frequent consequence.

The shame of having contracted a sexually transmitted infection, sometimes a deadly one, is common. Sexual violence increases the risk of HIV infection because it reduces the ability of the girls or woman to negotiate the use of a condom. Penetrative rape is also more likely to result in vaginal tears, which can spread the virus. During the Rwandan genocide, up to 70 per cent of raped women contracted HIV[39] and some commentators estimate that 25,000 Rwandan girls and women were *deliberately* infected with HIV.[40]

When instruments are used to penetrate girls and women, victims are left with vesico-vaginal or recto-vaginal fistulas, leading to urine or stool incontinence, vaginal stenosis and destruction of the urethra.[41] This was the paramount concern of a sixteen-year-old girl who was raped by ten Revolutionary United Front (RUF) rebels in a forest near Koidu in the eastern province of Sierra Leone in January 1997. She regarded her prospects of a fulfilling sexual life in the future as having been destroyed. In her words,

> I can no longer control my bladder or bowels as I was torn below. We stayed in the bush until ECOMOG [the armed force established by the Economic Community of West African States] took over Koidu. When we came out of the bush, even adults would run away from me and refuse to eat with me because I smelled so badly.

An operation to repair the damage failed.[42] Her experience was not unique: in most cases, traumatic fistulae are incurable.[43] The victims' subsequent incapacity to do heavy work or bear children reduces their 'value' to their families and communities as well as rendering them unmarriageable and infertile.

Perpetrator Shame

Finally, perpetrators often feel shame for their actions. This chapter began with Tarana Burke's MeToo, which she started in 2006. Burke understood that the fight for a world free of sexual harassment and violence would require the political and emotional labour of boys and men. This is not only because people of *all* genders can be victims of abuse, but because acts of *inflicting* harm on others are damaging for aggressors. This is not to excuse or minimize the actions of perpetrators of sexual harms: their agency is fundamentally different to the agency of those they victimize. It is, however, to observe that their worlds of sociability are adversely affected by their harmful acts.

Perpetrators know that what they are doing is wrong and ultimately shameful. At one extreme, raping another person could trigger cosmic or divine retribution. This was the belief of a soldier who had served in the armed forces of the Congo. He commented that

> You go and see a woman in the forest . . . It is bad. The woman that you are raping is somebody's woman . . . Also, we saw in some areas that they put a band around the women's wrists. If another man takes her, he has to die.

He swore that he had personally witnessed the effect of such a curse. He told a story about a soldier who

> went into the forest where he met a woman and raped her. When he came back, water/liquid started to pour from his body . . .
> We took him to the hospital, there they asked him 'what, tell us, what is this, what did you do?' 'I went to the forest and I raped a woman'. Just when he said that he died. So[,] you see, rape is something bad. If you rape you will not live long in this world.[44]

More typically, the shame of having perpetrated rape induces a guilty silence. Aggressors often beg victims not to tell anyone; they find it almost impossible to talk about what they have done. This was what journalist Peter Landesman observed when speaking to men who had participated in the Rwandan genocide. One of his interviewees spoke in detail about killing a woman. However,

> when I asked Lucien if he'd raped the woman, he fell silent and fought back tears. Every prisoner I spoke with described explicitly whom he killed and how. Not a single one admitted to raping a Tutsi woman . . . These men could somehow justify to themselves having murdered but not raped.

Landesman noted that 'the weight of that level of confession was obviously too much to bear.' He concluded that 'if there could be any tangible proof that rape was considered the more shameful crime, it was this.'[45]

Prosecutors working for the International Criminal Tribunal for Rwanda made similar observations. In the words of one,

> If you interview a witness who is a Hutu from the attackers' side, he will not tell you anything [about rape]. He will not admit anything due to the sensitivity of the crime. No one wants to admit publicly.[46]

This shame was not only evident in the aftermath of armed conflict. Similar shame was attached to rapists in prisons, where *sexual* violence towards children or women is reviled. Rapists are goaded, called 'skinners' or 'scum' and risk being sexually assaulted themselves.[47]

Perpetrator shame is one reason why abusers seek solace in alcohol, drugs and other numbing substances. As one Muslim internee at Trnopolje internment camp (established by Bosnian Serb military and police authorities in northern Bosnia and Herzegovina) recalled:

> As a doctor I was considered an authority, even by the Serbs, and in the first days many Serbian soldiers came to see me in the camp. They wept, they came to cry their hearts out, and they asked for apaurin [a sedative]. 'What's going on here?' they kept asking.[48]

Drawing attention to the suffering experienced by perpetrators of sexual violence does not excuse, or even mitigate, atrocious behaviour. It is important to be wary of the trope of 'perpetrators as victims', especially as it appears in the brutalizing context of combat. An example can be seen in some analyses of the mass rapes carried out by Red Army soldiers as they moved through Germany at the end of the Second World War. In the 1990s, these rapes were co-opted by revisionist historians who were attempting to reposition the German people as victims of that war, as opposed to its major instigator. This criticism was thrown (unfairly) at feminist Helke Sander, who in 1992 produced a film about the rape of German women by Allied forces entitled *Befreier und Befreite: Krieg, Vergewaltigungen, Kinder* (Liberators Take Liberties: War, Rapes, Children). Sander was accused of transforming German women into victims of the war rather than active participants in the atrocities of Nazism. The mass rape of German women was translated into a story whereby Germans were violated by a brutal Soviet culture, effectively drawing attention away from the enthusiastic involvement of German women in National Socialism.[49]

The political sidelining of liability for atrocities is not the only function performed by the rhetoric of 'perpetrators are victims': it can help alleviate the guilty consciences of individual aggressors as well. For example, decades after the Second World War, Japanese soldier Kondō Hajime came forward to testify alongside women who had been forced into sexual slavery for the Japanese Imperial Army. Although his motivations were partly compassionate, he insisted on his own status as a victim of militarism. He attempted to explain that he and his fellow soldiers only acted as they did because of ruthless military training, a starvation diet and heartless senior officers who sent them into combat unprepared. Hajime admitted that 'we committed deeds that are inconceivable to perform as human beings' and that these memories of mass rapes 'cannot be erased, even when sixty years have passed'. However, he trenchantly reminded his listeners that 'our hearts have [also] been tormented . . . The victims have gone through a lot, but perpetrators have also suffered tremendously.'[50]

It was a refrain often heard during the Winter Soldiers' Investigation in early 1971 when 109 American veterans testified about war crimes that they had committed during the conflict in Vietnam. These GIs provided a formidable list of the reasons why they acted in atrocious ways, including racism, peer pressure, fear of being punished by their comrades or senior officers, environmental confusion, retaliation and revenge, lack of training, failures in military leadership and so on. There are two problems with these excuses for rape. First, they cannot explain the high levels of violence directed at their own comrades (after all, just under one-third of American women who served in Vietnam were raped by fellow service personnel).[51] Second, the list of 'stressors' is so long that sexual atrocities quickly became overdetermined. The veterans at the Winter Soldiers' Investigation repeatedly made claims such as 'I think it's an atrocity *on the part of the United States Army*' and 'don't ever let *your government* do this to *you*.' The true victims (the raped, tortured and killed) were effectively effaced; the 'real victims' were the grunts – victims of U.S. government policy. Finally, explaining the motives or pressures that may have led to the rapes does not exculpate the perpetrators. Rape is rape whatever the traumas of the rapist.

Even more worrying is that, in recent years, some men espousing the 'perpetrators as victims' rhetoric have turned to social media to reiterate their claims. This may be dubbed 'hashtag anti-feminism'. Men's rights groups routinely claim that *they* are the ones being oppressed in a society that valorizes women over men and is too 'politically correct' to doubt women's accusations of rape. 'Hashtag *anti*-feminism' has great potential for harm.

The Limits of Hashtag Feminism

All is not well with 'hashtag feminism' either. While acknowledging that one important way to alleviate victim-shame is by creating forums – including online ones – where people can share their experiences and, as Burke put it, take comfort from the fact that 'they're not alone,'[52] there are dangers. Empathy is a learned practice. As such, it raises six very different problems.

First, online feminism can privilege the individual over the systemically abused community. With the rise of young, highly paid, feminist 'influencers' on social media, competition rather than compassion is the norm. Stories of pain become 'branded' commodities, with 'survivors' vying for the highest number of 'likes'. Disclosing stories of sexual abuse can become a form of neoliberal self-fashioning rather than a feminist strategy for social transformation. The political becomes personal.

Second, it ignores the fact that empathy is neither a predictable, nor even a common, response to witnessing the pain of others. One study of 82 girls and women who shared their experiences of sexual abuse via #BeenRapedNeverReported found that nearly three-quarters had subsequently been trolled or received other negative responses to their posts.[53] Another study revealed the astonishing fact that Twitter users who shamed victims and blamed them for their own violation were more likely to be retweeted than those who tweeted victim-supportive messages.[54] Disturbingly, some feminists have turned to reverse-trolling. Acting as 'digilantes', they use digital technologies to punish boys and men who troll girls and women sharing their experiences of abuse or harassment online.[55]

Third, should we be worried about the potential isolation of social media activism? When MeToo was established by Tarana Burke, its purpose was to ensure that survivors knew that they were not alone: they belonged to a community that would – together – support healing and personal growth in the context of systemic oppressions. However, large swathes of the movement have taken an 'individualist turn'. 'Speaking out' has become a 'good in-and-of itself'. It risks making victims once again responsible for their own healing.

Sociologist Alison Phipps is particularly eloquent in her critique of the commodification of 'experience'. She argues that turning individual experiences into a form of 'capital' ends up 'both reflect[ing] and perpetuat[ing] the neoliberal invisibility of structural dynamics: it situates all experiences as equal, and in the process fortifies existing inequalities.'[56] She warns that the turn to experience tends to 'reify personal narratives as the origin of explanation', therefore 'dehistoricising it and essentialising identities'. If we take 'experience as our starting point . . . we lose a focus on the historical conditions that shape and produce it and risk shoring up rather than contesting ideological systems.'[57]

Fourth, it is important to return to questions of multiple, interlocking oppressions. Digital practices of 'calling out' sexual abusers might gratifyingly reverse 'due process' by giving weight to the testimony of survivors of sexual abuse, but it also has the potential to undermine alliances between anti-sexist and anti-racist activists. After all, the abusers of many Black and minoritized women are Black or minoritized men. This makes feminist scholar Ashwini Tambe anxious. In her article entitled 'Reckoning with the Silences of #MeToo' (2018), she observes that

> The primary instrument of redress in #MeToo is public shaming and criminalization of the perpetrator. This is already too familiar a problem for black men. We know the history of how black men have been lynched based on unfounded allegations that they sexually violated white women. We know how many black men are unjustly incarcerated. The dynamics of #MeToo, in which due process has been reversed – with accusers' works taken more seriously than those of the accused – is a familiar problem in black communities. Maybe some black women want no part in this dynamic.[58]

It is a point well made.

Fifth, hashtag feminism can encourage a false sense of community: because 'we' share the same hurts or harms, then 'we' can 'know' the Other person. This is always dangerous.

Finally, online activism requires 'off-line action'. This is Nyabola's point when writing about anti-rape initiatives in Kenya. She contends that 'without the off-line platforms, it is difficult to push through policy-level change.' The hashtag campaigns were successful because

> There were one or more activists or advocates in the background who went to the hospital to procure pictures, who met the victims at the airport and escorted them to a safe house, who made sure that the victim was available for court appearances.[59]

In other words, hashtag feminism depends on on-the-ground feminists like Tarana Burke and Marai Larasi, working with their own communities to eradicate the shame, humiliation and fear that many victims are made to feel.

Acknowledging the shame that victims of sexual abuse experience is important if we are to effectively counter it. However, there are problems. Ironically, by emphasizing the view that rape is worse than death, feminists could be making the shame worse. As Phipps points out, isn't there the risk of '*produc*[*ing*] the sexual difference we seek to eliminate?'[60] In other words, by drawing attention to the way sexual abuse shames victim-survivors, we risk reinscribing ideas of female humiliation and vulnerability. We contribute to shoring up notions of male power over girls, women and other minoritized groups. The shamed bodies and minds of victim survivors come freighted with ideas about dependency and lack of agency. As such, they can invite paternalistic responses. 'Victims' are weaker beings, requiring the 'protection' of men or more privileged women.

It is important to observe, therefore, that victim-survivors and their families have actively worked against shame and shaming practices. Girls and women are not inevitably rendered passive through shame; many babies born of rape are loved by their mothers;[61] and rape survivors in military contexts might respond to their violation not by shame but by taking up weapons to fight.[62] Survivors are not objects of pity. They are shameless.

This is why shame needs to be turned on its head: shame belongs to those who inflict, not experience, harms. The insights of Tarana Burke are astute: sharing one's experience of abuse with other like-minded girls, women and 'queer folk' can forge bonds of solidarity. If hashtag feminism is to mean anything, it is that 'we are not alone.' The shame-making world is not inevitable. It can be changed, in part because victim-survivors are not wholly constituted by violence. Shame *bears witness* to injustice and, like anger and contempt, can be employed in political ways. Surviving rape, instead of attracting shame, should generate praise for the victim. The victim has survived and gives a lesson in courage necessary for a rape-free society. Shame is a particularly powerful emotion because it exists in societal contexts that deny the pervasiveness of sexual harms. In other words, victim-survivors feel ashamed because the silence around victimization conveys the message that they are not like other, more 'normal', people. This feeling of invisibility makes them reluctant to speak about their experiences and more likely to assume that others hold them in lower regard because of their abuse. In contrast, publicizing the extent of sexual abuse in our societies conveys the message that victim-survivors are everywhere. It creates a visibility that makes the internalization of the values of harm-supporters less likely. 'To confess one's shame is to destroy it,' contends philosopher Amanda Holmes.[63] Indeed, publicly reclaiming shame turns it into the opposite. After all, shame varies according to its audience. A victim-survivor may feel ashamed to speak in a room full of harm-ignoring, violence-minimizing or rape-excusing people, but not in a room full of feminists, activists or angry survivors. This is where the future lies.

TWO

(In)Justice

'P. R.' was a typical, jeans-wearing eighteen-year-old student in southern Italy. She was learning to drive. On 12 July 1992, 45-year-old Carmine Cristiano, her driving instructor, drove her to a secluded pathway where he threw her to the ground and raped her. She eventually told her parents of her ordeal, who took her to the police. Cristiano admitted to sexual intercourse with P. R. but claimed it was consensual. After a trial and an appeal, he was convicted and sentenced to two years and ten months in prison.

However, in February 1999, the conviction was overturned by the Corte di Cassazione, Italy's highest court. The Cassazione was sceptical about the fact that the victim had not reported the rape immediately. Because P. R. had not sustained any serious injuries, they questioned whether she had actively attempted to fight him off. The Justices contended that it was 'illogical to suggest that a girl would submit passively to a rape, which is a grave assault on the person'.[1] In other words, rape was so damaging to female honour that any girl or woman would have vigorously fought off any assailant, even at the risk of severe injuries or death. Bizarrely, the Justices added that 'it is a fact of common experience' that 'it is impossible to take off jeans . . . without the active cooperation of the person who is wearing them.'[2] In effect, having sexual intercourse with a girl or woman wearing jeans must have been consensual because removing that item of clothing required the wearer's assistance. The case was a stark reminder that women are not equal to men in law. It also draws attention to the persistence of discredited myths about rape, such as the belief that victims are prone to lie, that they will immediately report being assaulted, and that they are prepared to fight to the death to protect their 'honour'.

The decision sparked outrage across the political spectrum. Leftist prime minister Massimo D'Alema expressed his solidarity with those protesting the decision.[3] It did not go unnoticed that only ten (around 2 per cent) of the 420 Justices of the Cassazione were female.[4] On the political right, Alessandra Mussolini, the deputy of the National Alliance Party and the granddaughter of the fascist dictator Benito Mussolini (who, in 1936, had been responsible for drafting Italy's rape law), was also incensed. She encouraged female parliamentarians, government officials and media personalities to wear blue jeans until the decision was reversed. Their slogan became 'Jeans: An Alibi for Rape'. The conservative newspaper *Il Messaggero* maintained that the decision 'read like an instruction manual for aspiring rapists'. It sarcastically quipped that 'designers for years have not known they had in hand the most extraordinary antirape invention in the century'; blue jeans were the ultimate 'chastity belt'.[5] Throughout the world, feminists, anti-rape activists, human rights advocates, legislators and other socially aware men and women expressed their support for the victim. They initiated 'International Jeans for Justice Day' to promote a fair and rape-free society. The 'blue jeans' defence was only decisively rejected in 2008 when the Cassazione adjudicated in a case involving the sexual assault of a sixteen-year-old girl by her mother's partner. The court decided that blue jeans 'cannot be compared to a chastity belt'.[6]

This chapter explores justice and injustice in rape cases globally. What ideological, institutional, political, legal and practical factors limit the ability of victims with regard to having their voices heard and their suffering recognized in society and law? Of course, the injustices experienced by victims of sexual abuse in Italy are specific to Italian history and culture, but some of the overarching themes and tensions can be seen elsewhere in the world. Nevertheless, it is important to recognize that although the *form* of the problem is remarkably similar globally, the *content* is often different. The rest of this chapter explores some of the similarities and differences in accessing justice. It also seeks to undercut explanations for injustice that are based on 'culture'. As we will see, this requires nuanced analysis. After all, the problems faced by victims of sexual abuse in achieving justice *are* due, at least in part, to 'cultural' factors, including a region's history, legal and societal institutions, belief systems (including religious ones) and established gender relations. The problem arises because blaming unjust legal decisions on 'culture' has too often been used to explain sexual violence in the non-Western world: *their* 'culture' treats victims poorly, has inadequate systems of justice and is profoundly patriarchal, while *our* 'culture' makes mistakes, sometimes fails to live up to its high standards of law or is moving towards more progressive views even if we have not arrived yet. This chapter attempts the difficult balance, therefore, between pointing out cultural similarities and not ignoring local peculiarities.

Rape Fictions in Italy

Before turning to this global context, let's explore in greater detail (in)-justices in the treatment of sexual abuse in Italian justice systems and responses to the problems that have emerged. Rape is a serious problem in Italy. In 2019, it was estimated that more than 26 per cent of Italian women aged between sixteen and seventy years have experienced sexual violence.[7] The law has struggled to deal adequately with the scale of the crisis. Prior to 1996, legal responses to rape had been based on a law written in 1936 under the direction of Mussolini. It distinguished between 'acts of lust' and 'carnal violence'. The first included forced sexual conduct without penetration of or by the genitalia of either the victim or the accused; the latter involved forced sexual conduct *with* penetration and was considered much more serious, warranting higher penalties for the accused.[8] The distinction had significant consequences for rape victims. Not only did it wrongly assume that penetrative sexual acts were more harmful than non-penetrative ones, it also required victims to describe in court every intimate aspect of the assault.[9] For many, this was too humiliating an ordeal.

The rise of 'second-wave' feminism from the 1970s onwards drew attention to multiple failures in Italian justice systems. For example, until recently, there was widespread public agreement that rape within marriage was an impossibility: Italian husbands assumed they had unlimited access to their wives' bodies. In addition, punishments meted out to convicted rapists were minimal. In 1988, a man who had raped his daughters over a period of ten years was only fined $8,000.[10] That same year, a woman who had been brutally raped by fifteen young men was forced to flee her home after being labelled a 'slut who asked for what she got'. Because she was 'pretty' and wore a mini-skirt, it was assumed that she was partly responsible for being gang-raped. Her mother complained that 'One thing is certain. No one will marry my daughter now.'[11]

As during the 'blue jeans' fiasco, Italian feminists and their supporters could be heard loudly denouncing such prejudices. In 1979, 300,000

Italians petitioned the legislature, calling for a major reform of Italy's rape laws. In particular, they called for the reclassification of sexual offences, removing them from the section of the penal code entitled 'Delitti contro la morale pubblica e il buon costume' (or 'crimes against public morality and decency') and placing them in the section on 'Delitti contro la persona' (or 'crimes against the person'), which also dealt with murder, assault, threats and slavery.[12] This would require a recognition that sexual abuses harmed individual victims, not societal morality: victims were subjects, not objects. The reforms were only passed in 1996, after seventeen years of activism.

Part of the resistance to reform was due to entrenched ideas about female 'honour'. As is the case in many parts of the world, chastity was viewed as an Italian woman's most prized possession. This can be illustrated by looking at the trial of 'T. M.', who was accused of sexually assaulting 'S. V.', his fourteen-year-old stepdaughter. According to Italian law, T. M. was allowed to appeal his jail sentence on the grounds of *minore gravità*, or 'limited seriousness' – a legal concept that has never been defined. In February 2006, the Cassazione argued that the defendant was entitled to have his sentence reduced on the grounds that the court of appeal had failed to take into account the fact that S. V. had been sexually active with other men.[13] In other words, the sexual assault of fourteen-year-old S. V. was of *minore gravità* because she was not a virgin. Only 'innocent' girls and women were entitled to full protection under the law. This judgement also exposed distorted understandings of what constituted consent. The Cassazione ruled that S. V. had consented to sexual activity because, when her stepfather made it clear that he was going to sexually assault her, she 'chose' oral sex.[14]

Such erroneous beliefs affect some groups in Italian society more than others. Distorted views about sexual abuse were augmented in the Italian empire by virulent racism and a sense of colonial entitlement. Both provoked high levels of violence. Italian imperialists insisted that the normal rules of 'civilized' sexual conduct need not be applied to 'native women'. Given the fact that even the 'normal' was fundamentally unjust to its female citizens, this had a devastating impact on girls, boys and women in Eritrea, Ethiopia and Somalia from the late nineteenth century.

A particularly powerful indictment of colonial rapaciousness can be found in Ennio Flaiano's *Tempo di uccidere* (A Time to Kill), first published in 1947. The novel, which drew on Flaiano's time as a lieutenant in Ethiopia during the Italian invasion of 1935–6, centred on the experiences of an Italian officer named Enrico Silvestri. Keen to get relief from a painful toothache, Silvestri took a shortcut through the Ethiopian landscape. After stumbling upon a young Ethiopian woman swimming naked in a pool, he raped her and, later that night, unintentionally killed her. Over her grave, Silvestri addresses his victim, reflecting that 'It didn't seem to me that a life met by mistake (by mistake) [*sic*] would be worth so much.' Her 'life seemed more than a tree's and less than a woman's. Let's not forget that you were naked and were part and parcel of the scenery.'[15] The implication was that 'native' women matured early, they were sexually voracious, and the usual ways of obtaining consent did not apply. The empire and 'Africa' were liminal places, whose female inhabitants were scarcely human – their lives were worth 'more than a tree's and less than a woman's'.

Similar hierarchies of humanity persist in modern Italy, where minoritized girls and women continue to be accorded less respect than others, rendering them at significantly higher risk of being sexually abused. Equally, however, *perpetrators* of sexual violence in Italy are also racialized. For example, Roma boys and men are often vilified as rapists. Periodic panics about the alleged rapacious propensities of male Roma – often called by the pejorative terms *nomadi* or *Zingari* – circulate in the media and are spread by right-wing politicians and public figures. These rumours are deliberate attempts to mobilize violence and justify aggressive 'expulsion' laws against Roma communities.[16] In 2009, Prime Minister Silvio Berlusconi inflamed anxieties about 'foreign' men by sending an extra 30,000 soldiers to patrol the streets of Rome, claiming that rapes would continue to occur until there were 'as many soldiers as pretty girls'.[17] As historian Shannon Woodcock explains, this is a classic example of 'white men protecting white women from "other" men'.[18] Race and gender are intertwined. Woodcock contends that the stereotyping of 'sexually aggressive (hyper-masculine)' Roma boys and men simultaneously 'creates the ideal Italian woman as the object of masculine sexual aggression'. In this way, 'only white women of Italian ethnicity . . . are reported and imagined as objects to be raped.'[19] This has two negative effects: not only are non-white girls and women rendered unrapable, but even those girls and women whom racists are claiming to protect from violence (that is, 'pure' Italian women) are rendered vulnerable to abuses by white Italian men.

Silencing and Shame

To what extent do the themes that emerged in the last section echo those elsewhere in the world? As we shall see in the rest of this chapter, similar problems with systems of justice are encountered, although refracted through the lens of specific historical, institutional and cultural contexts. The Italian examples of (in)justice mentioned at the start of this chapter involved cases that reached the courts. My aim was to draw attention to some of the barriers that Italian girls and women faced when they sought legal remedies. What these examples fail to acknowledge, however, is that some victims of sexual violence would never be given the opportunity to disclose their personal experiences: following their ordeal, they were murdered. Rape-murder is rare in civilian contexts, although *fear of* such a fate terrifies a significant proportion of rape victims. Even more uncommon, killers might not be the rapists themselves, but members of victims' own families. This was the fate of some victims belonging to Muslim communities in Palestine, for instance: losing their chastity was so great a dishonour for the victim and her family that she deserved to die.[20]

Although rare in peacetime, the risk of being killed increases exponentially in times of armed conflict or state terror. This will be explored in depth in a later chapter, so I will just mention two examples here. During the 1994 genocide in Rwanda, between 5 and 10 per cent of the country's population were murdered; while some survivors testified to mass rape, the dead had no voice.[21] Large numbers of rape-murders happen in punitive dictatorships. In Argentina between 1976 and 1983, defenders of the military junta kidnapped and tortured up to 30,000 men, women and children, believed by the kidnappers to be political dissidents. It is unknown how many were raped before their forced 'disappearance'.[22]

Even those who survived sexual violence might have myriad reasons for not speaking about their ordeal. Recalling the details could resurrect painful memories, increase anxiety and trigger psychological disorders. It might also compel victims to instigate damaging regimes of self-management, such as drinking to excess and avoiding socializing at night. As we saw in the last chapter, it is common to feel an overwhelming sense of shame, although the degree of shame varies by region, religion, class and caste. It is particularly high in cultures that value purity in girls and women. Conservative, religious communities in the USA, for example, have historically placed great emphasis on the 'purity' of their women-folk. In the words of C. R. Carroll, writing from a southern state in the

USA in 1836, a woman should be clothed in 'chastity, pure as the driven snow, enveloping her form, so that the imagination can find nought to blush at'. In effect, publicly testifying to having been sexually assaulted inflicts a damning stain on a previously chaste woman's character.[23]

Clearly, disclosing painful experiences is also socially risky. It exposes victims to the gaze and judgement of other people. And empathetic responses are never guaranteed. Indeed, sympathy is a minority response. Distorted ideas about honour help explain dismissive or negative responses. Rather than being conceived of as a crime, rape could be relegated to a private attack (a *delito privado* in Guatemalan jurisprudence) on an individual's honour.[24] As such, the family's 'good name' had to be assuaged. This could be done by fathers or husbands dropping charges against alleged rapists, irrespective of the wishes of victims. Or victims might find themselves cajoled into marrying their abusers. This was the case in the USA, Europe and many South American nations well into the twentieth century.[25] In one exploration of statutory rape in New York City between 1896 and 1946, one in every four prosecutions included attempts to resolve the case through marriage even though 15 per cent of these court cases involved force.[26]

Notions of honour and the need to be chaste serve as excuses for police to actively discourage certain victims from taking their complaints further. Sometimes, this is due to misplaced sympathy, as when police believe that any subsequent court case might be more traumatizing for victims than not doing anything. This desire to spare the victim was one reason why, prior to 1999, perpetrators of rape in Taiwan could only be tried in court if the victim was willing to make a formal complaint and testify. Paradoxically, this was intended to *protect* women since admitting publicly to having lost one's 'chastity' was believed to inflict more harm on the girl or woman than the rape itself.[27]

Similarly, seeking justice for the victim might be considered less important than the risk of humiliating entire communities for failing to protect 'their' women. In the aftermath of the Holocaust, Jewish women who had been sexually abused in labour and extermination camps by fellow prisoners such as *Kapos* or *Funktionshäftling* (or camp functionaries) struggled to speak about it.[28] Admitting to having been raped in the camps was akin to testifying to gendered suffering that could disrupt attempts to reconstitute communities. Societal censure was also high in the aftermath of political conflicts. As ethnographer Kimberley Theidon observed during her time spent with the peoples of the Peruvian highlands, 'if there is a theme capable of producing silence, it is rape.'[29] Guatemala's Commission for Historical Clarification found that the 'suffering of women, victims of rape, in the majority of cases is not known even to their families'. When the facts became known, 'it is silenced or negated', which 'demonstrates the feeling of extreme shame on the part of the survivors and their communities'.[30] The issue of shame went even deeper in the Taiwan Criminal Code, which decreed that rapists would be punished more harshly if their victims attempted, or succeeded in committing, suicide. In this way, the law bolstered the view that girls or women who lost their 'chastity' had suffered such an incredible blow that they would kill themselves.[31]

Unfortunately, victims often internalized such attitudes, agreeing that the social stigma of referring to their violation outweighed the harm caused by the actual violence. As one Cambodian survivor of the Khmer Rouge explained,

> If a person was raped, she could not tell anyone. It was a shameful story. The value of a woman depends at that place [with virginity]. Even after the Khmer Rouge was finished, how could we tell our stories? We did not want to be judged by others as bad women because the Khmer Rouge enemy had raped us.[32]

Some victims internalized the fear that they had not resisted sufficiently, making them complicit in their own 'pollution'. Journalist Miriam Lewin had been imprisoned in one of the most infamous detention centres in Argentina and, in the aftermath, struggled to talk about her experiences. She alluded to the 'probable [social] condemnation' that prisoners like her faced. What they had been forced to endure was almost impossible to register. She explained that she was tormented by an 'inner voice' that insisted that there *must have been* some way to exercise 'a choice . . . a margin for resistance or consent in that situation'. She feared that the 'system of terror' was so severe that people who had not experienced it 'would certainly classify us as prostitutes and traitors if we talked'.[33]

Social pressures might have severe economic outcomes. In regions such as South Sudan where marriages were accompanied by a 'bride price' (that is, the brides' families would be given money, animals or goods in exchange for the marriage of their daughters), wives deserted by their husbands on the grounds that they had been raped might be required to return what had been given on their marriage. They would also lose custody of their children.[34] This was the case in many rural regions in Europe, including Ireland, up until the middle of the twentieth century.[35]

The social and economic risks of disclosure were especially daunting in societies where virginity was revered. One Palestinian woman recalled that, after her rape, she 'became a second-hand used thing. Nobody would agree to marry a second-hand woman.' She maintained that her rapists 'knew that by opening me' (an Arabic expression denoting the first intercourse) she 'would have no choice but to marry him'.[36] A sixteen-year-old Palestinian girl who attempted suicide after being raped by her cousin had a similar complaint. She explained that

> Nothing is left for a girl after she loses her virginity. All I see is my deep need to die and to run away from my shame (*a'ar*). He forced himself on me, and I couldn't even stop him. Death is the best solution for dirty girls like me. How can I look in my father's eyes without feeling the shame and fear? . . . All I can do is kill myself and bury the secret of my rape with me.[37]

This is one reason hymen repair is in high demand, despite its risks. Hymenorrhaphy, or the artificial restoration of hymens, is aggressively marketed to women in the Middle East, China, Southeast Asia and South America, as well as to conservative Christian women in the USA and Muslim women in North America and Europe.[38]

Of course, this emphasis on chastity was a double-edged sword. For girls and women possessing the demeanour and status of respectability and innocence (both of which were implicitly tied to issues of class and caste), testifying to having been violated could elicit sympathetic responses and even the punishment of their abusers. This helps to explain the supportive response of one court in Maharashtra (India) in 2005, where a rapist was convicted on the sole testimony of the victim. Court officials accepted the victim's account of what had happened, on the grounds that her testimony was 'quite natural, inspires confidence and merits acceptance'. After all, they concluded, in 'the traditional non-permissive bounds of society of India', it was inconceivable that a 'girl or woman of self-respect or dignity would dispose falsely implicating somebody of ravishing her chastity'. The victim must have been speaking the truth since publicly admitting to having been sexually abused risked 'sacrificing her future prospect of getting married and having family life', as well as exposing her to being 'ostracized and outcast from the society she belongs to and also from her family circle'.[39] While such a judgement was beneficial to *this* rape victim, it also entrenched misogynist ideas about female sexuality and the 'stain' left by sexual violation. It meant that women who *failed* to convincingly perform the chastity trope (for reasons of caste or class, for example) could be denied legal protections.

Importantly, though, not all cultures view the stigma of rape in terms of the victims' loss of virginity. The Dao and Hmông peoples of north-west Vietnam, for example, do not regard virginity as a highly prized attribute and young people often engage in premarital sex. Nevertheless, rape is highly stigmatizing on the grounds that it is proof that the family and clan were incapable of safeguarding 'their' womenfolk. Rape inflicts a major 'loss of face' and often leads to parents and the wider family being barred from communal functions such as rituals associated with crops. Marriage possibilities for victims are dramatically lowered: indeed, a woman who would have normally expected a bride-wealth of 120 silver coins might be willing to marry for no bride-wealth. Marriage to her abuser might be the safer option.[40]

'Just Worlds'

The emphasis on the victims' characteristics, as opposed to the aggressors' actions, encourages survivors of abuse to blame themselves, and be blamed by others, for having been violated. The assumption, which is common in the West, that people live in a 'just world' bolsters assumptions that victims *must* have acted in ways that brought suffering on themselves. Even if victims could not point to any specific social or moral infraction, a wrong must have been committed that made them deserving of abuse.

The strongest version of this 'just world' theory can be found in the Buddhist belief in 'karma'. In Vietnam, *luật nhân quả* means that social events come freighted with moral meaning. Bad events are directly connected to a family's *phúc đức tại mẫu* or 'merit and virtue', which not only stem from a person's own actions but from their previous lives and those of their family and ancestors. Since mothers are responsible for monitoring the morals of their families, they are equally dishonoured if their daughters are sexually abused. As ethnographer Nguyen Thu Huong explains in relation to the Kinh ethnic group in northern Vietnam, a mother who conducts herself modestly will bring 'happiness and good fortune to her family; a bad woman brings only tragedy and despair'.[41]

In Nepal, too, belief that bad karma is brought by sins committed in a person's prior life as well as those committed by dead ancestors (the latter being *pariwaarko karma* or 'family's karma') make kin reluctant to seek help after violence because this divulges their negative karma to the wider community and will have damaging social effects.[42] Because women are considered to have been less pious than men in their previous lives, they are at greater risk of distressing incidents, such as sexual abuse.[43] Similarly, in Cambodia, deeds committed in a previous life (*kam*) make girls and women responsible for their own suffering.[44] Astrological incompatibilities (*kuu kam*) between husbands and wives are believed to result in sexual and domestic violence, but it is the wife who is chided for not taking account of such incompatibilities prior to marriage.[45] Still other Cambodian girls and women are believed to 'invite' rapacious sex by bearing a mole or 'shy' birthmark on their vulva; they are truly 'women of misfortune'.[46]

The (in)justices of some spiritual beliefs can be illustrated further by turning to Cambodia, which has the highest incidence of sexual violence in the Asia-Pacific world (one in five men admit to raping a girl or woman).[47] Local explanations for such high levels include reference to a 'blighted endowment' or 'bad building', due to deeds committed in a previous life.[48] The risk of becoming a *perpetrator* is also destiny. If the parents of male infants who were wrapped in the chorio-amniotic membrane (caul) at birth fail to make an offering to the spiritual 'master-teacher of the caul cord' (*kruu samnom Sanvaa*), the boy might become sexually violent in adulthood.[49] Another 'harbinger of violence' was a birthmark on the tongue or penis – known as *pracruy* – which would manifest itself in later life as ruthlessly trapping women 'like elephant hunters lassoing their prey'.[50]

Spiritual beliefs clearly affect how victims respond to harm. The 'Buddhist path to liberation' in Japan mandates that victims exhibit endurance (*gamen*) and resignation.[51] This is particularly strong if their abuser is a person of higher social status and therefore commands deference.[52] When she interviewed Chinese victims of rape, Tsun-Yin Luo observed that forgiveness rather than legal or other forms of reprisal was given the highest priority; this was because victims were seeking to avoid a 'karmic vicious cycle'.[53] A similar response was found by researchers working with Muslim refugees. Although victims reported high levels of personal shame, they were unwilling to complain about abuse because to object to what 'God had written for you' was considered blasphemous.[54]

Protectors as Perpetrators

Risks emanating from spiritual entities in the *Other* World are compounded by those arising in *this* one. Reporting abuse to the authorities brings its own dangers. Retaliation by perpetrators or their supporters is a real threat. The short sentences given to sexual assailants who confessed in traditional Rwandan *gacaca* courts after the rapacious genocide of 1994 were an important reason why many victims were afraid to pursue justice.[55] In conservative, Islamic societies like Pakistan and Darfur (in western Sudan), reporting rape is especially hazardous: victims could even be charged with *zena* (that is, having sex outside of marriage) and subjected to penalties such as public whippings or imprisonment.[56]

Other practical problems include the fact that, throughout the world, sexual predators are respected community leaders, the police or governmental officials. Sexual abusers are often extremely powerful men. In the USA, he might even be the man who held the highest political office. They are often law enforcement officers. Although it is frequently said that poorly trained, under-resourced and corrupt or 'clientist' law enforcement agents in poorer countries are particularly prone to use their positions of power within communities to sexually abuse their residents, this should not blind us to the high levels of abuse committed by police and prison guards in the West. After all, European police forces have a poor record of sexual abuse. During the 1992–5 war in Bosnia, for example, the civilian police were subject to military authorities, which helps to explain their prominent role in the operation of rape camps.[57] The more vulnerable the population (for example, refugees, asylum seekers and undocumented migrants), the greater the likelihood that they will be exploited by those who are supposed to protect them. In one study of refugees and other undocumented migrants entering Belgium and the Netherlands in the 2010s, one-fifth of the perpetrators of sexual abuse were reception centre staff, police, lawyers and security guards.[58]

The role of officials in perpetrating abuse can be illustrated by looking at the geopolitical South. In India, the high-profile, brutal rapes of Mathura (1972), Rameeza Bee (1978), Maya Tyagi (1980) and Suman Rani (1984) were all committed by policemen. Civil wars, such as the one in El Salvador between 1979 and 1992, routinely see governmental and police authorities committing acts of sexual violence.[59] Chile's National Commission on Political Imprisonment and Torture Report (the Valech report), which recorded abuses carried out between 1973 and 1990 by officials of Augusto Pinochet's military dictatorship, found that sexual torture was common in nearly all police detention centres.[60] Rapacious behaviour by the police and prison staff is also documented in politically volatile nations such as the Philippines, South Africa, Kenya, Namibia and Rwanda.[61] When Rwandan mayor Jean-Paul Akayesu was convicted of the mass rape and murder of Tutsi women, it was found that the atrocities had occurred on mayoral premises. The Nigeria Police Force (with its colonial history of protecting British as opposed to Nigerian interests) was often accused of using rape or the threat of rape to extort money from girls and women stopped at checkpoints.[62] One policeman openly boasted that this was one of the 'fringe benefits' of the job.[63]

So-called 'peacekeeping' soldiers of the United Nations could also be sexually threatening, as Haitian women discovered in the aftermath of the 2010 earthquake. One-third of Haitian woman were subjected to sexual or physical violence that year and a large proportion named the perpetrators as the peacekeepers.[64] In the words of a Haitian woman in the 1990s who witnessed another woman being raped by two uniformed policemen, 'I did not report what happened to the police: what would have been the use? They were the ones responsible.'[65]

The police and military in South Africa are notorious for sexual aggression. An identical statement can be made about U.S. police and military, but the *context* within which these authorities have committed abuses is very different, which is why I focus on South Africa here. During apartheid, which lasted until 1994, the South African Police and the South African Defence Force routinely detained people without due cause. Indeed, they were explicitly permitted to do so under Section 29 of the 1982 Internal Security Act. Over 80 per cent of detainees reported being tortured, including having electric shocks to their nipples or genitals.[66] As Heather Reganass, the Director of South Africa's National Institute for Crime Prevention and Rehabilitation of Offenders, recalled, 'no black woman would go to a police station.' During apartheid, 'just to be seen near a police station might mean you were perceived as an informer, your home would be burnt down and you would be killed.'[67] In the face of a policing crisis in the late 1980s and early 1990s, 'Kitskonstables' or 'instant' police constables were enrolled into the police force, often being recruited from vigilante groups. After only a few weeks' training, they were sent to control crime in the townships and other predominantly Black neighbourhoods. Very quickly, they gained a reputation for raping vulnerable girls and women.[68] Male members of the anti-apartheid African National

Congress (ANC) also raped their female colleagues, who were reluctant to officially complain out of loyalty to the struggle.[69] Given that only one in four hundred rapes that were reported to the South African Police in the post-apartheid period ended in a conviction, the risks of reporting abuse were considerably greater than the likelihood of justice.[70]

The difficulties experienced by South African women in having their abuse taken seriously were exacerbated when the authorities were not simply members of the police or army, but men of high political status. This was starkly revealed during what has become known as the 'Zuma Affair'. In November 2005, the then-Deputy President Jacob Zuma was accused of raping 31-year-old Fezekile Ntsukela Kuzwayo, nicknamed 'Khwezi' ('Star'). He claimed that the sex was consensual. The trial turned into an ordeal for Khwezi. She was castigated for having worn a Kanga (colourful wrap) without underwear. When it was revealed that she had been raped three times when she was a child, she was told that she ought to have 'developed ways of resisting'. Bizarrely, Zuma himself used the 'culture defence', maintaining that, for Zulu men, 'leaving a woman in that state [of sexual arousal] was the worst thing a man could do . . . She could even have you arrested and charged with rape.'[71] Zuma was acquitted, to the glee of thousands of his supporters. Outside the courtroom, supporters brandished signs with words like 'Burn the Bitch' as Zuma performed the liberation song 'Umshini Wami' ('My Machine Gun'). He went on to become President of the African National Congress and then of South Africa.

In all these examples, men in authority personally perpetrated acts of sexual abuse. But there is another troubling aspect to the protector-as-perpetrator dynamic. Irrespective of the identity of the aggressors, reporting sexual assault to the authorities might have the undesirable effect of increasing the presence of police in the community. As mentioned at the beginning of this chapter in relation to the Roma people in Italy, immigrant groups can be in a particularly precarious position since reporting inter-group abuses has often elicited anti-immigrant sentiments. Similarly, women living in the favelas of Brazil might understandably avoid reporting infractions to the police, preferring instead to enlist the help of local gangs.[72] In Northern Ireland during 'the Troubles', being seen talking to the police was extremely unwise, and it was simply not an option for Palestinian women in the occupied territories to seek help from the Israeli police.[73] Even in communities where relations between the police and locals were relatively good, high levels of distrust towards the authorities meant that many victims refused to involve them. A Canadian study in 1999 interviewed 391 victims of sexual assaults who had not reported their assault. They found that just under half did not want the police involved; one-third did not believe that the police could do anything; and nearly one-fifth did not think the police would help even if approached.[74]

The fact that the same authorities who were tasked to protect people from harm were perpetrators of such harms should not surprise us. Many police hold inherently violent attitudes to sexuality.[75] They have very different ideas of what constitutes force or violence. Being accustomed to weapons, they are less intimidated by them. In addition, the police and other authorities share misogynistic prejudices held by the wider population. They probably adhere to even *more* pro-rape attitudes. As one study into the attitudes of police in New Zealand concluded, 'their investigation of rape complainants occurs in an organizational context characterised by excessive adherence to masculinist values'.[76]

One study in the 2010s of high-ranking police officers in Delhi found that 90 per cent excused rape on the grounds that the female victims had been in a public place alone, were dressed inappropriately or were in some other ways deserving of assault.[77] In 2002, the Delhi Police Commissioner R. G. Gupta even contended that crimes against women could be halved if women were 'careful in the way they dress, if they know their limits and if they do not exercise unsafe behavior'.[78] Yet again, victims are blamed for their own violation.

Medical Jurisprudence

In their fight for justice, victim-blaming attitudes are formidable hurdles that victims of sexual abuse must overcome. Law and public opinion continue to give moral weight to the victim's chastity, as well as her character and comportment. Instead of focusing on the behaviour of the accused, questions are asked about the accuser. Why did *she* act in particular ways? Why didn't *she* do this or that? Any action that the victim failed to take is seen as bestowing responsibility. Their bodies are expected to yield up unquestioned truth. The victim's every movement is expected to conform to a pre-established rape script, which (until recently) has been written by men who failed to appreciate the gravity of sexual assault, the humiliation (and often pain) of intimate medical examinations[79] and the diverse ways victims respond to rape.

Historically, some of the most hostile of these men were specialists in medical jurisprudence.[80] In 1815, for example, Onesiphorus W. Bartley's widely read *A Treatise on Forensic Medicine; or Medical Jurisprudence* observed that conception required a woman's orgasm. He argued that conception

> must depend on the exciting passion that predominates; to this
> effect, the *æstrum/veneris* must be excited to such a degree as
> to produce that mutual *orgasm* which is essentially necessary to
> impregnation; if any desponding or depressing passion presides,
> this will not be accomplished.

Since (he believed) female orgasm is impossible in rape, pregnancy is proof that she must have been under the 'cheering influence' of an 'exciting passion'.[81] Criminal trials could be delayed for a few months to see if the victim became pregnant; if she did, consent could be assumed.

Such views have not disappeared entirely. As late as August 2012, for instance, Todd Akin (U.S. Republican Representative for Missouri) insisted that pregnancy as a result of rape was 'really rare'. He claimed that 'If it's a legitimate rape [*sic*], the female body has ways of trying to shut the whole thing down.'[82] During debates in June 2013 over whether rape victims should be excluded from a bill that would ban abortion after twenty weeks of pregnancy, Republican Representative Trent Franks (Arizona) repeated the view that the number of pregnancies as a result of rape was very low.[83] Tea Party maverick Sharron Angle even advised women who became pregnant as a result of rape or incest to make 'a lemon situation into lemonade'.[84] In fact, some medical evidence suggests that rape victims are slightly *more* likely to become pregnant than women who have consensual sex.[85]

That such views can still be peddled in the twenty-first century is remarkable. In contrast, nineteenth- and early twentieth-century jurisprudence textbooks were full of such myths. The most common myth insisted that it was 'impossible to sheath a sword into a vibrating scabbard'. In other words, 'true' resistance is always effective.[86] The penis is coded as a weapon; the vagina is its passive receptacle, which merely by 'vibrating' could ward off attack. This meant that any women who *failed* to fight off an attack on her virtue could be assumed to have acquiesced or even actively consented.

This view was taken to an extreme by psychiatrists claiming that rape was a 'victim-precipitated' crime. In the *Journal of Criminal Law and*

Criminal Behavior in 1940, for instance, German criminal psychologist Hans von Hentig concluded that 'If there are criminals, it is evident that there are [also] born victims, self-harming and self-destroying.'[87] In 1957, distinguished Hungarian-French psychoanalyst George Devereux even claimed that female rape victims were partially 'on the side of the rapist'.[88] As American forensic psychiatrist Seymour Halleck put it in 1972, the rape victim 'frequently' played

> as large a role in precipitating the offense as the offender. Many rapes, particularly where the victim is known to the offender, might never have taken place had the 'victim' [*sic*] not been both flirtatious and ambivalent as to her desire for a sexual experience.[89]

These distorted views circulating in medical jurisprudence texts can be illustrated by looking at four textbooks published in India between 1911 and 1978. Muhammad Abdul Ghani's *Medical Jurisprudence: A Hand-Book for Police Officers and Students* was published in 1911. He questioned whether it was even possible to rape a resisting woman. In his words,

> a man of average size and weight could not perpetrate rape on a woman of average size and weight, in full possession of her faculties, if she wished to resist his doing so. In girls who have passed the age of puberty, a determined resistance may frustrate the attempt of even a powerful man.[90]

It was a view that was defended 67 years later in Bejoy Kumar Sengupta's manual. He ruled that 'under ordinary circumstances, it is impossible' to rape a resisting woman. He did, however, add that because resistance was 'less expected from those who lead a sheltered life, do not go out of home and face emergency', the physician should take into consideration 'the social status and the type of woman'.[91] In other words, middle- and upper-class women who alleged rape needed to be taken more seriously than their poorer sisters, who were effectively 'unrapeable'. As for women who claimed to have been raped while asleep, Sengupta counselled that 'it should be borne in mind that "Not all who have their eyes shut are asleep."'[92]

B. Sardar Singh's *A Manual of Medical Jurisprudence for Police Officers* (1916) went into greater detail. He argued that, in cases of sexual assault, 'the character of the prosecutrix and her parents is worth consideration.' If the victim or her family are of 'loose character', they

> may not hesitate in bringing a false charge of rape in order to extort money, to entangle an enemy or to avoid the detection of adultery. A respectable woman or her parents would not like to make a false complaint of this kind at the cost of their honour, but they might be induced to do so in order to white-wash her character if she was caught in the act of adultery.[93]

Suspicions that victims are prone to lie were echoed in Rames Chandra Ray's *Outlines of Medical Jurisprudence and the Treatment of Poisoning: For Students and Practitioners* (1925). When medically examining alleged rape victims, Ray advised physicians to ask themselves: 'Is she a masturbator?'[94] In bold letters, he warned '*Do not swallow her story* but judge if the wounds could have been caused otherwise than as suggested by the woman.'[95] Ray instructed physicians to also pay close attention to the victim's 'mental state', asking 'Is she emotional? or intoxicated? or was she drugged? Or insane? What are her feelings towards the accused?' In his view, 'an outraged woman is not likely to give a very accurate description and is likely to be confused and exaggerating. A designing female may tell a plausible story.'[96] In this way, rape victims faced an impossible dilemma: an incoherent account of their assault could be dismissed for being inaccurate while a coherent account could be dismissed as evidence of scheming. It is difficult to see how any rape victim could pass such a series of tests.

The Practicalities of (In)Justice

Abusers often hold high political office, or are responsible for law enforcement and laying out the principles of medical jurisprudence. But these predictors of (in)justice are amplified by some very practical constraints facing victims who are seeking help, let alone justice. Victims living in rural or inaccessible regions might be unable to attend police stations or magistrates' courts due to the lack of transport. It might be economically impossible to take sufficient time off work in order to draw the attention of authorities to their assault.[97] Victims might even find themselves dealing with police or legal representatives who are ignorant of the law or fail to appreciate the gravity of their complaints. As Joanne Fedler, legal adviser at Johannesburg's People Opposing Woman Abuse (POWA), discovered, many South African magistrates had not heard of the 1993 Prevention of Family Violence Act, so were not prepared to prosecute sexually violent husbands.[98] In other contexts, victims might prefer being dealt with by female police, while the police force was predominantly (or totally) male. For example, in 2000, less than 4 per cent of Japanese police were female.[99] Worst of all, justice systems might not even exist, as was the case during the 1991 to 2001 armed conflict in Sierra Leone that resulted in the demolition of the country's court system and police force.[100]

Accessing adequate police and prosecution services is only the start of a victim's difficulties. To achieve justice, there has to be an identifiable perpetrator, a victim who is credible to a judge and jurors, witnesses and sufficient evidence to warrant the expense of a trial. In the unlikely event of all these factors being present, victims routinely complain that the trial resembles a 'second assault'.[101] Defence councils are intimidating; victims might be questioned for hours; and (unique to rape trials) independent corroboration may be required. In no other kind of trial is a witness treated with such high levels of suspicion.

The problem is exacerbated by the nature of rape trials in many jurisdictions. Distorted assumptions based on the racial or ethnic identity of rape victims are pervasive. Colonial court officials in Kenya did not think that Kenyan women were much harmed by rape. In 1926, for example, Governor Grigg maintained that the death penalty for rape 'could not of course be imposed for rape upon a native woman because native opinion does not regard that offence as a matter of much gravity'.[102] In the words of another official writing three decades later, Europeans and Africans 'place different values on this particular offence and . . . in many cases it is regarded as little more than a breach of etiquette'.[103]

Some victims were thought not to suffer serious harms from assault. This was why, in a 1909 Congressional debate about the appropriate punishment for men who raped American Indian and Alaska Native women, one Representative argued that the 'morals of Indian women are not always as high as those of a white woman and consequently the punishment should be lighter against her'.[104] As late as 1968, this ruling was upheld by the Ninth Court of Appeals: it stated that men who raped non-Indigenous women would be subjected to higher penalties than men who raped Indigenous women.[105] In the USA until the late nineteenth century, Indigenous women were not even permitted to testify in courts of law.[106] Traditional tribunals in Namibia also don't allow women to speak – and all the headmen are male.[107] Elsewhere, such as in Darfur, the local version of Islamic law decrees that girls and women who wish to pursue a rape accusation have to present testimony from four male witnesses.[108] Complainants face hostile jurors or, even worse, judges who guffaw during their testimony.[109] In Taiwan, judges (who hear cases without a jury) may interrupt the victims' testimony in order to criticize their behaviour; they may openly display a 'disdainful attitude' towards victims and discriminate according to their occupation and education.[110] A casual attitude to privacy presents problems. In prosecuting the rapes in Rwanda, for example, victims were promised anonymity, only to discover subsequently that their names were published.[111] In the words of 'Grace', who testified in a Tanzanian court to rape during the Rwandan genocide, her 'testimony was supposed to be confidential', as was the fact that

> when I got back everyone seemed to know. People were constantly asking me questions about what I'd said, what the suspect had said, what was going to happen. I chose not to respond; I just kept to myself . . . But it was a really rough situation.[112]

The chief difficulty for victims giving evidence in court is proving that she *did not* consent: the burden of proof is on the victim, rather than the accused being required to prove that she *did* consent. This was not always the case. Brett Shadle has shown that court elders in Guisiland (Kenya) between the 1940s and the 1960s did not require rape victims to produce evidence that they had not been consenting parties to sexual intercourse. Unlike judges in courts in the West or in colonial British courts in Kenya, the accused men were required to prove that they had attained the woman's active consent. Shadle found that the idea that a woman would have 'morning-after regrets' or falsely claim rape was non-sensical for *ritongo* (court elders). Because most women engaged in sex before marriage, her

> sexual reputation was . . . more or less irrelevant. The courts generally believed that if a woman testified that she had said no, odds were good that she had in fact said no. It was thus incumbent on the man to prove consent.[113]

This is certainly not the case in nearly all other jurisdictions, where the burden of proof of non-consent lies with the victim. Her task is formidably difficult since, in times of peace, most sexual violence takes place in private. Whether it is the Nguyên Code in Vietnam or the famous instruction given to jurors in Britain and the USA that 'a charge of rape is easily to be made and hard to be proved and even harder to be defended,' accusers generally have to provide irrefutable physical evidence of having vigorously resisted in order to be believed.[114]

As we saw earlier, defining what constituted 'consent' was the central issue during the Italian trial of 'T. M.'. The appeal court reduced his sentence on the grounds that the fourteen-year-old victim had bargained with T. M. to engage in coerced oral sex in an attempt to avoid penetrative rape. This victim-blaming understanding of consent is not unique to the Italian judiciary. In 1992, a similar judgement was recorded in Travis County (south-central Texas, USA) when a grand jury refused to charge Joel Rene Valdez with rape. Valdez admitted that he was drunk when he entered the victim's bedroom, carrying a knife. When the victim pleaded with him to wear a condom because she was afraid of contracting HIV, he did so. After the rape, the naked victim snatched his knife and ran, screaming, to her neighbours. The grand jury concluded that, by begging the invader to wear a condom, the victim had consented to the sex.[115] The victim's one action, which was intended to minimize the harm to herself, rendered her culpable for her own frightening violation, unlike the multiple actions of Valdez. The verdict is more extraordinary since Valdez was a stranger-rapist wielding a knife. At the retrial, the victim – who agreed to be publicly named as Elizabeth Xan Wilson – observed that

> I'm not the little victim the grand jury expected. I'm not beaten up or maimed or even infected with the AIDS virus or pregnant. I find it sickening that in a very aware city with very aware people, the fact that I took extreme measures to protect my life means that I deserve to get raped.[116]

Her attacker was eventually sentenced to forty years for aggravated assault.

This chapter tells depressing stories of violent authorities, debilitating emotions, distorted beliefs (such as those surrounding ideas about female sexuality, chastity and honour) and a host of other barriers that victims of sexual abuse face when attempting to bring their abuse to public attention. Not all people who experience sexual harms have their pain acknowledged; some are seen as more worthy of attention than others. Is it any wonder that many victims preferred to 'bury their dishonour', as Serbian rape victims put it, rather than seek redress?[117]

It is important, however, to be reminded that change is possible. The final chapter in this book focuses on the power of resistance and solidarity but, even in the context of the stories of (in)justice told here, there are optimistic moments. Rape does not universally inflict stigma on victims and their families. After the conflict in Sierra Leone, for example, families were often so happy that their loved ones had survived that they welcomed them back eagerly.[118] Throughout the world, there have been attempts to expand legal and societal sympathy for victims of abuse. The distortions rehearsed in so many early medical jurisprudence textbooks and scholarly articles in forensic psychiatry have subsequently been excised. In India, widespread protests against high levels of sexual violence led the government to establish separate police stations and courts for such crimes.[119] Even the case which began this chapter – of the Italian student whose allegations of rape against her driving instructor were rejected on the grounds that 'it is impossible to take off jeans ... without the active cooperation of the person who is wearing them' – saw justice eventually secured by feminists, women's rights advocates, legal experts and the highest Italian court.[120] The final words, then, must go to Elizabeth Xan Wilson. During the final trial of the man who raped her, she told the jury that the public know her as 'the condom rape victim'. But, she contended, 'I am not the condom rape victim: I do not have the victim's mentality ... I am a survivor of rape.'[121]

THREE

Gender Troubles

Words wound. As George Orwell put it, 'if thought corrupts language, language can also corrupt thought.'[1] Words determine what we think about the world and how we experience it. They tell us what to feel and how to act. They expose underlying assumptions.

It is not surprising, therefore, that the words we use to talk about sexual violence are fraught with dangers. Rape discourse relies heavily on gender dichotomies ('she' as opposed to 'he') and agency ('victim' versus 'perpetrator'). Queer thinking has given us the 'singular they', while reflections on the Holocaust have accustomed us to add 'bystander' to the victim/perpetrator binary. Nevertheless, it is difficult to think and write about abusive encounters without both gendering the participants and employing agentic shortcuts. While Chapter Five will tackle the victim/perpetrator binary, this one seeks to disrupt the first of these unhelpful binaries, regarding gender. It focuses on the vulnerabilities experienced by people with non-normative gender identities, who are often relegated to footnotes in accounts of sexual violence. It also warns against the creation of new hierarchies of risk: sexual violence committed against cisgender males requires acknowledgement and theorizing too.

The key concept in this chapter is vulnerability. It comes from the Latin *vilnus*, meaning 'wound'. To be vulnerable is to be susceptible to wounding or injury. Of course, *all* sentient beings are vulnerable. This is not only because we are fleshy creatures accorded a finite span of life. It is also because of our fundamental dependency on others. In her essay 'Violence, Mourning, Politics' (2003), philosopher Judith Butler observes that people are constituted politically in part by virtue of the social vulnerability of our bodies . . . Loss and vulnerability seem to follow from our being socially constituted bodies, attached to others, at risk of losing these attachments, exposed to others, at risk of violence by virtue of that exposure.[2]

That said, human sociability means that some people – members of minoritized gender groups, for example – are more vulnerable to sexual victimization than others. This should not lead to the adoption of an essentialist or 'checklist' approach to vulnerability, whereby some groups (such as non-gender binary, or BME girls and women, for example) are automatically slotted into the riskier positions in any hierarchy of vulnerability. The labelling approach ends up stereotyping entire categories of people and can encourage responses that are patronizing and paternalistic. In the context of sexual violence, this checklist approach fails for another important reason: groups thought of as powerful – cisgendered men, for instance – might paradoxically discover that their socially-privileged status within society is precisely what allows the sexual abuse they suffer to be minimized.

This is why attention needs to be paid to layers of risk. A person is vulnerable to the extent to which she, he or they are unable to prevent harms to themselves. This is the lesson of Kimberlé Crenshaw's concept of intersectionality, which was discussed in the introductory chapter. Crenshaw observes that people come burdened with multiple vulnerabilities, some of which are intrinsic (such as skin colour, gender, disability or sexuality) while others are extrinsic or situational (such as residence in a prison, military barrack or slum). These multiple vulnerabilities are interlaced and mutually reinforcing. The specific traits, characteristics or identities they possess do not *in themselves* make people more or less vulnerable; people are *made* vulnerable by ideological, economic, political and spatial systems that construct and maintain hierarchies of power. Vulnerability is always interpersonal. Vulnerable people are rendered 'wound-able' *by* someone.

This chapter starts with the intersectional vulnerabilities of Black lesbians in the townships of South Africa. It then turns to other groups that experience a high risk of sexual violence because of their non-normative gender identity. Their vulnerability is not solely due to their membership of particular gendered communities, but also because they are situated in multiple personal and social contexts in which their needs and desires are not recognized by those around them. Finally, I turn to cisgendered males, who are generally regarded as the least sexually vulnerable persons – until they are raced and ghettoized, classed and criminalized, militarized and tortured. Crucially, in all these instances, intersectional vulnerabilities are affected by global regimes of power and, in particular, legacies of colonial subjugation and transnational armed conflict.

'Corrective' Rape

In April 2010, thirty-year-old Millicent Gaika of Gugulethu (a township on the edge of Cape Town) was returning home with friends after a night out. They were approached by her neighbour Andile Ngcoza. She told her friends to walk on while she chatted to him. Instead, he pushed her into a shack. For the next five hours, she was brutally beaten and raped. She later recounted that

> I thought he was going to kill me; he was like an animal. And he kept saying, 'I know you are a lesbian. You are not a man, you think you are, but I am going to show you, you are a woman. I am going to make you pregnant. I am going to kill you.'[3]

She survived. After the attack, she told a reporter that her attacker's supporters 'will say I'm trying to be a boy, that I even steal their girlfriends. So[,] no wonder I got raped. Serves me right, that's what they'll say.'[4]

Thanks in part to the support of the Luleki Sizwe Womyn's Project, a lesbian activist group, Gaika slowly recovered from her ordeal.[5] Ngcoza was subsequently arrested but, when the case came before the Wynberg Sexual Offences Court, he was released on a bail of only 60 rand (that is, the cost of a sandwich).[6] He fled and was not rearrested until 2013, when he was sentenced to 22 years in prison.[7]

Gaika is just one of thousands of South African lesbians, bisexuals, transpeople and asexuals subjected to 'corrective' or 'curative' rape.[8] The practice refers to a man or group of men raping a member of a sexual minority because they are seen as a threat to heteronormativity and cisgender dominance. The words used to discuss this form of violence are potentially wounding: after all, the terms 'corrective' or 'curative' rape adopt the vernacular of the *perpetrator* of the attack. They also imply that the victims' sexual identity or practices are improper, even wicked. However, the term 'homophobic sexual assault', which some scholars think ought to be used,[9] fails to capture the particularly invidious assumption held by aggressors that sadistic, penile penetration will convince lesbians of the superiority of heteronormative intercourse.

At the time of Gaika's ordeal, there were ten new cases of 'corrective' rape every week in Cape Town alone, a city of 2.5 million.[10] Some analysts estimate that there are at least five hundred victims of corrective rape every year in South Africa.[11] Its prevalence is all the more disturbing since South Africa was the first country in the world to make discrimination on the grounds of sexual orientation an offence under Section 9 of its 1996 Constitution. It was also the first African country to legalize same-sex marriage. The discrepancy between legislative liberalism and an underlying, hostile homophobia could not be starker.

South African lesbians and their supporters worldwide have responded to corrective rape through political lobbying, protest and activist art. Gaika's ordeal became a rallying point for feminists throughout the world. In a display of global solidarity, a petition was started by transnational, online activist communities asking South African President Jacob Zuma to take decisive action against the practice. A petition demanding that the government designate corrective rape a hate crime, therefore requiring the police and criminal justice systems to pay serious attention to every accusation, was signed by 170,000 supporters from 163 countries.[12] They were successful.

Artists have also fought to eliminate corrective rape. South African visual activist Zanele Muholi, and film-maker Peter Goldsmid, were determined to draw public opprobrium to the practice, while also celebrating the lives of South African lesbians. Their documentary *Difficult Love* (2010) not only focuses on the violence experienced by Black South African lesbians, including Millicent Gaika, but tells stories of love and resilience. Their message is that strong communities of LGBTQ people are flourishing despite incessant attacks upon them.

South Africa

Millicent Gaika was not alone. South Africa has the highest levels of rapes per capita during peacetime than any other country in the world, yet only 3 per cent of all rapes are ever reported to the police.[13] In part, the crisis in South Africa is due to the highly militarized nature of that nation during and after apartheid. The South African Defence Force, the South African Police, the army of the Inkatha Freedom Party, the army of the African National Congress and numerous armed right- and left-wing paramilitary groups have all contributed to creating a rapacious society. Under apartheid, rape was regularly used to terrorize Black populations. In the urban townships, there was a general sense of lawlessness, as the central function of the police and military was to 'control and contain' Black residents rather than to 'police and protect'.[14] The townships were also designed in ways that failed to provide female residents with private and safe living quarters.

The result has been soaring levels of sexualized violence. During apartheid, women of colour in South Africa were 4.7 times more likely to be rape victims than their white counterparts. In 2000, the South African *Sunday Times* published the results of a three-year survey of over 27,000 young men and women. They found that one in four young men admitted that, before they turned eighteen years of age, they had inflicted non-consensual sex on a girl or woman. Eighty per cent believed that women were responsible for sexual violence.[15]

When sexual identity is added to race and gender, the situation becomes even worse. Black lesbians and LGBTQ people are especially vulnerable. Eighty-six per cent of Black lesbians in South Africa live in fear of sexual assault, compared to 44 per cent of white lesbians.[16] Black lesbians are also less likely than other victims to see their assailants arrested and punished. This was one of Gaika's complaints. After all, Ngcoza was not her first assailant. Eight years earlier, Gaika had been gang-raped by four men. On that occasion, her attackers had been arrested and sentenced to between ten and fifteen years' imprisonment. However, she bitterly noted, 'after a few years, they got out and that was too little time . . . I saw them walking around here in Gugulethu again.'[17] As Soweto lesbian Zakhe Sowello observes, 'When you are raped you have a lot of evidence of your body. But when we try and report these crimes nothing happens, and then you see the boys who raped you walking free on the street.' This lack of access to justice is particularly upsetting because, as Sowello remonstrates, 'every day I am told that they are going to kill me, that they are going to rape me and after they rape me[,] I'll become a girl.'[18] According to Nkunzi Zandile Nkabinde, a lesbian *sangoma* (traditional healer), 'there are no safe lesbian spaces anywhere.'[19]

Lesbians who self-identify as 'butch' are in the greatest danger. In the words of 'Duduzile', a member of the Forum for Empowerment of Women (FEW), which was established by Black lesbians in Johannesburg in 2001,

If you are femme, it doesn't really show that you are a lesbian . . .
But when you are butch, it's when you dress like a man and you act
like a man in a way, and that's when you become maybe a target . . .
That's when they [men] see that you are born with the breasts and
all that, but you are acting differently . . . That's when they want
to prove a point to you that actually you are a woman, you know;
that's when they start raping you.[20]

The gendered impact of rape differed according to whether the victim
identified as butch lesbian, femme lesbian or heterosexual. Butch lesbians
suffer the *additional* harm of having their claims to masculinity attacked.[21]
As Muholi explained, the butch lesbians she spoke to were traumatized
because being overpowered and raped by a man 'cuts into their gendered
and sexualised selves'. Their 'masculine identities', she observed, 'are struc-
tured through the power they possess not to be touched intimately during
sexual encounters. Consequently, revealing intimate violation to anyone
is painful, and can be delegitimising and disempowering.'[22] Such harms
cement problematic ideas about masculinity as inherently inviolable, but
nevertheless express a specific form of suffering.

What explains the extremely high risk of lesbian, bisexual and asexual girls and women in South Africa experiencing acts of sexual hatred,
often carried out by neighbours, acquaintances and family members?[23]
Aggressors rage against what they regard as lesbian threats to their exclusive 'access' to the bodies of girls and women. In other words, cisgendered
men use sexual violence to 'warn off' lesbian encroachments into 'their'
territory.[24] They also appeal to the need for women to obey heteronormative rules – if not voluntarily, then by brutal force. As one South African
man explained, he could 'appreciate' why some men might engage in
corrective rape, even though he claimed not to have 'rack[ed]' a lesbian
himself. He contended that such rapes were intended to let lesbians
'know that they must be straight . . . Once she gets raped, I think she'll
know which way is nice.'[25]

This engrained sense of masculinist privilege is fuelled by deep-seated
homophobia, sometimes linked to colonialist religious movements. Prior
to the introduction of Messianic religious groups on the African continent, there was a broad acceptance of homosexuality.[26] Despite this,
aggressors contend that homosexuality had been imported into the
African continent from a morally corrupt West. In other words, they
claim that African societies had been contaminated by Western-backed

human rights activists and proponents of sexual liberation.[27] Accordingly, homosexuality is 'un-African'. For aggressors, it is their duty to turn lesbians into 'real African women'.[28]

It is ironic, therefore, that corrective rape in several African states has been invigorated by anti-gay lobbyists from the U.S. neoconservative Right, as well as by extremist Christian evangelicals. One of the most prominent of these evangelicals is Scott Lively, a pastor from Springfield, Massachusetts. In 2009, he was invited to address hundreds of Ugandan leaders, including parliamentarians. He informed audiences that the 'gay movement is an evil institution' whose goal was 'to defeat the marriage-based society and replace it with a culture of promiscuity'. Lively compared contemporary LGBTQ communities to 'the Spanish Inquisition, the French "Reign of Terror", the era of South African apartheid, and the two centuries of American slavery'. He even contended that gay people were the type of people 'it takes to run a gas chamber or to do a mass murder . . . The Rwandan stuff probably involved these guys.'[29]

Such inflammatory speeches appalled Kapya Kaoma, an Anglican priest from Zambia. In his report entitled *Globalizing the Culture Wars: U.S. Conservatives, African Churches, and Homophobia* (2009), Kaoma showed how U.S. conservatives mobilized African clergy 'in their domestic culture wars at a time when the demographic center of Christianity is shifting from the global North to the global South'. Kaoma lamented the fact that American evangelicals were promoting an anti-LGBTQ agenda that was leading to 'increased incidents of violence' against sexual and gender minorities. As a consequence, he warned, 'public, vicious forms of homophobic violence are now common.'[30]

Kaoma's accusations, which were directed at American evangelicals, undercut any notion that corrective rape against LGBTQ people is somehow unique to 'African cultures'. Indeed, the practice has been documented in places as dissimilar as North America, Latin America, Jamaica, Ecuador, Thailand and India.[31] In the Americas, special clinics claim to 'cure' the sin of homosexuality through forced heterosexual penetration combined with re-education. Homophobic parents in Ecuador can incarcerate their 'aberrant' children in such institutions, often for a minimum of six months at a cost of between $200 and $1,200 a month.[32]

Importantly, different meanings may be attached to corrective rape in these other contexts. Most notably, South African proponents defend the practice by referring to 'perverted' gender norms imported from the

West, while corrective rape elsewhere is posited as a *defence* of Christian values in the West. They quote biblical texts that declare that homosexuality is an 'abomination'. Proponents of 'corrective' practices are simply obeying God's Word.

For other North American supporters of corrective rape, the opposite rationale is given. Might the practice be defended on the ground of sexual liberation? In 1990, for example, a pastor who raped an asexual woman in Minnesota told her that coerced heterosexual intercourse was 'consistent with her treatment because it would remove her inhibitions' and finally 'set her free'.[33] This was also the excuse given by the man who attacked Julie Decker, now an activist in the USA. She was nineteen years old when a male 'friend' sexually assaulted her in an attempt to 'cure' her asexuality. Decker later recalled that people who perform corrective rape 'believe that they're just waking us up and that we'll thank them for it later'.[34] It was an echo of the comment made by the unnamed South African man who insisted that 'Once she gets raped, I think she'll know which way is nice.'[35] In this way, anti-queer violence is not only about homophobia but about misogyny.

Transgenderism

'Corrective rape' is usually framed in terms of attempts to impose a heteronormative gender identity on its victims, but it obviously has included a very strong element of punishment. Black South African lesbians like Gaika are very conscious of this motivation.

It is also a prominent theme in accounts of violence provided by transgender people. They, too, are targets of sexual violence based solely on their gender identity. Anti-transgender violence is especially salient in India and Nepal, where transgender people are assumed to be members of the lowest castes as well as sex workers. Hostility against intersex, transgender, and asexual peoples (called *kothis* and *hijras*) is relentless.[36] They are sexually assaulted by the police, army personnel, *mastams* (petty hoodlums) and, in Nepal, Maoist militants.[37] The severity of the violence is revealed in a report conducted by the People's Union for Civil Liberties in the Karnataka state, southern India. The authors concluded that sexual violence was 'constant [and] pervasive' in transgender lives. At the very least, the 'sexuality of the *hijra* . . . becomes a target of prurient curiosity', but it often leads to 'brutal violence'. Even the police constantly degrade *hijras* by asking them sexual questions, feeling up their breasts, stripping them, and in some cases raping them ... The police attitude seems to be that since *kothis* and *hijras* engage in sex work, they are not entitled to any rights of sexual citizenship.[38]

One *kothi* described being hauled into the police station one night and forced to engage in anal sex. He maintained that

I did not have condoms at the time since I was only in my underwear. I also could not talk about condoms. Even if we show condoms[,] they will beat us on our hands with a *lathi* [police stick].[39]

If *kothis* are found to be carrying condoms when arrested, the police use it as evidence that they are either sex workers or have been engaging in sexual activities in public places.[40] As a result, many *kothis* refuse to carry condoms, increasing their risk of HIV/AIDS and other diseases.

Sexual violence targeting transgender people exists throughout the world, often involving high levels of aggression similar to those experienced by *kothis* and *hijras*. One nationwide U.S. study found that 12 per cent of transgender children had been sexually assaulted while still in primary school.[41] Another U.S. study revealed that half of transgender people had experienced intimate partner violence.[42]

As elsewhere in the world, the U.S. justice systems are reluctant to acknowledge and respond to such violence. Courts routinely blame trans-victims for their own abuse. The most notorious example has been dubbed the 'trans panic defence'. *Perpetrators* of sexual abuse absolve themselves of responsibility on the grounds that they had been deceived into believing that they were engaging in a sexual liaison with a cisgendered person.[43] The view that trans-people provoke violence by not revealing their birth gender was even *defended* by academic Bradford Bigler in an article published in the respected *UCLA Law Review* in 2006. He contended that the 'nature of the sex to which the deceived party consents (for example, heterosexual sodomy)' was 'fundamentally different than the act in which the defendant actually engaged (here, homosexual sodomy)'. This means that the *victim* is guilty of fraud; the *aggressor* had simply panicked.[44] By such logic, transgender people are always defined by their anatomical sex as decided at birth, a denial both of their sense of self and their lived experience.[45]

Numerous barriers are placed in the way of trans and other queer people reporting sexual abuse. The most important is that disclosing one's gender identity to family, employers, landlords or the community can have damaging repercussions. Trans people are right to assume that it will provoke discriminatory practices. One-fifth of respondents surveyed by the National Discrimination Survey were refused medical care when their transgender identity was revealed, and 28 per cent reported being harassed in a medical setting.[46] In some states (including Montana and South Carolina), LGBTQ people are not allowed to apply for Protection Orders against violent partners; in other states, they are discouraged from doing so.[47] Transphobic tropes are routinely hurled at victims, including insinuations that they are so unattractive that sexual abuse is unlikely.[48] In the words of one trans woman, her boyfriend 'would tell me that no one would ever want a freak like me, that I am not a real woman, and that I am worthless'.[49] Unfortunately, transphobic views can be internalized by trans-people.

Prison is a particularly perilous place for trans women, especially since they are usually sent to male facilities. The most extensive research into this problem has been carried out in North America, perhaps because the USA has the highest level of incarceration of any nation in the world. A report commissioned by the California Department of Corrections concluded that sexual assault is thirteen times more prevalent among imprisoned transgender women compared to their cisgender male counterparts.[50] Nearly 60 per cent of transgender inmates in California prisons had been sexually assaulted; this contrasts with only 4 per cent of randomly selected inmates.[51] Transgender prisoners are often placed in 'protective custody' in segregated housing units, which is effectively solitary confinement.[52] They are routinely denied hormones, even if they had been taking them for decades.[53]

Even more disturbing, officers were *aware* of sexual assaults on cis-gendered prisoners in 60 per cent of cases, while they were *unaware* of the sexual assault of transgender prisoners in 71 per cent of cases. In a random sample of prisoners, 70 per cent of prisoners who were sexually assaulted were provided with medical assistance if they needed it; in the sample of transgender prisoners, medical attention was *not* provided when needed in 64 per cent of cases.[54] Prison guards and police might not even believe that trans women could be raped in the first place because they are not 'real women'.[55] Many transgender prisoners end up engaging in 'protective pairing', or sex with one inmate in order to be protected from others.[56]

Prison

These dispiriting tales of violence against minoritized genders and sexualities should not blind us to the high levels of vulnerability among other groups, including prisoners *of all genders and sexes*. In other words, although it is important to acknowledge that trans women in prison are at a particularly high risk, this should not lead us to dismiss the abuse of white, cisgendered men. Estimates of the percentage of prisoners of all genders who are raped in U.S. prisons vary from 1 per cent to over 20 per cent.[57] The pain inflicted on these prisoners is not only minimized but is even a source of comedy in a significant proportion of films depicting prison life.[58]

Official concerns about high and rising levels of sexual abuse in U.S. prisons came to a head in the 1990s, forcing the Department of Justice to initiate a study of 53 departments of corrections nationwide. The report, which was published in 1999, revealed that at least 45 per cent of facilities had been involved in either class actions or individual damage suits relating to sexual misconduct between staff and inmates. No training was given to staff or inmates on what constituted unacceptable sexual practices; most prisons did not even have policies in place prohibiting sexual conduct between staff and inmates.[59]

Numerous other studies have found that, although the main victims (and perpetrators) are boys and men, female inmates are also coerced into having sex with other inmates or staff. When placed in seclusion, they have their clothes taken away, allowing the male security officers manning the cameras to observe them naked.[60] Non-violent criminals of all genders are confined in cramped cells, which they are forced to share with criminals accustomed to using violence to enforce their will. Prisoners are increasingly encouraged to litigate against officials for failing to prevent sexual assaults, but they have found that complaining exposes them to even greater risks or increased surveillance.[61] They are branded 'snitches' and are liable to face retaliation from perpetrators and their friends.[62] As we saw with transgender prisoners, protective custody is also unhelpful. Since its main function is to punish prisoners who have violated prison rules, conditions are abysmal.[63] At the very least, protective custody means a loss of privileges (including educational and employment provisions) and reduced access to entertainment systems (such as television) or religious services.[64] Attempts by some prison authorities to reduce high levels of sexual victimization of gay prisoners by housing them in separate buildings is also ineffective. It requires LGBTQ prisoners to broadcast their sexuality, which can have devastating long-term consequences, especially for men who are Latino, Black and poor.[65]

Even if prisoners report being attacked, it is extremely rare for their assailants to be punished and, if they are, they are likely to be returned afterwards to the same section of the prison where their victims are housed. Guards and other officials simply advise victims to 'suck it up' or 'be a man'. Or they taunt them for being 'cry babies'. As one prison official informed a prisoner who had been sexually assaulted, 'I do not feel sorry for you. You're getting what you deserve.'[66] Another joked that 'here's another one the booty bandit got.'[67] Escape is impossible.

Of course, vulnerability is not evenly distributed. Male prisoners who are labelled 'effeminate', are disabled, are younger or of smaller body build than most other inmates are at greater risk.[68] Sexual identity also matters. We have already seen this with regard to transgender prisoners. But other sexual minorities find themselves exposed as well. Officials often assume that a homosexual sexual orientation makes all sex consensual.[69] In 2008, the U.S. Bureau Justice Statistics revealed that homosexual and bisexual men in state prisons were ten to eleven times more likely than heterosexual prisoners to be sexually victimized by other inmates (34 to 39 per cent compared with just over 3 per cent).[70] Interestingly, there were no differences in inmate-on-inmate victimization among imprisoned lesbian, bisexual and heterosexual women (victimization levels for all were 13 per cent).[71] Another study, focusing on correctional facilities in California, took into account not only sexual identity but ethnicity as well. They found that 67 per cent of gay inmates in the random sample reported having been sexually assaulted compared with 2 per cent of heterosexual inmates. Half of gay inmates who were assaulted were African Americans, compared with 83 per cent of Black heterosexual inmates.[72] In other words, being gay raised the risk of sexual assault, but so too did being 'heterosexual while Black'.

Male Vulnerability

So far, this chapter has explored vulnerability to sexual violence experienced by minoritized gender groups, such as lesbian and transgender women, as well as imprisoned men and women. But what about *non-incarcerated* gay and cisgendered men? The fact that, prior to the rise of gay liberation from the 1970s on and the decriminalization of homosexuality, gay men tended to be portrayed as perpetrators of sexual violence (particularly against children) should not encourage us to ignore their victimhood. Similarly, acknowledging the prominent role played by cisgender men in committing acts of sexualized aggression does not mean that those who are sexually victimized can be overlooked.

Like lesbians and transgender women, gay men face huge barriers to having their abuse recognized. Gay communities can be anxious that 'washing their dirty linen in public' will further stigmatize them. This is not irrational. After all, as late as 1973, the American Psychiatric Association classified homosexuality as a disorder, as did the World Health Organization until 1992. Today, 78 countries criminalize sexual activity by lesbian, gay, bisexual, transgender or intersex people.[73] Abuse is even hurled at them by men in the highest political offices: President Robert Mugabe of Zimbabwe, for example, did not hesitate to call homosexuals 'worse than pigs and dogs', threatening to 'punish [them] severely'.[74] Legal systems routinely conflate consensual gay sex and forced intercourse, prosecuting both under the same sodomy statutes. This means that, in jurisdictions as diverse as Malawi, Puerto Rico and more than a dozen U.S. states, gay victims who complain of sexual abuse to the police can be arrested and punished.[75]

Cisgender boys and men experience similar abuse. In many jurisdictions, including China before 1999, rape is an offence against the chastity of girls and women; therefore, by definition, only females could be raped. Boys and men are assumed not to have 'chastity issues' because they always 'want it'.[76] Medical personnel have been complicit in such distorted views. By assuming that victims are female, they fail to even *ask* male patients about possible victimization.[77] The fact that few male victims are left with physical injuries (for example, only 10 per cent of victims of sexual torture in Sri Lanka sustained genital scarring) also reduces the likelihood of their suffering being medically diagnosed.[78]

This denial that boys and men are potential victims can be illustrated by looking at the ways in which international human rights organizations assess victimhood. In one survey of 4,076 NGOs working on sexual violence during armed conflicts, only 3 per cent mentioned male victims, and usually in a brief note.[79] Indeed, some international aid organizations are unapologetically reluctant to publicize male-on-male rape. In 2010, for instance, the Refugee Law Project based at Kampala in Uganda produced a documentary called *Gender against Men, exploring rape against men in armed conflicts.* Director Chris Dolan was frustrated when aid agencies attempted to halt the screening on the grounds that publicizing rape against *both* men and women was a 'zero-sum game'. In other words, they assumed that funding for victims of sexual violence in armed conflicts was a 'pre-defined cake'. Dolan was told that if 'you start talking about men [being sexually abused], you're going to somehow eat a chunk of this cake that's taken them a long time to bake'.[80]

It is a view that has been echoed by many second-wave feminists from the 1970s onwards. They, too, were worried that offering help and support to male victims of sexual abuse would divert precious resources away from female victims. In one study conducted in a large U.S. city in the 1990s, of the thirty agencies who provided services for victims of sexual assault, eleven (37 per cent) did not admit male victims, claiming that they 'were not set up to treat men'.[81] Nineteen were 'amenable' to helping male victims, but only four had actually done so in the past year.[82] Gay and trans victims also often complain about the cold reception they receive from domestic and sexual violence shelters.[83]

The refusal to acknowledge the extent of male-on-male sexual abuse is exacerbated by language. Violence aimed against male genital organs and reproductive systems is often categorized in *asexual* terms.[84] For example, the Peruvian Truth and Reconciliation Commission coded male experiences of sexual humiliation, genital mutilation and other forms of sexual torture as non-sexual crimes: they were categorized under headings such as 'torture', rather than 'sexual violence'. When researchers reanalysed the original testimonies, they found that over one-fifth of victims of sexual violence were men, while the original coders had categorized only 2 per cent of victims of sexual abuse as being male.[85]

How can we explain such discrepancies? In part, this is because researchers and human rights activists assume that the sexual torture of men will involve forced penetrative sex. As Harry van Tienhoven of the Refuge Health Care Centre in Utrecht observed, physicians and nurses 'had become familiar with sexual violence against women, and because this usually implies rape, they assumed that sexual violence against men would take the same form, namely anal rape'.[86] Male victims internalize such assumptions.[87] For example, Eric Stener Carlson was employed by the International Criminal Tribunal for the Former Yugoslavia in the Sexual Assault Investigation team. He reported that some men who had been tortured by being 'beaten on the testicles' failed to report the crime. This was 'not because they are afraid of revealing sexual assault, but because what happened to them does not fit their conception of sexual assault'. Carlson claimed that the refusal to see such violence as *sexual* was due to the fact that 'being hit in the testicles during peacetime is generally considered a "normal" occurrence', especially in sport.[88] As a result, the seriousness of such abuse is minimized.

This is a common assumption. A bar-room fight in which a man repeatedly kicks another in the genitals is regarded as 'simple assault', not a 'sexual' one. Within the navy and army, as well as in public schools and fraternities, 'hazing' is a 'rite of passage', even when it involves men forcibly inserting objects inside their victims' anuses. Highly sexualized ceremonies initiating men into fraternities or sports clubs are also seen through the lens of 'social bonding'.

As a result, when scholars *do* focus attention on the sexual violation of cisgender boys and men, they reveal unexpected results. For example, the National Intimate Partner and Sexual Violence Survey for 2010 found similar levels of non-consensual sex for men and women (around 1.2 million for each sex) in the previous year.[89] When boys and men are asked directly about whether they had experienced 'unwanted sexual experiences' with girls and women, the proportion saying 'yes' is high. Admittedly, caution is needed when interpreting these statistics. After all, in regions of the world where gender expectations involve active male and passive female roles, young men might feel pressurized into sex *whenever* a woman initiates sex.[90] *By definition*, she is 'aggressive'. With this caveat in mind, evidence that boys and young men experience 'unwanted' sex is significant. A U.S. National Crime Victimization Survey household study (1992–2000) found that 9 per cent of victims of sexual assault and rape are men, and that 46 per cent of male victims claimed to have been abused by a female.[91] The same survey found that while 30 per cent of women report their rape to the police, only 15 per cent of men do. Men are more likely to report the assault when the perpetrator was a man (22 per cent reported) than a woman (only 7 per cent reported).[92] This may be because male-on-male assaults are regarded as more physically, emotionally and sexually injurious. In 2016 and 2017, Barbara Krahé and her colleagues found that sexual victimization studies in Greece showed *higher* levels among young men than young women.[93] Another study of men aged between 12 and 19 years in Burkina Faso, Ghana, Malawi and Uganda in 2004 discovered that between 4 and 12 per cent of men were 'not willing at all' during their first sexual encounter.[94] In India, the Caribbean, Ghana, Namibia, South Africa and Tanzania levels ranged from 2 to 16 per cent.[95] In Peru, 20 per cent of men studied had experienced unwanted sex, compared with 30 per cent in Cameroon and 44 per cent of schoolboys in South Africa.[96] For some, the pressure to have sex came not from women but from male friends who taunted them for being virgins.

Finally, there are three other contexts in which boys and men are vulnerable to sexual abuse: slavery, religious organizations (especially Christian ones) and armed conflicts. By definition, enslaved people do not own their bodies. There is a large literature exposing the systematic sexual abuse of enslaved girls and women.[97] Less frequently discussed is the sexual abuse of enslaved men. In part, the reason why abuse has been erased from history is a distorted view about masculinity generally; the belief that men are always keen for sex and, therefore, always consenting partners (at least for cisgendered men in heterosexual encounters). Legal and societal definitions of sexual violence that rename sexual violence against men as different to the rape of girls and women also contribute. Other reasons for these abuses are specific to the institution of slavery: racist beliefs in the hypersexuality of Black men, for example, as well as the pervasive assumption that male enslavers are heterosexual and female enslavers are either victims of patriarchy or sexually passive.

Definitional distortions are also part of the reason for the neglect of these forms of abuse. The castration of enslaved men, for example, is not discussed as *sexual* violence but simply 'violence'. The stripping of enslaved men prior to being whipped is similarly referred to in the context of punishment while its sexualized aspects are ignored. As enslaved Virginian Isaac Williams recalled in *A North-Side View of Slavery* (1856), his enslaver would strip both Williams and his wife naked before whipping them.[98] These punishments routinely bruised and scarred genitals. Enslaved men were also forced to have sex with enslaved women in order to bear children, but historians have usually not categorized this as non-consensual sex. In the words of Virginian enslaver Mr Gholson, in a speech in the Legislature on 18 January 1832,

> It has always (perhaps erroneously) been considered by steady and old-fashioned people, that the owner of land had a reasonable right to its annual profits; the owner of orchards, to their annual fruits; the owner of *brood mares*, to their product; and the owner of *female slaves, to their increase.*

The enslaver's 'rights of property' are 'founded in wisdom and justice'. It leads him to forgo

> the service of the female slave; has her nursed and attended during the period of her gestation, and raises the helpless and infant offspring. The value of the property justifies the expense; and I do not hesitate to say, that in its *increase consists much of our wealth*.[99]

In other words, forced maternity of the enslaved women – often involving the coerced sexual labour of enslaved men – further increases the fortune of the person who enslaved them. Testimony was also given by William J. Anderson from Mississippi. About the man who enslaved him, Anderson recalled that

> His humane feelings were all absorbed in his avaricious pursuit of wealth. He kept a close watch over his slaves by night to keep them at home . . . I have known him to make four men leave their wives for nothing, and would not let them come and see them any more on the peril of being shot down like dogs; he then made the women marry other men against their will. Oh, see what it is to be a slave? A man, like the brute, is driven, whipped, sold, comes and goes at his master's bidding.[100]

According to another, if 'either one showed any reluctance, the master [*sic*] would make the couple consummate the relation in his presence'.[101]

White women were active in the sexual abuse of enslaved men as well as enslaved women. The extent of this abuse has been revealed by historian Thomas A. Foster in *Rethinking Rufus: Sexual Violations of Enslaved Men* (2019), who laments the continued assumption that white plantation women lacked sexual agency, despite playing leading roles in the institution of slavery.[102] In fact, white women were known to compel enslaved Black men to sleep with them, sometimes under threat of whipping or being sold to well-known sadistic slaveholders. They occasionally also promised freedom.[103]

If the first vulnerable context for the sexual abuse of boys and men is enslavement, the second is Christian institutions. In recent decades, and throughout the world, the Catholic Church has been rocked by revelations of widespread sexual coercion. According to one estimate, 6 per cent of Catholic priests in America have personally abused minors.[104] The child abuse scandal in the Catholic Church has implicated everyone from the Pope downwards. A very high proportion of victims are boys. For example, in the USA between 1850 and 2002, four out of five victims were male.[105] Many scholars have sought to understand how the abuse could have continued for so long without being exposed. They have pointed to the Church's emphasis on hierarchy and obedience, which inhibited criticism. Justice had also been impeded by the fact that bishops relied on 'diocesan lawyers, insurance companies, and sometimes questionable treatment centers to direct their handling of sexual abuse cases'.[106] Catholic parents failed to believe that parish priests – as men of God – would act in sexually abusive ways.[107] It was unimaginable to many pious, homophobic parents that their *boys* were at risk. Other scholars point to the fact that many priests entered seminaries at the age of fourteen so had never actually lived in 'the world'. They harboured a strong sense of entitlement, including the view that 'normal' rules did not apply to them. A deep sense of loyalty to the Church and, in times of declining religiosity, a reluctance to either 'air dirty linen' in public or to question the suitability of ordinates also played major roles.[108] Crucially, the Church preaches a belief in redemption: we are all sinners, but we can also all be redeemed.[109]

The third context in which boys and men are sexually abused is during armed conflict. The statistics are shocking. A survey published in the *Journal of the American Medical Association* in 2010 found that 22 per cent of men in eastern Congo reported conflict-related sexual violence. The comparable percentage for women was slightly higher, at 30 per cent.[110] During the armed conflict in Uganda, men were

> forced to penetrate holes in banana trees that run with acidic sap, to sit with their genitals over a fire, to drag rocks tied to their penis, to give oral sex to queues of soldiers, [and] to be penetrated with screwdrivers and sticks.[111]

In Liberia, a cross-sectional population study found that one-third of male former combatants had suffered sexual violence.[112] In North and South Kivu and Ituri (DRC), 21 per cent of men in general and half of former male combatants had experienced sexual violence.[113] In Sri Lanka, estimates range from 9 to 21 per cent.[114] In all these conflicts, it was extremely rare for perpetrators to be accused, let alone prosecuted.

Sexual violence against men in military conflicts can also be genocidal, in much the same way as the wartime rape of women. During the war in the former Yugoslavia, for example, men in the detention camps in Bosnia and Herzegovina were sexually humiliated, raped, genitally mutilated, castrated, sterilized and coerced into sexually assaulting members of their own families – all acts deliberately aimed at ensuring that they were unable to procreate.[115] Serbian torturers (both male and female) would beat detainees on their testicles, saying 'you'll never make Ustasha/Muslim children again' – a taunt they also used against their female victims.[116]

Similar atrocities occurred during the genocide in Rwanda. Boys as young as seven were forced to have sex with their mothers or sisters.[117] Others were castrated.[118] One Tutsi man, who was raped by three men and had his reproductive organs mutilated, heard soldiers bragging that by making the men impotent, the Tutsis would eventually die out.[119] In 1998, the International Criminal Tribunal for Rwanda ruled that rape was genocidal and a crime against humanity when it 'brought harm to a group through the violation of women's bodies'.[120] A similar claim could be made for the men who were sexually mutilated. Not only were these male victims prevented from reproducing, but they were also cast out from male society, becoming 'de facto' female. In the words of one male survivor of sexual abuse during the war in the Democratic Republic of the Congo, one of the rapists kept repeating, 'you're no longer a man, you are going to become one of our women.'[121] A similar calamity was experienced by 'Polidor', from Kazimia in South Kivu. He was married with four children when soldiers of the Burundian insurgent group raided his village. Polidor described the soldiers entering his home and, in the presence of his children, raping him and his pregnant wife. He recalled that, during his rape, 'they kept saying "you're no longer a man, you are going to become one of our women."' He confessed that he was 'not able to have sexual relations any more'.[122] The shame and stigma inflicted by such abuse not only strips men of their role as 'protectors' of their own families, but destroys the cohesion of the entire community.

The highest levels of male-on-male sexual abuse occur in regimes employing torture.[123] During the Greek dictatorship, a study of 28 male prisoners found that 43 per cent had been subjected to genital trauma.[124] A survey conducted by the Rehabilitation and Research Centre for Torture Victims in Denmark revealed even higher levels: 69 per cent of 148 torture victims had been tortured sexually.[125] Of 434 prisoners who had been held in custody during the conflict in El Salvador, over three-quarters reported having been subjected to at least one instance of sexual torture.[126] More than one-fifth of 184 Sri Lankan Tamil men seeking asylum in London and referred to the Medical Foundation for the Care of Victims of Torture in 1997–8 had been sexually abused. Most (68 per cent) had been assaulted on their genitals, while others were given electric shocks on their genitals, had sticks pushed up their anus (often with chillies rubbed on the stick first) and were forced to masturbate in public.[127] Such forms of sexual torture rarely leave any physical trace but cause lasting sexual dysfunction.

How do people make sense of the sexual abuse of men? One of the disturbing answers to this question is that the sexual abuse of boys and men is regarded as especially aberrant, unlike similar abuses inflicted on girls and women. During the 1971 war of independence of Bangladesh, for example, men were raped by soldiers of the Pakistani Army. As one liberation fighter informed anthropologist Nayanika Mookherjee, the rape of men was considered barbarous: only men from 'the frontier' (not 'the plains') would commit such vile acts. As this fighter explained, on the Asian plains, male-on-male rape was 'totally unnatural'. For men living on the plains, 'it is more natural to rape women . . . Rape of men is more a culture of the frontier.'[128] In other words, raping girls and women was 'natural'; men who raped other men must hail from more 'primitive', frontier cultures. As a consequence, Mookherjee found that it was 'easier to talk [to fighters] about the rape of women' since such conversations helped to 'mobilize heterosexual men to join the guerrilla forces, defeat the Pakistani army, recover raped women and build the nation after the war'. In contrast, the 'violated male body' had to remain 'excluded from the national narrative'.[129]

Because it is considered 'unnatural', the sexual abuse of boys and men is especially damaging. It breaches heteronormative rules. As one American counsellor maintained, 'straight men don't want to be seen as gay, so they don't report.'[130] This is exacerbated by the fact that, even during the most brutal attacks, male victims sometimes become aroused, even ejaculate.[131] Might they have *unconsciously* 'wanted it', hostile commentators asked?[132] Homophobia is a powerful disincentive to reporting male-on-male (as well as female-on-female) abuse.[133]

Finally, because men are regarded as the protectors of the community, their sexual abuse, public sexualized humiliation and castration is extremely damaging for the community. The dishonour is attached not only to the victim but to his family and community as well, which is why *victims* who report incidents might be beaten by their own families.[134]

To admit to having been sexually assaulted by a woman is even more humiliating: men are assumed to be the initiators of sexual relations and, if coerced, to be able to resist effectively. As Salome Atim, gender officer for the Refugee Project in the Democratic Republic of the Congo, contended, African men are not vulnerable. They 'never break down or cry. A man must be a leader and provide for the whole family. When he fails to reach that set standard, society perceives that there is something wrong.'[135] Sexually abused men attempt to hide their 'disgrace'; unable to do so themselves, they beg others to inform their wives. When wives are told their husband's secret, they responded by asking 'So now how am I going to live with him? As what? Is this still a husband? Is it a wife? ... If he can be raped, who is protecting me?'[136]

This chapter began with Orwell's claim that language can 'corrupt thought'. This aphorism is relevant to all speaking and thinking about sexual violence. It is particularly revelatory in the context of gender dichotomies ('she' as opposed to 'he'), which erase the lives of queer bodies. All people can be rendered vulnerable by power, colonial subjugation and armed conflict. Vulnerability should not be treated therefore as an immutable trait attached to specific *types* of people. The harms of sexual violence extend well beyond the usual 'checklist' approach. Members of supposedly privileged groups – white cis-men, for instance – can also be rendered suffering victims. It is crucial, in other words, to avoid construing minoritized groups as nothing more than the sum of their different vulnerabilities. A 'vulnerable subjecthood' approach insists that if minoritized people are not afraid of abuse, they are delusional. Such an approach provokes fear and anxiety. It encourages LGBTQ people to remain in (or return to) the closet; it closes down the tears and fears of cis-male victims. It contributes to silencing practices and makes safety the responsibility of 'at risk' people. It is profoundly disempowering.

Like thousands of Black lesbians living in South African townships, Millicent Gaika (with whom I started this chapter) knew that she was vulnerable to 'corrective rape' on account of living within a particular skin and geopolitical environment, as well as her gendered identity as a male-identified lesbian. Crucially, though, the 'gender troubles' of lesbians like Gaika are not *the result of* their sexual or gender identities, but arise from the *reception* of those identities by other people. In other words, sexual violence does not simply respond to vulnerability: it *creates* vulnerability.

In contrast, *minoritized* communities (as opposed to minori*ty* people) routinely fight back. Black South African lesbians, for instance, have been effective in forging communities that are joyful as well as empowering. As in Zanele Muholi's artistic projects, discussed earlier, which seek to celebrate the lives of Black queers, any analyses of vulnerabilities must also be studies of the diverse ways in which LGBTQ people, as well as others who are *made* vulnerable in sexually abusive ways, 'express our gendered, racialized, and classed selves' in forging communities of resistance and love.[137] It is within these communities and coalitions that hope lies.

FOUR

Conjugal Cruelty

For I am going anyway,
Whatever you say or do –
Although you try, so hard, to bind me
With tears, fists, works, guilts
And my still existing love for you –
I am going anyway,
Out of nightmares
Into the sun.

Judy Gemmel, 'Into the Sun', 1975[1]

Judy Gemmel's 1975 poem 'Into the Sun' represented a heartfelt cry by a wife determined to leave her abusive husband. It was published at an important time for Australian feminism, when increasing numbers of women were publicly protesting against their subordinate position. Married women were especially conscious that their wedding vows stripped them of rights over their own bodies. They could prosecute their husbands for physical assault, but not for forced sexual intercourse. A married woman was legally assumed to have consented to each and every act of vaginal intercourse with her husband. Legally, she could never accuse him of raping her. This was called the 'marital rape exemption', whereby a husband cannot, by law, rape his wife since by marriage he is entitled to sexual intercourse with her.

This chapter explores this marital rape exemption as well as some of the campaigns to overturn it. Although I start with Australian debates, the difficulties these feminists and reformers faced when attempting to criminalize rape within marriage have been replicated throughout the world. For women, marriage has always come freighted with inequities, whether this includes the disproportionate distribution of domestic labour or the casual sense of sexual entitlement held by husbands. This is why it is important to devote an entire chapter to this most pernicious form of sexual abuse: after all, husbands coercing their wives into sex is the most tolerated form of violence. It has even been vigorously defended. Philosopher of language John L. Austin has argued that the words 'I do', spoken at a wedding ceremony, are one of the paradigmatic examples of a performative speech act: the words themselves act on the world or consummate an action. By saying 'I do', a woman not only marries a man but surrenders future rights to say 'I don't' to him. In the guise of offering conjugal fulfilment and sanctuary to wives, matrimony extends to them a lifetime of sexual servitude.

The (im)possibility of rape within marriage provides a lens from which to explore attitudes about the rights of women over their own bodies. The chapter starts by exploring debates in Australia in the 1970s and 1980s, after which it turns to the historical context of these debates. Nineteenth-century philosophical and political texts were influential in setting the agenda for later debates about the marital rape exemption. The chapter will then briefly survey the status of the marital rape exemption globally, followed by an analysis of the common arguments used *against* criminalizing marital rape. It will conclude by looking at some of the strategies that feminists, reformers and jurists have employed to ensure that husbands are held accountable for their abuses. In that final section, I will focus on progressive attempts to criminalize rape in Namibia. This example allows us to question the limitations of legislative reforms when not accompanied by fundamental shifts in public attitudes.

Before proceeding, however, it is important to issue a word of caution about the language used to discuss these topics. Legal terminologies about the immunity from prosecution of husbands who rape their wives employ phrases such as 'spousal rape' and 'marital rape exemption'. Although it is impossible to avoid using these terms here, their gender-neutrality is deceptive. It would be more accurate to use phrases such as 'rape by *husbands*' (not 'spouses') and '*husbands*' rape exemption'. After all, wives do not need to be exempted from prosecution since, first, they do not 'rape' in the legally defined sense of coerced penetrative contact and, second, it is relatively uncommon for them to sexually compel their husbands into having sex. Equally problematic are laws (as in Greece) that criminalize sexual coercion under the guise of abuse *against family members*, rather than against *women*.[2] Identifying husbands as the main abusers within marriage is not to deny that some men are sexually victimized by their wives. It is to acknowledge, however, huge gender disparities in domestic violence.

Australian Contexts

In the 1970s and 1980s, Australian feminists were dismayed to hear prominent politicians defending the rights of husbands to unrestricted access to their wives' sexed bodies. For example, in a parliamentary debate on 8 April 1981, Liberal MP Nathanael Orr contended that repealing the marital rape exemption for husbands would threaten the basis of marriage. He claimed that, by the marriage contract, 'a responsibility is accepted that each has an equal right to the other person's body.' He was anxious about criminalizing spousal rape on the grounds that 'one does not know what might be done by a bitchy woman or a woman who for some reason has a bad liver.' After all,

> In a bedroom situation, what court can work out what really happened where somebody is out of sorts and a bit of a scrap occurs at home and the wife goes to the local police station and says 'I have been raped'? Who is going to unscramble that situation, particularly where there is no history on either side? Recently the Parliament dealt with anti-discrimination legislation. This is the worst form of discrimination against men that can exist.[3]

Orr's arguments were particularly underhand since he employed an equal-rights model of husband–wife relations. On the one hand, he insisted that *each* partner in the marriage has inalienable rights over the other's body and yet, on the other hand, he argued that criminalizing forced marital sex would discriminate against only one party – the husband. Rights discourse is deeply flawed if it can be used to bolster white male privilege.

Other conservative politicians and the 'morality police' quickly lined up to defeat attempts to eradicate the marital rape exemption. One of these was Mrs Beverley Cains, MP for the Family Team in the Australian Capital Territory's House of Assembly. In 1985, she published a letter in the *Canberra Times* entitled 'Nonsense Talked about Rape in Marriage'.

Cains insisted that the harm of rape was not so much that it was physically damaging or even that it 'violates a woman's bodily integrity'.
Rather, rape is an offence because it

> threatens to beget an extra-marital pregnancy and it violates
> the victim's psychological unity with her present, past or future
> husband and children. It is thus an offence not only against the
> abused woman but against marriage and the family as innate
> elements of her sexuality.

It was a classic example of categorizing women not as people in their
own right but only in relation to their husbands and children. In the
context of marriage, Cains continued, it was clear (at least to her) that
being raped by one's own husband 'does not violate a woman' in the same
'manner or degree' as other forms of rape since, by definition, marriage
'implies consent to continuing sexual intercourse'. She was prepared to
admit that 'no partner should be obliged to be always sexually available
to the other,' but contended that 'a husband's forcing intercourse on the
wife with whom he shares a bed is, in terms of normal perceptions or
right and wrong, a private indignity rather than a civil offence.'[4] Cains
was keen to identify herself as a married woman, signing her name with
a 'Mrs'. Other Australian wives at the time expressed such views. They
argued that the two sexes were engaged in a kind of trade-off: husbands
provided financial support; wives, sexual services. It was a view of marriage that came uncomfortably close to prostitution. Still others accepted
that a husband had 'some right to expect sexual intercourse, provided
his demands are reasonable and not violent or excessive'. Wives should
simply 'put up with it'.[5]

Australian feminists recognized that they had a fight on their hands.
This was not simply an issue about whether women, by marriage, automatically lost all rights of sexual autonomy; it was also about women's
rights and freedoms more broadly. A critical turning point in feminist
activism against sexual violence in Australia was a meeting on 9 and 10
March 1974 in the Teachers' Federation Auditorium in Sydney. Sexual
violence was a key topic and, as was happening throughout the world in
the 1970s, women were increasingly prepared to speak publicly about
being abused. Leading socialist-feminist activist Joyce Stevens attended
the 1974 meeting and, a decade later, recalled that it was 'an exercise in
mass consciousness-raising'. She described how

One hundred and thirty-eight women, many of whom had been unable to reveal physical and sexual assaults to their closest friends or family, rose to talk, some making their debut in public speaking as well. Women sat taut, breathlessly silent as speakers struggled to overcome grief and pain.[6]

A few days later, a group of feminists led by Anne Summers, Jennifer Dakers and Bessie Guthrie entered two deserted buildings in Glebe (Sydney) and converted them into 'Elsie Women's Refuge Night Shelter'. It was the first women's refuge in Australia. Elsie opened on 16 March 1974, after which abused and homeless women and children began arriving.[7] As with similar initiatives, the Australian refuge movement struggled financially. In order to finance their activities at Elsie, Summers even sold marijuana. In her memoir *Ducks on the Pond*, she admitted that 'I can't say today that I am proud of what I did, but it is difficult to overestimate the desperation of those days and the responsibility we felt to the women to whom we had promised refuge.' She also justified her actions on the grounds that she was 'merely redistributing money the inner-city crowd would have spent anyway, to a service that was in dire need'.[8]

Their activism paid off. Within a year, there were twelve refuges in Australia, including the Melbourne Women's Liberation Halfway House, the Brisbane Women's Centre, the Naomi Women's Shelter in Adelaide, Nardine Wimmin's Refuge in Perth and the Marrickville Women's Refuge (which is now the Aboriginal Women and Children's Crisis Services) in inner west Sydney.[9] A 1976 survey of over 1,000 women who had taken shelter in the Elsie and Marrickville refuges found that more than 70 per cent had been victims of marital rape.[10]

The rapid expansion of the refuge movement exposed the needs of women who were being sexually abused by their husbands. Feminist initiatives had been necessary because state and commonwealth governments failed to recognize the scale of the problem. After all, marital rape was not a crime in most states and sexually abused wives were not even allowed to apply for emergency housing. The police were reluctant to intervene in what they called 'domestics'. Anti-rape feminists persevered and, from 1975, began to have limited success when the Commonwealth made some funding available. This was more than simply a matter of money: as refuge activist Catherine Gander maintained, it was also 'about gaining political recognition that domestic violence was not a "private" matter'.[11]

Nevertheless, relying on refuges was nothing more than a palliative solution to a huge underlying problem. More fundamental changes were required. Law needed to be reformed. Australian feminists drew attention to the fact that the immunity of a husband from being prosecuted for rape of his wife was based on a 1736 ruling by the jurist Sir Matthew Hale. According to Hale, a wife gave lifelong consent to sexual intercourse with her husband. In his words,

> The husband cannot be guilty of a rape committed by himself upon his lawful wife, for by their mutual matrimonial consent and contract the wife hath given up herself in this kind unto her husband which she cannot retract.[12]

Feminists and their supporters pointed out that the biblical metaphor that Hale (a devout Puritan) was employing was an inappropriate basis for twentieth-century law. According to the Bible, after fashioning Eve out of Adam's rib, God decreed: 'Therefore shall a man leave his father and his mother, and shall cleave unto his wife: and they shall be one flesh' (Genesis 2:24). God's subsequent curse of Eve included the phrase that 'thy desire shall be to thy husband, and he shall rule over thee' (Genesis 3:16). Feminists also observed that Hale had been active in witchcraft trials, sentencing two women to death in 1662 for the crime.[13]

Hale was not the only source of authority in these matters. Equally important was Sir William Blackstone – another famous jurist – who pronounced on the marital rape exemption in 1765. As Blackstone explained, 'by marriage, the husband and wife are one person in law.' He insisted that 'The very being or legal existence of the woman is suspended during marriage, or at least it is incorporated and consolidated into that of the husband: under whose wing, protection, and *cover*, she performs every thing [*sic*].'[14] According to this doctrine, known as the 'unities' doctrine, the legal existence of a wife is inextricably merged into that of the husband. Her legal existence, including her sexed body, is identical to his.

Was this appropriate for the modern world? Feminists pointed out that eighteenth-century law and society was so different to that of the twentieth century that the pronouncements of these jurists were obsolete. At the time Hale and Blackstone were writing, women lacked basic rights to property and education; they had no access to political rights. Except in rare circumstances, divorce was impossible. Women only gained these rights in the nineteenth century. Given such difference, the pronouncements of Hale and Blackstone should not be allowed to legitimate the subordination of late twentieth-century women.

Australian feminists were aware that legal remonstrations were not enough. The views of women themselves had to change. One of the most creative ways Australian feminists made arguments against the marital rape exemption was through film. In 1980, independent film-makers Susan Lambert, Sarah Gibson, Martha Ansara and Pat Fiske released their short film *Behind Closed Doors*. As with the funding of refuge centres, financing the film had been difficult since they had no access to governmental grants. They used what was then a novel approach: an early, rough version of the film was shown at women's centres, with audiences encouraged to donate money to develop it. This early form of crowd-sourcing ensured that the film was responsive to collective communities of women.[15] As Lambert later recalled, the film 'authenticated for us that working from your own experiences, and trusting your own instinctive and creative feelings', can 'produce something that has really radical potential'.[16] It was 'a discussion starter', Gibson added.[17]

Behind Closed Doors opens with the image of an orderly bedroom, evoking the romantic hopes and dreams of women embarking on conjugal life. Gradually, however, the colours change to red (denoting injuries), then to blue (sexual violence). Glass is shattered; a mournful saxophone plays. The bed becomes dishevelled; a pair of men's trousers and a belt appear on it, along with a torn negligee. No actual women are shown but audiences hear the voices of women who had experienced domestic abuse and rape. A Greek chorus of women are heard talking about the 'inner secrets that live behind closed doors'.[18] These abused wives are determined not to suffer any longer. While they use different words to Gemmel, whose poem introduced this chapter, the refuge women speak about similar themes:

> Although you try, so hard, to bind me
> With tears, fists, works, guilts
> And my still existing love for you –
> I am going anyway.[19]

When the women in *Behind Closed Doors* decide to leave their abusive husbands, order is restored in the bedroom.

The film was not only an activist tool. It was also aimed at women who had experienced domestic violence and marital rape, providing them with a way to discuss their experiences. For this reason, the directors had been careful to avoid any hint of voyeurism. As curator Susan Charlton explained, abused women could use the film because 'they weren't being eroticised as victims . . . It had voices rather than pictures of women.'[20] The film also refused to perpetuate distorted views about the identity of both abusers and abused. In a screening of the film at a workshop for women held at the Filmmakers Co-Op, a reviewer noted that the film

> manages to successfully challenge many of the myths regarding domestic violence. It makes a distinct break with the working class stereotypes – wife bashed by alcoholic/alienated and/or unemployed husband – mainly because at no time is the bruised and battered face of any woman seen on the screen.[21]

By using voiceovers, audiences were 'left with the indisputable realisation that it could happen to any woman, in any domestic situation.'[22]

Admittedly, there is a problem with this 'everywoman' argument: Australian women are unevenly at risk of domestic abuse. Indigenous women, for example, are 'multiply burdened'. According to a 2010 report, Aboriginal women are forty times more likely to be subjected to family violence than other women.[23] And this is an underestimate due to the isolation of many indigenous communities and their distrust of official law enforcement.

Although the directors of *Behind Closed Doors* insisted that abused wives were 'everywoman', they were equally keen not to portray 'everyman' as abusive. As Lambert put it, they did not want *Behind Closed Doors* to be 'read purely and simply as a separatist film; that this happens to women and is done to them by men, so men are the enemy, and the solution is to divide them.'[24] They also worried that some audiences might simplistically conclude that the solution was more refuges, rather than a fundamental revolution in gender relationships.

Change was painfully slow. South Australia took the lead in 1976, with an energetic campaign aimed at repealing the marital rape exemption. It was led by feminists, but also won the support of the progressive Attorney General, Peter Duncan, who insisted that 'every adult person must be given the right to consent to sexual intercourse both within and outside marriage.'[25] Unfortunately, reportage of the campaign was often skewed: Melbourne's *Herald* reported Duncan's words under the heading

'Man and Wife Bill Sparks a Rumble'. The man is the fully human, against whom the woman is defined as wife.

Other aspects of the repeal campaign were driven by a politics of emotion. Politicians in the South Australian Legislative Assembly were emotionally moved when, during a debate on 11 November 1976, MP Anne Levy read accounts by women who had suffered marital rape. They heard that one 35-year-old woman with two children told Levy that 'my husband raped me often. Once, he pushed a carrot up my anus and I was bleeding.' A 26-year-old woman with five children informed her that 'If you talked the wrong way or annoyed him, you got a belting and then he would want to go to bed . . . He raped me several times in front of the kids.'[26] Combined with detailed critiques of the law, these testimonies were effective. In 1976, South Australia became the first *common law* jurisdiction in the world to decree that marital rape was a criminal offence. However, there still had to be 'aggravating circumstances', a clause that was not removed until 1992.[27] South Australia's lead in repealing immunity for husbands was followed by New South Wales in May 1981.[28] By 1992, the marital rape exemption had been repealed in all Australian jurisdictions. Feminists and other activists celebrated, but they were aware that this was only a legal victory. After all, few husbands were actually prosecuted and, while only 5 per cent of rapes reported to the Australian police end in a conviction,[29] the proportion is even lower in the case of marital rape.

Global Cruelty to Wives

The rape of wives by their husbands is endemic in societies which sexualize power. As we will see shortly, nineteenth-century philosophers and feminists set out powerful reasons why it was morally reprehensible. Their arguments emerged in contexts in which women were increasingly seen as persons in their own right and not merely in relation to their fathers or husbands. However, their words went unheeded legally until 1926, when Russia became the first country to criminalize marital rape under civil law. This was followed by Czechoslovakia in 1950 and Poland in 1969. In the case of communist Russia and Czechoslovakia, the decision was based on the view that curtailing sexual freedoms undermined individual rights of self-determination and was opposed to socialist beliefs. In Poland, the exemption of husbands from rape legislation was included in the 1932 Criminal Code. In Chapter XXXII of the Code, rape was within the section on 'offences against morality'. Since sexual relations were only acceptable between married persons, it could not be immoral. During the 1969 reforms of the Code, rape was placed in the section on 'offences against freedom'. Since wives possessed sexual freedoms in socialist countries, they could be raped by their husbands.[30]

The rest of the world was tardy in following their example. It is *still* not a crime for a husband to rape his wife in 48 countries today. In half of those, the marital rape exemption is explicitly *endorsed* in law. Spousal rape did not begin to be abolished in American jurisdictions until 1976 (Nebraska) and it took until 1993 for North Carolina to be the last state to follow. The possibility of convicting a husband of marital rape was only introduced in Italy in 1976, France in 1984, Spain in 1989, England and Wales in 1992 and Germany in 1997. In Greece, marital rape only became an offence as late as 2006. As in Australia, the legal *possibility* of prosecuting violent husbands does not necessarily translate into actual prosecutions. In Greece, only 6 to 10 per cent of women subjected to domestic violence in 2013 complained to the police and conviction rates remain extremely low.[31] Similarly, in South Africa, marital rape was criminalized in 1993 but the first successful prosecution did not happen until nineteen years later.[32] Police everywhere remain reluctant to pursue 'domestics' and they typically encourage wives to attempt reconciliation rather than prosecution.[33]

The lack of legal prohibitions, and their limitations where they exist, are significant since the rape of wives by their husbands is commonplace. For example, in Turkey, the marital rape exemption was eradicated in 2006, at a time when 36 per cent of married women experienced marital rape 'sometimes' and 16 per cent experienced it 'often'.[34] Article 5 of South Africa's 'Prevention of Family Violence Act' (1993) decreed that 'a husband may be convicted of marital rape.'[35] However, a 1999 survey of 1,394 male workers in Cape Town found that 15 per cent of men admitted having raped or attempted to rape a wife or girlfriend on one or more occasions in the previous ten years.[36] A similar study, this time of young men living in greater Johannesburg, showed that one in three believed that 'forcing sex with someone you know is never sexual violence.'[37] Clearly, legislating against marital rape alone will never change attitudes or practices.

These statistics are even more worrying because of the huge barriers to reporting abuse. In many periods of history and in jurisdictions where marital rape is not a crime, statistics are simply not collected. This led historian A. James Hammerton to conclude that the high proportion of court cases in nineteenth-century Britain brought by wives against their husbands for 'assault and battery' were actually instances of marital rape. He observed that many of these assaults took place in bed 'with no explanation of precipitating arguments'. It is a reasonable assumption that many wives were using evidence of physical assault to punish sexually abusive husbands.[38]

Barriers to reporting one's husband for rape are as strong today as in the past. Battered wives know that they will not achieve justice. Penalties for raping one's wife still remain significantly lower than for non-spousal rape. In societies where relatively little value is placed on romantic love (such as parts of South Asia), it can be extremely difficult for a woman to be taken seriously when she complains about a sexually aggressive husband.[39] As we saw in the Australian case study at the start of this chapter, judges and jurors often express concern that women are lying about husband-assaults in order to leverage better divorce settlements. Might battered wives really be vengeful women? Crucially, husbands wield formidable power over their wives. This was what infuriated Joanne Fedler, legal adviser at Johannesburg's People Opposing Woman Abuse (POWA). She found that abusive husbands routinely intimidated their wives, telling them to 'Say Goodbye to your children, because you'll never see them again.' Wives were also informed that

> 'A court is not going to award custody to a lunatic like you'; 'leave me and I swear I'll leave my job. I'd rather starve than pay maintenance to you'; 'Next time I'll shoot you and then me – the law won't convict a dead man'; 'Call the police, see if I care – do you think a policeman doesn't beat his wife?'[40]

Immense financial as well as familial pressures are powerful disincentives to making any complaint.

Certain groups of women face specific barriers to reporting, as Bipasha Ahmed, Paula Reavey and Anamika Majumdar argue in their research on the experiences of South Asian women living in the UK. While warning against homogenizing the experiences of 'South Asian' women as well as adopting stereotypes of them as 'compliant', Ahmed, Reavey and Majumdar observed that, in these close-knit communities, wives were under huge moral pressure to stay in abusive marriages in order to sustain family honour (*izzat*) and avoid communal shaming.[41]

For women who had migrated to Britain to marry, their precariousness was increased by dependency on their husbands' 'documents'.[42] In Britain, this was particularly important because of the 'one-year rule' in immigration law which means that a woman coming to the UK to join her spouse must live with him for at least one year before applying for residency. This could be devastating for women living with violent husbands.[43] Crucially, Ahmed, Reavey and Majumdar draw attention to the particular difficulties South Asian women face due to the lack of a 'gender community' within the family.[44] Unlike most white British women, South Asian women have different spatial issues to navigate, including the very public nature of 'private' spaces (that is, inhabited by members of the extended family, including mothers-in-law). They found that 'more often than not, it was older female family members such as mothers and mothers-in-law' who 'were able to exert power which effectively colluded with the violence'.[45] While discourses about 'romantic love' and 'individual rights' can be employed by white, middle-class women to defend their decision to leave the marital home, these are denied to South Asian women, for whom deference to older members of the family (including older women) was paramount.

Defending Marital Rape

Defenders of the marital rape exemption have been creative in devising rationales for ignoring sexual abuse. The main argument is 'love'. It is difficult to reconcile 'good men' (for example, previously devoted partners) with 'bad deeds' (forcing sex). Many commentators simply refuse to believe that a wife can be psychologically harmed by being coerced to have sex with a man with whom she had previously been intimate. They might even believe that women were naturally masochistic so, in the words of one prominent jurist in the 1950s, 'resistance during preliminary love-making greatly increases the sexual pleasure of some women.'[46]

However, most late twentieth-century arguments supporting the retention of a husband's exemption from rape prosecutions can be categorized under four headings: the nature of the marital contract, gender norms, protection of the family and risks to husbands. Admittedly, generalizations and categorizations emphasize similarities. There are huge differences as well as subtle deviations in the rationales evoked both regionally and across time, let alone those emerging within micro-cultures (religious or minority-ethnic ones, for example). In a chapter of this size, I can only plead that the four categories are simply short-hand attempts to summarize complex worlds of conjugal cruelty. To help alleviate the risks of dissolving differences, this section will conclude by looking briefly at some very specific rationales employed in Ghana.

The first type of argument defending the marital rape exemption focuses on established beliefs about the nature of marriage between a 'man and wife'. The phrase itself is revealing. It identifies the 'man' as the individuated human to whom a 'wife' is appended. As in British-based common law systems, a woman's personhood is thought to merge into her husband's on marriage. In the words of a Rwandan proverb, *Abagore ntibafite ubwoko* or 'wives don't have an identity'.[47] According to this logic, a man cannot be 'violent' towards his own property: a husband is as incapable of raping his wife as an owner of property is of stealing from himself.

The second reason refers to ideas about gender roles within marriage. The wife has a duty to submit to her husband's embraces, whatever her inclination, and the husband has a right to chastise her. These views are widely held. In one 2002–3 survey of 1,835 women in northern Tanzania, 97 per cent of the women agreed that it was a wife's duty to have sex with her husband.[48] This greatly reduces the likelihood that a wife would admit to having been subjected to forced sex by her husband. The other side to this gender roles argument is that husbands are 'naturally' inclined to violence against disobedient wives. This can be illustrated by turning to Japanese courts where, despite the fact that the Penal Code does *not* exempt husbands from rape accusations by their wives, marital rape is rarely prosecuted.[49] In 1985, for example, the Hachiôji Branch of the Tokyo District Court ruled against a woman who sought to divorce her husband on the grounds that he had used violence to have sex with her. The court accepted that the husband's actions 'involved a certain degree of violence' but contended that it was 'within the range of the degree of force used in fights among ordinary married couples and thus it does not warrant special consideration' by the court. The ruling even chastised the wife, maintaining that if she had been 'slightly more considerate of the defendant, discussed the matter with him more and made attempts to resolve his sexual frustration to a certain degree, this would not have happened'. The court ruled that 'it is with the plaintiff [the wife] that responsibility lies.'[50]

A further elaboration of this 'gender roles' argument can be heard in former colonialist or imperial jurisdictions. There, opponents of the criminalization of marital rape maintain that the idea that wives and husbands have separate identities is colonialist: it is an attempt by the 'West' to impose their 'cultural' norms on the 'rest'. As some Indian critics claimed, abolishing the exemption was 'going the way of the West'.[51] In other words, female integrity over their own sexed bodies is a foreign import.

The third, and related, rationale is the need to protect the family. In the words of a Brazilian proverb, *entre marido e mulher não se mete a colher* ('between husband and wife don't interfere' or, literally, 'don't place a spoon').[52] Discarding the marital rape exemption would spread familial disharmony. During the debates in South Australia, opposition was most vocal by members of the Festival of Light, an organization that also opposed homosexuality and abortion. In the words of David Phillips, Chairman of Festival of Light, criminalizing marital rape would 'deal a crushing blow' to the family. Bizarrely, he argued that this was because

> A husband, who is consistently and unreasonably refused inter-course by a vindictive wife, could be pushed into ignoring his wife through fear of reprisal and seek adulterous relationships instead. By weakening the resolve of the partners to repair the crack in their marriage, criminal charges would act like a sledge hammer on a wedge.[53]

Phillips's argument, therefore, depends on the belief that male sexual desire is like a pressure pot: denied 'release' in one way, it will seek another. It also reflects distorted views about feminine deceitfulness. If angered or humiliated, wives would use the laws maliciously to punish abusive husbands. Such wives were not only 'vindictive' but responsible for their husbands' committing adultery.

This was also what a politician belonging to the conservative Mexican Partido Acción Nacional feared. 'What they ask for is ridiculous,' he exclaimed, adding, 'who will believe that rape within marriage exists? That's like[:] careful with your wife, she might get upset and sue you!'[54] A similar response could be heard during debates about the reform of marriage laws in India. The 2005 Protection for Women from Domestic Violence Act, which was the first civil law in India to criminalize domestic violence, was attacked by opponents for threatening to destroy the family and punish in-laws.[55] Indian judges accused its anti-cruelty provision of being an 'instrument of family destruction; a veritable "legal terrorism": far worse than the original ailment it was designed to remedy'.[56] In Taiwan, too, when the first 'Sexual Assault Prevention Act' was put before the Congress in March 1994, the phrase proposing the 'right to sexual autonomy between spouses' was denounced as 'a bill that destroys domestic harmony' since, some reasoned, it was well known that 'marital spats are quickly solved in bed'.[57]

Finally, many arguments claim that overturning the marital rape exemption is dangerous because of husbands' irrepressible sexual needs. As distinguished British legal academic Glanville Williams contended in the early 1990s, 'We are speaking of a biological activity, strongly baited by nature.' He admitted that a husband might 'occasionally . . . continue to exercise what he regards as his right when his wife refuses him' but insisted that this should not be regarded as an act of sexual violence. 'What is wrong with his demand', Williams insisted, is 'not so much the act requested, but its timing, or the manner of the demand'. The 'fearsome stigma of rape' is 'too great a punishment for husbands who use their strength in these circumstances'.[58]

These four general rationales for marital rape can be illustrated – and some variations introduced – by turning to debates in Ghana. The extent of the problem for Ghanaian wives has been aptly characterized in a novel entitled *Changes: A Love Story* (1991) by Ama Ata Aidoo. Aidoo's novel includes a scene in which Esi is raped by her husband Oko. In a country in which over eighty different languages are spoken, Aidoo reflects on the impact of language on the way Ghanaian women understand marital rape. She asks,

> How would you describe marital rape in Akan? . . . 'Igho?
> . . . Yoruba? . . . 'Wolaf? . . . or 'Temne?' . . . Kikuyu? . . . or
> Ki-Swahili?' . . . Chi-Shona? . . . 'Zulu? . . . or Xhosa? Or . . .
> But marital rape? No. The society could not possibly have an
> indigenous word or phrase for it.[59]

Without an indigenous word meaning 'marital rape', how could a woman speak about it?

Part of the problem facing wives in Ghana results from the payment of large dowries to the brides' families. This encourages the assumption that the husband has 'bought' his wife and therefore has a right to insist on unquestioned obedience.[60] Wives often internalize such gender roles. As one Ghanaian woman explained,

> When he forces because he is in need, it does not amount to rape.
> First of all[,] I must ask myself why I married him. If we were not
> married, I will never have sex with him[,] so marriage is primarily
> for sex.

This woman also expressed a concern about sexually transmitted infections. She mentioned that she had heard stories that some men 'have sex with their female aids' as soon as 'they get to the office' in the morning. By refusing to have sex with her husband, she worried that she would be 'exposing my husband to this risk ... In the end he will bring me AIDS on a silver platter because I would have exposed him to it through denial.'[61] This was a serious concern for Ghanaian wives, not least because the law recognizes polygamous marriages, also potentially exposing women to sexual diseases.[62] Fundamentally, it blames wives for the actions of their husbands.

In 2007, when the question of allowing the prosecution of sexually coercive husbands was debated in parliament, Ghanaian politicians maintained that it would represent an unwarranted interference of the state into marital relationships. The criminalization of rape within marriage would disturb both the 'sanctity of marriage' and the privacy of the family.[63] As Edward Mahama, a physician and prominent politician, reasoned, 'If we talk about marital rape, it means we are going into the bedroom, and we have no right to go there ... You can't legislate on such issues.'[64] The law was also 'anti-Ghanaian'.[65] According to some chiefs in the Upper East region of Ghana, prohibiting marital rape might be suitable for 'urban dwellers' but, in the rest of the country, it was a 'foreign imposition'.[66]

Ghanaian opponents of the repeal of the marital rape exemption failed. In 2007, the law was changed to allow the prosecution of husbands. But legislative decrees do not necessarily affect thoughts and behaviours. A 2015 study by sociologist Phebemary Makafui Adodo-Samani found that only 3 per cent of married Ghanaian men and 18 per cent of married Ghanaian women believed that non-consensual sex acts in marriage constitute rape.[67] Adodo-Samani explained this finding in terms of the weak social status of Ghanaian women, the privatization of marital sex abuse and 'Ghanaian socialisation'.[68] Although Adodo-Samani comes precariously close to blaming Ghanaian 'culture', her arguments about the 'private' nature of the family and female status point to very real problems.

Overturning the Rape Exemption

Although this chapter has devoted considerable attention on the arguments of men and women who *support* the marital rape exception, *opposition* to rape within marriage can be traced to the mid-nineteenth century.[69] Where there is power, there is always resistance. This has become the rallying crying of Foucauldian scholars, based on Michel Foucault's argument in the *Histoire de la sexualité* (1976) that defiance is inherent to power relations. A husband's immunity from rape prosecutions is no exception.

Early opposition was registered by utilitarian John Stuart Mill, the most influential English-speaking philosopher of the nineteenth century. Mill attacked the assumption that a husband owned his wife's body. In 'The Subjection of Women' (1869), Mill railed against the fact that a wife could be forced into having sexual intercourse. He argued that this placed married women in a worse situation than enslaved women, who could 'refuse to her master the last familiarity' (in theory, but not in practice). Mill provocatively concluded that marriage was 'the only actual bondage known to our law. There remain no legal slaves, except the mistress of every house.'[70]

Other feminists of the period could also be heard speaking publicly against a wife's sexual enslavement by her husband. Prominent American women's rights campaigner Elizabeth Cady Stanton insisted that a woman's rights over her body were the first step towards gaining economic and political equality. As she informed the 1854 women's rights convention in Albany, the marriage contract was 'instant civil death to one of the parties'. By marriage, women were stripped of everything that was important: the wife 'can own nothing, sell nothing. She has no right even to the wages she earns; her [sexed] person, her time, her services, are the property of another.'[71] This meant that marriage was nothing more than 'legalised prostitution'.

It was no coincidence that many of these early feminists arguing for the right to the bodily integrity of women were active in both abolitionist movements and pro-birth-control campaigns. Like Mill, they maintained that there were links between the patriarchal ownership of the bodies of enslaved people and wives. Stanton and fellow campaigner Susan B. Anthony referred to married women forced to flee their violent husbands as 'fugitive wives: running to Indiana and Connecticut divorce mills, like slaves to their Canada, from marriages worse than plantation slavery.'[72]

Of course, it was a comparison that discounted the extremes of abuse suffered by enslaved women, but as political rhetoric it was powerful. These feminists were also uncomfortably aware that the marital rape exemption meant compulsory maternity for many women. At a time where there was no reliable birth control and maternal death rates in childbirth were high, it was crucial that a woman's 'no' was respected. Since divorce was prohibited, rape in marriage was not only a public health issue; it was also a matter of life and death for many women.

The pleas by people like Mill, Stanton and Anthony in the 1850s and 1860s for marriages to be based on mutual respect and love were confined mainly to feminist circles. By the 1870s, however, reformers from a much broader range of philosophical and political perspectives began imploring husbands to change their bedroom behaviour. For many commentators, forcing a wife to have sex was wrong because it harmed the *husband*. The effects on husbands were thought to be similar to those of obsessive masturbation. Aggressive husbands were warned that their actions would give them heart palpitations, impair their digestion and cause general weakness. Even worse, they would suffer spermatorrhoea (that is, the involuntary drooling of semen without erection) and their 'genetic powers' would 'lose their vigor'.[73] Even the children of forced sex within marriage would inherit their fathers' weakness, having been endowed before birth with 'lustful passions and morbid appetites'.[74]

For many husbands, these arguments were convincing. They tied into a new 'cult of masculinity' that was emerging from the end of the nineteenth century.[75] The domestic sphere was being reconceptualized as a restful location where husbands could forge companionate relationships with their wives. Male dominance in the home went unquestioned, but 'modern' husbands professed to be happy to at least discuss the sexual and other desires of their wives.

Admittedly, such reconceptualizations of relationships between husbands and wives did not alter underlying assumptions about the husband as the 'head of the household', let alone dent the marital rape exemption. For those things to happen, feminist lobbying, coupled with the rise and increased intervention of women in politics and law, was necessary. This gathered pace from the 1970s. Married or not, feminists argued that a woman's body belonged to one person: herself. The assumption that a husband had any control over his wife's body was simply one more example of patriarchal rule. These points were part of wider arguments about rape. Feminist attention shifted from the sexual aspects of rape towards its foundation in regimes of power and domination – a move that created a space to critique the authority of husbands over wives.

Feminist research was also exposing the extent of the problem. Notably, sociologist and activist Diana E. H. Russell published her landmark *Rape in Marriage* in 1987, based on interviews with 930 women from San Francisco. Of the 644 women who were or had been married, 74 per cent stated that they had been forced by their husband into having sex and 13 per cent accused their partner of rape or sexual abuse. Russell was able to show that victims of marital rape were harmed in similar ways to other victims of rape. The main difference was that wives suffered *additional* feelings of betrayal, inability to trust and isolation.[76] A host of other research shows that, contrary to myth, wives sustained *more* severe physical injuries than did other rape victims.[77] According to another study, over half of victims of marital rape suffered severe long-term effects, compared with 39 per cent of victims of stranger rape.[78] Rape was a hidden form of traumatic assault.

The first step was convincing legislators that eighteenth-century rulings about marital relations were obsolete. The second step was to show that the law was 'capable of evolving in the lights of changing social, economic and cultural developments', as the Scottish judge Henry Shanks Keith noted during the 1991 debates in the House of Lords. Lord Keith argued that Hale's views should no longer be a guide to current law since 'the state of women, and particularly the married woman, has changed out of all recognition' from Hale's time. Marriage was now a 'partnership of equals, and no longer one in which the wife must be the subservient chattel of the husband'. No 'reasonable person' would believe that simply by marriage she was giving her husband 'her irrevocable consent to sexual intercourse . . . under all circumstances and irrespective of the state of her health or how she happens to be feeling at the time'.[79] After strenuous lobbying, the marital rape exemption was finally abolished in Scotland in 1989 and in the rest of the UK in 1992.

This chapter began with the attempts by Australian feminists to get public recognition of violence against wives and, in particular, to repeal the exemption from prosecution given to husbands who rape their wives. Like others seeking to criminalize marital rape, they recognized that criminalization and the provision of refuges were only the first step in overhauling relationships between men and women. Perhaps the abolition of marriage itself would be necessary if men and women were to become truly equal.

There were always tensions in the movement. One of these focuses on the way the debate is gendered. Until recently, attempts to revolutionize husband/wife relationships have focused exclusively on the threats *to* wives *by* husbands. This has been questioned. Although there are unquestionably gender disparities in domestic violence, it is also a fact that some wives sexually abuse their husbands. Men's rights groups have distorted the statistics. Not only do they claim that such abuse is much more common than it is, they also use these distortions in profoundly anti-womanist ways to further bolster white male supremacy. However, the fact that sexually aggressive wives cannot simply be overlooked has generated tensions within the refuge movement as well as feminism more broadly. When the Elsie refuge was taken over by the St Vincent de Paul Society in 2014, it was announced that it would remain a service catering only to women and children.[80] Male victims of domestic sexual violence would be excluded.

The other tension relates to the over-reliance on criminal justice systems to change behaviours. South Australia was the first common law jurisdiction to criminalize marital rape, but it led to very few prosecutions, let alone convictions. Optimists simply claimed that the value of the reform was the way it led to public discussion 'in pubs, in front of television, in buses, in the corner deli, between husbands and wives, between wives and wives, in discussions between men in the workplace, between women in the workplace', as a former press secretary and general policy adviser to Attorney General Peter Duncan contended.[81]

A less rosy view was evident in the context of reforms in Namibia. That country's 'Combating Rape Act' of 2000 is one of the most progressive pieces of anti-rape legislation in the world. It does much more than criminalize marital rape. It also employs an expansive definition of rape; rejects the British-colonialist common law legacy that distinguishes between 'real' rape and other forms; does not make gender distinctions for 'victims' or 'perpetrators'; disallows reference to the victim's previous sexual history; does not require that victims prove non-consent; and accepts evidential rules similar to those required for other crimes.[82] However, rape in Namibia has not subsided and some even argue it is becoming more widespread and brutal.

The painful lesson emerging from the failures of liberal feminism is that a reliance on law does not address underlying gender inequalities and the oppression of women. Despite all the reforms – the prosecution of rapist-husbands, the establishment of shelters, the education of police and instructions to jurors and civil protection orders – the effect for battered and abused wives has been limited. This is the dilemma we will address in the last chapter of this book.

FIVE

Mothers and Monsters

Girls and women are generally assumed to be objects rather than agents of sexual violence. They are cast in the role of 'angels in the house', 'icons of innocence' and nurturers of children and communities. Too often, scholarship on sexual violence has bolstered such ideas. After all, the foundations of knowledge about sexual violence were, and remain, the radical insights of feminists in the 1970s and 1980s. The most prominent thinkers in this tradition maintained a strict binary-gender divide in their conceptualization of rape: they thought in terms of male perpetrators and female victims. Masculinity itself was portrayed as contaminated by its investment in aggressive forms of sexual expression. An extreme version of this can be seen in Catharine MacKinnon's claim that men want

> women bound, women battered, women tortured, women humiliated, women degraded and defiled, women killed. Or, to be fair to the soft core, [they want] women sexually available, have-able, there for them, wanting to be taken and used, with perhaps just a little light bondage.

MacKinnon quipped that 'part of the male interest in keeping women down lies in the fact that it gets men up.'[1]

Such rhetoric is false; it is also dangerous. Male-bashing doesn't help us understand the complexity of aggressive sexual encounters. It is certainly not conducive to engaging in constructive dialogue with boys and men. Equally important, it consigns girls and women to a position of eternal victims: by virtue of being female, we are already and always the wounded, subjugated gender. As social critic Sharon Marcus perceptively observed, taking 'male violence or female vulnerability as the first and last instances in any explanation of rape' makes 'the identities of rapist and raped pre-exist the rape itself'.[2] Clearly, we need more subtle ways of thinking about gender, agency and subjection. This is why this chapter takes as its fundamental premise that there is nothing essentially violent in masculinity or passive in femininity. Mapping masculinity and femininity onto physiologically male and female bodies also represents a limited understanding of gender, and one that needs to be replaced by a more nuanced view of gender as performative in the sense mapped out by philosopher Judith Butler and other queer scholars. As we shall see, acts of sexual abuse are products of gendered labour, and that labour is political.

Female Perpetrators

Feminists can no longer ignore the fact that girls and women inflict sexual suffering on other people. Admittedly, there are good pragmatic reasons to be wary about focusing on sexually violent women. Second-wave feminists observed that exposing the extent of male violence against girls and women led some of their adversaries to seek out examples of sexually aggressive women: 'the media', journalist Michele Landsberg complained, 'have never been more relieved and satisfied than when they can point to a woman who is "just as bad" or "even worse"' than their male counterparts'.[3] Focusing on such women effectively depoliticizes gendered critiques of the most common abusers, who are cisgendered male.

More worrying for feminists is the rise and rise of men's rights activism. These pro-male activists use distorted statistics about female perpetration of sexual abuse to push a radical anti-womanist agenda.[4] Not surprisingly, the Southern Poverty Law Center, which monitors hate groups, lists many of these men's rights groups as organizations pedalling hatred.[5] A hard-headed feminist politics might not wish to tip the 'justice balance' against girls, women and minoritized genders even more than it already is.

However, in this chapter, I contend that the dangers of creating hierarchies of victims are greater than the risks of either minimizing male-led violence or depoliticizing it. Acknowledging and alleviating the full universe of suffering is crucial to any feminist politics. A feminism that turns a blind eye to the vulnerability of the full range of bodies, of all genders, is politically weakened.

Wars on Terror

Much of the literature on female-perpetrated sexual violence points to the extremely high levels occurring during civil-war-type conflicts in the geopolitical South. I will be returning to these conflicts later in this chapter. However, it is important to observe that sexually aggressive women are not rare in the West, although commentators too often portray such women as atypical, even perverse, *individuals* rather than members of sexually belligerent *cultures*.

The U.S. 'War on Terror' provides numerous examples of sexually aggressive women. A 2005 Pentagon investigation led by Vice Admiral Albert T. Church III into the U.S. military prison in Guantánamo Bay (Cuba) exposed the ways in which some female interrogators were using sexualized tactics to extort information. One interrogator 'made inappropriate contact with a detainee by running her fingers through the detainee's hair and making sexually suggestive comments and body movements, including sitting on the detainee's lap'. The Church Report stated that this was not 'indecent assault' as defined in the Manual for Courts-Martial 'because the interrogator did not perpetrate the act with the intent to gratify her own sexual desires'. As a result, she was simply 'given a written admonishment'. Church referred to another female interrogator who wiped 'dye from a red magic marker on the detainee's shirt', telling him that 'the red stain was menstrual blood.' She received a 'verbal reprimand'.[6] Such practices were witnessed by Erik Saar, an interpreter at Guantánamo Bay. In his account of his time in the facility, he saw a female interrogator smearing (fake) menstrual blood on a Muslim detainee's face while he screamed hysterically.[7] Kristine Huskey, a lawyer representing Guantánamo detainees, noted that they had been

> forced to strip naked in front of female guards; some have had
> their private parts touched and squeezed; some have been offered
> sex in exchange for cooperation; some have been threatened
> with rape. One of my clients told of an interrogator pulling out a
> condom and threatening to use it on him unless he 'cooperated'.[8]

A female interrogator would 'blow cigarette smoke in his face, rub his neck, call him handsome, "talk dirty" by speaking of sex acts, make sexual sounds, and take her shirt off so [the] client could see her breasts and nipples'.[9] Another lawyer at Guantánamo described how a detainee started crying when describing the way a female interrogator made suggestive comments. He was 'truly afraid', she recalled, because 'he feared that she would rape him.'[10] As one official admitted, in places like Guantánamo, good interrogators 'take initiative and are a little creative'.[11]

Public outrage about the use of such tactics in Guantánamo Bay and Afghanistan was muted, unlike the uproar caused by the photographic exposure of sexualized torture in Iraq. The photographs had been handed to the army's Criminal Investigations Division on 13 January 2004 by military policeman Specialist Joseph Darby, who had been stationed at the Baghdad Correctional Facility (Abu Ghraib). CBS News's '60 Minutes II' exposed the scandal on 28 April 2004 while journalist Seymour Hersh's articles in the *New Yorker* were published in April–May that year.

Most of the sexualized abuse was carried out by male guards and soldiers, not women. They sodomized detainees, sexually assaulted them with truncheons and phosphorescent tubes, required them to be naked in public, put female underwear on their heads, compelled them to masturbate and forced fathers and sons to engage in sexual acts with each other. The homophobic nature of much of the abuse was blatant, as was the aim to transform the male prisoners into terrified and racialized 'women'.

Less publicized was the sexual humiliation, rape and impregnation of *female* detainees by male U.S. guards in detention centres throughout Iraq. In December 2003, a female detainee known as 'Noor' smuggled a note out of Abu Ghraib complaining about the rapes to Iraqi lawyer Amal Kadham Swadi. Noor begged the Iraqi resistance to bomb the jail to spare them further shame.[12] Some abused detainees were reported to have committed suicide, while others were subjected to 'honour' killings by their families after being released.

The actions of these male abusers were condemned, although many commentators dismissed the abuses as nothing more than martial masculinity taken to an extreme. In contrast, public dismay focused on the photographs showing white American *women* perpetrating sexual abuse. Photographs of Private Lynndie England, Private Megan Ambuhl and Specialist Sabrina Harman sent shock waves through women's rights groups. In a chapter entitled 'Feminism's Assumptions Upended' (2004), prominent activist and columnist Barbara Ehrenreich confessed that her response to seeing the Abu Ghraib photographs showed that she still retained 'some illusions about women'. Although she had never believed that women were 'innately gentler and less aggressive than men', she had harboured a different kind of 'feminist naiveté' – that is, the assumption that men were 'the perpetual perpetrators', with women their 'perpetual victims'. In Ehrenreich's words, many feminists held that male sexual violence against women was

> the root of all injustice. Rape has repeatedly been an instrument of war and, to some feminists, it was beginning to look as if war was an extension of rape. There seemed to be at least some evidence that male sexual sadism was connected to our species' tragic propensity for violence. That was before we had seen female sexual sadism in action.

What she saw in the Abu Ghraib exposés destroyed her belief in women's moral superiority to men.[13]

Ehrenreich's disquiet stemmed from a reluctance among academics and other commentators to address female aggression in the U.S. armed forces.[14] Feminist scholars have focused on the injustice of not allowing women to serve in combatant roles, the barriers to military women being promoted to higher ranks and the pervasiveness of sexual harassment and rape of female soldiers *within* the military. Acknowledging that female members of the armed forces were responsible for *perpetrating* violence against other people – including girls and women throughout the world – was obscured by these other concerns.

In contrast, the visual evidence of the abuses in Iraq could not be ignored; clearly, martial femininity included sexual bellicosity. As philosopher Bonnie Mann remarked, in an increasingly democratic military, 'the American woman is given the phallus' and is 'invited to participate in the militarized masculine aesthetic along with the men'. As such, women are permitted 'to become the one who penetrates the racialized other'.[15]

This does not mean that female-perpetrated sexual abuse is identical to its male equivalent. Violence is gendered. The male guards in U.S. military facilities in Iraq, Afghanistan and Cuba engaged in overtly aggressive, often penetrative, acts; the women flashed their breasts, danced semi-naked and smeared fake menstrual fluids. It was *female* sexuality that was being weaponized.

Crucially, these were *deliberate*, gendered tactics. The Church Report of 2005 conceded that the sexualized abuses carried out by female interrogators in Guantánamo Bay raised 'problematic issues concerning cultural and religious sensitivities'.[16] Prior to being deployed in the 'War on Terror', U.S. military personnel were given 'cultural awareness' training. Journalists Philip Gourevitch and Errol Morris explained that this included being taught that Arab men were 'sexual prudes, with a particular hangup about being seen naked in public, especially by women. What better way to break an Arab, then, than to strip him, tie him up, and have a woman laugh at him?'[17] Gourevitch and Morris contended that the female participants in the abuses were 'not expected to wrest prisoners into stress positions or otherwise overpower them'. Their purpose was to inflict suffering on detainees simply by being present as witnesses.[18] Army Specialist Charles Graner, the primary instigator of the abuse, admitted that having female interrogators watching was 'just so they'd know – Hey, here's a female and, you know, she watching.'[19] England agreed, noting that 'one of the things they wanted was [for] females to be there so they knew they were being humiliated by having females see them naked.'[20] Abu Ghraib detainee Dhia al-Shweiri understood this all too clearly. He noted that the abuses, including those involving U.S. women, were attempts to 'humiliate us, break our pride'. 'We are men,' he insisted, adding that

> It's OK if they beat me. Beatings don't hurt us, it's just a blow. But no one would want their manhood to be shattered . . . They want us to feel as though we were women, the way women feel, and this is the worse insult, to feel like a woman.[21]

In this way, women in the U.S. military feminized the enemy through the imposition of Western, heteronormative sexual 'freedoms', combined with white, racial privilege. Muslim preacher Sheik Mohammed Bashir expressed this point bluntly when he noted that U.S. military personnel were articulating 'the freedom of rape, the freedom of nudity, and the freedom of humiliation'.[22]

An Artistic Response

Since 2004, there has been a proliferation of analyses in newspapers, edited collections and academic books seeking to understand how 'ordinary' American women like England, Ambuhl and Harman could sexually abuse male Iraqi detainees.[23] Similar academic analyses have been published exploring the sexual abuse perpetrated by American women in Afghanistan, Guantánamo Bay and elsewhere during the 'War on Terror'.

Some of the most insightful responses, however, have been artistic. In 2005, during New York's Performa05 (the first visual art performance biennial in the USA), performance artist Coco Fusco presented an early version of what was to become 'A Room of One's Own: Women and Power in the New America'. It was a powerful reflection on sexual violence perpetrated by American women in the armed forces.

The performance opened on a stage furnished with a podium, flanked by an American flag and two screens. One screen displayed a PowerPoint presentation, projecting slogans, charts, photographs and drawings; the other was a simulated CCTV video of a male detainee wearing an orange jumpsuit in an interrogation room. The central element of the performance involved Sergeant Fusco (played by Latina artist Coco Fusco) delivering a lecture to a room of military and official personnel. During her speech, she would periodically leave the stage to bark out commands in pidgin Arabic to the terrified detainee on the CCTV. Sergeant Fusco's speech began by saying

> Ladies and gentlemen, it was the great British writer Virginia Woolf who argued that every woman had to have a room of her own in order to manifest her strengths . . . At the onset of the new millennium, American women finally have what they need to demarcate their prowess. The War on Terror offers an unprecedented opportunity to the women of this country.[24]

She was, of course, referring to Woolf's classic essay *A Room of One's Own* (1929), which contended that, to succeed in a male-dominated world, women needed money and a room of their own within which they could be truly creative. In Fusco's Brechtian performance, American women were being allowed to occupy rooms of their own. But they were interrogation rooms.

Within prison cells, female interrogators could express what Sergeant Fusco called 'tactical creativity'. Rather than resorting to physical torture, women could exploit the terrorists' own supposedly 'perverse cultural conditioning' to intimidate detainees. Sergeant Fusco was drawing on anthropologist Raphael Patai's book *The Arab Mind* (1973), a racist text that was widely discussed among pro-war Washington conservatives prior to the invasion of Iraq.[25] Patai had argued that 'Arab culture' was sexually repressive and that 'the biggest weakness of Arabs is shame and humiliation.' Therefore, sexualized torture was a particularly effective interrogation weapon.[26] This book was to become 'the bible of the neocons on Arab behavior'.[27]

In Fusco's play, the abusive tactics advocated were those employed by American women in detention centres during the 'War on Terror': that is, forcing detainees to undress or masturbate in front of them, flashing their breasts, sitting on their laps and smearing (fake) menstrual blood on their faces. Sergeant Fusco maintained that 'even a hardened Islamic terrorist' could 'be disarmed through the tactical use of *certain lewd phrases and gestures* particularly when performed by a Western female who is preferably in her 20s and physically fit'.[28] These 'lewd phrases' included 'YOUR SISTER'S VAGINA OR FUCK YOU' and 'dicksucker'.[29] At one stage during Sergeant Fusco's speech, photographs of women wearing burkas alongside others of women with their faces uncovered appeared on the PowerPoint screen. These images prompted Sergeant Fusco to inform her audience that 'one of our principal goals in bringing democracy to Afghanistan has been to liberate Afghan women.'[30] It was a play on feminist critic Gayatri Chakravorty Spivak's famous quip about 'white men saving brown women from brown men': militarized, white *women* in the developed world were bringing 'freedom' to developing-world 'brown women' by sexually abusing 'brown men'. The 'strategic deployment of female interrogators', Sergeant Fusco maintained, 'represents a giant leap for womankind'.[31]

Coco Fusco's performance was a stark warning of the potential impact of 'equality feminism': it gives women the equal right to sexually abuse, torture and kill members of any group that the government designates an 'enemy'. Fusco was encouraging feminists to reflect on their complicity in perpetrating violence on people elsewhere in the world.

Global Exposés of Female Perpetrators

'A Room of One's Own: Women and Power in the New America' draws attention to three arguments: sexually abusive acts are not monopolized by the male gender; there is no strict dichotomy between the status of perpetrator and victim; context is paramount. All three arguments come into focus when analysing female-perpetrated sexualized violence throughout the world.

It is no coincidence that sexually abusive women flourish in the context of war. Armed conflicts and sexual torture are related phenomena, snaring militarized women as well as men into practices that they might otherwise abhor. Although not technically a 'war zone', social disarray is so high in parts of Haiti that levels of armed violence, including gang rape perpetrated by women belonging to armed criminal gangs and paramilitaries, rival those occurring in civil wars.[32] In Haiti and elsewhere, female perpetrators of sexual violence generally act *alongside* male leaders. This is not surprising since, during most armed conflicts, the people occupying positions of power that give them the authority to order and carry out abusive practices are male. The subordinate position of (most) women in the military means that they lack many opportunities to take the initiative in promoting sexual abuse. Exceptions included Simone Gbagbo of the Côte d'Ivoire in 2010–11 (discussed below), Indira Vrbanjac Kameric and Biljana Plavšic. Kameric was one of the commanders of a women's detention camp housed in the Polet sports stadium in Bosanski Brod. Witnesses testified that she used to 'take women to the front line where countless soldiers raped them all night'.[33] Plavšic was a former acting President of the Serbian Republic of Bosnia and Herzegovina. At the International Criminal Tribunal for the Former Yugoslavia, she pleaded guilty to acts of persecution as a crime against humanity. Plavšic was also accused of responsibility for acts of sexual violence carried out in detention facilities centres in Zvornik (the Ekonomija farm) and the camp at Čelopek. She was sentenced to eleven years' imprisonment.[34] However, Plavšic's violence was routinely underplayed by claims that she was naively entangled in a 'man's game' that exploited her.[35] Commentators also focused on her relationship with the brutal Serbian paramilitary commander Željko Ražnatović (known as 'Arkan'), with its sexualized overtones.

Some of the most *publicized* instances of female-perpetrated sexual violence have occurred in African states such as Liberia during the civil war, where women used objects to rape other women and to injure the genitals of both male and female prisoners.[36] But the attention paid to female-perpetrated sexual violence in Rwanda during the 1994 genocide exceeds all other. Hutu women could be heard broadcasting incitements to rape and murder Tutsi Rwandans on the Milles Collines radio station.[37] They sexually abused young Tutsi boys.[38] They lured other women into situations where they could be violated, often participating in the rapes by holding the victims down. They would even sing while women were raped and killed.[39] Legal scholar Nicole Hogg interviewed 71 Rwandan women who had been detained for their involvement in the genocide and found that half had been involved in killing while 27 per cent had exposed the hiding places of Tutsis or 'handed someone over' to the killers.[40] The *gacaca* courts (community courts) tried around 2 million suspects, of whom 10 per cent were women.[41] As one female genocide suspect admitted to Hogg, women participated in the genocide by 'refusing to hide Tutsis' and 'assisting the killers'. They cooked them food, even brought meals to the roadblocks.[42] In carrying out such tasks, they were (at the very least) colluding in the sexual abuse of the Tutsi girls and women, and they often actively participated in the rapes. Clearly, for these aggressive women, Hutu nationalism overrode gender-identification.

The conflict in the Democratic Republic of the Congo (DRC) exposed comparable patterns. According to one study, 17 per cent of the survivors of sexual violence perpetrated by the Mai-Mai (community-based militia groups) claimed that women had been perpetrators.[43] Another survey in North and South Kivu and Ituri (DRC) maintained that 41 per cent of female rape victims and 10 per cent of male victims were assaulted by a woman.[44]

Similar observations have been made in the context of the eleven-year-long civil war in Sierra Leone (1991–2002). Women participated in one in four of the gang rapes.[45] Female rebels subjected female abductees to virginity tests and manually raped them before handing them over to male rebels. Some even forced captive men to choose between engaging in sexual intercourse or being killed.[46] According to international relations scholar Dara Kay Cohen, most of the gang rapes in Sierra Leone were committed by members of the Revolutionary United Front, one-quarter of whom were female.[47] She came to the startling conclusion that there was a positive correlation between the proportion of women in an armed group and the extent of sexual violence committed by them. In other words, 'groups with more women not only committed rape but actually committed *more* rape than did groups with fewer women.'[48] Nationalist and ethnic ideologies exerted a formidable power over women as well as men: they easily trumped female solidarity.

Cohen's discussion of sexual violence during the civil war in Sierra Leone draws attention to another issue: girls and women were both perpetrators *and* victims of sexual violence during armed conflicts. Power inequalities and injustices experienced by female victims made them turn into perpetrators. This is how some scholars have explained England, Ambuhl and Harman's behaviour. In terms of gender, class, age and military rank, all three women were subordinate members of a hyper-masculine, military culture. Within military as well as civil hierarchies, they were relatively powerless. For example, at the time of the scandal, England was 21 years old. She had been raised in an impoverished family, experienced developmental difficulties and was poorly educated. The army employed her as a military file clerk. She was also being bullied by Graner, her boyfriend. Graner outranked England, was fourteen years older and had a history of violence. His wife had obtained three protection orders against him.[49] England repeatedly denied that she could have exercised significant agency, claiming that Graner had pressurized her into participating. She was embedded in an institution in which refusing to participate in the activities of the group – even when those activities clearly constituted torture – would have taken a level of moral courage that she did not possess.[50]

Without dismissing them totally, such arguments are problematic. Importantly, they threaten to strip female perpetrators of agency altogether: women become pawns in a story that belongs either to more powerful men or to an amorphous, 'patriarchal' military. Even powerful military women could be absolved from responsibility. For example, Brigadier General Janis Karpinski was the commanding officer of all sixteen detention facilities in Iraq. After the scandal was exposed, she refused to admit liability for the abuses, despite the fact that she oversaw the Abu Ghraib prison and her lack of leadership facilitated the abuses. In her memoir entitled *One Woman's Army*, Karpinski based her claim that she was not answerable for the abuses on the grounds that she had been scapegoated as a reservist and a woman.

Constrained Agency

Drawing attention to the inequities that girls and women face in everyday life has been used politically to minimize their responsibility for acting in sexually atrocious ways. This argument becomes stronger when female perpetrators of sexual violence have themselves been victims of sexual atrocities. The starkest examples are girls and women abducted, press-ganged or otherwise forced into the Revolutionary United Front in Sierra Leone and the Lord's Resistance Army in northern Uganda. All were subjected to extreme violence by their own comrades. Upon joining, nearly all the female 'recruits' were immediately 'disvirginalized' by gang rape.[51] They were forced into 'bush marriage' and around half subsequently gave birth.[52] This severed their ties to their previous life and made desertion extremely difficult.

However, recruits were also required to participate in killing, mutilating and raping other people; any reluctance or signs of distress could result in them being gang-raped or murdered.[53] Cohen even argues that sexual violence *both* against members of their own group *and* against rival groups is a central means for forging cohesive intragroup dynamics in armed groups with low levels of cohesion.[54] Some female soldiers enthusiastically joined in the violence against other girls and women, hoping that their cooperation would mean that their male comrades would spare them similar insults.[55] Whatever their motivation, all were forced to navigate complex social and military contexts by employing tactical agency under conditions not of their own making. This involved negotiating with fellow captives, commanders, 'bush husbands' and boyfriends, as well as making strategic alliances with NGOs, medical professionals and peacekeepers.

Rehabilitation of these victim-perpetrators presents their birth-communities with formidable problems. Families and local villagers were often hostile to their return. This is not surprising since these girl and woman soldiers had perpetrated numerous acts of terror – often against members of their own communities – and they had broken various taboos, including those relating to premarital sex and pregnancy.[56] Marriage was unlikely. They were rendered social outcasts.

It has been a deliberate policy of NGOs and rehabilitation groups not to publicly disclose the fact that a large proportion of victims of rape and other atrocities had also perpetrated such abuses. They have strong incentives to emphasize the 'victim' status of the girls and women they seek to support. Human rights activists, charities and other Western philanthropists seek to support individuals who are unequivocally *casualties* of conflict. The more 'innocent', the better. Hence the emphasis placed on the rape of children, unmarried girls and women, pregnant women and the elderly, as well as the interest shown in infants born of rape. These groups are viewed as 'not responsible' for any carnage, an argument that is problematic because it denies their complicity while also opening up the possibility of talking about victims who *are* responsible for the violations inflicted upon them. Western interventionist organizations have pragmatic reasons for taking this stance. Donors are keen to fund programmes supporting rape *victims*; they are reluctant to donate money to help girls and women who were not only rape victims, but perpetrators of sexual abuses, combatants and lovers of their 'bush husbands'.[57] In Uganda and Sierra Leone, even governmental campaigns espousing DDR

– that is, 'disarmament, demobilization and reintegration' – refused to go beyond the 'victim' paradigm. They frequently assumed that female members of militias were *casualties* of the armed conflicts, never 'soldiers', despite the fact that in conflicts like the one in Sierra Leone between 10 and 50 per cent of combatants were female.[58]

For critics anxious to acknowledge female victim-perpetrators of sexual violence, the dichotomy between agency and subjection has been problematic. In many armed conflicts, appealing to a Western neoliberal rhetoric of 'choice' makes no sense: girls and women were faced with the 'choice' of raping, mutilating or murdering other girls and women or *being* raped, mutilated or murdered. Victims may identify with the oppressor, in exchange for privileges or basic survival. Their 'choices' were radically constrained.

This is what Primo Levi called the 'gray zone'. In his reflections on the Holocaust, during which certain prisoners became implicated in the atrocity, Levi observed that oppressors need auxiliaries – and they recognize that the best way to enforce compliance is 'to burden them with guilt, cover them with blood, compromise them as much as possible, thus establishing a bond of complicity so that they can no longer turn back'.[59] Levi insisted that 'I believe that no one is authorized to judge them, not those who lived through the experience of the Lager and even less those who did not.'[60] It was an argument elaborated on by philosopher Claudia Card. She notes that grey zones develop 'wherever oppression is severe and long-lasting' and are 'inhabited by victims of evil who become complicit in perpetrating on others the evils that threaten to engulf themselves'.[61] She points out that 'oppressive social structures . . . offer an inhospitable context for the development of good character.'[62] Resistance is possible but, she warns, 'outsiders are rarely, if ever, in a position to judge when.'[63]

This is not to deny the possibility of manipulating bad situations to good ends. Exercising agency is still possible, albeit within extreme limits. The exceptional decisions of many girls, women and other minoritized groups caught up in armed conflicts to shelter vulnerable people *despite* the extreme risks are testimonies to the possibility of moral action. The stark dichotomy between agency and subjection fails to do justice to the complexity of people's lives.

Pauline Nyiramasuhuko

Attempting to make sense of sexually violent girls and women is difficult, exposing many contradictions. This is largely because violent femininity is assumed to be contrary to what is 'natural' for their sex. In 2007, international relations scholars Laura Sjoberg and Caron E. Gentry published *Mothers, Monsters, Whores: Women's Violence in Global Politics*, which was republished in 2013 and again in 2015 in a revised form.[64] They argue that violent women have been conceptualized according to one of three discourses: mothers, monsters or whores. Accounts drawing on motherhood describe female violence as arising from 'a need to belong, a need to nurture, and a way of taking care of and being loyal to men'. It is maternity 'gone awry'. In contrast, commentators who view violent women as 'monsters' contend that they are irrational, even insane, and cannot be held fully responsible for their actions. They are scarcely human. The 'whore narrative' locates female evil in their perverted sexuality.[65]

In the context of *sexual* violence, all three ways of narrating stories about abusive women can be heard – and often coincide. Interestingly, the three models are used in contradictory ways – that is, both to explain *and* deny female violence. A prominent example is the commentary about Pauline Nyiramasuhuko, the most vilified female perpetrator of sexual violence in the 1990s. Nyiramasuhuko had been born into a subsistence farming family in Butare (Rwanda) but worked her way up to become a social worker lecturing on female empowerment throughout Rwanda. The peak of her career came when she was appointed the National Minister of Family and Women's Affairs in Prime Minister Jean Kambanda's interim government. Her local community were proud of her achievements, nicknaming her 'Butare's favourite daughter'.

Nyiramasuhuko's triumphs, however, have been overshadowed by her participation in the Rwandan genocide. She ordered soldiers and *Interahamwe* ('those who fight together') to round up thousands of Tutsi children, men and women in her hometown for the purpose of sexual assault, rape, physical abuse and slaughter.[66] Dressed in army fatigues, she told the *Interahamwe* that 'before you kill the women, you need to rape them.'[67] She even handed out condoms. Her incitement of sexual violence was not incidental to the terror; it was a deliberate policy. Nyiramasuhuko was central to the genocidal programme of the Rwandan government. As former Prime Minister Kambanda confirmed during his trial at the

International Criminal Tribunal for Rwanda (ICTR), Nyiramasuhuko was one of the five members of his 'inner sanctum' which planned and ordered the genocide.[68] The genocidal intent of the mass rapes was summarized by one woman who survived the atrocities. She

> remembered two things most of all: the stamens from the banana trees they used to violate her, leaving her body mutilated, and the single sentence one of the men used: 'We're going to kill all the Tutsis, and one day Hutu children will have to ask what did a Tutsi child look like?'[69]

When Nyiramasuhuko was charged with genocide in June 2001, international curiosity was enormous. Standing beside her in the dock was her son Arsène Shalom Ntahobali (who was a student and part-time manager of Hotel Ihuliro as well as commander of the local *Interahamwe*), Sylvain Nsabimana, Alphonse Nteziryayo, Joseph Kanyabashi and Elie Ndayambaje. The trial, which became known as the 'Butare Trial' because most of the defendants held positions of authority in that *préfecture*, lasted ten years. Nearly two hundred witnesses gave evidence, and the transcript came to more than 125,000 pages.[70] Unusually, there were five women on the team of prosecutors.[71]

On 24 June 2011, Nyiramasuhuko was convicted of conspiracy to commit genocide, extermination as a crime against humanity, rape as a crime against humanity, outrages upon personal dignity as a war crime and violence to life, health and the physical or mental well-being of persons as a war crime.[72] This made her the first woman to be charged and convicted in an international court with genocide and crimes against humanity, although it is important to note that between 12,000 and 20,000 women have been prosecuted for genocide-related crimes in local courts or the *gacaca* (so-called 'traditional' justice systems).[73] Nyiramasuhuko was sentenced to life imprisonment.

Journalists reporting on the Rwandan trials were obsessed with female defendants such as Nyiramasuhuko, even though it was extremely common for *male* governmental officials and military personnel to incite men to rape. They also treated female defendants very differently to male ones. In particular, they fixated on Nyiramasuhuko's appearance. In the *Christian Science Monitor*, Donna Harman began her article by stating that Nyiramasuhuko 'looks more like someone's dear greataunt than what she is alleged to be: a high-level organizer of Rwanda's 1994 genocide who authorized the rape and murder of countless men and women'. Harman noted that Nyiramasuhuko had 'her hair pulled neatly back, her heavy glasses beside her on the table'. She was 'wearing a green flowery dress one day, a pressed cream-colored skirt and blouse set the next' and, while listening 'stoically to the litany of accusations against her', Nyiramasuhuko adjusted 'one of the shoulder pads of her pretty dress and jots a note'.[74] In contrast, journalists did not find it relevant to provide detailed descriptions of the clothing and appearance of the men on trial.

The fact that Nyiramasuhuko's son (Arsène Shalom Ntahobali) was on trial alongside her for his role in the mass rapes and murders also fascinated journalists. However, mother-and-son defendants were viewed differently to father-and-son ones. Legal scholar Mark A. Drumbl observed that during the 2003 genocide trial of the Reverend Elizaphan Ntakirutimana and his son Gérard, the two men were referred to as 'pastor and son'. In contrast, Nyiramasuhuko and her son were referred to as 'mother and son' rather than 'Minister and son'.[75] For senior male defendants, vocation was seen as germane; for females, maternity.

These differences in narratives about female aggressors are due to gendered understandings of sexual violence. Time and again, journalistic, legal and political commentators circled around a single question: how could a *woman* have committed such crimes? At the end of this chapter, I will suggest that this is the wrong question, as it essentializes both femininity and masculinity, as well as being based on a mistaken understanding of the meaning of gender. However, the preoccupation with the feminine identities of sexually aggressive women is probably inevitable because gender tends to be conceptualized in binary ways. Masculinity is aggressive; femininity is passive. Women who act aggressively are aberrant: they are 'like men'.

This helps explain why commentators frequently draw attention to the dynamics of military institutions, which are strongly gendered male. As a result, female members are required to act or pretend to act *more* aggressively than their male counterparts, if only to stake a claim for their right to be militarily active. In other words, like the female perpetrators in Abu Ghraib, Nyiramasuhuko's willingness to inflict sexual torture has been interpreted as a way to assert herself as a powerful woman in government. This was exacerbated in Nyiramasuhuko's case by the fact that she harboured a secret: her great-grandfather was a Tutsi, which meant that, according to her patrilineage, she was Tutsi. Nyiramasuhuko's sister Vineranda observed that 'Pauline was afraid that maybe the government would find out. And she was among many men in the government. And she had money and a position. She didn't want to lose that.'[76]

Still other commentators emphasize the other side of the binary: rather than seeking to 'join the men', sexually violent women were acting in accordance with *feminine* precepts. In the case of Nyiramasuhuko, her willingness to incite sexual violence against Tutsi women drew on gendered assumptions about female rivalry. Jealousy was a female foible. For example, ICTR investigator Maxwell Nkole maintained that Nyiramasuhuko

> was convinced by the propaganda, especially the propaganda that caused divisions between women. The myth of the beautiful, arrogant Tutsi woman led to jealousy by Hutu women and an inferiority complex among Hutu women. This seems to have come through in the way she treated Tutsi women.[77]

Such allegedly 'innate' feminine traits were related to ideas about motherhood. Numerous commentators drew attention to the fact that Nyiramasuhuko was a mother of four children as well as being a grand-mother. Canadian-based Rwandan journalist Chantal Mudahogora was blunt about the importance of motherhood. She maintained that the focus on Nyiramasuhuko's role as a mother was appropriate 'not only because of her alleged active participation in genocide and her crucial position within the government' but because being a mother entails a host of 'social criteria and expectations'.[78]

However, this emphasis on motherhood was contradictory. It was used *both* as proof that she could not have committed the sexual crimes (because she was, in the words of Nyiramasuhuko's defence council, 'very nice, a mother hen')[79] *and* proof that, if she *had* ordered the rapes and murders, she was particularly odious.[80] In other words, sexually violent women straddle *both* motherhood and monstrousness. The first narra-tive was the one adopted by Nyiramasuhuko and her supporters. She proffered her identity as a mother as evidence that she was, by defin-ition, incapable of atrocious behaviours. She told a BBC reporter that 'I am ready to talk to the person who says I could have killed. I cannot even kill a chicken. If there is such a person who says that a woman, a mother, killed then I'll confront that person.'[81] Nyiramasuhuko's hus-band (Maurice Ntahobari) and her mother supported this argument. Ntahobari told a *New York Times* reporter that Nyiramasuhuko was 'committed to promoting equality between men and women. It is not culturally possible for a Rwandan woman to make her son rape other women. It just couldn't have taken place.'[82] Nyiramasuhuko's mother echoed this view, maintaining that 'it is unimaginable that she did these things. She wouldn't order people to rape and kill. After all, Pauline is a mother.'[83]

Opponents argued otherwise. Wasn't it obviously the case that mothers who *do* act atrociously are *ipso facto* deviant, even pathologically sadistic? Court papers called Nyiramasuhuko a woman of 'unfathomable depravity and sadism'.[84] Judithe Kanakuze, the National Co-ordinator of Réseau des Femmes, even cast doubt on whether she was a woman at all, insisting that 'she always acted like a man.'[85] It was a view supported by Rwandan lawyer Vincent Karangura. When he was interviewed by legal adviser Nicole Hogg, Karangura maintained that the female genocide suspects were 'evil'. He observed that many people presumed that

> women are good by nature, that is, hospitable, welcoming, mild, and incapable of committing atrocities. So, women who really participated, that is, those who were violent or surpassed the expectations of them, and who cannot be explained away as innocent, are not understood. They are treated, not like men, not like women, but something else, like monsters.[86]

Real women and mothers could not carry out such crimes: they were not fully human.

These ways of making sense of sexually aggressive women during armed conflicts are not unique to debates about Nyiramasuhuko. Similar narratives appear in discussions about the culpability of Simone Gbagbo, for example, who was indicted by the International Criminal Court accused of committing 'crimes against humanity' in Côte d'Ivoire in 2010–11. The indictment included rape and other forms of sexual violence, persecution and murder committed against supporters of her husband's rival for the presidency.[87] She had ordered the violence and coordinated the pro-Gbagbo forces.[88] While Gbagbo's abuses were often placed in the context of her husband (she was acting in support of her husband, as 'good wives' do),[89] she was also painted as monster. She was Côte d'Ivoire's 'Bloody Lady'.[90] Similar tropes appeared in accounts about Lynndie England's aggression. England was routinely pathologized: she had an 'overly compliant' personality, argued a psychologist during her court-martial, which made her particularly vulnerable to a person like Graner.[91] She was described as a 'phallic female', 'tomboyish' and a 'leash-girl', who turned out to be 'something other than a natural lady'.[92] She was the 'sex sadist of Baghdad', according to a particularly sensationalist headline in *The Star*.[93] Writing in *Newsweek* in May 2004, Evan Thomas asked: 'How did a wispy tomboy behave like a monster at Abu Ghraib?'[94] Linda Chavez, the President of the Center for Equal Opportunity, sought to blame England's actions on the 'sexual tension' that was inevitable in 'the new sex-integrated military'. She contended that 'putting young men and women at their sexual prime in close proximity to each other 24 hours a day increases sexual tension.'[95] Similarly, the 'sexual pervert' narrative was employed in relation to Karpinski. She was widely denigrated as a 'bull dyke', not because her detractors really believed that she was sexually attracted to women but because any woman who allows sexual abuse to take place must be 'deviant' in some way.[96] In this way, homophobia serves the torture project.

Everyday Violence

The existence of female perpetrators of sexual violence during the USA's 'War on Terror' and during civil conflicts in Rwanda, Sierra Leone and Uganda (to name just a few) cannot be explained in terms of a few pathologically evil women. Neither gender dysfunction nor narratives of 'mothers, monsters, and the mad' help make sense of these perpetrators. Even explanations that draw attention to some of the unique factors of armed conflicts – such as the lowering of social restraints, the availability of weapons, environmental confusions and paroxysms of ideological hatred and fear – are inadequate in explaining female sexual aggression.

This is particularly true since women commit sexually abusive crimes in times of peace, as well as war. Admittedly, most of the well-publicized cases relate to extremely violent female rapist-murderers, such as Myra Hindley (1960s) and Rose West (1970s and 1980s) in Britain and Karla Homolka (1990s) in Canada. These women may very well be psychiatrically disturbed.

If we broaden our lens, however, to look at more 'typical' female sexual offenders, a picture emerges that is closer to the 'everyday' male sex criminal. The most rigorous study in recent years was conducted by Franca Cortoni, Kelly M. Babchishin and Clémence Rat and published in the journal *Criminal Justice and Behavior* in 2017. Unlike many other studies, which were based on offender populations, victim groups or self-report by university students, and often conflated serious sexual abuse with prostitution and harassment offences, these researchers carried out a large meta-analysis of data. They focused on official data and large-scale victimization surveys from Australia, Belgium, Canada, England, Wales, France, Ireland, New Zealand, Norway, Scotland, Spain, Switzerland and the USA between 2000 and 2013.[97]

Cortoni, Babchishin and Rat found that prevalence rates of female sexual offenders ranged from 0.4 per cent to just under 7 per cent in official sources but from 3 per cent to one-quarter in victimization surveys.[98] Furthermore, compared to male sex offenders, female ones were much more likely to target male victims. According to victimization studies, 40 per cent of male victims reported that their abuser was a female compared with only 4 per cent of the female victims.[99] When only victimization data was looked at, females constituted 12 per cent of all sexual offenders.[100] This means that a huge proportion of female-perpetrated sexual offences are never reported to the police. Interestingly, victims were *increasingly* willing to report being sexually abused by a woman, but this 'does not seem to have translated into increased *official* reporting'. Cortoni, Babchishin and Rat speculated that this might be because

> the criminal justice system is not yet ready to fully acknowledge that women commit sexual offenses. For example, there is a tendency among professionals to not consider the possibility that sexual abuse by a woman may have occurred, particularly if the woman is the child's mother.

They hoped that increased awareness of female-perpetrated abuse would not only change the ways professionals responded to accusations but would also help victims feel 'less ostracized when they attempt to report their victimization at the hands of a woman'.[101] Chillingly, they observed that only 10 to 20 per cent of *male* sexual offenders come to the attention of the police; it is not rash, therefore, to wonder whether the proportion of *female* offenders who attract official concerns might not only be similarly high, but may even be *higher* than their male counterparts due to greater reluctance of victims to admit to having been abused by a woman.[102]

⊕

This returns us to a question that underpins this chapter: why is the existence of female perpetrators either ignored by many scholars or relegated to a footnote? As already mentioned, the assumption that women are the more pacifistic sex has meant that many researchers fail to even ask victims to identify the gender of their assailants. High levels of female perpetration of sexual violence are especially prominent during armed conflicts in the geopolitical South, luring many developed-world scholars to identify the abuses perpetrated by predominantly white female women during the 'War on Terror' as 'bad apples' or otherwise inadequate individuals. Unfortunately, the other side to this is that by focusing on female abusers during armed conflicts in Rwanda, Sierra Leone, the Democratic Republic of the Congo, Uganda, Liberia and so on, research on sexual abuse in those regions in times of *peace* has been overlooked.

The debates have also had the unhelpful consequence of reinforcing a limited understanding of gender as consisting of biological men and biological women. By this, I am not alluding to the paucity of research on the experiences of non-binary people, although that is certainly the case. Rather, I am suggesting that the dichotomy of cis-male versus cis-female fails to acknowledge the fluidity of gender norms, practices and identities. Women can also enforce and perpetuate masculine norms. The point is well made by philosopher Judith Butler, who contends that

> When the constructed status of gender is theorized as radically independent of [physiological] sex, gender itself becomes a free-floating artifice, with the consequences that *man* and *masculine* might just as easily signify a female body as a male one, and *woman* and *feminine* a male body as easily as a female one.[103]

When Barbara Ehrenreich lamented that women like Lynndie England were behaving as 'men', and when Coco Fusco railed against 'equality feminism', which sought to give women the rights of men, including the rights to engage in sexualized torture in 'rooms of their own', they were reinforcing a stereotypical gender binary. This is also the problem in many analyses of the genocidal rapism of Pauline Nyiramasuhuko which focus on her status as a woman, mother and grandmother. Such analyses fail to do justice to the complexities of Nyiramasuhuko's life, the social, political and ideological contexts in which she was operating and her performance as a powerful, political persona. She was acting very much like other people of all genders during a carefully orchestrated genocide.

Denying the existence of sexually violent women does not help their victims. It also damages pacificist cis-men by shoring up a militarist and aggressive masculinist stereotype. Although the vast majority of people who inflict sexual harms on others are gendered male, nevertheless, a significant minority are female. 'Perpetrators' and 'victims' are brought into being within historical, material and ideological contexts that often blur or eradicate altogether agent/subject distinctions. Failing to recognize sexual wounds inflicted by girls and women, who might also be embedded in sexually harmful worlds, will not only limit our understanding of this form of violence, but will undermine any attempts to forge peaceful societies.

SIX

Reckonings

*Two hundred Indian women killed their rapist on the courtroom floor of
Nagpur in 2004. When Police tried to arrest lead perpetrators // the women
responded 'arrest us all'...*

Arrest us all   On the red puddle // on the white courthouse floor
Arrest us all   We sawed his penis off // & tore his house // to rubble

Look // the streets are swarming // in protests   [welcome home]...

Christopher Soto, 'In Support of Violence' (2016)[1]

By 2004, the women of Kasturba Nagar in northern India decided that
they had suffered enough. For more than a decade, Akku Yadav (born
Bharat Kalicharan) had terrorized the three hundred families belonging
to their community. Yadav and his gang had beaten, tortured, mutilated
and murdered men, women and children. They had invaded people's
homes, extorted money and stolen property. Gang rape (often in public)
had frequently been employed to humiliate and intimidate them. At
least forty women and girls (some as young as ten years of age) had been
sexually assaulted.[2] In the words of one resident, 'a rape victim lives in
every other house.'[3]

Yadav's victims had attempted to stop him. Despite the formidable
stigma attached to being raped, they had reported his violence to the
authorities, only to find their complaints ignored by the police or dismissed by court officials. Yadav was skilled at manipulating men in power,
bribing them with cash and alcohol. He was also of a higher caste than

his victims, most of whom were Dalits (previously known as 'untouchables'). His freedoms were valued much more highly than those of his economically struggling victims.

This changed in August 2004. Yadav had raped a young girl and demanded money from another. When Yadav heard that a 25-year-old Dalit woman called Usha Narayane had reported these actions to the police, he arrived at her home with forty members of his gang threatening to 'throw acid' in her face so she would no longer be 'in a position to file any more complaints!' He warned Narayane that 'If we ever meet you, you don't know what we'll do to you! Gang rape is nothing! You can't imagine what we'll do to you!' Narayane called the police. But, as had happened before, they never arrived. When she feared that he was going to break into her home, Narayane turned on the gas and threatened to blow up herself and her assailants. Yadav left, but the community decided that they had had enough. Hundreds of men and women picked up rocks and sticks and began attacking Yadav and members of his gang. After they burnt down his house, Yadav was taken into police custody for his own protection.

A few days later, on 13 August, Yadav appeared before the Nagpur District Court. When it became clear that he would be acquitted again, two hundred local women entered the courtroom. Yadav was full of bravado, threatening to teach each of them a lesson. When he called one woman (whom he had previously raped) a prostitute, she removed her sandal and began beating him, screaming that 'We can't both live on this Earth together. It's you or me.'[4] At this point, the other women in the courtroom spontaneously rose up in fury. They overpowered the guards and court officials, threw chilli powder in Yadav's face and cut off his penis with a kitchen knife. He was stabbed at least seventy times.[5] Vigilantism was the only way these women could achieve justice.

None of the women were apologetic. They defended their lethal vigilantism on the grounds of 'social justice' and the 'freedom struggle'.[6] As trade union activist V. Chandra explained, 'we have all waited for police to act, but nothing happens. The molestations and rapes go on.'[7] Activist Usha Narayane agreed, maintaining that the police and politicians were 'in cahoots with the criminals', providing them with 'protection'. She asked

How are we in the wrong? Courts take ages to give a decision. We may die before they give a decision. What is the point of going to courts? We gave 15 years to the courts. Now, the women of

Kasturbanager [*sic*] have given a clear message to the courts. You could not do it; we have done it. How are we in the wrong?[8]

To people who criticized them, the women retorted, 'there is no justice for the poor. What if this had happened to a minister's wife or daughter? So, we decided to do it ourselves.'[9]

A small number of women were charged with lynching Yadav but there was insufficient evidence to convict them. Even if the case had been pursued in the courts, the chance that these women would have been convicted was low: they were being hailed as heroines within the community. Hundreds of women were prepared to confess en masse to having carried out the murder. The retired High Court judge Bhau Vahane publicly supported the women, admitting that 'they were left with no alternative but to finish Akku. The women repeatedly pleaded with the police for their security. But the police failed to protect them.'[10] A group of one hundred lawyers based in Nagpur announced that the accused women should be treated as victims, not perpetrators of violence.[11]

By beginning this chapter with the vigilantism carried out by the women of Kasturba Nagar, I seek to draw attention to the difficulties that victims experience when sexual abuse is systematic and systemic, as it is for Dalit and Adivasi women in India. But I also aim to question assumptions that victims are passive subjects. When faced with the impotence of the law to remedy their grievances, victim-survivors can act with retributive fury.

But what about the negative side of vigilantism? The violent actions of the women of Kasturba Nagar cannot be compared with some murderous mobs elsewhere in India or in the USA, where thousands of Black Americans were lynched as a result of *false* accusations of rape. And what about formal justice? The law is not free from justified accusations of racism and classism. These prejudices were in part enhanced by the introduction of scientific experts into the courtroom. Since the mid-nineteenth century, the question as to whether perpetrators of sexual violence are 'mad or bad' has had a significant impact on punishment regimes. It could determine whether an offender was incarcerated or treated in a psychiatric hospital. Diagnostic classifications such as 'paedophile' and 'psychopath' have been employed in contradictory ways to ensure that violent men of colour are either denigrated as 'degenerates' (for which the only response is lifelong incarceration) or seen as not being psychically sophisticated enough to warrant psychiatric treatment.

Without understanding the compounding effects of caste, class, race and respectability, it is impossible to understand the differential punishments handed out to boys and men who act in sexually aggressive ways.

Caste

The women of Kasturba Nagar were 'multiply burdened' on account of their gender, economic standing and, most crucially, caste. Every day of their lives, they were made aware of their lowly position in the hierarchy of humanity. This was particularly painful when they were sexually assaulted. They rapidly discovered that they had no recourse in law. After all, Yadav was allowed to act with immunity because of caste privilege, financial and political power and his ability to marshal other violent men into his gang. His case was not unique. In numerous other trials, men accused of raping lower-caste women were given immunity from prosecution. In the state of Rajasthan in 1992, for example, five men of the Gurjar (milkmen) caste were tried for the gang rape of Bhanwari Devi, of the lower Kumhar (potter) caste. As a *saathin* ('friend') of the Women's Development Project, Bhanwari was attacked for attempting to prevent a child marriage taking place in her assailant's family. The judge refused to believe that men of the Gurjar caste would demean themselves enough to sexually abuse a woman from an 'inferior' caste. When he acquitted one of the assailants, he professed his belief that 'Indian culture has not fallen to such low depths' as to allow 'an innocent, rustic man' to 'turn into a man of evil conduct who disregards caste and age differences – and becomes animal enough to assault a woman'.[12] In other words, because Gurjars were not 'animals', they would never have sexual relations (let alone sadistic, non-consensual sex) with lower-caste women. The other side to this dynamic is the erasure of the agency of abused women. Caste privilege, observes historian Anupama Rao, is 'overdetermined', meaning that the bodies of Dalit women are seen as 'collectively mute, and capable of bearing penetration and other modes of marking upper-caste hegemony without the intervention of desire and/or sexuality'.[13] In effect, they invited abuse.

Internationally, the impact of caste on the treatment of rape victims was exposed most starkly after the gang rape and murder of Jyoti Singh in 2012. Singh was an ambitious, upwardly mobile, physiotherapy intern who was gang-raped and tortured in a private bus in which she was travelling with her male friend Awindra Pandey. What became known as the 'Delhi Gang Rape' case incited protests throughout India and internationally. Within less than a year, her assailants had been tried and sentenced to death. This was unprecedentedly fast in Indian judicial history.[14]

It led to the central government reviewing the treatment of rape victims, especially the slowness of bringing the accused to court. The seriousness of concern can be seen by the fact that the Commission to investigate rape was led by J. S. Verma (former Chief Justice of the Supreme Court), Leila Seth (retired Justice) and Gopal Subramanium (Solicitor General). One of the chief reforms proposed in the 'Justice Verma Report' was to introduce 'fast-track courts' to streamline and accelerate procedures dealing with sexual violence trials, as well as the introduction of training. Liberia and Zambia have also introduced specialized sexual violence courts, to good effect. This was an important reform both in deterring potential offenders and sending out a sign that gender-based crimes were regarded as particularly heinous.

The vehement national and international protests occasioned by Singh's rape-murder raise some awkward questions. What if the six perpetrators had been prominent men, rather than lower-caste, itinerant slum dwellers?[15] Would there have been such a response if Singh had been of a lower caste? What if she had been a resident of a deprived community in Kasturba Nagar, as were Yadav's victims? Dalit activists maintained that caste bias meant that Singh's rape and murder could be condemned and mourned while the routine abuse of poor women is overlooked. As Anu Ramdas explained in *Savari* (the activist website of lower-caste women), protests against the rape and rape-murder of 'dalit and adivasi women in Vachati, in Chattisgarh, in Haryana, in Manipur, in jail, in thanas [police stations], in courts and in villages all over the country' are ignored.[16] Of course, what happened to Singh was appalling but, Ramdas argued, the 'selective national exclamation of horror against this urban gang rape furthers the normalization of rapes and gang rapes of dalit and adivasi women'.[17]

There is a further problem. The international attention paid to Singh's rape and murder was underpinned by colonialist prejudices. Western media portrayed the assailants as members of a 'backward and misogynist culture', thus playing into the West's obsession with 'white men saving brown women from brown men'.[18] After all, as sociologist Poulami Roychowdhury pointed out, before being discarded at the side of the road, Singh's male friend had been stripped naked and beaten so severely that his leg snapped. But, she drily commented, 'white men are not in the business of saving brown men from brown men.'[19]

Vigilantism

The killing of Yadav by the women of Kasturba Nagar encourages us to think anew about lethal vigilantism. Is it legitimate for victims to assassinate men who are known by the community, police and local politicians to be thugs, torturers, rapists and murderers but are treated as above the law? What if the legal system is so overburdened that, despite sincere attempts to prosecute offenders, they cannot cope? After all, at the time of Yadav's murder, Indian courts were swamped with cases: according to one estimate, with around 20 million court cases waiting to be heard.[20] Is extra-judicial punishment, even execution, an excusable action if there are no alternatives?

For many girls and women in India the answer is 'yes'. India is home to the largest female vigilante group in the world.[21] The Pink Sari (or *Gulabi*) gang was formed in 2010 and boasts over 20,000 members. Led by Sampat Pal, Gulabi is based in Uttar Pradesh, one of the poorest regions in northern India, but has spread throughout the country. Members wear bright pink saris and carry *lathis* or long, heavy sticks, which they use to beat men who abuse girls and women.[22] They also intervene to help women sort out other problems, including those arising from land disputes, inheritance, child marriages and female education. They have even hijacked trucks of food in order to distribute it to poor families.

Although called a 'gang', members of Gulabi act more like a collective. They use the language of self-defence.[23] They have flourished because caste, class, gender and religion mean that members have little chance of seeing their abusers convicted and punished in formal courts of law. As anthropologist Atreyee Sen argues, the Gulabi is a legitimate socio-political movement that uses 'ethical violence' to remedy injustices in the lives of members and friends.[24] She quotes one member explaining that 'First we go to the police and beg them to do something. But the administration won't listen to poor people, so we end up taking matters into our own hands.'[25] A slow and corrupt legal system, coupled with a weak government, makes the use of communal justice the only viable option. Vigilantism is how lower-caste Indians gain access to rights and entitlements.

The Pink Saris are a notable example of vigilantism in modern India, but the practice has a long history throughout the world. Historically, vigilantism linked to sexual abuse tended to be carried out by *individuals* outraged by violent men within their neighbourhood or village. Most vigilantes were not part of an organized *movement* (as are members of Gulabi) but respond to specific local troublemakers. Throughout nineteenth-century Europe, sexual abusers could find themselves paraded around the village to local jeers, the windows of their homes would be broken and their credit was rejected in the market square. Some examples can be taken from nineteenth-century Britain. In 1846, the 'atrocious rape' of two 'unfortunate women' near Shap in Cumbria, northwest England, excited local passions so much that the carriage carrying the four perpetrators to the penitentiary was forced to stop numerous times. Agitated crowds of men, women and children lined the streets 'to show their disgust at the heinous conduct of the prisoners'. One witness reported that 'it was feared from the strong feeling evinced against them that an attempt would be made to do them some personal injury.' At one stage, 'the yells, hisses, groans and execrations of the assembled crowd were so violent as to render it necessary to obtain the assistance of the police to protect the men.'[26] Similar scenes were witnessed in London forty years later in response to 48-year-old Thomas Gibney being charged with sexually assaulting nineteen girls aged between eight and fifteen years. The girls were described as 'the daughters of respectable persons – tradesmen and others'. Their parents 'endeavoured to lynch' Gibney and 'nearly succeeded in tearing him from the hands of the police'.[27] In all such cases, reportage focused on the unblemished 'innocence' and naivety of the victims. As Dalit and Adivasi women were all too aware, public reputation and perceived virtue are required if public outrage is to be elicited.

Vigilantism is an understandable response when formal policing mechanisms are undeveloped, overwhelmed or believed to be too lenient. In pre-colonial Kenya, for example, women would hold 'shaming parties', entering the homes of men believed to be sexually abusive, seizing some of their property and humiliating them.[28] No clear distinction could be drawn between vigilantism and community policing. Today, in parts of Nigeria, police or other security forces simply do not exist despite high levels of sexual crime, making vigilantism the only way to achieve justice and accountability.[29] In northern Peru, *rondas campesinas* (peasant patrols) were formed to deal with what was believed to be a dramatic increase of crime. As one Bolivian argued, 'There is no justice in Bolivia. At least for the poor there isn't. You have to have money to get justice.'[30] After bitter civil conflicts, as in South Africa, Northern Ireland and Liberia, vigilantism flourished partly because police and justice systems were severely weakened or discredited. Thus, in Guatemala, where lynching is called *justicia a mano propia* (justice by one's own hand), it became widespread after the end of the civil war in 1996 and was supported by three-quarters of the population.[31] Informal pacts were even made between vigilante groups and the police, as happens in South Africa. In such cases, the police accept the rights of families and local communities to administer beatings to men accused of sexual offences before they step in to cart offenders off to prison.[32]

In more recent years, however, vigilantism against sex offenders has undergone two major changes. In the UK and USA, tabloid newspapers have taken it on themselves to orchestrate vigilante campaigns. The most notorious in recent decades was coordinated by the UK's *News of the World*. Their 'For Sarah' crusade was named after eight-year-old Sarah Payne, who was abducted, sexually assaulted and murdered in July 2000. The newspaper published the names, photos and addresses of convicted paedophiles who were living in the community. This led to the proliferation of vigilante groups, who targeted the homes of those named. At least two men committed suicide and other innocent families were forced to flee from their homes. In one case in Newport, a female physician was forced into hiding after vigilantes confused the words paedophile and paediatrician.

The other major shift is that vigilantism has been increasingly individualized. Rather than being a *community* response to sexual violence, it has become an individual's 'payback' against male aggression. This is particularly prevalent in the USA where handguns are marketed to women as a major means of exacting personal justice against men who threaten to rape them. The most prolific advocate is Paxton Quigley, formerly Director of Community Relations for Playboy Enterprises. Between 1989 and 2010, she published a series of books with titles such as *Armed and Female: 12 Million American Women Own Guns. Should You?* (1989 and 1990), *Not an Easy Target* (1995), *Stayin' Alive: Armed and Female in an Unsafe World* (2005) and *Armed and Female: Taking Control* (2010).[33] She explained that 'coming from a liberal, mid-western, anti-gun background', she 'made an about-face when her best friend was raped one morning in her home in Los Angeles'. She 'vowed not to let it happen to her' and set off on a mission to ensure that women could defend themselves.[34] This has involved her teaching the use of firearms to nearly 7,000 women in more than twenty states.[35] Quigley's books are crammed with lurid descriptions of rape. In the 1989 edition of *Armed and Female* (which has been called the 'bible of gun self defense for women'),[36] she tells readers that 'if you are over the age of twelve and female, be prepared to be criminally assaulted some time in your life.'[37] She devotes an entire chapter to the consequences of rape, contending that 'the most succinct expression of the effect of rape upon its victims is that rape approaches a death experience.'[38] In all her case studies, the assailants are strangers and, although she is careful to never mention race, references to 'inner cities' suggest that they are coded as Black or Latinx.[39] Furthermore, she doesn't want to be mistaken for a 'women's libber': indeed, she implies that feminism is to blame for the soaring levels of rape.[40] The trend for women to purchase handguns, she contends, 'Began in the late 1960s, with more women living alone and working outside the home and having more disposable income. In turn, women have become accessible targets, not only for rape, but for robbery and assault.'[41]

As Quigley complains in *Stayin' Alive*, 'most women are just too afraid to take responsibility and prepare themselves against a possible life-threatening situation.'[42] She even takes it upon herself to *require* victims of rape to speak. In *Armed and Female: 12 Million American Women Own Guns. Should You?* (1989), Quigley writes about talking to a woman who had 'buried her rape experience for sixteen years'. In Quigley's words,

> When I spoke to her, she had just completed a year of therapy and a defensive-tactics course. A reticent woman who hid behind large tinted glasses and layers of clothing, Donna at first wanted only to discuss the theories she had learned concerning rape. My probing for her experience and her feelings made her nervous and even more theoretical. Finally, she accepted my desire to know her story and how her experience affected her life.[43]

Quigley then goes on to tell Donna's story of rape over two pages. Donna was coerced (by Quigley's own telling) into publicizing her rape and then required to arm herself in defence against future violations. Unlike the self-defence classes established by feminist groups at the time, Quigley abstracts women's experience of sexual violence from broader gender oppression and from female solidarity movements: her focus is individualistic and socially conservative.

Why Seek Non-Judicial Justice?

Why do victims and their supporters seek non-judicial justice? In North America and the UK, vigilantism is about the expression of moral outrage, individual power and celebrity culture. In the USA, advocating vigilantism can be lucrative, as sales of Quigley's books attest. It can also rake in cash if co-opted by the entertainment industry. Paedophile 'hunters' typically pose online as children, luring their prey into setting up a meeting, then exposing them. Sometimes, they administer a beating before reporting them to the police. Often, they livestream the encounters, even though many of their targets have committed no crime.[44] Vigilantes in this tradition are active in the USA, where groups such as Perverted-Justice (PeeJ) advertised their tactics in NBC's popular reality TV show *To Catch a Predator*. Similar groups are also active in Germany, the Netherlands, Canada, Australia and Cambodia. There are at least 75 'paedophile hunting' groups in the UK alone.[45] This was brought to public attention in 2014 with the broadcast of a Channel Four documentary called *The Paedophile Hunter*, featuring Nuneaton-based Stinson Hunter, a so-called 'legend' in the field. Vigilante activities have been accused of impeding justice, diverting resources from legal law-enforcement agencies and encouraging offenders to become even more secretive. Their lack of accountability and their biased reporting (often claiming to be 100 per cent effective and ignoring instances of miscarriages of justice or suicides of their victims) make their activities particularly alarming.

Online forms of informal policing in wealthy countries are reliant on stable, non-corrupt police systems. They operate on the assumption that once paedophiles have been 'cornered' they can be handed over to the police, who will ensure that they are punished. This is not the case in many other regions of the world, however, where vigilantism is an important resource if justice systems are corrupt, highly bureaucratic, expensive and conducted in non-indigenous languages. Vigilantism is more common in areas where there are few lawyers, most of whom are based in the large cities, leaving vast swathes of the country without access to a formal system of justice. It is a cheap and quick way to deter sexually violent criminals and organized gangs. In such contexts, vigilantism can enjoy social legitimacy, giving the dispossessed some sense of agency.

However, vigilantism is of less help in effecting social change. Although it makes emotional sense, it has minimal effects in the longer term. It can even contribute to disorder. There have been legitimate criticisms of white feminists whose acts of feminist empowerment have sometimes opened the door to being misused by racist vigilantes. For example, in 1984, Valerie Amos (now a leading British politician) and Pratibha Parmar (activist and film-maker) warned white feminists about the impact that 'Take Back the Night' had on their communities. They pointed to 'the complicity of many white feminists with the racist media and the police'. They criticized the silence of white feminists 'when public hysteria was periodically whipped up through images of white women as innocent victims of black rapists'. In their words,

> When women marched through Black inner city areas to 'Reclaim the Night' they played into the hands of the racist media and the fascist organizations, some of whom immediately formed vigilante groups patrolling the streets 'protecting' innocent white women by beating up black men.[46]

There is also the common problem of 'good' vigilantes turning 'bad', as in the case of the Bakassi Boys in Nigeria. When they were first formed, they garnered widespread support from local communities, but this changed when their activities showed that they were biased and unaccountable to anyone.[47] Their presence impeded institutional reform of police and legal systems.

Even the poor, low-caste women of Kasturba Nagar discovered the limitations of vigilantism. They were pleased when their actions drew international as well as national attention to their plight. But the death of Yadav, the dispersal of his gang and the establishment of a well-funded community project did nothing to stem systemic gender or economic inequalities, let alone raise the status of low-caste women and their families either locally or nationally. Communal retribution leaves underlying inequalities undisturbed. It might be gratifyingly retributive but will never change a culture of sexualized violence. Even the Gulabi gang, with its commitment to humiliating sexual predators, remains content with simply *improving* the way men treat women and children rather than undermining fundamental gender disparities.[48]

Lynching

There is also a vicious side to the extra-judicial killings of suspected rapists. It is easy to be sympathetic to actions that empower systematically disempowered communities. But these forms of vigilantism are not typical. More usually, vigilante justice serves to *cement* patriarchal caste, class, racial and religious power regimes.

This is most noticeable with vigilante groups linked to extremist or anti-feminist movements. One example is the killing of suspected rapist Syed Sharif Khan, who was dragged from prison, stripped, beaten and hanged in Dimapur (India) in 2015. Sociologist Poulami Roychowdhury argued that Khan became a target for the lynch mob less because he was suspected of being a rapist (as were many other men) than because of local anger directed against Muslim traders from the state of Assam.[49] Indeed, nationalist political groups routinely use vigilantism-rape as a political tool. For example, Hindu nationalists propagate the notion that Muslim men are rapists to encourage extra-judicial killings.[50] In Roychowdhury's words, 'the politics of race can *rationalize* social inequality, rather than undermine it . . . Politics itself is not a gender-neutral mechanism of resistance.'[51]

Nowhere is the extra-judicial killing of alleged rapists on the grounds of race more brutally exemplified than in the American South, where false accusations that African American men had raped white girls or women resulted in mass acts of lynching. Between 1882 and 1968, at least 3,446 African Americans in the USA were lynched. The third-highest reason given (after homicide and 'all other causes') was rape.[52] Furthermore, in the 1930s, one survey found that 64 per cent of people living in the southern states of the USA believed that lynching men for rape was warranted.[53]

For some legal commentators, extra-juridical killings were understandable, even justified. Writing in the *Yale Law Journal* in 1897, William Reynolds from Baltimore, Maryland, believed that lethal vigilantism against alleged rapists was an 'evil' but explicable. After all, he reminded readers, white Americans resorted to lynch law out of 'a natural desire to shield the victim of outrageous assaults from the ordeal of . . . testifying' in court, especially since 'this humiliation must be greatly intensified by the wrong having been committed by a negro.' He explained that

Given a case where a crime of this sort has been committed and where a man has been caught whom the woman identified as her assailant, unless she be a person of notoriously abandoned character, it will be very hard to convince the average citizen living in her neighbourhood, that it is not a far less evil to anticipate the sentence of the law by promptly lynching the accused.

He insisted that this 'popular feeling would of course be much stronger if the man charged with the crime should be a negro'.[54] He urged jurists to allow rape victims to make their complaints privately.

Other public figures such as Rebecca Felton and Luther Rosser openly defended lynch mobs, using inflammatory, racist rhetoric. Felton was leader of the Georgia Chapter of the Women's Christian Temperance Union and the first woman elected to the U.S. Senate. In the 1890s, she argued that

> If it needs lynching to protect woman's dearest possession from human beasts, then I say lynch a thousand times a week if necessary. The poor girl would choose death in preference to such ignominy, and I say a quick rope to assaulters![55]

Twenty-four years later, in 1921, lawyer Rosser spelled out the racist logic behind lynching in detail. He informed members of the American Bar Association that white Americans lacked confidence that the legal system would deal efficiently with 'bestial' criminals. Rosser blamed African American 'troublemakers' (by which he meant civil rights leaders) for encouraging the 'ignorant negro' to dream of social equality and even intermarriage with white American women. According to Rosser, African Americans used to be 'simple, trusting, polite, goodnatured and hopeful'. But 'militants' had

> bereft him, so far as they were able, of all these simple, lovable qualities and, in their stead, they gave him unrest, suspicion, hate, a diseased and inflamed ego, an ill-balanced ambition to strut and bluster in place and position for which he had no aptitude by mental or moral equipment or by tradition or training.

Rosser contended that it was easy to predict the tragic result. The typical African American man had become lazy, disgruntled and determined to 'gratify his lust' with any white women he chose. In such circumstances, Rosser ranted, was it any wonder that the white American population had become 'beguiled . . . into lynching'? He contended that whenever

> a woman, innocent and of good repute, is ravished, mutilated and murdered, and especially by a brutal, ignorant member of an inferior and socially ostracized race, then nothing but Divine Providence . . . can hold the fury of the mob.

It was of little avail to argue that justice could be found within the courts, Rosser noted. The law was 'too calm in its procedure' to terrify the potential Black rapist. It was 'not equal' to 'Judge Lynch in striking terror'.[56] As such extreme rhetoric suggests, rape was much more than an attack on a woman; it was an assault on the entire structure of white power and authority.

Race and Class in Formal Justice Systems

Are formal modes of justice less biased? In the USA, the extra-judicial lynching of African American men gradually declined after the 1950s, as state courts proved willing to carry out the executions themselves. As Jeffrey J. Pokorak explains, the decrease in the number of Black men lynched for alleged rape was 'inversely proportionate to the number of *legal* executions of Black men for the rape of White women'. In other words, 'where there once was mob violence to act on White gendered racism regarding rape, there would now be the law'.[57]

Pokorak is making a valid point. However, when *class* is added to the argument, things become more complex. To understand responses to sexual violence in the USA, it is important to recognize that race is not the only vector of power/powerlessness: class was also important, as was the perceived respectability of victims. Diane Miller Sommerville's *Rape and Race in the Nineteenth-Century South* (2004) analysed 152 cases of enslaved men convicted of rape in Virginia between 1800 and 1865, while Lisa Lindquist Dorr looked at rape cases in Virginia between 1900 and 1960.[58] They both found that the responses of jurors and judges to Black-on-white rape were not always punitive. Of the 152 enslaved men convicted of rape or attempted rape in Sommerville's study, only 76 (half) were executed. If one focuses solely on race, a much higher proportion of death sentences would have been predicted. It seems that white, racist southerners were 'extending leniency to slave rapists', Sommerville concluded.[59] She argued that this could only be explained by drawing attention to the class and assumed propriety of *victims*. Most victims of rape cases appearing before law courts were white, working-class women, who were often reproached for breaching social rules. Self-designated 'respectable' members of white communities were as keen to control these women as they were to control Black men. In Sommerville's words, 'class interests often combined with misogyny to forge a formidable obstacle to an expediated, successful prosecution and execution of a black man for rape.'[60] Dorr concurred, noting that trials of Black rapists were an opportunity for community leaders to put *both* African American men *and* white women 'in their place', bolstering white patriarchal power.[61]

The racial bias of U.S. systems of justice is not unique. Race-specific laws and punishments for sexual abuse are common throughout the world. In the Solomon Islands and New Guinea in the early twentieth century, for instance, Black men who raped white women were flogged or sentenced to death while white men who raped Black women had impunity.[62] In Natal, it was not considered remarkable for a judge in 1868 to sentence a Black man convicted of assault with intent to rape a white woman to fourteen years' imprisonment with hard labour and one hundred lashes. He admitted, though, that 'I shrink from giving the whip to a European if it can be helped. It seems to degrade him and make him feel less a man for the remainder of his life.'[63] Not so if the offender was Black. The conditions in which this offender would have spent his life in prison would also be different to those experienced by white prisoners. For example, in the 1860s, while white prisoners were fed a diet of 424 ounces (12 kg) of food, Black ones were only allocated 272 (7.7 kg).[64] In 1955, Natal's Minister of Justice told the Free State National Party Congress that during his time in office 'not a single reprieve had been granted to a Non-European man sentenced to death for the rape of a European woman.'[65] As late as 1970, there had never been an execution of a white man in South Africa for the rape of a woman of colour.[66]

The Racialized Medicalization of Rape

Racist and class biases in formal as well as informal legal systems were amplified by the medicalization of rape. As we saw in an earlier chapter, from the mid-nineteenth century, courtrooms were increasingly eliciting 'expert opinions' from medical professionals. Questions about whether sex criminals should be sent to prisons or psychiatric hospitals came laden with assumptions based on race and class. Not all sexually aggressive boys and men were deemed to be suffering from a mental illness; some were pathologized but believed to be sane, albeit deeply 'tainted'. Numerous examples of these processes could be given, but I will focus on three theories: the ideas of Austrian psychiatrist Richard von Krafft-Ebing (the nineteenth-century 'father' of classifications of 'perverted' sexuality), the invention of 'sexual psychopathy' in North America from the 1930s, and the substitution of 'culture' for 'psychiatric illness' in French debates about '*les tournantes*'.

One of the most influential psychiatrists responsible for the pathologization of sexual deviance was Krafft-Ebing, a professor of psychiatry at the universities of Strasbourg, Graz and then Vienna. In his 1886 classic *Psychopathia Sexualis: eine Klinisch-Forensische Studie* (Sexual Psychopathy: A Clinical-Forensic Study), Krafft-Ebing invented a series of diagnostic terms for 'perverted' sexual identities. These included sexual sadism (from the Marquis de Sade) and paedophilia (from the Greek *pais*, meaning 'child', and *philia*, meaning 'love').

How did Krafft-Ebing characterize sadists and paedophiles? Along with Italian criminologist Cesare Lombroso, he believed that most were degenerates. Krafft-Ebing espoused a kind of evolutionary principle in which *moral* traits were passed down generations, in a similar way to physical and intellectual ones.[67] Krafft-Ebing illustrated this by referring to a series of case studies of paedophiles discussed by Czech physician Joseph von Maschka. One of these – a patient called 'K' – was described as

> an imbecile, and physically deformed, being scarcely 1.5 metres tall; cranium rachitic [associated with rickets] and hydrocephalic; teeth bad, – furrowed, defective, and irregular. Large lips, idiotic expression, stuttering speech, and an awkward attitude complete the picture of psychophysical degeneration. K. behaves like a child discovered in some mischievous act. Scarcely any growth of beard. Genitals well and normally developed. He has a superficial consciousness of having done something improper, but he is unconscious of the moral, social, and legal significance of his crimes.[68]

This is a classic description of a degenerate, with its emphasis on arrested physical as well as moral development. Krafft-Ebing also believed that sexual degenerates might be suffering from mania and epilepsy.[69] They were plagued by 'satyriasis', or uncontrollable sexual urges. In short, they were human monsters, coded poor and 'foreign'. There was no cure – if they offended, execution or lifelong imprisonment were the only solutions.

A similar attempt to categorize sexually violent men was introduced in 1930s America with the invention of 'sexual psychopathy'. This is my second example. Psychopaths were believed to be men 'lacking in the balance of fundamental instincts, emotions and sentiments common to mankind', and therefore incapable of acting in socially responsible ways.[70] They rarely felt guilty for their violent actions. In psychoanalytical language, the psychopath's Ego (or conscience) was too weak to resist the sexual and aggressive impulses of the Id (the source of 'animalistic drives').[71]

Jurists recognized the value of enshrining the diagnosis of 'sexual psychopath' in law. From the mid-1930s, U.S. states began introducing sexual psychopath legislation to deal with persistent and violent offenders. Although these laws varied state by state, in most cases an offender *prior to conviction* would be given a hearing in front of a jury and if psychiatrists testified that he suffered from a 'criminal sexual psychopathic perversion', he could be committed to the psychiatric hospital or wing of the prison. Once psychiatrists within the hospital were willing to claim that the offender was 'cured', he could be either placed on probation and released or returned to court and sentenced for the original crime.

However, the uses of these laws were highly raced: psychopathic statutes were rarely applied to African American paedophiles and rapists. This was because psychiatrists charged with diagnosing 'sexual psychopathy' assumed that Black sex offenders were psychologically different to their white counterparts. In 1954, Albert Ellis, Ruth R. Doorbar and Robert Johnston III, all of whom worked at the State of Jersey's Diagnostic Center, even went so far as to claim that statutory rape was 'virtually a normal and expected part of the culture of many New Jersey Negroes'. They explained that while 'the white offender tends to be a severely emotionally disturbed individual, with several serious psychiatric symptoms,' African American offenders tended to be 'undisturbed emotionally'. Feeling 'less guilt, shame, and self-deprecation' for their crimes, Black rapists were less emotionally disturbed by them, they claimed.[72] As a result, there was a vast racial discrepancy in the proportion of sexually violent men sent to hospital rather than prison: in the State of

Washington, 90 per cent of the men committed under the sexual psychopath law were white.[73] Black sexual offenders were much more likely to be regarded as vicious criminals while their white equivalents are categorized as psychologically deviant. The former were sent to the electric chair or prison; the latter, to the therapeutic couch.

My third example looks at recent debates in France. Aggression committed by men from minority ethnic communities is blamed on their 'culture', rather than any mental illness or pathology. This approach is similar to that of Ellis, Doorbar and Johnston III at the State of Jersey's Diagnostic Center, who also assumed that violence committed by ethnic minorities was culturally 'normal', rather than pathological. In France, this bias has been embraced by the mass media. From 2000, angry statements began emerging about '*les tournantes*', or gang rapes committed by young men of North African origins in the *banlieues* of Paris. These particularly vicious rapes – usually involving oral or anal assaults in order, bizarrely, to preserve the virginity of victims – generated a public panic. White French commentators began protesting about 'Arab culture', which they claimed was leading to widespread sexual violation of young girls. Certain high-profile cases, such as the rape-murder of Sohane Benziane, excited interest, which was stirred up by commentators such as Samira Bellil, who went on to publish *Dans l'enfer des tournantes* (2003; In Gang-Rape Hell). The film *La Squale* (2000) also propagated the idea of immigrant and 'Arab' neighbourhoods as inherently violent, while pro-republican feminists established the movement entitled Ni Putes Ni Soumises (Neither Whores nor Submissive); the latter's slogan *Ni voile, ni viol*, or 'neither veil nor rape', explicitly identified the perpetrators as belonging to particular cultural and religious groups.[74] 'Arab culture' was assumed to be a single, homogeneous entity, and sexual aggression was located in a specific place: the *banlieues*, which were seen as hotbeds of other 'Islamic' foibles, including honour killings, female circumcision and forced marriage.

Despite clear evidence that males of all ages and social classes committed rape,[75] attention in France focused on immigrant boys and men. In contrast, white, middle-class, heterosexual men were seen as protectors of French womanhood. 'Other' ethnic groups were considered inferior, accused of failing to assimilate 'civilized' sexual practices and of being incapable of controlling their 'natural instincts' for sexual expression. A psychiatrist brought in to give evidence at a 2010 rape trial in which a Peruvian man used the 'it is part of my culture' defence testified that the claim was 'not perverse; it is a heavy cultural heritage'. The defendant even told the psychiatrist that 'The French ought to give me classes so that I understand that women are equal to men.'[76] This was racism being 'used in the fight against sexism', as anthropologist Homa Hoodfar observed.[77]

This chapter started by exploring the motivations of two hundred women from Kasturba Nagar who murdered a man who had raped members of their community. The women openly justified their violence on the grounds that he was a serial sexual abuser, extortionist, torturer and killer in a neighbourhood where his victims could never attract the attention of the police or justice systems. They claimed that they had been pushed to the absolute limits of endurance, making vigilantism the only way to restore some kind of semblance of agency and moral economy. Like members of the Gulabi gang, the women took matters into their own hands. Their vigilantism was not simply an act of violence: it was a *response* to acts of systemic violence that were ubiquitous in their community. In contrast, lynching mobs in the USA from the mid-nineteenth century, as well as politically and religiously motivated 'rough justice' in India and the USA today, deliberately eschew formal law enforcement institutions in their pursuit of revenge.

This is not to ignore the fact that formal justice systems are institutionally racist and classist, as I have shown. When alienists and psychiatrists began appearing as 'experts' in courtrooms, they were biased against minoritized boys and men accused of sexual crimes. European, British and American psychiatrists from the nineteenth century to the late twentieth century created diagnostic systems that routinely assumed that sexual predators and paedophiles were poor men from ethnic minorities. These biases had dramatic impacts on court decisions and the legal dispensing of punishment.

Finally, feminists and other anti-rape activists are right to draw attention to the failures of legal systems to defend victims of sex crimes. The law is parsimonious in dispensing justice to rape victims. In some jurisdictions – British courts, for example – victims of sexual abuse are *less* likely to see their assailants prosecuted than ever before. In 1977, one in three reported rapes resulted in a conviction. By 1985, this was 24 per cent and it was just one in ten by 1996.[78] Today, it is one in twenty. In 2020, Dame Vera Baird (the Victims' Commissioner for England and Wales) warned that the Crown Prosecution Service were prosecuting 52 per cent fewer cases than they had done just two years earlier. Baird argued that 'we are facing the decriminalisation of rape'.[79] Rapists who end up being convicted in a court of law must regard themselves as exceptionally unlucky.

These debates about prosecuting and punishing sexual abusers have led many feminists to question their own assumptions about justice. In particular, debates about the appropriate response to perpetrators of sexual abuse have become fraught within feminist and other activist circles. Arguments take two forms. First, should feminists seek to increase penalties meted out to offenders within the prison system? While second-wave feminists fought to persuade courts to impose lengthy terms of imprisonment on sex offenders, many activists today warn against 'carceral feminism' (sometimes known as 'governance feminism') on the grounds that 'lock 'em up and throw away the key' approaches disproportionately penalize poor men from ethnic minorities. Punitive responses to sex offenders are risky. They encourage a feminism that is secure in its own privileges. Feminists of colour regularly remind white, middle-class feminists of the dangers of encouraging greater state regimentation of their communities. They argue that retributive justice will not solve the problem of gender-based violence; indeed, it may exacerbate it by producing angry men. I return to these questions in the final chapter, which asks: what can be done?

The second debate has been about feminist vigilantism. As we saw with regard to the women of Kasturba Nagar who murdered Yadav, there was considerable feminist sympathy for their actions. The Clinton Global Initiative, the M. Night Shyamalan Foundation and the National Institute for Women, Children, and Youth Development even gave Usha Narayane (the young woman who had stood up to Yadav in August 2004) financial support to establish the Kasturba Nagar Community Project. This project trains both women and men in skills such as catering, cooking, milk processing, ceramics, cardboard-box manufacturing and IT.[80] Many activists believed that fighting violence with violence was the only option available to the women of Kasturba Nagar. In the twenty-first century, feminist 'fairy tales' have tended to present similar arguments. Films such as *The Girl with the Dragon Tattoo* (2011) and *Snow White and the Huntsman* (2012) feature rape survivors who turn to vigilantism to terrorize their abusers. These films are interpreted as films of empowerment when they perhaps should be viewed as depictions that *enlist* patriarchal violence rather than *resist* it. As womanist activist Audre Lorde has argued, the 'master's tools' will never dismantle the master's house. They may allow us temporarily to beat him at his own game, but they will never enable us to bring genuine change. And this fact is only threatening to those women who still define the master's house as their only source of support.[81]

She encourages us all to 'make common cause with those others identified as outside the structures in order to define and seek a world in which we can all flourish'. It is a call for solidarity as much as dialogue.

SEVEN

Militarized Rape

Between 1932 and 1945, the largest incident of sex trafficking in modern history was planned, organized and systematically implemented by the Japanese Imperial Army. The misnamed 'comfort stations' were populated by around 160,000 girls and women, called *ianfu* (or *jūgunianfu*) in Japanese. They were military sexual slaves. They had been kidnapped, had their families threatened or were tricked by false promises of employment in war factories, hospitals or restaurants. Eighty per cent were Koreans, but Filipino, Chinese, Taiwanese, Indonesian, Dutch and Japanese women were also subjected to this form of abuse. They were enslaved in regulated brothels, military barracks, blockhouses and mountain caves in Japan, Taiwan, Korea, Manchuria, Sakhalin, Guangdong, Myanmar, the Philippines, Indonesia, Malaysia, Sumatra, Papua New Guinea and the Pacific Islands.

Military sex slaves endured a brutal existence. They were raped numerous times a day; some suffered this abuse for five years.[1] It is estimated that only one-quarter to one-third of *ianfu* survived.[2] Victims were often left with serious physical injuries, sexually transmitted infections, tuberculosis, mental disorders and infertility. The effects could last a lifetime. In the words of Hwang Kuen Soo, 'We were treated like pigs, dogs. My life was ruined and I am emotionally crippled. I never tried to marry. The thought and sight of men nauseated me.'[3] Returning home at the end of the war was also distressing. Many were denigrated as 'dirty women', even collaborators, by their communities.[4] They ended up as displaced persons, rejected and excluded from their home communities. As Yi Yōngsuk, a Korean woman who was 24 when the war ended, explained,

A ship came to take us home. I didn't want to return, but I had to get on board as all Koreans had been ordered by the government to return home. The ship was filled with comfort women. I had no family, no relatives, and no home to go to. It would be impossible for me to find a husband. I thought it would be better to drown than to return to my country, but I didn't have the courage to throw myself overboard.[5]

For Hwang Kuen Soo and Yi Yŏngsuk, no amount of financial payment would compensate them for their experiences. They pleaded simply to have their ordeal acknowledged by the Japanese government.

How did the Japanese military and political leaders justify the establishment of 'comfort stations'? They claimed that sexual slavery would improve the morale of their troops, curb soaring levels of rape in occupied areas, increase revenue through military brothels and reduce sexually transmitted infections among their own men. They designated 'comfort stations' as 'hygienic public convenience facilities'.[6] In 1993, conservative female journalist Uezaka Fuyuko explained that *ianfu* were 'a necessary evil during the war era in order to maintain the minimum security and order . . . This problem is nobody else's fault, but rather the inevitable extension of war business.'[7] This was also the view of Nakasone Yasuhiro, one of the military leaders who introduced the rape camps and went on to become prime minister of Japan (1982–7). He admitted that soldiers were beginning to 'assault the native women or indulged in gambling'. This was why, he explained, 'I made strenuous efforts to establish a comfort station for them,' since the men were 'just like potatoes jostling each other in a washbowl'.[8] Aware that what they were doing was a sexual atrocity, Japanese officers intentionally attempted to hide the shameful reality of what they were doing. Official documents listed the *ianfu* as 'military supplies'.

In Japan and Korea, post-war governments were reluctant to acknowledge the existence of surviving *ianfu*, let alone provide compensation. This was not the case in Dutch Indonesia, where, between 1948 and 1949, the authorities publicly tried a number of high-ranking Japanese officers for their role in sexual enslavement. Once convicted, they were imprisoned. One officer was executed; others committed ritual suicide to avoid imprisonment.[9]

In contrast to Dutch Indonesia, a very different response was encountered in Korea, where *ianfu* faced formidable hurdles in their struggles for justice. As late as 2007, Prime Minister Abe Shinzō even denied the existence of *ianfu* altogether, even though Yoshimi Yoshiake, a professor at Japan's Chuo University, published official documents in November 1991 and January 1992 proving that it had been an official policy. Many wealthy, urban Koreans found it difficult to empathize with *ianfu*, most of whom originated from poor, rural communities.[10] Dismissal of their claims was based on gender as well as class: the *ianfu* were a 'poor woman's problem'.

Nationalism was key. Girls and women were regarded as embodiments of a nation's morals and ethnic purity; those who had been forced into sex slavery were expected to stay silent and were reprimanded when they attempted to speak. Their sufferings were used to bolster anti-Japanese sentiment and pro-Korean nationalism. *Ianfu* became political pawns in a competition between Japanese and Korean men, sidelining the female victims. Historian Vicki Sung-yeon Kwon even observed that speaking publicly about the sexual slavery of Korean women might (ironically) *strengthen* 'both anti-colonial and patriarchal nationalism' by construing the abuses 'as a wound to national pride rather than a violation of women's human rights'. This was because 'in patriarchal nationalism, men are the subject of the nation and women, the object, the possession of the men.'[11]

The problem was compounded by the fact that Korea had been part of the Japanese empire. As a result, the sexual labour of Korean women could be seen as part of the war effort: they were a 'voluntary corps' or *deishintai*. Hyanah Yang drew attention to this aspect. She noted that, unlike the mass rapes in the former Yugoslavia,

> colonial Korean women's bodies were not clearly located in the position of enemy. Since the primary aim in the invention of the comfort women was the successful prosecution of the war, Korean women's bodies were treated simply as military supply, a resource to enable the Japanese victory.

The 'greater East Asia Co-Prosperity Sphere' was built on sexual violence.[12] This meant that the issue was profoundly political for successive Korean governments. After all, many members of the government had actively collaborated with the Japanese colonial regime.[13] Some Koreans had profited from the procurement and transportation of sex slaves.

The post-war political economy also encouraged repression of the atrocities. The Korean economy was dependent on Japanese technology for economic growth and faced a huge trade imbalance with Japan (as late as 1992, this amounted to $79 billion).[14] Since 1951, Korean and Japanese politicians had attempted to negotiate a general post-war settlement. It came to fruition in 1965 when the Japan–South Korea Claims Settlement Act was passed. By prioritizing the economy, this Act meant that further claims for damages inflicted on Korea while it had been part of the Japanese empire were foreclosed.[15] That included compensation for the women who had been forced into sexual slavery. There was a moral element to these negotiations: successive Korean governments were conscious that attacking the Japanese government for engaging in sexual slavery sat awkwardly alongside Korean governments' involvement in supplying American Army bases with brothels. Desperate for foreign currency, Korean governments turned a blind eye to sex tourism.

Criminal accountability of the Japanese had a wider geopolitical context. During the Cold War, the USA needed Japanese help in its struggle against communist regimes in the Soviet Union, China and North Korea. U.S. governments were all too willing to tolerate the image of Japan as a victim after the devastating losses caused by the atomic bombing of Hiroshima and Nagasaki. They therefore discouraged South Korea from pursuing a more aggressive course.

The main arguments against recognizing and (financially or symbolically) compensating the *ianfu* included the view that both colonized and colonizers were victims, atrocities are inevitable in times of war and not all the women had been forced. A small proportion had even indeed been paid for their sex labour, albeit a pittance. The newspaper *Sankei* quoted a Korean proverb exhorting people to 'keep a lid on something smelly'.[16]

The role of historical memory was also mobilized. Shouldn't ugly and shameful aspects of history be forgotten? Was resurrecting the past insulting to surviving veterans and dead ancestors? In 2012, the veterans' Korean Liberation Association certainly thought so when they opposed the creation of a museum in Seoul in honour of the military sexual slaves. They argued that the museum was a 'defamation of character' for those who had fought for independence.[17] Their lobbying failed: the 'War and Human Rights Museum' opened in May 2012.

The view that shameful aspects of history should be suppressed was linked to debates about Japanese history textbooks. In Japan, these books are produced by teams of writers and must be approved by the Ministry of Education. In 1963, historian Saburō Ienaga's textbook *Shin Nihonshi* (A New History of Japan) was rejected by the Ministry on the grounds that it was 'excessively critical'. Ienaga was asked to delete three hundred sections, including his mention of wartime rape atrocities and sexual enslavement. The Ministry reasoned that 'the violation of women is something that has happened on every battlefield in every era of human history. This is not an issue that needs to be taken up with respect to the Japanese Army in particular.'[18] The debate was reignited in 1995 by the Liberalist History Research Group, launched by university scholars Fujioka Nobukatsu and Nishio Kanji. They argued that the historiography of Japan during the Second World War had been one-sided.[19] The following year, they resumed their attacks under the auspices of the Council for the Creation of New History Textbooks. One of their demands was the erasure of all mentions of 'comfort women.'[20]

Despite such opposition, the abuses committed against *ianfu* gradually came to public attention. In 1979, Yamatani Tetsuo released the film *An Old Lady in Okinawa: Testimony of a Military Comfort Woman*, which told the story of Pae Pong-gi, the first Korean comfort woman to be publicly named.[21] By 1990, the Korean Council for the Women Drafted for Military Sexual Slavery by Japan had been formed. The Korean Council was a coalition of women's, human rights, labour and religious (both Christian and Buddhist) groups.

The increased willingness of *ianfu* to testify publicly about their experiences was decisive, however. On 14 August 1991, after more than half a century of silence, 67-year-old Kim Hak-sun came forward to identify herself as a former sex slave. She travelled around Japan telling audiences that she was willing to become a 'living witness' because her 'blood boiled when I heard the Japanese government denying its role in the *Chōngshindae* system'. She acknowledged that her bravery stemmed in part from being a childless widow, with no family to shame.

Hak-sun's descriptions of what had happened to her resonated with people throughout the world. Hak-sun reported that, at the age of seventeen, she had been kidnapped in Beijing and taken to Manchuria, where she was sexually enslaved. She testified that 'When I refused to have sex with soldiers, they said that they would kill me because I was under orders from the Emperor, the commanding officer, and the soldier himself, a soldier of the Japanese Imperial Army.' She admitted that her 'whole body and soul still shiver just thinking and talking about my experience as a *Chōngshindae* woman.'[22]

Hak-sun's example emboldened others. The following year, the Korean Council published *Witness of the Victims of Military Sexual*

Slavery. It included a song entitled 'Katusa' (Struggle), composed by Yi Yang-su. The words went:

> I can't live with this bitterness
> Give me back my youth
> Apologize and make reparations,
> Japan, apologize and make reparations for
> Taking us and trampling on us
> Mother, father, can you hear
> Your daughters crying
> Now my Korean brothers and sisters help me along.[23]

Interestingly, perpetrators of abuse also felt it was time to come forward. Many confessed via anonymous telephone lines. Others, such as Yoshida Seiji (who had been the chief of the National Service Recruitment Branch in Shimonoseki, southern Japan), came out more openly. In two books, he admitted that between 1942 and 1945 he had 'hunted' down around 5,000 Korean girls and women for the sex trade.[24] He was remorseful.

Change was slow. In 1993, Cabinet Chief Secretary Yohei Kono accepted that the Japanese military had been responsible for the military sexual slavery of Korean and other women. He offered an apology. Three years later, the United Nations condemned Japan's policy of sexual enslavement. However, the Japanese government only offered a limited apology, including an $8.3 million reparation fund, at the end of 2015. It was seen as too little, too late.

Is Wartime Sexual Violence Unique?

The history of sexual slavery by the Japanese military exemplifies some of the most emblematic features of militarized rape. It is an example of the extremes of wartime sexual cruelty, political excesses and historical neglect. The *ianfu* are also a stark reminder that wartime sexual violence does not exist in a cultural, political and economic vacuum. Sexually abusive ideologies and practices, as well as the political, economic and cultural institutions that maintain them, are rooted in pre-war histories. These are just some of the issues that will be addressed in the rest of this chapter.

It is important to note, however, that rape in times of armed conflict has distinctive features. Mass rape in wartime requires significant planning: combatants must be brutalized; propaganda, disseminated; abusive infrastructures, marshalled; racial and other inter-communal prejudices, drummed up. Crucially, rape at war is often extensive and systematic. It is sometimes genocidal.[25]

Wartime rape is also intrinsically political. Reports of rape have enormous propaganda value, especially when involving victims who can be politically construed as 'innocent' – young girls, for instance.[26] Rape stories are routinely mobilized for both defensive and expansionist militaristic purposes. During the First World War, for example, rumours about the 'rape of the Hun' were deliberately spread by the Allies in an attempt to mobilize hatred and convince other nations to commit troops to the conflict. The best known of these attempts is Viscount James Bryce's *Report of the Committee on Alleged German Outrages* (1915), which testified to German atrocities, including the mass rapes of girls and nuns.[27] Similarly, in France, posters, pamphlets and newspaper articles repeatedly portrayed the invasion of Belgium and France in terms of sexual violation. The historian Ruth Harris noted that France 'became a frail and ravished *jeune fille* [young woman], weeping and broken on the floor as the uhlan, the helmeted German cavalryman, leaves the bedroom'.[28]

Artists were also mobilized. These included the Dutch painter and caricaturist Louis Raemaekers, who created cartoons depicting German atrocities. His aim was to persuade governments in the USA and the Netherlands to give up their neutrality and side with the Allies in the war effort. His sketch entitled 'Seduction' showed a German soldier with a pistol to a woman's head, clearly with rapacious intent. Raemaekers's cartoons proved extremely popular. After being published in the *Amsterdam Telegraaf*, they were exhibited throughout the world and served as virulently anti-German propaganda. It was, as J. Murray Allison contended in his 1919 compilation of Raemaekers's cartoons, an example of beauty being 'drowned in a bestial orgy of force . . . the pencil in his hands becomes an avenging sword.'[29] The art of rape, as well as the material reality of actual rape, became a weapon of war.

The most shocking aspect of sexual violence in armed conflicts is not that it is planned. Nor that it is intrinsically political. It is the extent to which war radically lowers the threshold at which sexual violence can take place and dramatically alters the nature of that violence. Of course, it is right to be wary of a 'politics of exception', the view that wartime rape is worse than endemic abuse in times of peace. Or the 'politics of accountancy', the view that only once *this* threshold of victims is reached can it be labelled an atrocity. However, it is indisputable that certain aspects of armed conflicts increase risk. War magnifies existing inequalities between the sexes, which makes sexual violence more likely. Men within the community, as well as invading strangers, speedily arm themselves with a range of weapons, increasing their ability to coerce others. Male 'protectors' may be absent. This often pushes girls and women to engage in 'survival sex'. They might hastily accept offers of marriage in the hope that husbands will provide some level of protection. Many of the usual mechanisms for deterring sexual violence are diminished or disappear altogether: these include the dismantling of policing and legal systems and the absence of village elders, religious spokesmen and others who might potentially encourage restraint. As a result, in armed conflicts, rules against violent behaviour become extraordinarily relaxed.

There is nothing 'private' in incidents of mass rape during armed conflicts.[30] Rape becomes an intensely *public* display of brutality. It is often an extension of other forms of extraordinary violence, such as the destruction of property, beatings, abductions, strip searches, torture and murder. Compared to times of peace, wartime rape increases the number of men and women willing and able to inflict sexual cruelty. Rape can even be valorized as a patriotic act and one that facilitates emotional bonding between perpetrators.[31] As politics scholar Miranda Alison put it, gang rape in wartime 'bonds men together in a complicity (in fact a shared *awareness* of responsibility) that makes loyalty to the group vital'.[32] Historian Regina Mühlhäuser elaborates. She notes that 'In the life-threatening situation of combat, where men are extremely dependent on one another, gang rapes confirm the inextricable bonds between them and the reliability of their hierarchies.' Men 'meet one another in the body of a woman' and, 'in this process, they reaffirm their masculinity and sexual potency.'[33] Hierarchies are enacted; military rank (and therefore power) decides *who* rapes *which* women and *when*.[34] Officers are given licence to rape the most 'valued' victims first.

Wartime rape communicates a powerful message between men *in general*. It has symbolic value as an insult to the masculinity of the enemy. In the words of anthropologist Veena Das, women's bodies become 'a sign through which men communicated with each other'.[35] These women's rape is an indictment of their male associates who have patently failed to fulfil the unwritten 'gender contract' under which men fight to protect women, who, in turn, provide them with nurture. As 'biological reproducers of the collectivity' and 'transmitters of its culture', Alison argues, the sexual abuse of women is a potent declaration of dominance.[36] As sociologist Ruth Seifert put it, the rape of women is 'the symbolic rape of the body of [the] community'.[37] Public acts of rape are intended not only to physically destroy populations but to destroy religious and cultural symbols too. This was the case with the mass rape of Malay-indigenous girls and Guatemalan women: the rapists' intention was to eradicate any basis for social cohesion within the community.[38] Wartime rape generates disorder by violating deeply held norms associated with gender, family and community.[39] That is why it is such an effective weapon of war.

The Extent of Sexual Violence in War

Sexual violence is an ingrained part of armed conflicts. During the First World War, the most thoroughly documented instances of mass rape took place in Belgium and Russia. As we have already seen, from the late 1930s, rape and enforced prostitution was a feature of the Japanese invasion of China. Japanese soldiers also engaged in the mass rape of non-*ianfu*. In Nanjing, for example, over 20,000 women were raped in 1937 alone. As a further way of humiliating and destroying communities, fathers were forced to rape their own daughters, brothers to sexually assault sisters, and sons to molest mothers.[40] Shirō Azuma participated in such atrocities. He recalled that he and his comrades 'felt no shame . . . No guilt', explaining that

> When we entered a village, the first thing we'd do was steal food, then we'd take the women and rape them, and finally we'd kill all the men, women, and children to make sure they couldn't slip away and tell the Chinese troops where we were.

Chillingly, he noted that they killed the victims because 'otherwise, we wouldn't have been able to sleep at night'.[41] The statement implies that they might have felt some shame after all.

The 1937 mass rapes in Nanjing were examples of what took place to varying degrees in all theatres of war between 1939 and 1945. Every invading army proved to be rapacious.[42] Military sexual slavery was not a prerogative only of the Japanese Imperial Army. At least 35,000 Jewish prisoners at Ravensbrück camp alone were forced to work in brothels during the war, often 'servicing' over seven men a day.[43] Notorious mass rapes took place in Germany, Russia, Korea, China, Japan, Italy and the

Philippines. In many cases, the victims were presented as though they were culpable for the attacks carried out on them. Even the mass rapes carried out by the Red Army as they made their way through Eastern Europe near the end of the Second World War were presented in this way. In Budapest, approximately 50,000 women were raped by Russian soldiers;[44] during the Red Army's march into Germany, an estimated 1.9 million women were sexually violated.[45] In Berlin, approximately one in every three women was raped and over 10,000 died as a result of sexual assault. Thousands committed suicide.[46] Boris Slutsky was a poet who served as a *politruk* of a Red Army infantry platoon between 1941 and 1945. In his memoir, entitled *Things That Happened*, he dismissed any suggestion of suffering, claiming that

> In Europe the women surrendered themselves and were unfaithful sooner than anyone else . . . The Hungarian women loved the Russians in their turn, and . . . along with the dark fear that parted the knees of matrons and mothers of families, there was also the affectionate nature of young women and the desperate tenderness of the women soldiers, who gave themselves to the men who had killed their husbands.[47]

American troops were not exempt from engaging in such atrocities. According to one estimate, American rape levels in France and Germany towards the end of that war were between 300 and 400 per cent greater than rape rates in civilian America.[48] Sociologist J. Robert Lilly deduced that between 14,000 and 17,000 women were raped by American military personnel between 1942 and 1945.[49]

The catalogue of sexual violence in armed conflicts seems endless. In 1947, the partition of Punjab between India and Pakistan led to mass rapes.[50] During nine months in 1971–2, some estimates suggest that Pakistani soldiers, while attempting to crush the Bengali nationalist rebellion, raped around 200,000 Bengali women. Some scholars believe that twice that number of women were sexually assaulted.[51] Around 80 per cent of the victims were Muslim.[52] In the 1990s, there was widespread rape as well as torture and killings in Timor and Guatemala. The humiliation for the victims was enhanced by requiring them to mimic consensual, domestic interactions. For example, during the civil war in Guatemala, soldiers carrying out mass rapes would often insist that their victims cook them a meal and dance to marimba music.[53]

Although I will be warning against characterizations of 'African wars' as especially rapacious, this should not lead to minimizing the effects of high levels of sexual violence during particular conflicts in that region. During the Rwandan genocide of 1994, between half and 90 per cent of surviving Tutsi girls and women had been sexually attacked.[54] An unknown number of Hutu girls and women were also sexually assaulted, generally because they associated with Tutsi women or were in the 'wrong place at the wrong time while female'.[55] Similar levels of sexual violence were observed during and immediately after the war in Liberia, where between 50 and 90 per cent of women reported having been subjected to sexual assault at least once.[56] Half of the victims in Liberia were aged between ten and fifteen years.[57] Crucially, between 10 and 40 per cent of members of the fighting forces were children.[58] They not only experienced and witnessed atrocities, but participated in acts of extreme cruelty.

In recent years, research has focused on armed conflicts spurred by the financial needs of international conglomerates. In other words, in recent armed conflicts, rape is inflicted on vulnerable populations by greedy, global capitalists. A notable example is agribusiness companies in Ecuador, who employed mercenaries to sexually abuse indigenous Yuracruz girls and women to drive them and their families from resource-rich land. According to one estimate, half of Yuracruz women have been sexually assaulted.[59]

Another form has been called 'petro-violence', or the use of rape to expel populations from regions that reap massive profits for state and multinational oil companies. During the Biafra War in Nigeria, rape was 'more than just a "tool" of war', explains feminist scholar Heather M. Turcotte: it was 'the condition on which global oil politics' were 'made possible'.[60] Similarly, in the Democratic Republic of the Congo (DRC), rape was a means of 'clearing' land for the mining of coltan, diamonds and gold. Coltan is particularly important since it is indispensable for mobile phones, personal computers, automotive electronics and cameras. Eighty per cent of the world's coltan is in the DRC.[61] According to the UN, at the end of the 1990s the Rwandan military may have been selling coltan for as much as $20 million each month.[62] In the words of international relations scholar Sara Meger,

> Because of the greater ease globalization provides to transnational
> trade and mutual cooperation, nonstate actors have greater
> access to eager regional and international buyers, which provides

strong incentive to use violence as a means of achieving economic objectives.[63]

Also beset by internal political ambition, the weakness of state authorities and ethnic rivalries, the DRC is the worst place in the world to be a woman.[64] One thousand girls and women are raped every day; today, there are over 200,000 surviving rape victims in the DRC, one-third of whom are children under the age of eighteen.[65]

These armed conflicts are just a few examples. Other regions that have seen sexual violence reach such extreme levels that it amounts to femicide include Afghanistan, Algeria, Argentina, Bangladesh, Bosnia, Brazil, Burma, Cambodia, Croatia, Cyprus, East Timor, El Salvador, Haiti, India, Indonesia, Kosovo, Kuwait, Liberia, Mozambique, Nicaragua, Peru, Serbia, Turkey, Uganda, Vietnam, Zaire and Zimbabwe.

Law and Genocidal Rape

Despite such high levels of sexual violence throughout the world, rules against wartime rape are remarkably recent. Sexual violence has been proscribed in civilian contexts since the first codification of law; this is not the case with military law. For centuries, the rape of women in war was considered a bounty for the victors, a price paid for by the marginalized. In the West, this changed in 1863 when the Lieber Code was introduced for the U.S. Union Army, decreeing that a soldier who raped a woman could be 'lawfully killed on the spot'.[66]

International law has also been sluggish in responding. In 1907, Article 46 of the 'Laws and Customs of War on Land (Hague IV)' prohibited the violation of 'family honour' while Article 27 of the Fourth Geneva Conventions of 1949 ruled that 'women shall be especially protected against any attack on their honour, in particular against rape, enforced prostitution, or any form of indecent assault.' However, the war crimes trials in Nuremberg ignored rape and other gender-based crimes altogether.[67] The International Military Tribunal for the Far East prosecuted rape, but as 'inhumane treatment' and 'failure to respect family honour and rights', rather than as a major war crime.[68] The Japanese leaders responsible for sexual violence perpetrated against 160,000 *ianfu* were overlooked.

The trigger-point for international attention to wartime sexual violence was the 1991–2 conflict in the former Yugoslavia. Indeed, debates about law, genocide and sexual violence continue to be reflected through the lens of that war. Mass rapes took place on all sides, but systematic and widespread violations were perpetrated by Serbian forces against Muslim women, Catholics and Croats. According to some estimates, nearly 20,000 girls and women were raped.[69] They were violated in their homes, incarcerated in detention camps established explicitly for the purpose of rape, forced into prostitution and, at rape camps like the one at Foca, deliberately impregnated, then forced to bring the foetus to term and give birth.[70] Every side made use of these acts in their propaganda: the Serbian press vilified Croat and Muslim men as orientalized rapists while the Croatian and Bosnian media did the same to the Serbs. Croatian nationalist groups argued that 'rape is a distinctly Serbian weapon for which all Serbs – even feminists who oppose the war – are culpable.'[71] One Croatian periodical accused anti-war feminists of treachery: 'Croatian feminists rape Croatia!', screamed one headline.[72] In the words of gender scholar Dubravka Zarkov, 'raped women became flags waved by the warring parties.'[73]

The co-option of the experiences of women in the former Yugoslavia were part of broader debates about the way some local as well as international groups were exploiting the suffering of violated women. The non-nationalist Zagreb Women's Lobby found it necessary to publish a 'Letter of Intentions' to women's organizations as well as peace movements throughout the world. In it, they voiced concern over the way sexually violated women were being 'used in political propaganda with the aim of spreading hatred and revenge, thus leading to further violence against women'.[74] The feminist group 'Women in Black' similarly warned against 'the politics of instrumentalization of victims'. They refused to become tangled up in arguments about 'who is the real victim, or who has the greatest right to call themselves victims'. They pointed out that 'A victim is a victim, and to her the number of other victims does not decrease her own suffering and pain.' Admittedly, they continued, 'we happen to live in Belgrade and happen to work with women who happen to have Serbian names, and happen to be prisoners of war and victims of rape.' However, when faced with

> courageous, exhausted and traumatized women, we cannot in any way see them as less victims than any women of different nationality. They tell us of all kinds of atrocities, systematic rapes, death threats and other horrors . . . it is not the nationality but the body of men which have destroyed their joy of life.[75]

It was an impassioned plea, but it risked casting *all* women as victims, thus excusing some for the active role they played in the carnage.[76]

Alongside such anxieties were debates about 'rape as a weapon of war', which was sometimes called 'rape warfare' or 'strategic rape'.[77] 'Rape as a weapon of war' should not be allowed, however, to dominate the history of sexual violence. As Alison reminds us, such a focus 'misses so much'. It

> means that sexual violence that occurs during conflicts but does not stem from a directed military strategy is either obscured from view or is, troublingly, assumed to be part of a military strategy instead of the deeper structures of power in any given society.[78]

That said, rape as a weapon of war was a prominent aspect in the wars of the former Yugoslavia. Commentators kept asking whether the high levels of sexual violence during that conflict should be considered 'ethnic cleansing' by Serbian forces. There is general agreement that the mass rapes were part of an attempt to clear territories of Bosnian Muslims and Croats, with the intention of destroying their cultures. In the words of Kelly Dawn Askin, legal consultant and adviser to the International Criminal Tribunal for the former Yugoslavia (ICTY), the methods of achieving ethnic cleansing were

> not limited to physical elimination. For instance, a person may be sexually assaulted in order to be humiliated or emotionally destroyed or to be proven submissive or subordinate; a person may be raped in order to cause chaos or terror and/or to make people flee the area, effectively destroying the group; a woman may be raped in order to forcibly impregnate her with a different ethnic gene.

These were all 'different tactics but with the same objective – destroying or removing the unwanted group'.[79]

The second point of contention was whether 'ethnic cleansing' should be considered a form of genocide. Were the widespread, systematic rapes conducted by Serbian forces genocidal or were they simply a dramatic extension of 'everyday rape'? Was there a risk of ignoring the rapes carried out by non-Serbians? The first time that the ICTY held that rape constituted a grave breach of international humanitarian law (rather than a breach of the Geneva Convention) concerned a Croat defendant (Furundzija), while the second prosecution involved a Bosnian Muslim defendant who raped Serbian women at Čelebići (Foča).[80] Did some victims' suffering count for more than others'?

An important plank in the argument that the Serbian rape campaigns were genocidal lay in the deliberate impregnation of women who were then forced to give birth to what the rapists claimed would be 'little Chetniks'. According to some commentators, these acts of forced impregnation were nothing less than the 'occupation' of women's wombs.[81] For others, the genocide lay in the assumption that infants born of rape would be genetically Serbian. This is deeply problematical, and not solely for obvious physiological reasons. The chief problem is that it accepts the rapists' belief that ethnicity is biological and paternal. As legal expert Karen Engle complained, the belief that 'if a Muslim egg were inseminated with a Serbian sperm, a Serbian child would ensue' too often went unchallenged.[82] Scholars like Robyn Charli Carpenter warned that the argument

> reifies both the false logic of genetics that brought about the rapes and the patriarchal attitude that labels any child born of rape as automatically 'other', rejected, stigmatized, and unwanted by the culture that claims the mother's reproductive identity.[83]

The socially constructed notion of biology, favouring the male, was particularly stark in the context of Bosnia, where there was little to differentiate Bosnian Muslims and Serbs genetically and where, prior to the war, around one-third of marriages in the region were inter-group.[84]

What few people doubted was that the exceptionally high levels of rape and its deliberate deployment by military forces required revisions to international law. In 2001, both the Statute of the International Criminal Tribunal for the former Yugoslavia and the Statute of the International Criminal Tribunal for Rwanda recognized rape as a crime against humanity, as opposed to a violation of men's property rights or an inhumane act.[85] In the words of philosopher Debra Bergoffen, by

> identifying rape, like torture, as a crime against humanity, the ruling affirms the principle of embodied subjectivity. It goes beyond past rulings on torture, however, in attending to the sexual realities of embodiment and in insisting that violating a *woman's* sexual integrity is a crime against humanity.[86]

International scholars were jubilant; sexually violent perpetrators barely noticed.

'Africa's World Wars'?

The high levels of sexual violence during the break-up of Yugoslavia are often seen as exceptional in Europe. In contrast, analyses of mass rape during armed conflicts in the geopolitical South typically eschew the 'politics of exception' for a narrative that assumes that 'African wars are culturally rapacious'. This assumption is based on colonialist and racist misconceptions. When researchers at the Peace Research Institute in Oslo examined all 48 armed conflicts in Africa (involving 236 organized armed groups) between 1989 and 2009, they found that 64 per cent of armed groups did not engage in sexual violence.[87] In their research into rape committed by combatants in the geopolitical South, Dara Kay Cohen, Amelia Hoover Green and Elisabeth Jean Wood observed that

> rape by combatants is widespread in some conflicts but not others, that armed groups even within the same war do not perpetuate sexual violence to the same extent or in the same form, and that an armed group that refrains from sexual violence at one stage of a war might perpetuate it on a large scale at other times.[88]

In other words, there was as much variety in levels of sexual violence in armed conflicts in the geopolitical South as elsewhere in the world. They cited research into 86 major civil wars around the world between 1980 and 2009, concluding that

> Eighteen wars had at least one year of massive reported rape, thirty-five of at least one year with numerous reported rapes, eighteen of isolated reports of rape, and fifteen of no reports. Of wars with some reports, 38 percent had asymmetric reports of rape – that is, only one side perpetrated the violence. In sum, it was more common for both states and nonstate actors to perpetrate rape, whereas rape by only armed state actors was less frequent, and rape by only rebel actors relatively rare. Notably . . . armed state actors are more likely than rebel groups to be reported as perpetrating high levels of sexual violence.[89]

They also set out to dismantle the idea that Africa was especially prone to rapacious warfare. Admittedly, sub-Saharan Africa 'experienced the most civil conflict' but 'only 36 per cent (ten of twenty-eight) of wars in this region showed evidence of the highest level of wartime rape.' In contrast, 44 per cent (that is, four out of nine) of armed conflicts in Eastern Europe 'reported the highest level of rape'. In their words, 'on a per-conflict basis, eastern European civil wars were more likely than sub-Saharan African conflicts to feature reports of massive levels of rape.'[90] Furthermore, 64 per cent of state actors in African wars perpetrated sexual violence compared with less than one-third of rebel groups and militias.[91] They explained this surprising finding by the fact that rebel groups are more dependent upon local populations for food, water and other resources: it was important not to alienate locals whom they may later rely on if they become the government.

False assumptions about 'African wars' are compounded by two other biases. The first is a partiality in reporting trials of wartime perpetrators of atrocities. This was a criticism made by transnational legal scholar Mark A. Drumbl. After the genocide in Rwanda, he observed that Western attention was paid to Hutu men and women who were tried in international tribunals rather than local ones. For example, numerous legal commentators claimed that Pauline Nyiramasuhuko (whom I discussed in an earlier chapter) was the first woman convicted for genocide and rape. This ignores the thousands of other women who were tried in Rwandan courts. One of these was Agnès Ntamabyaliro, who was also a high-profile Minister in the Cabinet and was given a life sentence for genocide. Drumbl noted that this

> reveals the powerful tendency to view international justice as the only justice, or at least iconically as the first-best form thereof, which fuels the disregard often accorded to national initiatives, especially those undertaken within the post-conflict society itself.

It cements the 'much-vaunted superiority of enlightened internationalism over clumsy localism'.[92]

The second problem is that much reporting on sexual atrocities in the geopolitical South risks cementing stereotypes about rapacious 'Black men', 'violent tribal groups' and 'patriarchal African culture'. Too much research on the conflict in the Congo, for example, slips into a 'Conradian landscape' animated by a 'primitive "heart of darkness"'.[93] While Western perpetrators of sexual atrocities and sexualized torture are discursively constructed as examples of 'bad apples' or men and women suffering from PTSD, when identical atrocities are carried out by armed men in the geopolitical South they are explained according to alleged 'rapacious *cultures*'.

Negative reportage of rapacious 'Black men' during armed conflicts can be juxtaposed against explanations given for similar behaviour by 'White men'. While 'African' sexual violence is positioned as part of 'African' cultures, not so mass rape and other atrocities committed by American troops, for example. This was discussed in Chapter One in connection with the 1971 Winter Soldiers' Investigation. These American soldiers excused their rapacious behaviours by blaming racism, peer pressure, unfamiliar environments, lack of training, revenge, weak military leadership and PTSD. What they did not mention was 'American culture'.

This is not to deny the reality of 'combat stressors'. But it is to point to the additional role played by 'American culture' in the sexual atrocities perpetrated by members of the U.S. military during deployment as well as in training. The men testifying during the Winter Soldiers' Investigation and in thousands of other contexts admitted to committing sexual and other atrocities against Vietnamese women, but they were also perpetrating abuse against their own comrades. A survey of 558 American women who had served in Vietnam revealed that 48 per cent of them had been subjected to personal violence by their male comrades during their military service. Thirty per cent had been raped, 35 per cent had been physically assaulted and 16 per cent had been *both* raped and physically assaulted during their service.[94] Today, between 30 and 40 per cent of women in the U.S. military have been sexually abused by their own comrades.[95] In other words, when committing acts of sexual violence, male service personnnel targeted a gender; when faced with an officially designated enemy, they targeted an ethnicity as well as gender.

Aftermaths

The political uses of accounts of rape are not only important in mobilizing support for armed conflict, but for reframing memories of war in its aftermath. This was prominent in post-1945 West Germany, whose founding myth circled around the rape of 'innocent' German women by 'Asiatic hordes', thus overlooking the active involvement of German women in the Holocaust.[96] It also distorted the motivations of German soldiers committing atrocities on the Eastern Front. As historian Heide

Fehrenbach put it, German troops were not portrayed as 'convinced Nazi ideologues fighting *for* Hitler, but rather desperate husbands, fathers, brothers, and sons attempting to protect their women and families – and indeed the "Christian West" – from the cruel vengeance of a savage foe.'[97]

Rape narratives fulfilled similar political functions in the Soviet Union, East Germany and Hungary following the Second World War. It was only after the collapse of Communism that many people felt able to talk about militarized sexual violence. Tight controls over the press and mass media ensured that harrowing accounts had to be buried. In many communist states, governments had promoted an idealized version of history in which the Red Army liberated (rather than sexually victimized) populations. When rape was discussed, as in Hungary, for example, such talk could be dismissed as a politically inspired attack on communism.[98] For many Hungarian Jews and others, stories about mass rapes carried out by the Red Army were outrageous attempts by conservative nationalists who wanted to forget how active Hungarians had been in promoting fascist ideologies and enabling the Holocaust.[99]

Active 'forgetting' was often justified in terms of rebuilding societies after conflict. This was what a Bengali freedom fighter meant when he spoke about Bangladesh's 1971 war of independence from Pakistan. He acknowledged that 'this talk about women and rape is okay to an extent' but said that it should not be encouraged. After all, he maintained, 'the kind of history that should be written about the war is the glorious victory of the Bangladeshis against the Pakistanis. Rape happened in the war. But this is not something to tell the future generation.'[100]

In the aftermath of war, acknowledging mass rape could be deeply unpopular, and not only because it drew attention away from heroic narratives. It could be treacherous. This was what Kondō Hajime discovered. During the Second Sino-Japanese War, he had been involved in the gang rape of a Chinese woman when stationed in Shanx. When he testified to atrocities, ultra-nationalists pilloried him and called him a traitor for besmirching the honour of the Japanese forces.[101] As we saw at the start of this chapter, the military sex slaves of the Japanese Imperial Army also found themselves treated as 'collaborators' in the aftermath of the war.[102]

The victorious side could demand that the girls and women they 'saved' engage in sexual intercourse with them as a 'reward'. This was what some survivors of the genocide in Rwanda discovered when they were housed in displaced persons' camps guarded by members of the Rwandan Patriotic Army.[103] There is also increased risk from international NGOs and humanitarian workers, who exploit the vulnerability of girls and women in post-conflict societies. Between 2005 and 2017, approximately 2,000 reports of sexual abuse by UN peacekeepers were reported.[104] In Monrovia (Liberia), a survey in 2012 revealed that 44 per cent of female respondents admitted to having engaged in transactional sex with UN peacekeepers.[105]

Continued violence in the aftermath of military conflicts is not surprising. Former combatants typically experience high levels of PTSD, alcohol and drug abuse and joblessness. During the war, they had become accustomed to using violence to achieve their goals. In refugee camps, defeated men are often frustrated and angry; they are keen to reassert their authority over women. As one Congolese man living in a refugee settlement in Uganda in 2016 complained during a group discussion convened by women's rights advocate Pearl Atuhaire,

> While we were still in Congo, my wife used to respect me and never denied me sex at any point. But since we arrived here, because of the strong message of women's emancipation and women's rights in Uganda, my wife has become big-headed. She sometimes denies me sex! Yet she is my wife! And I am entitled to conjugal rights from my wife ... Once, she even told me that I had raped her because I forcefully had sex with her. How is it possible that someone can rape his wife?[106]

The other men in the group burst into laughter.

Victims of wartime sexual violence cannot be silenced forever, although recognition could take decades. The Korean *ianfu* with whom I began this chapter are prominent examples not only of protest and memory-keeping, but also of transnational solidarity. This can be illustrated by the unveiling of *P'yŏnghwaŭi Sonyŏsang* in 2011. The 'Statue of the Girl for Peace' is the creation of South Korean artists Kim Seokyung and Kim Eunsung. However, it was originally the brainchild of the Korean Council for the Women Drafted for Military Sexual Slavery, a non-governmental body who, since 1992, have organized regular protests in front of the Japanese embassy in Seoul. It is a bronze sculpture paying tribute to survivors of military sexual slavery. It shows a young, barefoot Korean girl who had been used as a sexual slave sitting on a chair. Behind her is a shadow of how she would look decades later – that is, a prematurely aged woman. Her fists are clenched. She has unevenly cut hair. The bird that sits on her shoulder 'symbolizes the victim's spirit', explains art historian Vicki Sung-yeon Kwon: it 'cannot leave this life for reincarnation because the issue has not been resolved'.[107] Next to the young *ianfu* is another chair: it is empty.

Sonyŏsang has elicited empathetic responses. Visitors stroke the bronze *ianfu* and, in winter, place scarfs around her neck or socks on her cold feet. They adorn the empty chair with flowers. The sculpture has been replicated in at least 66 places in South Korea, as well as in the USA, Canada, Australia and China. Performance artists have turned themselves into 'Living Sonyŏsang' in public squares in London, Munich and Chicago.[108]

One of these artists is Shimada Yoshiko from Japan. In 1993, she had etched 'A House of Comfort', which juxtaposed photographs of some 'comfort women', a military brothel and a semi-naked woman. Her most well-known tribute to the *ianfu*, however, took place in 2012 when she performed 'Becoming a Statue of a Japanese Comfort Woman' outside the Japanese Embassy in London. This was followed by performances throughout Japan, including at the contested Yasukuni shrine. Her enactments involved wearing a Japanese kimono, painting herself bronze and adopting the same posture as the girl in the *Sonyŏsang* statue, including placing an empty chair beside her. By wearing the Japanese kimono rather than the Korean *hanbok*, Yoshiko was drawing attention to the fact that Japanese women were also sexually enslaved.[109] Yoshiko does not speak during these performances, occasionally taping up her mouth to indicate the forced nature of the sexual slaves' silence.[110]

Successive Korean and Japanese authorities have sought to get rid of the *Sonyŏsang*. In 2015, the Korean government even made an agreement with the Japanese government to 'make an effort' to remove the statue from the front of the Japanese embassy, in return for ¥1 billion (£7.6 million) to establish the Foundation for Reconciliation and Healing.[111] Activists were furious. Crowds rallied in front of the original statue as well as replicas. During a protest in front of the *Sonyŏsang* replica in Dong District in eastern South Korea, a photograph of a protester hugging the statue in an effort to prevent police officers from carting it away triggered widespread public sympathy and forced city administrators to back down.[112] In Seoul, students at the Ewha Women's High School even established the 'Chumŏktokki' (Hand A) group, which set out to install *Sonyŏsang* replicas in one hundred schools. In the words of one student interviewed by Kwon, 'the sonyŏ were at our age. Wouldn't they be us in the past?'[113]

Although *Sonyŏsang* has been a focal point for South Korean anti-rape and pacifist activism, former *ianfu* did not remain fixated on their own pasts. They expressed solidarity with other abused Korean girls and women, including sex workers catering to soldiers in the American bases in Korea, low-paid labourers and servants and people who had been imprisoned under the reunification movement.[114] Their actions generated rich transnational seams of solidarity. Former *ianfu* quickly recognized that their struggles to have their suffering recognized was shared by victims of wartime sexual violence throughout the world. As survivor Kim Bok-Dong admitted, 'It still hurts to remember the past and tell the painful stories of my experience in public,' but 'by attending seminars around the world, talking about my experiences, and meeting various people, I have come to recognize that there are many people who suffered like I did.'[115] Along with survivor Gil Won-ok, Bok-Dong established the *Nabi Kigeum* (Butterfly Fund), raising money for other victim-survivors, such as those in the Congo. They explained that the fund set out to 'stop violence against women in armed conflicts, promote a strong solidarity among us and our friends, set history right, heal the wounds of the victims, and uphold truth and justice'. They chose the butterfly as their symbol since 'the fluttering butterfly stirs its wings with all its power to fly high[,] free from discrimination, subjugation, and violence.'[116]

Solidarity also went in the other direction. Japanese feminists recognized that they needed to do more than simply acknowledge the sufferings that Japanese men and women had inflicted on other women; they also had to work for justice. Suzuki Yuko explained that 'our own liberation is bound together with correcting injustices done to these Korean sisters, thus affirming our own identity as women and as caring human beings.'[117] Dalit women from India had a similar response. Disillusioned by mainstream Indian feminists, whom they reproached for caste-based biases which ignored the needs of Dalit women, Dalit activists sought to develop communities of solidarity with Korean *ianfu*. The 1994 Asia Tribunal on Women's Human Rights in Tokyo presented opportunities for dialogue. Ruth Manorama and Babamma Basappa travelled to Tokyo to share their experiences and expertise. Manorama was a Dalit women's rights activist from Bangalore who later established the National

Federation of Dalit Women. Basappa was from Karnataka, where she had been a *devadasi*, a form of caste-based prostitution in which young girls are dedicated to a goddess to serve in a temple for their entire lives. Manorama, Basappa and former *ianfu* began identifying similarities between caste-based sexual slavery and its wartime equivalent. Both forms of violence were made possible by hierarchies of caste and rank, as well as being 'cultural mechanism[s]' for the perpetration of abuse, as historical-anthropologist Purvi Mehta later explained.[118] Speaking at the Tribunal, one activist contended that

> It is from the edges that the women are speaking, knowing that from the margins of power, we see the world differently. We need to find a new terrain, walking with other people on the edges – the indigenous, the Dalits, the disabled, the dispossessed.[119]

Sexual slaves found empowerment through becoming global human rights activists.

EIGHT

Trauma

Today, it is a truism that all victims of sexual violation will suffer trau-matic aftermaths. The devastating psychological effects of rape are given considerably more weight than any physical or social harms. The trauma of rape is so engrained that rape victims who claim to be emotion-ally unaffected are thought to be 'in denial' and are warned to anticipate delayed reactions. Some therapists have even argued that *all* women are suffering from post-traumatic stress disorder (PTSD) or 'insidious trauma'. As one feminist argued, every woman is a PTSD sufferer, due to the stress of knowing that 'they may be raped at any time and by anyone.'[1]

PTSD and, less commonly, rape trauma syndrome (RTS) have become such an integral part of the lexicon around victimhood that it may seem perverse to question it. But that is what this chapter will do. Its central claim is that the ways we understand the after-effects of rape in the West today are, first, historically and, second, culturally problematic. This is why, when I write about rape in this chapter, I will be using the term 'bad event' rather than '*traumatic* event'. This is obviously not to deny that rape victims in earlier periods and different regions of the world experience *intense* distress in the aftermath of abuse. However, the language, beliefs, significance and bodily reactions to sexual violation are not universal. Variations in physiological and emotional responses to a 'bad event' such as rape are not superficial historical and cultural peculiarities: they pro-foundly affect the *meaning* and *experience* of the 'bad event'. As a result, they have consequences for strategies involving individual healing and social transformation.

Historical Responses to Rape

In the early decades of the nineteenth century, the English city of Manchester was being transformed into the 'workshop of the world' thanks to an industrial revolution centred on the cotton mills. It was a turbulent time for impoverished workers. The exploitation of children and women was particularly egregious: not only did they work long hours in often appalling conditions, but they also had to deal with a casual misogyny expressed by the boys and men with whom they had dealings. Nevertheless, the rape of seventeen-year-old, unmarried mill worker Mary Ann Houay by five young men was regarded as particularly shocking. Newspapers agreed to report Houay's 'melancholy narrative', but only 'as far as we can reduce such truly disgusting particulars to a narratable form'.

Houay's harrowing experience occurred on Wednesday 9 October 1833. Mid-afternoon, she left the Birley and Kirk cotton mill (where she had been working a 'short time') and returned home. A few hours later, her mother sent her on an errand, after which she went to meet a friend outside Mr Moreland's factory. When she discovered that workers at Moreland's had not been 'loosed' yet, she turned to return home – only to be approached by David Tetley, who attempted to persuade her to accompany him elsewhere. She flatly refused. Emboldened by the appearance of John Armstrong, the two men pushed her to nearby waste ground, threw her on the ground, roughly held her by the throat and raped her. In the intervals of consciousness, Houay became aware that three other men were participating in the rape. These were twenty-year-old John Openshaw (the eldest), John Cork and Joseph Wellings. Each of them raped her a number of times. On the last occasion, Openshow turned her naked body onto her stomach and 'flogged her severely with his braces' shouting 'You — bitch'. 'The brute' then 'made water upon her'.

Houay's assailants were quickly apprehended. Not only did she know both Tetley and Cork since they worked alongside her at the factory, but the five young men had openly bragged about what they had done. The morning after Houay's ordeal, Wellings, Cork and Openshaw had 'laughed and joked about what had occurred', boasting that they had been 'having a lark with that crazy b----r that works at Birley's'. They were so proud of their violence that they even took one male friend to the waste ground to point out the site of their exploit. This friend testified that 'they all laughed heartily, and talked over the matter as a most excellent joke.'

In court, the young men were less jovial. Shortly after he had been arrested, Cork had told the policeman that he wished he had killed the 'silly girl'. However, in court he behaved with 'respectful propriety', although he 'burst into tears' when told that they might be executed. Tetley showed 'angry impatience' and 'did not seem to be aware of the perilous situation in which he was placed'. Wellings was 'respectful' but easily distracted by goings-on in the courtroom. Only eighteen-year-old Armstrong (whom journalists called an 'unhappy stripling') seemed aware of their likely fate. He 'laboured under strong excitement', often 'shed tears' and would have fainted 'had not water been promptly applied'. Journalists marvelled that, except for Openshaw, they were 'all fine youths, and evince nothing in their appearance to justify the slightest suspicion of malignity'.

The fact that the perpetrators of the 'outrage' were so young, in employment and did not look like brutal rapists might have led members of the court to doubt the truthfulness of Houay's testimony. Houay's actions after the multiple rapes also could have raised questions. After all, Houay had not immediately reported her brutal violation. She admitted that she 'could not for shame' tell her mother. Houay even went to work the following day, knowing that she might come across at least two of her abusers. Eventually, though, Houay 'felt very ill; a blindness sometimes came over her, and she could not see her work'. Distress coupled with these physical omens led her to tell her married sister, who reported the incident to the police.

Despite the innocent appearance of the young assailants, the lack of corroborating evidence, Houay's lowly status as an unmarried mill worker, and the fact that she delayed reporting the 'outrage', her account was considered to be totally believable. This is because Houay conformed to many of the stereotypes of a 'true' rape victim in early nineteenth-century Britain. Journalists observed that she was 'delicately formed' and 'though not handsome, exhibits a simplicity of expression by no means unprepossessing'. She also comported herself in a manner that people in the 1830s believed pointed to 'real' victimhood. The 'wretched' victim's 'indisposition' (which meant that she was unable to attend court the first day of the trial) worked in her favour, as did the fact that, when she appeared, 'wine, salts, and other restoratives were constantly administered to keep her from sinking under the effort.'[2]

Houay's account of being raped was credible for people in early nineteenth-century Britain for reasons that are very different to 'believability' tropes in the West today. In particular, it deviated signi-ficantly from the 'psychological trauma' paradigm of modern times. The most important aspect of Houay's response to her rape was her adherence to an 'insensibility' script. Victims of rape in nineteenth-century England were required to have been rendered 'insensible' during the assault. Crucially, insensible did not necessarily mean unconscious. Rather, insen-sibility was an infliction of the physiological nervous system: it was a somatic affliction that resulted in a 'sinking' of the self. The 'sensible' body was seductive and either invited abuse or would have been able to repulse any attack. The 'insensible' rape victim testified to 'true' vio-lation. The emphasis on Houay's 'delicacy', then, was not only proof of her inability to fight off the rapists, but – crucially – also of her virtue and moral 'simplicity'. Only the 'nervous', 'insensible' body could speak of sexual violation.

Strangely to modern ears, rape victims like Houay claimed to be 'insensible' *in order* to be able to talk about their experiences. Unlike the modern notion of hysteria as involving a silencing or the muddling of a person's ability to communicate some terrible harm, in this earlier period, hysteria was associated with speech, a truthful recitation of suf-fering. Ironically, it was precisely the testimony of the insensible body that *enabled* women to speak of violation: it provided incontrovertible proof of their moral virtue.

Houay's blindness also attested to her authenticity. Clinicians today would call post-trauma somatic symptoms such as blindness a form of 'conversion hysteria': that is, traumatized victims 'converted' their wish not to 'see' what had happened to them into a literal inability to see – that is, blindness. Conversion hysteria is relatively uncommon in the West today – perhaps because widespread knowledge about psychological responses to 'bad events' makes this basic physiological response seem unnecessarily blunt. But in nineteenth-century Britain, there was nothing 'unsophisti-cated' about somatic conversion of distress into physiological ailments. Indeed, the body and mind were seen as inseparable entities, meaning that mental distress would *inevitably* be registered on the corporeal body.

Finally, Houay's story was described as a 'melancholy narrative'. Disorders such as melancholy were believed at the time to be due to either a stoppage or an excess of nervous vibrations, which had a direct impact on mental symptoms or 'vapours' within the body. The brutal, physical attack on Houay's body would inevitably affect her nerves, plunging her into melancholia.

Invention of Psychological Trauma

Houay's responses to sexual assault in 1833 are a world away from the language of 'trauma' that was to develop later in the century. The 'trauma model' that is familiar to us today is essentially an invention of the 1860s. In Houay's time, trauma retained its original Greek ($\tau\rho\alpha\nu\mu\alpha$) meaning a bodily injury. The legacy of this definition is still seen in the term 'trauma wards' for the emergency rooms in hospitals.

In 1866, however, British surgeon John Eric Erichsen reconceptualized trauma, taking it away from its original meaning of an external wound to an internal, 'psychological' one. He did this after observing the responses of people after railway accidents (this was when railways were still a new and anxiety-inducing technology). Erichsen argued that nightmares, uncontrollable trembling and other symptoms were not due to any physical injury, but to emotional ones. He identified an inner psychological response to an external 'bad event'. From this time, the notion of 'trauma' catapulted into mainstream Western understandings of the self, quickly being applied to every 'bad event'. It is assumed that every 'bad event' is traumatizing – so much so that 'bad events' are called 'traumatic events': they are subjectively experienced as 'trauma'. In other words, even in the West, 'trauma' was *not* the way people responded to 'bad events' prior to the 1860s.

The traumatic aftermaths of sexual violence were widely acknowledged in European psychiatric discourses. In *Étude médico-légale sur les attentats aux mœurs* (A Medico-Legal Study of Sexual Assault, 1878), eminent French forensic physician Ambroise Tardieu documented hundreds of cases of sexual abuse (mainly of children), carefully delineating the serious psychological consequences of assault.[3] French neurologist Jean-Martin Charcot never paid much attention to sexual assault as a causal factor in the neuroses of his female patients (perhaps not surprising since, for Charcot, the 'bad event' was simply a trigger for a pathology that was fundamentally hereditary), but Freud drew on his work to make such connections. Freud's early work insisted that the 'ultimate cause of hysteria always is the sexual seduction of a child by an adult'.[4] The work of pioneering French psychologist Pierre Janet and Hungarian psychoanalyst Sándor Ferenczi also provided innumerable examples of the psychic effects of sexual assault.[5]

Despite this scholarship into the psychological effects of rape on its victims, together with the rise and rise of 'trauma' as a common way of talking about human responses to 'bad events' such as rape, such things had little impact on the way most victims of rape were treated in Britain and North America until second-wave feminist activity of the 1970s onwards. Indeed, the theoretical, psychoanalytically inspired, European research on rape trauma was ignored by many medical professionals in the USA and UK. An American study carried out in the early 1960s revealed that even Health Departments in areas with the highest rates of sexual assault had *no* programmes in place to provide 'follow-up assistance' to rape victims.[6] In 1974, when a distinguished panel of American physicians, hospital administrators and other medical personnel met to discuss the psychological needs of rape victims, they found that only 2 of the 66 hospitals surveyed showed 'any awareness of the possible need for psychological services following a rape' and 'no hospital routinely offered any type of counselling.'[7] Even the title of their discussions – '*Alleged Rape*' – sent a signal that victims might be lying. Indeed, in emergency wards and hospitals throughout the USA, the care of rape victims was often the responsibility of the chaplaincy, not medical personnel.[8]

This neglect of the emotional repercussions of sexual assault is mirrored in Britain. As late as 1957, a 548-page study on *Sexual Offences* by the Cambridge Department of Criminal Science devoted only a couple of sentences to the emotional responses of rape victims. Even these sentences were embedded in a section entitled 'Physical Consequences to the Victim', in which the attention focused primarily on bodily injuries, sexually transmitted diseases and pregnancy.[9]

This changed because of effective argumentation and lobbying by feminists in the 1970s and 1980s. Two pioneers were psychiatric nurse Ann Wolbert Burgess and sociologist Lynda Lytle Holmstrom, who met in 1972 and resolved to make a difference to the lives of rape victims. They began working in the emergency services department at Boston City Hospital, providing crisis counselling, telephone follow-up and support in court. In total, they talked to 146 rape victims.[10] In 1974, Holmstrom and Burgess published an article on their findings in the prestigious *American Journal of Psychiatry*. It was to become one of the most influential medical articles in the twentieth-century history of sexual violence. Entitled 'Rape Trauma Syndrome', it was a detailed analysis of 92 rape victims admitted to the emergency room of Boston City Hospital. Crucially, they proposed a new diagnosis called 'rape trauma syndrome' (RTS), which they defined as an 'acute stress reaction to a life-threatening situation.'[11]

Why was the invention of RTS so important? First, until this time, the responses of adult women to rape were pathologized: accusers were called hysterics or perhaps even nymphomaniacs. Physicians, psychiatrists, psychoanalysts and sexologists routinely assumed that women who acted 'hysterical' after reporting having been sexually assaulted must have been making false accusations. In contrast, Burgess and Holmstrom insisted that extreme emotional disturbance after sexual assault was *normal*. They observed that women responded to rape in a wide variety of ways, none of which should be used to deny the reality of their assaults. They were not the first to make this argument. Four years earlier, Sandra Sutherland and Donald J. Scherl had published 'Patterns of Response among Victims of Rape' in the *American Journal of Orthopsychiatry*, which was the first major attempt to delineate the 'normal' and predictable psychological after-effects of rape.[12] But Burgess and Holmstrom took this further: they provided more evidence, popularized it subsequently in numerous medical journals and bravely insisted that even laughing might be an appropriate coping device for some victims.

Second, Burgess and Holmstrom were contributing to widespread feminist criticism about the way physicians routinely disregarded women's emotional reactions. From the 1970s onwards, there had been numerous complaints about the treatment of girls and women who reported being sexually assaulted. However, Burgess and Holmstrom did not simply want rape victims to be subsumed under broader categories of trauma. They insisted on the *specific* nature of *sexual* attacks, claiming that rape wasn't just another generic 'bad event' (like a car crash or skiing accident). Any diagnosis had to refer specifically to a girl's or woman's *sexual* integrity: it was '*rape* trauma syndrome'.

Finally, the diagnosis of RTS called for radically new ways of treating such victims: treatment couldn't simply stop when the victim left the emergency room. Physicians and other (largely male) medical professionals were believed to be too busy and uncaring to provide post-critical care services: nurses were essential to the recovery of rape victims. Training had to be introduced; status bestowed on those qualified. Forensic nursing was introduced as a professional specialism. The first Sexual Assault Nurse Examiners (SANE) were introduced in the late 1970s in four U.S. states. Within two decades, 86 SANE programmes were underway in the USA and Canada.[13] The speed with which attitudes and practices changed can be judged by looking at the title of Burgess and Holmstrom's landmark book. In its first edition in 1974, it was called *Rape: Victims of*

Crisis. Five years later, it was republished as *Rape: Crisis and Recovery*, representing a shift towards feminist empowerment.

A similar trend can be seen in the British context. From 1976, British activists began opening 'Rape Crisis Centres' in general hospitals and local communities, offering physical help as well as psychological counselling to victims.[14] Even the police adopted RTS after policeman Ian Blair (who subsequently went on to become the Commissioner of Police of the Metropolis, the highest-ranking officer in London's Metropolitan Police Service) published *Investigating Rape: A New Approach for Police* (1985). Blair lamented the fact that, unlike in the USA, 'little appears to be known about rape trauma syndrome in the United Kingdom.' He studiously read Burgess and Holmstrom's research and believed not only that RTS was real, but that police officers needed to be trained in order to recognize it. Such training was crucial, he maintained, because the ways victims are treated by the police

> will have a major impact on the severity of the trauma they may suffer. If police treatment reinforces or reduces feelings of guilt and self-blame, it is likely to affect the ability of the witness to provide evidence and her effectiveness in doing so.[15]

All was not well, though. Although Burgess and Holmstrom had argued that the divergent responses of rape victims were *normal*, in practice RTS became a psychiatric diagnosis that could be used to pathologize rape victims. As a diagnosis, it was eventually superseded by the diagnosis of post-traumatic stress disorder when, in 1980, PTSD was included in the third edition of the *Diagnostic and Statistical Manual of Mental Disorders* (DSM), the so-called 'Bible' of American psychiatry due to its global hegemony over the field of diagnosis. The symptoms of PTSD included painful and intrusive memories of the 'bad event', nightmares, dissociative states, psychic numbing, feeling estranged from other people, excessive autonomic arousal, impaired memory, difficulties concentrating and (in contexts where people died) survivor's guilt.[16]

The PTSD diagnosis had been developed in the context of war-related suffering experienced when American soldiers returned from Vietnam. Veterans had been extremely active in lobbying for its inclusion, in part because it would give them access to health insurance and counselling. However, from its conception, PTSD was defined in relation to *both* war and rape. According to DSM-III, the 'essential feature' in a PTSD diagnosis is 'the development of characteristic symptoms following a psychologically traumatic event that is generally outside the range of usual human relationships'. It stipulated that 'the trauma may be experienced alone (rape or assault) or in the company of groups of people (military combat)'.[17] Although it then listed other 'bad events' that might trigger trauma responses, military combat and rape were always at the forefront of the diagnosis. These were the Master-Traumas: combat for men, rape for women.

'Culture-Bound Syndromes'

This chapter began by exploring the *historically* differentiated nature of responses to 'bad events'. After being raped in 1833, Mary Ann Houay was affected by 'vapours', which rendered her 'insensible'. It was followed by the somaticization of her distress, in the forms of blindness and 'sinking'. I contrasted this with the trauma model of responding to 'bad events', which was developed from the 1860s but applied to female rape victims from the 1970s onwards. Rape trauma syndrome had morphed into PTSD by 1980. As opposed to somatic and 'insensibility' understandings of responses to 'bad events' such as rape, the trauma model emphasized internal, psychological 'wounds'.

However, there is a problem with this story: even in the present day, the trauma model does not apply to peoples universally. It is a Eurocentric, developed-world characterization of responses to 'bad events'. The symptoms by which PTSD is to be diagnosed according to the DSM are culturally specific. In other words, the symptoms are not based on a 'natural' or universal physiology but are influenced by cultural norms.[18]

That there would be major cultural variations in responses to 'bad events' like rape should come as no surprise. As I argue in *The Story of Pain*, it is not the case that a person 'feels' or experiences a 'bad event', *after which* affective, cognitive and interpersonal processes 'kick in' – responding and interpreting the event. Affect, cognition and relational exchanges operate simultaneously and are in constant dialogue. Trauma is not a reified entity that impinges upon a person independently of personal, social and environmental contexts. That is, the harm and suffering resulting from sexual violation is profoundly affected by environmental contexts, ideological beliefs and interpersonal interactions. The languages used to communicate suffering (to oneself as much as to others) emerge from bodily experiences and environmental interactions. Bodies are actively engaged in communicative processes and social interactions that constitute painful experiences. And culture collaborates in the creation of physiological bodies and language.[19] In short: responses to rape are affected by everything in that person's world.

The culturally varied responses of people to 'bad events', such as violence and illness, have been studied since the middle of the twentieth century, becoming a leading theme in psychiatry from the 1990s.[20] The field came to clinical attention during the Third World Congress of Psychiatry in 1961 when psychiatrist Pow Meng Yap spoke about 'atypical culture-bound, psychogenic psychosis'. A few years later, he widened the concept to 'culture-bound syndromes', which (along with 'idioms of distress') are the terms used today.[21] Culture-bound symptoms and diagnoses take as their fundamental premise that it is a 'category fallacy' to take a 'nosological category developed for a particular cultural group' and apply it to 'members of another culture for whom it lacks coherence and its validity has not been established', as anthropologist Arthur Kleinman explained in 1987.[22]

One of the diagnoses that have generated sustained critique is PTSD. Are the symptoms of PTSD universally experienced in the aftermath of a 'bad event' such as war, torture and rape? No, contends Derek Summerfield of the Medical Foundation for the Care of Victims of Torture. He argued that, despite the mass murders and rapes that took place during the conflicts in Bosnia and Rwanda, PTSD was a 'pseudocondition'.[23] Drawing on his extensive experience working with peasants who had been subjected to violence, including rape, during the war in Nicaragua, Summerfield maintained that it was important to recognize that although certain symptoms might *appear* similar to those experienced by people in other stressful contexts, the *meaning* attached to the symptoms was significantly different. He admitted that 'PTSD features were common' among the displaced peasants, but these symptoms

> were not what the subjects themselves were attending to. These people were undoubtedly fearful, grieving and weary, but not psychological casualties in any sense meaningful to them; they were active and effective in maintaining their social worlds as best they could in the face of poverty and continuing threat of further attacks.[24]

It was a point reiterated by Brandon Kohrt and Daniel J. Hruschka in the context of their research in Nepal. They maintained that if researchers *looked for* PTSD, they would find it in all distressed populations. However, 'the mere identification of PTSD symptoms in a population has questionable therapeutic value . . . Understanding personal or social meanings and experiences of distress associated with traumatic events also is necessary for effective treatment.'[25] They contended that if local psychological frameworks are ignored 'there is risk of unintended consequences such as denigration of local support systems, pathologizing and stigmatizing already vulnerable individuals and shifting resources from social and structural interventions.'[26]

Other researchers similarly concluded that human responses to 'bad events' might be manifested in ways that had no parallel in the West. For example, in sub-Saharan Africa people with mental health problems present with somatic conditions.[27] The Quechua-speaking, indigenous Andean people of Peru experienced exceptionally high levels of violence (including sexual abuse) perpetrated by Shining Path guerrillas and Peruvian military counter-insurgents. One-quarter exhibited PTSD symptoms, but they also complained of symptoms such as *llaki* and *ñakary*, for which there is no English translation.[28] The Mayans escaping the massacres, rapes and razing of villages as a result of the 36-year-long civil conflict in Guatemala experienced syndromes such as *sustos*, which translates as 'soul-loss'. It occurred 'when an individual is suddenly frightened or startled while in a spiritually weakened state, causing a separation of body and soul'.[29] Symptoms include weakness, loss of appetite, headaches, nightmares, fever and diarrhoea. Treatment 'can be administered by family members or healers through sweeping with eggs or herbal mixtures and other healing rituals, such as invoking benign spirits and praying for the return of the lost soul'.[30] Other refugees from the conflict in Guatemala experienced *ataques de nervios*, or nervous attacks, causing extreme anger or grief. During such attacks, sufferers would shout, experience heart palpitations, shake and faint.[31]

Similarly, in Latino cultures, where attention is paid to 'nerves', victims of 'bad events' describe feeling dizzy and numb, as well as becoming weak in the legs and arms.[32] In places as different as Liberia, Darfur and Haiti, heart and head metaphors are prominent when people describe their suffering.[33] In Southeast Asian cultures, where the head is highly esteemed, distressing experiences typically manifest as a headache.[34] The Korean women who were sexually enslaved by the Japanese military expressed *Han*, or a sense of unresolved pain and anguish caused by suffering injustices that had not been acknowledged. The symptoms of *Han* include heart palpitations, dizziness and dyspepsia, as well as an overwhelming sense of oppression and loneliness.[35] As *minjung* (or 'the people's) theologian Suh Nam-dong explains, it was

> a feeling of unresolved resentment against injustices suffered, a sense of helplessness because of the overwhelming odds against one, a feeling of acute pain in one's guts and bowels, making the whole body writhe and squirm, and an obstinate urge to take revenge and to right the wrong – all these combined.[36]

The comfort women described their greatest *Han* as not having been able to marry and have children.[37] In many Asian societies, emotional upsets are linked to the wind, which causes havoc throughout sufferers' bodies.[38] In Cambodia, this wind-like substance is called *khyâl*, which, in healthy states, flows uninterrupted through the body, exiting naturally through the skin or by burping. 'Bad events', though, can cause the flow to stop or be diverted towards the head, leading to a *khyâl* attack.[39] The post-rape symptoms of a survivor diagnosed with PTSD compared with a survivor during a *khyâl* spell are substantially different forms of suffering. Not only do they exhibit different symptoms, but they also elicit radically different responses from people around them.[40]

The existence of culture-bound syndromes, with their very different symptoms, is only one of the limitations of trauma-based definitions. PTSD's Anglo-European centricity also manifests itself in the definition's insistence on a sudden, seismic event that is 'outside the range of usual human relationships', as DSM-III put it. In other words, the diagnosis of PTSD excludes 'bad events' that are endemic to a society or to an individual's life experiences. After all, the syndrome is called *post*-traumatic stress disorder. The idea that there is an 'after', a 'post-', to abuse is based on an assumption that there is a non-assaultive 'before'. It assumes that violence is an event limited in time and distinguishable from everyday life. But in many parts of the world, this is simply not the case. Vulnerable people might *themselves* not register an occurrence as distressing simply because it is so typical. Nightmares, excessive sweating, trembling and flashbacks might similarly be interpreted as ordinary happenings. In other words, the language of psychological trauma might not make much sense to people for whom 'bad events' like sexualized abuse are endemic and related to issues such as poverty, patriarchy and racial prejudice.

Furthermore, in regions where sexual violence is endemic, resilience rather than trauma might be the culturally appropriate response. In Kinyarwanda (a language spoken by at least 12 million people in Rwanda, Eastern Democratic Republic of the Congo and parts of southern Uganda), there is not even a word for 'stress'. In the aftermath of sexual atrocity and murder, emphasis was placed on *kwihangana* (withstanding), *kwongera kubaho* (living again) and *gukomeza ubuzima* (continuing living).[41] As one survivor explained,

> To strengthen yourself, you feel that you don't let the suffering make you fade away; otherwise, you could die. You hurry up and go through it. You do not linger in that pain. But, as it goes, *kwihangana* causes you to feel that you brought force inside yourself . . . You eventually realize that you are not the only one who has suffered because there are other people with whom you share your problems. This then makes you withstand and you no longer experience these feelings.[42]

Indeed, clinical trauma is not an inevitable aftermath of sexual assault. For example, in a survey in 2000 of refugees from the 36-year civil conflict in Guatemala, which saw extensive sexual violence as well as other atrocities, the researchers found high levels of resilience. The refugees described their health in positive terms, with over 8 per cent saying their health was 'excellent' or 'very good', 28 per cent saying it was 'good' and 54 per cent saying their health was 'okay'. Only 8 per cent said it was 'bad'.[43]

These cultural variations did not go unnoticed by the authors of the different editions of the DSM. In the run-up to the publication of DSM-IV (which eventually came out in 1994), there was increasing awareness of the need to ensure that the manual continued to be regarded as 'universal' and thus had global relevance.[44] As a consequence, the authors introduced some 'culture-bound syndromes'. Not coincidentally, given the Western orientation of the manual, these culturally specific categories were relegated to the ninth appendix at the end of the manual. In other words, the 'norm' was Anglo-European, against which 'other' cultures were compared and assumed to be 'specific' rather than 'universal'. The placement of the diagnoses is crucial because it represents the ability of one group (American psychiatrists, for instance) to define their own local characteristics as 'global' while designating another group's characteristics (Latinx psychiatrists, for instance) as 'local'. But PTSD is as much a 'local idiom of distress', with social, political, medical and legal origins, as the other cultural illnesses. As critical psychiatrist James Phillips wondered, could it be the case that 'some of the diagnoses, in the *main* body of the text, were compromised by unacknowledged cultural differences'?[45] Cultural differences, he contended, might 'defeat the possibility of codifying such difference into a neat, medical nosological category' and yet the 'notion of a Trauma Disorder NOS [not otherwise specified] category satisfies no one'.[46] In effect, what the various editions of the DSM were doing was medicalizing distress according to a liberal, Western paradigm. In his book *Crazy Like Us* (2010), journalist Ethan Watters made the argument even stronger, calling this the 'globalization of the American psyche'.[47]

Political Work Performed by 'Trauma'

The concept of 'trauma' does a formidable amount of political and ideological work. Despite widespread awareness of the existence of culture-bound symptoms, PTSD and rape trauma syndrome have been exported globally. The application of the concept of 'trauma' to rape victims everywhere has had four significant effects. It has affected the way rape victims are expected to comport themselves in the aftermath of abuse, led to the pathologization of victims, influenced treatment regimes and, finally, cemented hierarchies of power.

First, the trauma model as modelled by psychiatric and legal professionals in the West requires rape victims to comport themselves in specified ways if they are to have their complaints taken seriously. It has mandated the performance of a narrow range of social scripts. Rape victims have to act *as victims*: distressed, passive and chaste. The model insists that rape victims are traumatized: by definition, they cannot be in good mental health. There is also no room for bitterness, revenge or political agitation. Expressions of rage turn victims into 'rabble-rousers' or 'women with a feminist agenda'.

The requirement that victims of rape must behave as traumatized collapses their complex lives and identities into 'rape space' or 'embodiments of risk'.[48] They are required to define themselves in terms of the actions of the perpetrator, a position that is profoundly disempowering. Victimization becomes an inner turmoil rather than an external event, among many others. In the words of feminist critic Carine M. Mardorossian, they become 'irremediably and unidirectionally shaped by the traumatic experience of rape and hence incapable of dealing with anything but their own inner turmoil'.[49] This effect is particularly acute for victims of wartime rape in which there are often multiple perpetrators of sexual violence as well as mass killings. The prioritization of the 'rape' aspect in causing 'traumatic stress' narrows the victims' experience. They become identified by one label – 'rape victim' – rather than their multiple identities as a homeless person, bereaved mother or widow.

Second, rape victims, as opposed to the perpetrators, are pathologized. This was not always the case. After all, PTSD was included in the 1980 edition of DSM-III with the aim of turning *perpetrators* of atrocities into mentally ill patients who were deserving of disability pensions and psychiatric therapy. In more recent decades, however, the pathology of perpetrators has taken second place to that of victims. Although sexually sadistic 'stranger rapists' retain the 'mentally ill' label, 'ordinary' offenders are discussed in social terms, that is, broad-brush characterizations of power dynamics or masculinities in crisis. Their behaviour is part of cultures of masculinity rather than psychiatric illness.

In contrast, the opposite has happened for *victims* of their abuse. They are increasingly dependent upon a PTSD diagnosis if their suffering is to be acknowledged. In other words, they have to concede that they have been rendered mentally ill. Sexually abused women can only access treatment if they accept a psychiatric diagnosis. The diagnosis is also necessary to access free or subsidized counselling, a more sympathetic hearing in a court case or health insurance. Indeed, the fact that some women do *not* have symptoms of PTSD has been used in court as evidence that they could not have been assaulted. This weaponization of psychiatric diagnoses requires victims to brand themselves with the term PTSD, even though PTSD-type trauma is only one of the many negative aftermaths of sexual assault. Other responses to 'bad events', such as crying or sleeplessness, become 'signs' of something else. The medicalization of rape victims *does* make suffering visible (rape trauma), but it does so at the cost of reinscribing women with the stigma of victimhood. Furthermore, these processes are biased against less privileged victims. Typically, it is high-status, educated victims who can access the psychiatric experts necessary for the effective medical and legal uses of PTSD.

Third, the globalization of trauma affects psychological treatment regimes. In particular, it privileges speech as the royal road to post-abuse recovery and empowerment. But the assumption that survivor testimony leads to a 'coming to terms' emerged from histories of religious confession, as well as secular frames of meaning such as psychoanalysis and cognitive behaviourist therapy. Both treatment regimes privilege more articulate and educated victims. As feminists Linda Alcoff and Laura Gray argue in 'Survivor Discourse: Transgression or Recuperation?' (1993), 'breaking the silence' can become 'a coercive imperative on survivors to confess, to recount our assaults, to give details, and even to do so publicly. Our refusal to comply might then be read as weakness of will or as re-enacted victimization.'[50] Scholars Beth Goldblatt and Sheila Meintjes agreed. In the context of the refusal of many women to admit to rape in front of South Africa's Truth and Reconciliation Commission, they observed that the victims were already in a lowly position in society, so asking them to 'give up their privacy' meant 'pressuring women to give up the mechanisms that they had developed to deal with the trauma of sexual violence.'[51] It was a comment echoed by Jessica Duart, who asked:

> What about the loss of pride that they will experience at the time when they talk about it? How are we going to deal with that issue? The incident may have happened 10 years earlier and the woman may have dealt with the trauma by herself without ever having lost the loss of pride. Now that woman is being asked to recreate that loss of pride.[52]

Alcoff and Gray argue the need to acknowledge that 'survival itself sometimes necessitates a refusal to recount or even a refusal to disclose and deal with the assault or abuse.' Disclosure could be more emotionally, financially and physically damning to women than silence.[53]

The emphasis on survivor discourse also ignores other social practices in which a contemplative silence or rites of forgetting protect the victim's dignity. This can be seen in widely divergent contexts. In nineteenth-century Mexico, for example, victims of sexual abuse protected themselves by refusing to talk about being harmed since only shameless women would talk publicly about sexual matters.[54] A similar comment could be made in the context of late twentieth-century Rwanda.[55]

What feminists in the West might label 'silencing' has a different meaning elsewhere. Refugees from Mozambique valorized 'forgetting', while in Ethiopia 'active forgetting' was considered to be curative.[56] This is not to exaggerate the divide between 'the West and the Rest'. After all, half of all female Mayan refugees and nearly 40 per cent of all male Mayan refugees from the civil war in Guatemala reported that talking about their bad experiences was palliative.[57] One Cambodian victim-survivor expressed the advantages of telling her story particularly eloquently. She noted that

> Previously, I had felt secretly ashamed in front of other people. After I shared my story [with members of a psychosocial support organization], I didn't mind anymore sharing openly with the villagers. They must have all along known the real truth – that, when we were called to be killed or punished, the women were also raped. I am an old woman now, and no one discriminated against me for telling this story. In fact, my neighbors admire me for speaking out.[58]

But confessional discourse requires the adoption and framing of the experience along rigid lines shaped by legal doctrines or moralistic codes, which may not be in keeping with an individual woman's process of self-creation. Trauma counselling, which had been developed on the basis of the American experience in Vietnam, has been imposed upon cultures with very different ways of thinking about sex, violence and interrelationships between the two.

There is a wider problem with the imposition of a trauma model on all victims of sexual abuse: it mandates short-term, individualized treatments, such as trauma counselling or Cognitive Behavioural Therapy (CBT). For communities that had experienced extreme life events, such approaches could even be viewed as insulting. Was it any wonder that refugees from Bosnia or Somalia regarded CBT and exposure therapies as 'tricks'?[59] As Neil Boothby, expert on forced migration, concluded, it was not a surprise that applying 'western models of psychotherapy' that had been developed 'in stable and affluent social contexts' failed when 'applied in unstable and impoverished settings'.[60] Spirit exorcism, prayer, storytelling, the 'laying on' of hands, rebalancing of *yin* and *yang* forces and other traditional healing processes would have been more effective approaches for victims of rape and other atrocities.[61] This was also the point being made by cross-cultural psychologists Nick Higginbotham and Anthony J. Marsella in the context of their work on Southeast Asia. They contend that replacing 'indigenous conceptions of disorder' with 'modern psychiatry's purely secular discourse' is unhelpful. It 'forces a kind of epistemological break with traditional formulations embodied in many non-Western cosmologies'.[62] It effortlessly slips into a form of therapeutic governance or cultural imperialism, thus perpetuating paternalistic and neocolonial practices.

Finally, as all these critiques imply, the globalization of trauma has cemented Western hierarchies of authority. It has led to the imposition of particular kinds of knowledge on victims of rape and their carers, substituting local cosmologies for a culturally specific expertise. In Summerfield's words, concepts like PTSD and its treatment regimes

> aggrandise the Western agencies and their 'experts' who from afar define the condition and bring the cure. There is no evidence that war-affected populations are seeking these imported approaches which appear to ignore their own traditions, meaning, systems, and active priorities.[63]

There is big money in these projects – indeed, one of the main ways for large, Western-based NGOs to fund their programmes is by packaging them as tackling PTSD-suffering rape victims.[64] Even more disturbing, victims of sexual torture might be *required* to exhibit or enact the symptoms of PTSD if they are to be granted medical or legal help, asylum and other benefits.[65]

Today, it is assumed that all victims of sexual violence will suffer similar forms of psychological trauma – whether these types are linked to diagnoses like PTSD and rape trauma syndrome or more broadly dubbed 'traumatic responses'. It was not always so. This chapter started with Houay's response to multiple-perpetrator rape, which has almost no resemblance to rape trauma syndrome as espoused in the West from the 1970s onwards. Furthermore, despite the global spread of PTSD diagnostic practices (often introduced by NGOs and Western 'experts' to countries in the geopolitical South), more attention should be paid to culturally specific responses to sexual violation.

Clearly, trauma is a normative concept. It distinguishes 'normal' abuse (for example, practices that routinely pressure girls, women and other minoritized groups into having sex) from what is excessive and therefore 'traumatizing'. Victimhood becomes tied to the sufferer's identity – her very selfhood – rather than a description of some harmful event. It adheres to an individual psyche rather than a structural or social failing. As such, it is depersonalized. As a result, violence is privatized; material violence, thrust aside. It shifts attention from the external wound to the inner one.

Finally, a distinction must be made between experiencing a distressing event and becoming pathologically ill because of it to the extent that the person subsequently develops a 'disorder'. In other words, experiencing a 'bad event' such as rape can (and often does) inspire creative behaviour, bolster the development of closer interpersonal bonds with allies and encourage a clearer sense of self.

NINE

A Rape-Free World

'Youn-ede-lòt'
('Helping one another' in Haitian)

This book has bombarded readers with a lot of grim stories, surveys and statistics. So: now for the good news. It doesn't have to be this way. Through the creation and cultivation of effective coalitions and strategies of resistance, it is possible to forge rape-free futures for everyone.

It is not going to be easy. The most debilitating myth for people seeking to forge a world without sexual abuse is the assertion that violence is inherent to male sexuality. Many commentators claim that this form of violence is 'deeply wired' in evolutionary terms, or that it is culturally omnipresent.[1] When writing this book, some friends even accused me of being hopelessly utopian to believe in a world in which rape has been eradicated. But that is my contention. After all, to be human is to seek companionship, collaboration, friendship and love.

This is why the first step in eradicating sexual violence is to acknowledge that we don't have to accept that it is inevitable. As we saw in an earlier chapter, even in armed conflicts, there are wide variations in the nature and degree of sexual violence – with some conflicts experiencing very little.[2] Rape was prevalent on a vast scale in Punjab in 1947, for instance, but not during the communal violence of the 1980s and 1990s.[3] Although rape levels are high during what international scholar Mary Kaldor has called 'new wars' – that is, counter-insurgencies or guerrilla wars, and where the lines between armed forces and organized crime are blurred[4] – they are low in those armed groups that possess a strong degree of internal discipline and ideological values.[5]

In peacetime contexts, too, anthropologists and ethnographers such as Peggy Reeves Sanday, Maria-Barbara Watson-Franke and Christine Helliwell have drawn attention to societies where rape is non-existent, at low levels or highly stigmatized. Most famously, Sanday's ethnographic research and analysis of the Human Relations Area Files (which supports and disseminates cross-cultural research) has revealed that discourses favourable to rape are not present in all cultures.[6] Watson-Franke worked in communities in North and South America, Oceania, Asia and Africa where rape was unknown or very rare. Rape was regarded as 'a shameful act which puts a man's virility and his humanity in question'.[7] Helliwell's research was based in the Dayak community of Gerai in Indonesian Borneo. She criticizes feminists for assuming that rape of women by men is universal, and that 'the same "biological" bodily differences between men and women exist everywhere,'[8] Gerai men have a higher status than women, but, Helliwell explains, this does not translate into the idea that power and potency are manifest through the penis nor that 'men's genitals' are 'able to brutalize women's genitals'.[9] Indeed, Gerai men and women are 'not understood as fundamentally different types of persons: there is no sense of a dichotomized masculinity and femininity.'[10] Male aggression is not valued highly, and even the 'Western notion of conception as involving an aggressive active male cell (the sperm) seeking out and penetrating a passive, immobile female cell (the egg)' is absent.[11] As Helliwell explains, 'The idea of having sex with someone who does not need you to have sex with them' is 'almost unthinkable'.[12]

Such research has been criticized for its small sample size and focus on band and tribal societies. However, ignoring the low levels of sexual violence in these societies naturalizes Western practices and experiences of rape. Sanday, Watson-Franke and Helliwell point to the fact that rape thrives in situations of structural inequality. Low levels of militarization and high levels of sexual equality and female economic power are characteristic of communities with relatively low levels of rape. They point to one of the conclusions of this book: that is, that sexual abuse is fomented within contexts of inequity and masculinism.

Local Contexts; Global Impacts

A reasonable retort to the work of anthropologists and ethnologists like Sanday, Watson-Franke and Helliwell is: 'but, *where I live*, sexual violence is rampant, and people are hurting.' What can we do?

Effective solutions to high levels of sexual violence are difficult to pinpoint – not because there are no positive ways forward, but for the opposite reason. The strategies open to us are legion. The awe-inspiring, creative diversity of human existence offers an exhilarating range of options for anti-rape activists, if we can only demonstrate a keenness to listen and a willingness to learn. Crucially, the task of imagining, thinking, planning and acting on forging rape-free worlds requires us to pay attention to our *local* contexts within *global* economic, ideological and political frameworks. My point is that the cumulative effect of local change is global transformation.

In the next few pages, my proposals for working towards a rape-free world are not intended to *prescribe* what strategies activists should adopt. After all, the transversalist approach that animates all my work (and which I will be discussing at the end of this chapter) is vehemently hostile to universalist approaches. Rather this chapter aims to suggest a milieu within which effective activism might emerge.

My emphasis on local specificities within global frames of vision also means that the rest of this chapter will inevitably draw on my own personal, localized position as well as my political identification as a socialist feminist. My worldview has been fundamentally shaped by a childhood in New Zealand, Zambia, Solomon Islands and (most important in terms of my political orientation) Haiti. These early frames – historically and geographically specific – have been moulded by interactions with other people, material objects and localities (particularly Britain and Greece). They have led me to be sceptical about the commitment and capacity of criminal justice systems to effectively challenge pervasive rape cultures. This is not to deny that legal and other legislative initiatives are crucial in drawing public attention to the extent and seriousness of sexual violence. Certain legal approaches (such as restorative justice) are consistent with feminist ambitions. The law may also be effective in establishing officially agreed norms of behaviour, such as the wrongness of a husband coercing his wife into sex or an employer sexually harassing his employee. However, it fails to dent persistent assumptions of male entitlement and its accompanying casual misogyny.

This book has already addressed some of the harms caused by relying on the penal state to enforce good behaviour. Ironically, carceral types of anti-rape feminism dramatically *increase* levels of sexual assault, especially as suffered by boys, men and non-binary genders. No one seriously believes that imprisonment is a deterrent, either. Sexually aggressive men either don't accept that what they are doing is wrong or don't think they will be caught and punished (and they are right). The idea that prison sentences can rehabilitate sexual offenders has repeatedly been debunked. Indeed, in most prisons worldwide, wardens don't even bother to pretend that rehabilitation schemes are operational. It is more plausible to argue that incarcerating sexual offenders boosts their anger and brutalizes them further. Equally germane is the fact that legislative reforms inequitably criminalize certain populations. Retributive justice disproportionately targets people of colour and those already disenfranchised, such as the poor, mentally ill and those belonging to gender minorities. The online anti-harassment initiative 'Hollaback!' (which was established in 2005 and is currently operating in sixteen countries worldwide) expresses this anti-carceral point eloquently: 'replacing sexist oppression with racist oppression is not a proper Hollaback.'[13]

I also cannot summon enthusiasm for palliative solutions to sexual violence. Prison reform (such as introducing more surveillance within jails, encouraging conjugal visits or providing prisoners with information on how to litigate against prison officials who fail to prevent sexual abuse) simply nudges the problem elsewhere.[14] Outside of carceral institutions, a lot of attention has been paid to providing victims with shelter, counselling, legal advice and long-term mechanisms for day-to-day flourishing. These are crucial but leave the central problem intact. They may – unwittingly – bolster patronizing or victim-blaming sentiments. Requiring people who are at risk of assault to police their own behaviour by comporting themselves modestly, upgrading their security and (as in the USA, South Africa and India)[15] paying insurance premiums to ensure that, if assaulted, they can afford the appropriate legal advice, treatments and counselling is damaging at best. Advising girls and women to 'stay at home' is equally unhelpful. Household survival often depends upon female labour in the fields, forests and marketplaces. And domestic spheres are crowded with abusers.[16]

Other palliative solutions focus on the vulnerable body. Much feminist energy has been devoted to ensuring that victims of sexual assault have their medical, psychological, contraceptive and forensic needs catered for. Again, this is important, although, as many scholars have observed, such reform movements are easily co-opted by professional services that are more concerned with ameliorating difficult lives or punishing perpetrators than with eradicating sexual violence. This is neatly encapsulated in the subtitles of two important books by Kristin Bumiller and Rose Corrigan, respectively: *How Neoliberalism Appropriated the Feminist Movement against Sexual Violence* and *Rape Reform and the Failure of Success*.[17] The central difficulty with 'tweaking' the system is that it can end up naturalizing oppression. Survival? Yes. But at a cost.

Situated Knowledges

To create rape-free worlds, more radical labour is required. I have taken inspiration from feminists battling sexual violence in contexts where inequities and multiple oppressions are particularly stark, thus demanding urgent and deeply rooted action. Their 'situated knowledges', as philosopher Donna Haraway puts it, incite inventive ways of thinking about anti-rape activism.[18] Sociologist Chandra Talpade Mohanty even maintains that, in developing both theoretical knowledge and revolutionary practices, marginalized communities possess an 'epistemic advantage' over more privileged ones. Of course, she is not making the naive claim that 'all marginalized locations yield crucial knowledge about power and inequity.' Rather, her point is that 'the lives, experiences, and struggles of girls and women of the Two-Thirds World . . . demystify capitalism in its racial and sexual dimensions.' This provides 'productive and necessary avenues of theorizing and enacting capitalist resistance.'[19] Haraway has made a similar contention. She acknowledges that the 'positionings of the subjugated are not exempt from critical reexamination, decoding, deconstruction, and interpretation'. Nevertheless, they are 'preferred' because

> They are least likely to allow denial of the critical and interpretive core of all knowledge . . . They are knowledgeable of modes of denial through repression, forgetting, and disappearing acts – ways of being nowhere while claiming to see comprehensively.

Subjugated peoples, Haraway continues, are more likely to see through the 'god trick' of universalism with all 'its dazzling – and, therefore, blinding – illuminations'. She argues that '"subjugated" standpoints are preferred because they seem to promise more adequate, sustained, objective transforming accounts of the world.'[20]

Part of the reason why both Mohanty and Haraway demand that activists pay attention to the 'situated knowledges' of subjugated peoples is because they are committed to the view that all forms of tyranny are interlinked. It will never be enough for activists to work along only one dimension of oppression – misogyny, for example – because systems of domination are multi-layered and co-constituted. Abuse is not a discrete or singular event. In order to effectively tackle rape, it is important to recognize that sexual violence is not (only) 'personal'. Nor is it (solely) 'personal-political' or even (specifically) a tool of gendered oppression. Because sexual violence cannot be detached from other political, economic and sociocultural inequities, attempts to eradicate it require activists to move attention away from individual perpetrators and victims towards systemic injustices, fuelled by sexism, racism, colonialism, economic injustice, heteronormativity, transphobia, militarism, climate denial and neoliberal capitalisms. In other words, campaigns against gender violence cannot exist, thrive or transform the world without alliances with other progressive causes.

This can be illustrated by looking at REMTE ('Red Latinoamericana Mujeres Transformando la Economía', or the 'Red Latin-American Network of Women Transforming the Economy'), an example of a coalition that takes the fundamental embeddedness of oppression seriously. REMTE was established in 1997 and initially comprised women's movements in Chile, Colombia, Mexico, Nicaragua and Peru, before spreading to eleven Latin American countries and having strong ties with other transnational movements, including the World March of Women.[21] Their chief argument is that only by transforming the economy will other oppressive features of women's lives be alleviated. In other words, they recognize the inextricable link between macro-level oppression and micro-level transformations. In the words of one REMTE activist, 'Our urgent task is to link the fight against violence aimed at women with the global struggle against neoliberal capitalism.'[22] Crucially, REMTE has made alliances with other women's movements, including those focusing on the commodification of women and global sex tourism, peasant groups, people of African descent, anti-poverty groups, men's groups and anti-globalization organizations.[23] This willingness to successfully pursue collaborations has been central to their effectiveness. As one activist explained, 'the idea is to look for a meeting point (*un punto de encuetro*) and to construct a shared discourse.'[24] In an assessment of feminist campaigns in Latin America, anthropologists Sally Cole and Lynne Phillips acknowledged major divisions between groups targeting sexual violence. They observe that 'some groups interpreted gender-based violence as a health issue whereas others view it as a development issue, and still others understand it to be a product of a powerful economic system.' These differences could have resulted in 'an oppositional "politics of difference"' that would have divided and weakened their effectiveness. Instead, REMTE recognized 'the importance of strategic coalitions across difference'. Only by forging such coalitions could 'violence against women' be 'successfully recognized as a global, regional, and national issue for which serious attention and resources were necessary'.[25]

Locality, Diversity, Pleasure and the Body

REMTE points to a central argument for this book: effective movements against gender violence need to celebrate difference, even though this will inevitably fuel disagreements and dissent *within* activist movements. I will be elaborating on this point in the final section of this chapter, drawing on the concept of transversalism. However, before turning to this overarching premise for effective resistance, I want to briefly address four other tenets for transnational campaigns against sexual violence. These are: locality, diversity, pleasure and the body.

Anti-rape strategies must attend to *local* needs and engage the political labour of *local* activists. They cannot be outsourced to (or directed by) outsiders. This will require paying attention to micro-practices of resistance against sexual violence – often carried out by minoritized people who lack access to prominent speaking platforms and the global media. Crucially, small, localized movements are not simply pockets of proto-resistance waiting to be noticed, developed and enhanced by one of the 'authorized feminisms': they are a vital component of the global movement to create a rape-free world.

One example of effective local engagement can be seen by turning to the political labour of Haitian feminists. Organizations such as HAVH (Haitians against Violence at Home), Solidarite Fanm Ayisen ('Haitian Women's Solidarity Group'), Kay Fanm ('Women's House') and Dwa Fanm ('Women's Rights') engage in educational campaigns, educating women about domestic violence and the remedies available to them.[26] In the aftermath of the 2010 earthquake, the grassroots work done by Komisyon Fanm Viktim Pou Viktim ('Commission of Women Victims for Victims') and Fanm Viktim, Leve Kanpe ('Women Victims, Get Up Stand Up') in Haiti was vital in helping women and their families endure the catastrophe. While foreign NGOs and multinational aid organizations squandered billions of dollars, these local groups intervened in pragmatic ways: they encouraged girls and women to share their experiences of sexual violence, provided medical assistance and counselling to victims, organized security for women walking to and from toilets at night and led protest marches.[27] In scale, their actions were small; in effect, life-changing.

Justice is not only locally relevant, but culturally variable. By necessity, anti-rape initiatives will be *diverse*. This is meant in many ways but let me just mention two. First, they need to be inclusive in terms of *personnel*. This includes ensuring that anti-rape activism responds to the desire of many boys and men to be welcomed as co-workers in anti-rape movements. Anti-rape activists cannot afford to alienate any potential allies. In the final analysis, political attempts to reduce and finally eliminate sexual aggression must start with the main perpetrators: cisgendered boys and men.

Second, *strategies* for eradicating rape must also be diverse. There is no singular template. This does mean, however, that different feminist strategies will be in conflict with each other. For example, anti-rape activism carried out by Native American women in the USA may be incompatible with white, liberal feminist ideals. As Native American gender scholar Sarah Deer explains, 'simply replicating the Anglo-American model' will 'fail to address the unique nature and context of sexual violence as experienced by Native women'. Indeed, she contends, White feminist ways of addressing violence might even *exacerbate* the rape crisis in their communities.[28]

Different communities also have different priorities. While many feminists in 'the West' may urge activists in the geopolitical South to focus on changes (they call them 'reforms') to rape laws, this might not be a top priority for indigenous feminists. The anti-statism and anti-nationalism of many First World feminists may also not be in step with Third World ones. Indeed, as philosopher Ranjoo Seodu Herr forcefully argues, for many Third World feminists, the nation-state is an important site of struggle against violence. While she appeals to her colleagues not to 'relinquish the national political arena to patriarchal nationalists', she also urges them to 'insist that they are as authentic as any other member of their nation and demand their right to participate in national discourses'.[29]

Religion is another area of dissent for feminists contesting rape in different parts of the globe. Many secular feminists are hostile to religious interventions into sexual violence on the grounds that Judaeo-Christian and Islamic values and practices have been pivotal to women-hating ideologies. But this is disputed by other feminists. Islamic feminism is a powerful force in much of the world. In Cambodia, Buddhist temples are places where abused people can find refuge and recovery.[30] Magical designs created by Buddhist monks and traditional healers on cloth or metal – called *yantra* – are worn to protect people from sexual violence, while, in the aftermath of abuse, spiritual rituals have healing powers.[31] Mayan survivors of the civil war in Guatemala were also supported by traditional healers. Their medicinal plants and healing rituals – *limpias* (cleansings) – enabled survivors of sexual and other atrocities to develop resilience.[32] In Haiti, vodou teachings are routinely employed in anti-rape and domestic violence initiatives.[33] Vodou is a particularly potent force for good due to its historical links with anti-enslavement movements, as well as the way vodou beliefs emphasize the role of spirits in everyday community relationships, the prominent role played by women in spiritual worlds and the equality of men and women. Vodou creates *fanm vanyan* ('strong women').

If the first two tenets are locality and diversity, the third is the embrace of pleasure. Anti-rape activism is often tiring, dispiriting and depressing. That is inevitable. But more positive and creative approaches are important if girls, women and other oppressed people are to be empowered, while also encouraging the involvement of boys, men and other potential oppressors. While not minimizing the seriousness of the task ahead – after all, femicide is rampant in the USA as well as other countries throughout the world – anti-rape activism must be enticing, even seductive, if it is to change people's hearts and minds.

Activists are emboldened by art, literature, poetry, film, performance theatre and music. The poet Adrienne Rich has reflected on the importance of all forms of artistic expression, not as 'a privileged and sequestered rendering of human suffering' but as a form of 'resistance, which totalising systems want to quell'. She insists that art and literature are capable of 'reaching into us for what is still passionate, still unintimidated, still unquenched'. The former British prime minister Margaret Thatcher famously coined the phrase 'There is no alternative' in aid of her neoliberal policies, which earned them the nickname 'TINA'. However, Rich argued that the 'imagination's roads open before us, giving the lie to that brutal dictum, "There is no alternative."' Rich maintained that when 'poetry lays its hand on our shoulders we are, to an almost physical degree, touched and moved'.[34]

Rich's claim that creative activism emotionally 'moves' people 'to an almost physical degree' is apposite. Activism is most effective when it is 'hands on'. The bodily presence of other people – survivors who share their stories, for example – is formidable. This was what Marta Hillers, the author-survivor of the memoir *A Woman in Berlin*, was alluding to when she discussed how girls and women coped in the aftermath of the 1945 mass rapes in Berlin. Hillers argued that experiences of being raped – often numerous times – were 'something we overcame collectively'. Survivors 'help each other by speaking about it, airing their pain, and allowing others to air theirs'.[35]

The visceral way survivors 'spit out what they've suffered', as Hillers put it, has materialized in recent years in the context of #MeToo and its transnational equivalences. For all its undisputed influence, however, hashtag feminism has (ironically) a potential to exchange social exchange for individualized, isolated encounters in front of computer screens. It is important to emphasize, therefore, that hashtag protests facilitate and supplement, rather than replace, the power of people massing together to protest and demand change. The presence of recalcitrant bodies linked together in solidarity has a subversive force that cannot be replaced by online assignations. Physical bodies are actively engaged in processes of resistance; the social interactions that emerge in relation with other bodies during protests are in themselves political. As philosopher Maurice Merleau-Ponty argued, 'a body is not just something we own, it is something we are.'[36]

This can be illustrated by exploring transnational performances of the Chilean dance/song 'Un Violador en Tu Camino' ('A Rapist in Your Path'). This crowd-performance piece was created by the feminist collective Las Tesis from Valparaíso and initially performed on 25 November 2019 as part of the International Day for the Elimination of Violence against Women. Groups of women gather in public squares and perform a simple but compelling dance (including squatting in the position they are compelled to take during police searches) while singing. Part of the lyrics runs:

> It's femicide.
> Impunity for my killer.
> It's our disappearances.
> It's rape!
> And it's not my fault, not where I was, not how I dressed. [× 3] . . .
> And the rapist WAS you
> And the rapist IS you.

It's the cops,
It's the judges,
It's the system,
It's the President,
This oppressive state is a macho rapist.

Women across the globe have adapted the performance to their own local contexts. Key to the action is the insistence that the problem is multi-layered – the *system* is the problem, but *you* (the men being addressed) are responsible. It is an empowering spectacle of solidarity and protest that spurns hierarchies. Bodies influence the way people think. Recalcitrant bodies spawn recalcitrant politics.

Transversalism

So far in this chapter, I have pointed to four central tenets for any trans-national campaign against sexual violence: acknowledging locality, diversity, pleasure and the body. These tenets nestle within the over-arching concept of transversalism, with its promise of going beyond or passing through (the Latin root of 'trans') universalism. This is what I turn to in my concluding reflections.

If we are to create rape-free worlds, we will need to harness the polit-ical, economic and cultural labour of *all* progressive groups. This is not straightforward. Although sexual violence is an unequivocal 'wrong', this does not mean that it will be easy to establish coalitions. As we saw in the introduction to this book, even the most basic question – 'what is sexual violence?' – is contested. Does it include female genital cutting, for example?

Strategies also divide us. Those radical feminists who believe that sexual violence is caused by the mass consumption of pornography by males are unlikely to be converted by sex-positive feminists who argue for *better* (rather than less) pornography. Those who believe that the solution to pervasive rape cultures is a return to family values will not sud-denly be persuaded by those who celebrate erotic liberation. The divide between American socialist-lesbian-feminists and Cuban socialist femin-ists who marginalized homosexuality is a chasm.[37] The vigilantism that is necessary in parts of the world with weak law enforcement systems is repudiated by feminists in the West, while the carceral feminism of many white feminists is (rightly) deemed racist. Some believe that *male* anti-rape activists will distort anti-rape movements, draining resources from girls and women towards the politically dominant gender. Others (like myself) believe that the inclusion of all genders is indispensable for radical transformations. As we have seen throughout this book, there is no universalist standpoint on which people who seek to eradicate sexual violence can agree: knowledges are local and diverse.

So how is feminist solidarity going to be forged? I have found inspiration in transversalism. The concept was coined by activists in Bologna during the early 1990s and had proved useful in encouraging productive dialogues between Palestinian and Israeli feminists. Nira Yuval-Davis, along with other scholars who employ transversalism in their work, are interested in how people who regard each other as adversaries can come to a mutual understanding in the interests of a shared goal. In the context of this chapter, that shared objective is to eradicate sexual violence.

Transversalism starts from the basic belief that each person recognizes the world from their own position and that, as a consequence, all knowledge is partial and incomplete.[38] Yuval-Davis pleads for a shift from identity politics ('who' we are) to goal-orientated politics ('what we want to achieve').[39] This shift does not require activists to repudiate their self-identities: after all, even though each of our identities is complex and in flux, we come freighted with personal histories, social and economic contexts and accidental as well as intentional encounters. Transversalism requires activists to acknowledge our situated knowledges while eagerly responding to the knowledges of others. As Yuval-Davis maintains, 'it is vital in any form of coalition and solidarity politics to keep one's own perspective on things, while empathizing and respecting others.'[40] This involves acknowledging one's own intersectional position in historical time (what Yuval-Davis calls 'rooting') and paying attention to what matters for others (that is, 'shifting' in response to other people's thoughts, needs and desires).[41] In the words of feminist international legal scholar Hilary Charlesworth, 'each woman remains "rooted" in her own history and identity while "shifting" to understand the roots of other women in the dialogue.' There are two conditions: transversalism 'should not mean losing one's own roots and values nor should it homogenize "other" women'. Charlesworth explains that transversalism 'differs from universalism by allowing multiple points of departure rather than assuming that there is a universal bedrock of values in all societies'.[42] In other words, transversalism draws attention to the fact that universalism is nothing more than disguised ethnocentrism. It exchanges hierarchical models founded on positions of dominance for what literary scholars Françoise Lionnet and Shu-Mei Shih call 'horizontal communication'.[43] Fantasies of unity and homogeneity are jettisoned. The task of creating anti-rape coalitions requires the acceptance of difference, predicated on a recognition of the grounded positionalities of participants, strategically united by one goal: eradicating the harms of sexual violence.

What this means is that feminists should abandon the precept of shared female identity in the interests of solidarity based on the acknowledgement of difference and disagreement. Indeed, this can be stated more strongly: recognizing that we each possess 'unfinished, situated knowledges' is the very basis of successful coalitions. In Haraway's words, the

> knowing self is partial in all its guises, never finished, whole, simply there and original; it is always constructed and stitched together imperfectly, and _therefore able to join with another, to see together without claiming to be another._[44]

This argument can be made at individual as well as group levels. Individuals are constituted in interaction with other people. Selfhood is flexible, dialectic and co-constitutive. This means that the relations that create our subjective sense of self are not natural but are constructed in relations of power, including domination. Creating effective coalitions to combat sexual violence cannot succeed if we fail to acknowledge power and if we suppress difference. As cultural studies scholar Linnell Secombe put it,

> It is not disagreement, resistance, and agitation that destroy community. It is rather the repression or suppression of difference and disagreement in the name of unity and consensus which destroys the engagement and interrelation of community.[45]

This is well known to activists from minoritized communities. As we saw in an earlier chapter, even enslaved female leaders in early America warned about the limitations of assuming that women could unite over 'shared interests'. Bitter experience exposes the fact that attempts to forge 'common ground' will favour the socially, economically and politically dominant 'partners'. This is why anti-rape coalitions must address questions of inclusion. Political philosopher Iris Marion Young defined inclusion as the extent to which people affected by decisions – which, in the context of this chapter, are strategic decisions about the best way to achieve the shared goal of eradicating sexual violence – 'have been included in the decision making process and have had the opportunity to influence the outcomes'. Inclusive feminist practice requires anti-rape activists to 'encourage the particular perspectives of relatively marginalized or disadvantaged social groups to receive specific expression'.[46] To achieve this, relations of domination *within* coalitions need to be addressed explicitly and platforms created where marginalized communities can not only speak, but critique their socially, economically and politically dominant allies.

Because universalism, essentialism and identity politics create barriers to effective anti-rape coalitions, activists should abandon attempts to collaborate only with those 'like us'. This is not to say we should cease to argue with opponents who share our goals but not necessarily our political and epistemological approaches. Dissent is inherent in what it means to be political creatures within local, diverse and situated knowledges. In the interests of transnational solidarity, however, these will be pursued separately (and vigorously) from the broader goals of establishing coalitions that focus on eradicating sexual violence.

I am optimistic. Every community has a wealth of knowledge that can be used to address its particular needs and desires for a rape-free world. The rich tapestries of public and private resistance that are open to us are inspiring. They are hope-inducing. Wherever we are situated – as academics, homemakers, labourers, shopkeepers, secretaries, publishers, journalists, civil servants, teachers, students, entertainers, novelists, artists, lawyers, doctors, scientists, the unemployed and so on – we can make a difference in our local contexts. Each chapter of this book provides concrete examples of people doing just that. Effective activism requires each of us to exploit our specific proclivities, skills and spheres of influence. Intersectionality (which reminds us of difference) and transversalism (which provides ways of acting together while embracing difference) are powerful tools towards achieving a shared goal – a rape-free world. Transversalism emphasizes the need to pay attention to interpersonal and inter-communal differences: it encourages uneasy coalitions, not mergers. The true enactment of solidarity requires reciprocal exchanges focusing on political, economic and social projects that will reduce or eradicate sexual violence. It is a task that will require the political, ideological and discursive labour of every global citizen.

References

INTRODUCTION: THE GLOBAL CRISIS

1 Wanda Coleman, *Imagoes* (Santa Barbara, CA, 1983), pp. 112–24.
2 Catharine A. MacKinnon, *Toward a Feminist Theory of the State* (Cambridge, 1989), p. 172.
3 Pauline B. Bart and Patricia H. O'Brien, *Stopping Rape: Successful Survival Strategies* (New York, 1985), p. 1.
4 Lee Madigan and Nancy C. Gamble, *The Second Rape: Society's Continued Betrayal of the Victim* (New York, 1991), pp. 21–2.
5 Susan Brownmiller, *Against Our Will: Men, Women, and Rape* (New York, 1975), pp. 14–15.
6 Kimberlé Crenshaw, 'Demarginalizing the Intersection of Race and Sex: A Black Feminist Critique of Antidiscrimination Doctrine, Feminist Theory, and Antiracist Politics', *University of Chicago Legal Forum*, 139 (1989), pp. 139–68.
7 Ibid., p. 140.
8 J. Clifford Edgar and Jas. C. Johnson, 'Medico-Legal Consideration of Rape', in *Medical Jurisprudence, Forensic Medicine and Toxiocology*, vol. II, ed. R. A. Witthaus and Tracy C. Becker (New York, 1894), p. 420.
9 Stephen Robertson, *Crimes against Children: Sexual Violence and Legal Culture in New York City, 1880–1960* (Chapel Hill, NC, 2005), and Stephen Robertson, 'Shifting the Scene of the Crime: Sodomy and the American History of Sexual Violence', *Journal of the History of Sexuality*, XIX/2 (May 2010), p. 240.
10 V.A.C. Gattrell and T. B. Hadden, 'Criminal Statistics and Their Interpretation', in *Nineteenth-Century Society: Essays in the Use of Quantitative Methods for the Study of Social Data*, ed. E. A. Wrigley (London, 1972), pp. 336–96.
11 Régine Michelle Jean-Charles, *Conflict Bodies: The Politics of Rape Representation in the Francophone Imaginary* (Columbus, OH, 2014), p. 5.
12 Nonhlanhla Mkhize et al., *The Country We Want to Live in: Hate Crimes and Homophobia in the Lives of Black Lesbian South Africans* (Cape Town, 2010), p. 29, at https://open.uct.ac.za, accessed 1 December 2020.
13 Ibid.
14 R. Charli Carpenter, *Forgetting Children Born of War: Setting the Human Rights Agenda in Bosnia and Beyond* (New York, 2010), p. 59.
15 Ibid.

16 Jovanka Stojsavljevic, 'Women, Conflict, and Culture in Former Yugoslavia', *Gender and Development*, III/1 (February 1995), p. 40.

17 Catharine MacKinnon, 'Turning Rape into Pornography: Postmodern Genocide', *Ms.*, IV/1 (July/August 1993), pp. 24–30.

18 Ibid., p. 28.

19 Wendy Hesford, 'Reading Rape Stories: Material Rhetoric and the Trauma of Representation', *College English*, LXII/2 (November 2004), p. 119.

20 Ibid., pp. 120–21.

21 Wendy S. Hesford, 'Documenting Violations: Rhetorical Witnessing and the Spectacle of Suffering', *Biography*, XXVII/1 (2004), p. 121.

22 Guitele J. Rahill, Manisha Joshi and Whitney Shadowens, 'Best Intentions Are Not Best Practices: Lessons Learned While Conducting Health Research with Trauma-Impacted Female Victims of Nonpartner Sexual Violence in Haiti', *Journal of Black Psychology*, XLIV/7 (22 November 2018), p. 606.

23 Ibid.

24 Ibid.

25 Jean-Charles, *Conflict Bodies*, p. 3.

26 Rahill, Joshi and Shadowens, 'Best Intentions Are Not Best Practices', p. 614.

27 Nivedita Menon, 'Harvard to the Rescue!', *Kafila* (16 February 2013), at https://kafila.online, accessed 11 April 2020.

28 Jamie Campbell, 'German Professor Rejects Indian Student Due to the Country's "Rape Problem"', *The Independent* (9 March 2015), at www.independent.co.uk, accessed 1 December 2020.

29 Suruchi Thapar-Björkert and Madina Tlostanova, 'Identifying to Dis-Identify: Occidentalist Feminism, the Delhi Gang Rape Case, and Its Internal Others', *Gender, Place, and Culture: A Journal of Feminist Geography*, XXV/7 (2018), p. 1034.

30 Ibid., p. 1032.

31 Ibid., p. 1034.

32 Kelly Ashew, '[Review]. Umoja: No Men Allowed by Elizabeth Tadic', *African Studies Review*, LVII/3 (December 2014), p. 271.

33 Ibid., p. 272.

34 Human Rights Watch, *Shattered Lives: Sexual Violence during the Rwandan Genocide and Its Aftermath* (New York, 1996), unpaginated but at footnote 61, at www.hrw.org.

35 Unnamed court interpreter speaking on 26 June 2006 to Jonneke Koomen, '"Without These Women, the Tribunal Cannot Do Anything": The Politics of Witness Testimony on Sexual Violence at the International Criminal Tribunal for Rwanda', *Signs: Journal of Women in Culture and Society*, XXXVIII/2 (Winter 2013), pp. 265–6. Also see James Dawes, *That the World May Know: Bearing Witness to Atrocity* (Cambridge, MA, 2007), pp. 22–3.

36 Pascha Bueno-Hansen, *Feminism and Human Rights Struggles in Peru: Decolonizing Transitional Justice* (Urbana, IL, 2015), p. 123.

37 Manisha Joshi et al., 'Language of Sexual Violence in Haiti: Perceptions of Victims, Community-Level Workers, and Health Care Providers', *Journal of Health Care for the Poor and Underserved*, XXV/4 (November 2014), pp. 1623–40.

38 Iain McLean and Stephen L'Heureux, 'Sexual Assault Services in Japan and the UK', *Japan Forum*, XIX/2 (2007), p. 251.

39 Toma Shibata, 'Japan's Wartime Mass-Rape Camps and Continuing Sexual Human-Rights Violations', *u.s.-Japan Women's Journal. English Supplement*, XVI (1999), pp. 50–51.

40 Laura Hyun Yi Kang, 'Conjuring "Comfort Women": Mediated Affiliations and Disciplined Subjects in Korean/American Transnationality', *Journal of Asian and African Studies* (February 2003), p. 43.

41 Radhika Coomaraswamy, 'Report of the Special Rapporteur on Violence against Women, Its Causes and Consequences, Ms Radhika Coomaraswamy, in Accordance with Commission on Human Rights Resolution 1994/45' (Geneva, 1996), p. 4, at https://digitallibrary.un.org, accessed 1 December 2020.

42 Inderpal Grewal and Caren Kaplan, 'Introduction: Transnational Feminist Practices and Questions of Postmodernity', in *Scattered Hegemonies: Postmodernity and Transnational Feminist Practices*, ed. Inderpal Grewal and Caren Kaplan (Minneapolis, MN, 1994), pp. 17–18.

1 SHAME

1 Adrienne Cecile Rich, 'Rape', in *Diving into the Wreck: Poems, 1971–72* (New York, 1973), pp. 44–5.

2 'JustBeInc', at https://justbeinc.wixsite.com, accessed 1 October 2020, and 'Tarana Burke: Biography', at www.biography.com, accessed 1 October 2020.

3 Colleen Walsh, 'Me Too Founder Discusses Where We Go from Here', *Harvard Gazette* (21 February 2020), at https://news.harvard.edu, accessed 1 October 2020.

4 J. R. Thorpe, 'This Is How Many People Have Posted "Me Too" since October, According to New Data', *Bustle* (1 December 2017), at www.bustle.com, accessed 1 October 2020.

5 Ibid.

6 Ibid.

7 Meg Jing Zeng, 'From #MeToo to #RiceBunny: How Social Media Users Are Campaigning in China', *The Conversation* (6 February 2018), at https://theconversation.com, accessed 1 October 2020.

8 Ibid.

9 Leigh Gilmore, 'Frames of Witness: The Kavanaugh Hearings, Survivor Testimony, and #MeToo', *Biography*, XLII/3 (2019), p. 610.

10 Ibid., p. 620.

11 Angela Davis, 'Joan Little: The Dialectics of Rape', *Ms. Magazine* (1975), at https://overthrowpalacehome.files.wordpress.com, accessed 1 October 2020.

12 'Memphis Riots and Massacres', House of Representatives, 39th Congress, 1st session, Report No. 101 (25 July 1866), p. 5.

13 Marai Larasi, quoted in Jessie Thompson, 'Pearl Mackie and Marai Larasi on Why UK Actresses and Activists are Saying Time's Up', *Evening Standard* (6 April 2018), at www.standard.co.uk, accessed 1 October 2020.

14 'The Combahee River Collective Statement' (April 1977), at www.circuitous.org, accessed 1 October 2020.

15 Ann Cvetkovich, *An Archive of Feelings: Trauma, Sexuality, and Lesbian Public Cultures* (Durham, NC, 2004), p. 36.

16 Helen B. Lewis, *Shame and Guilt in Neurosis* (New York, 1971), and Frantz Fanon, *Black Skin, White Masks*, trans. Charles Lam Markmann (New York, 1967).

17 Nanjala Nyabola, 'Kenyan Feminisms in the Digital Age', *Women's Studies Quarterly*, XLVI/3–4 (Fall/Winter 2018), p. 262.

18 Ibid., pp. 262–3.

19 Charles B. Dew, 'Speaking of Slavery', *Virginia Quarterly Review*, LIII/4 (Autumn 1977), p. 790.

20 Ruth Harris, 'The "Child of the Barbarian": Rape, Race and Nationalism in France during the First World War', *Past and Present*, 141 (November 1993), p. 170.

21 Contribution of M. Tissier, *Chronique médicale*, XXII (1915), p. 250, cited in Harris, 'The "Child of the Barbarian"', p. 196.

22 Katherine Stefatos, 'The Psyche and the Body: Political Persecution and Gender Violence against Women in the Greek Civil War', *Journal of Modern Greek Studies*, XXIX/2 (October 2011), p. 265.

23 Robert S. McKelvey, *The Dust of Life: America's Children Abandoned in Vietnam* (Seattle, WA, 1999).

24 Louise Branson, 'Victims of War', *Chicago Tribune* (24 January 1993), at http://articles.chicagotribune.com, and Patricia A. Weitsman, 'The Politics of Identity and Sexual Violence: A Review of Bosnia and Rwanda', *Human Rights Quarterly*, XXX/3 (August 2008), p. 567.

25 Helena Smith, 'Revealed: The Cruel Fate of War's Rape Babies', *The Observer* [London] (16 April 2000), p. 1.

26 James C. McKinley Jr, 'Legacy of Rwanda Violence: The Thousands Born of Rape', *New York Times* (25 September 1996), p. A1, at www.nytimes.com; Emily Wax, 'Rwandans Are Struggling to Love Children of Hate', *Washington Post* (28 March 2004), p. A1, at www.genocidewatch.org; Peter K. Landesman, 'A Woman's Work', *New York Times Magazine* (15 September 2002), at www.nytimes.com.

27 Lydia Polgreen, 'Darfur's Babies of Rape Are on Trial from Birth', *New York Times* (11 February 2005), p. A1, at www.nytimes.com.

28 Pascha Bueno-Hansen, *Feminism and Human Rights Struggles in Peru: Decolonizing Transitional Justice* (Urbana, IL, 2015), p. 120.

29 Allison Ruby Reid-Cunningham, 'Rape as a Weapon of Genocide', *Genocide Studies and Prevention*, III/3 (Winter 2008), p. 283. Also see Lynda E. Boose, 'Crossing the River Drina: Bosnian Rape Camps, Turkish Impalement, and Serbian Cultural Memory', *Signs: Journal of Women in Culture and Society*, XXVIII/1 (2008), pp. 71–99.

30 McKinley, 'Legacy of Rwanda Violence', p. A1.

31 Yasmin Saikia, *Women, War, and the Making of Bangladesh: Remembering 1971* (Durham, NC, 2011).

32 'Sonya', cited by Karmen Erjaavee and Zala Volčič, '"Target", "Cancer", and "Warrior": Exploring Painful Metaphors of Self-Presentation Used by Girls Born of War Rape', *Discourse and Society*, XXI/5 (September 2010), p. 532.

33 Robyn Charli Carpenter, 'Forced Maternity, Children's Rights, and the Genocide Convention: A Theoretical Analysis', *Journal of Genocide Research*, II/2 (2000), p. 228, and Robyn Carpenter, 'Surfacing Children: Limitations of Genocidal Rape Discourse', *Human Rights Quarterly*, XXII/2 (May 2000), p. 467.

34 Bueno-Hansen, *Feminism and Human Rights Struggles in Peru*, p. 118.

35 This is a large literature, but see Dylan G. Gee et al., 'Early Developmental

Emergence of Human Amygdala-Prefrontal Connectivity after Maternal Deprivation', *Proceedings of the National Academy of Sciences of the United States of America*, CX/39 (24 September 2013), pp. 15638–43, and Marinus H. van Ijzendoorn, Maartji P. C. Luijk and Femmie Juffer, 'IQ of Children Growing Up in Children's Homes: A Meta-Analysis on IQ Delays in Orphanages', *Merrill-Palmer Quarterly*, LIV/3 (July 2008), pp. 341–66.

36 Dontella Lorch, 'Wave of Rape Adds New Horror to Rwanda's Trail of Brutality', *New York Times* (15 May 1995), at www.nytimes.com.

37 Carol J. Williams, 'Bosnia's Orphans of Rape: Innocent Legacy of Hatred', *LA Times* (24 July 1993), p. A1, at http://articles.latimes.com.

38 Ananya Jahanara Kabir, 'Double Violation? (Not) Talking About Sexual Violence in Contemporary South Asia', in *Feminism, Literature, and Rape Narratives: Violence and Violation*, ed. Sorcha Gunne and Zoë Brigley Thompson (New York, 2010), p. 156.

39 Patricia A. Weitsman, 'The Politics of Identity and Sexual Violence: A Review of Bosnia and Rwanda', *Human Rights Quarterly*, XXX/3 (August 2008), p. 577, and Peter K. Landesman, 'A Woman's Work', *New York Times Magazine* (15 September 2002), p. 6, at www.nytimes.com, accessed 1 October 2020.

40 Mary Kayitesi-Blewitt, 'Funding Development in Rwanda: The Survivors' Perspective', *Development in Practice*, XVI/3–4 (June 2006), p. 316.

41 Jennifer F. Klot, Judith D. Auberbach and Miranda R. Berry, 'Sexual Violence and HIV Transmission: Summary Proceedings of a Scientific Research Planning Meeting', *American Journal of Reproductive Immunology*, LXIX/1 (February 2013), p. 8.

42 'R. T.' cited in Human Rights Watch, *'We'll Kill You If You Cry': Sexual Violence in the Sierra Leone Conflict* (Washington, DC, 2003), p. 29.

43 Klot, Auberbach and Berry, 'Sexual Violence and HIV Transmission', p. 8.

44 Maria Eriksson Baaz and Maria Stern, 'Why Do Soldiers Rape? Masculinity, Violence, and Sexuality in the Armed Forces in the Congo (DRC)', *International Studies Quarterly*, LIII/2 (June 2009), p. 512.

45 Interview of Lucien Simbayobewe in Landesman, 'A Woman's Work', p. 20, p. 6, at www.nytimes.com.

46 'Cee', an ICTR prosecutor interviewed on 17 July 2005 by Jonneke Koomen, '"Without These Women, the Tribunal Cannot Do Anything": The Politics of Witness Testimony on Sexual Violence at the International Criminal Tribunal for Rwanda', *Signs: Journal of Women in Culture and Society*, XXXVIII/2 (Winter 2013), p. 259.

47 Christopher D. Man and John P. Cronan, 'Forecasting Sexual Abuse in Prison: The Prison Subculture of Masculinity as a Backdrop for "Deliberate Indifference"', *Journal of Criminal Law and Criminology*, XCII/1 (Fall 2001), p. 174, and Rosemary Ruicciardelli and Mackenzie Moir, 'Stigmatized among the Stigmatized: Sex Offenders in Canadian Penitentiaries', *Canadian Journal of Criminology and Criminal Justice*, LV/3 (July 2013), pp. 353–85.

48 Cited in Lisa S. Price, 'Finding the Man in the Soldier-Rapist: Some Reflections on Comprehension and Accountability', *Women's Studies International Forum*, XXIV/2 (2001), p. 217.

49 Atina Grossmann, 'Remarks on Current Trends and Directions in German Women's History', *Women in German Yearbook*, 12 (1996), pp. 11–25, and Elizabeth Heineman, 'The Hour of the Woman: Memories of Germany's "Crisis

Years" and West German National Identity', *American Historical Review*, CI/3 (April 1996), pp. 354–95.

50 Cited in Yuki Terazawa, 'The Transnational Campaigns for Redress for Wartime Rape by the Japanese Military: Cases for Survivors in Shanxi Province', *NWSA Journal*, XVIII/3 (Fall 2006), p. 141.

51 Megan MacKenzie, *Beyond the Band of Brothers: The U.S. Military and the Myth That Women Can't Fight* (Cambridge, 2015).

52 Walsh, 'Me Too Founder Discusses Where We Go from Here'.

53 Kaitlynn Mendes, Jessica Ringrose and Jessalynn Keller, '#MeToo and the Promise and Pitfalls of Challenging Rape Culture through Digital Feminist Activism', *European Journal of Women's Studies*, XXV/2 (May 2018), pp. 236–46 (p. 11 at www.researchgate.net, accessed 1 October 2020).

54 Megan Stubbs-Richardson, Nicole E. Rader and Arthur G. Cosby, 'Tweeting Rape Cultures: Examining Portrayals of Victim Blaming in Discussions of Sexual Assault Cases on Twitter', *Feminism and Psychology*, XXVIII/1 (2018), p. 90.

55 Mendes, Ringrose and Keller, '#MeToo and the Promise and Pitfalls of Challenging Rape Culture' (p. 12 at www.researchgate.net, accessed 1 October 2020).

56 Alison Phipps, 'Whose Personal Is More Political? Experience in Contemporary Feminist Politics', *Feminist Theory*, XVII/3 (2016), p. 303.

57 Ibid., pp. 306–7. For an early analysis of this problem, see Joan W. Scott's classic essay 'The Evidence of Experience', *Critical Inquiry*, XVII/4 (Summer 1991), pp. 773–97.

58 Ashwini Tambe, 'Reckoning with the Silences of #MeToo', *Feminist Studies*, XLIV/1 (2018), p. 200.

59 Nyabola, 'Kenyan Feminisms in the Digital Age', p. 271.

60 Alison Phipps, '"Every Woman Knows a Weinstein": Political Whiteness and White Woundedness in #MeToo and Public Feminisms around Sexual Violence', *Feminist Formations*, XXXI/2 (Summer 2019), p. 4.

61 R. Charli Carpenter, *Forgetting Children Born of War: Setting the Human Rights Agenda in Bosnia and Beyond* (New York, 2010), p. 63.

62 Ibid.

63 Amanda Holmes, 'That Which Cannot Be Shared: On the Politics of Shame', *Journal of Speculative Philosophy*, XXIX/3 (2015), pp. 415–16.

2 (IN)JUSTICE

1 Cited in Kitty Calavita, 'Blue Jeans, Rape, and the De-Constitutive Power of Law', *Law and Society Review,* XXXV/1 (2001), p. 93. Also see Rachel A. Van Cleave, 'Sex, Lies, and Honor in Italian Rape Law', *Suffolk University Law Journal*, XXXVIII/2 (2005), p. 452.

2 Calavita, 'Blue Jeans, Rape, and the De-Constitutive Power of Law', p. 89.

3 Ibid., p. 90.

4 Ibid., p. 92.

5 Cited ibid., p. 94.

6 Benedetta Faedi Buramy, 'Rape, Blue Jeans, and Judicial Developments in Italy' (San Francisco, 2009), at http://digitalcommons.law.ggu.edu, accessed 1 September 2020.

7 Giulio D'Urso et al., 'Risk Factors Related to Cognitive Distortions toward Women and Moral Disengagement: A Study on Sex Offenders', *Sexuality and Culture*, 23 (2019), p. 544.

8 Rachel A. Van Cleave, 'Renaissance Redux: Chastity and Punishment in Italian Rape Law', *Ohio State Journal of Criminal Law*, VI/1 (2008), p. 338.

9 Ibid., pp. 338–9.

10 Clare Pedrick, 'Italian Rape Case Stirs Public Rage', *Dallas Morning News* (15 June 1988), p. 1C, cited in Amy Jo Everhart, 'Predicting the Effect of Italy's Long-Awaited Rape Law Reform in the Land of Machismo', *Vanderbilt Journal of Transnational Law*, XIII/3 (March 1998), p. 685.

11 Ibid.

12 Van Cleave, 'Renaissance Redux', p. 338.

13 Ibid., p. 335.

14 Ibid., p. 344.

15 Ennio Flaiano, *Tempo di uccidere* [1947] (Milan, 1973), p. 34. Note that the film version turns the rape into an amorous encounter.

16 Shannon Woodcock, 'Gender as Catalyst for Violence against Roma in Contemporary Italy', *Patterns of Prejudice*, XLIV/5 (2010), p. 475.

17 'Critics Say Berlusconi's Response to Rape Cases Flippant', *ABC News* (26 January 2009), cited at www.abc.net.au, accessed 1 September 2020.

18 Woodcock, 'Gender as Catalyst', p. 479.

19 Ibid., p. 485.

20 Nadera Shalhoub-Kevorkian, 'Towards a Cultural Definition of Rape: Dilemmas in Dealing with Rape Victims in Palestinian Society', *Women's Studies International Forum*, XXII/2 (1999), pp. 166–70.

21 Helen M. Hintjens, 'Explaining the 1994 Genocide in Rwanda', *Journal of Modern African Studies*, XXXVII/2 (June 1999), p. 241.

22 Alison Brysk, 'The Politics of Measurement: The Contested Count of the Disappeared in Argentina', *Human Rights Quarterly*, XVI/4 (November 1994), pp. 685–6.

23 C. R. Carroll, 'Woman', *Southern Literary Journal*, III (November 1836), pp. 181–2, cited in Peter W. Bardaglio, 'Rape and the Law in the Old South: "Calculated to Excite Indignation in Every Heart"', *Journal of Southern History*, LX/4 (November 1994), p. 754.

24 David Carey Jr, 'Forced and Forbidden Sex: Rape and Sexual Freedom in Dictatorial Guatemala', *The Americas*, LXIX/3 (January 2013), p. 359.

25 For a discussion, see Stephen Robertson, 'Seduction, Sexual Violence, and Marriage in New York City, 1886–1955', *Law and History Review*, XXIV/2 (Summer 2006), pp. 331–73; Sonya Lipsett-Rivera, 'The Intersection of Rape and Marriage in Late-Colonial and Early National Mexico', *Colonial Latin American Historical Review*, VI/4 (Fall 1997), pp. 559–90.

26 Robertson, 'Seduction, Sexual Violence, and Marriage', p. 334.

27 Marietta Sze-Chie Fa, 'Rape Myths in American and Chinese Law and Legal Systems: Do Tradition and Culture Make the Difference?', *Maryland Series in Contemporary Asian Studies*, 4 (2007), p. 79.

28 Steven T. Katz, 'Thoughts on the Intersection of Rape and *Rassenschande* during the Holocaust', *Modern Judaism*, XXXII/3 (October 2012), p. 297.

29 Kimberley Theidon, *Entre prójimos. El conflict armado interno y la política de la reconciliación en el Perú* (Lima, 2004), p. 109.

30 Comisión para el Esclarecimiento Histórico, *Guatemala, memoria del silenció*, vol. III (Guatemala, 1999), p. 21, quoted in Jean Franco, 'Rape and Human Rights', *PMLA*, CXXI/5 (October 2006), p. 1663.

31 Fa, 'Rape Myths', p. 78.

32 Theresa De Langis, 'Speaking Private Memory to Public Power: Oral History and Breaking the Silence on Sexual and Gender-Based Violence during the Khmer Rouge Genocide', in *Beyond Women's Words: Feminisms and the Practices of Oral History in the Twenty-First Century*, ed. Katrina Srigley, Stacey Zembrzycki and Franca Iacovetta (London, 2018), p. 165.

33 Cited in Mariana Joffily, 'Sexual Violence in the Military Dictatorships of Latin America: Who Wants to Know?', *Sur International Journal on Human Rights*, 24 (2016), p. 168.

34 Maureen Murphy, Mary Ellsberg and Manuel Contreras-Urbana, 'Nowhere to Go: Disclosure and Help-Seeking Behaviors for Survivors of Violence against Women and Girls in South Sudan', *Conflict and Health*, XIV/6 (2020), p. 2.

35 See my 'The Mocking of Margaret and the Misfortune of Mary: Sexual Violence in Irish History, 1830s to the 1890s', *Canadian Journal of Irish Studies/Revue canadienne d'études irlandaises*, 43 (2021).

36 Shalhoub-Kevorkian, 'Towards a Cultural Definition of Rape', p. 163.

37 Ibid.

38 Thomas Eich, 'A Tiny Membrane Defending "Us" against "Them": Arabic Internet Debate about Hymenorrhaphy in Sunni Islamic Law', *Culture, Health, and Sexuality*, XII/7 (October 2010), p. 755.

39 'Vishnu @ Undrya vs State of Maharashtra on 24 November 2005', at https://indiankanoon.org, accessed 3 April 2020.

40 Nguyen Thu Huong, 'At the Intersection of Gender, Sexuality, and Politics: The Disposition of Rape Cases among Some Ethnic Minority Groups of Northern Vietnam', *Journal of Social Issues in Southeast Asia*, XXVIII/1 (March 2013), pp. 139–40.

41 Nguyen Thu Huong, 'Rape Disclosure: The Interplay of Gender, Culture, and Kinship in Contemporary Vietnam', *Culture, Health, and Sexuality*, 14.S1 (November 2012), p. S43.

42 Brandon Kohrt and Daniel J. Hruschka, 'Nepali Concepts of Psychological Trauma: The Role of Idioms of Distress, Ethnopsychology and Ethnophysiology in Alleviating Suffering and Preventing Stigma', *Culture, Medicine, and Psychiatry*, 34 (2010), pp. 332 and 337.

43 Ibid., p. 238.

44 Maurice Eisenbruch, 'The Cultural Epigenesis of Gender-Based Violence in Cambodia: Local and Buddhist Perspectives', *Culture, Medicine, and Psychiatry*, XLII/2 (2018), p. 315.

45 Ibid.

46 Ibid., p. 326.

47 E. Fulu et al., 'Why Do Some Men Use Violence against Women and How Can We Prevent It? Quantitative Findings from the United Nations Multi-Country Cross-Sectional Study on Men and Violence in Asia and the Pacific' (Bangkok, 2013), p. 9. Also see E. Fulu et al., 'Prevalence of and Factors Associated with Male Perpetration of Intimate Partner Violence: Findings from the UN Multi-Country Cross-Sectional Study on Men and Violence in Asia and the Pacific', *The Lancet Global Health*, 1 (2013), pp. e187–e207.

48 Eisenbruch, 'The Cultural Epigenesis of Gender-Based Violence in Cambodia', p. 319.

49 Ibid., pp. 324–5.

50 Ibid., p. 325.

51 Akira Yamagami, paraphrased by John P. J. Dussich, 'Decisions Not to Report Sexual Assault: A Comparative Study among Women Living in Japan Who Are Japanese, Korean, Chinese, and English-Speaking', *International Journal of Offender Therapy and Comparative Criminology*, XLV/3 (2001), p. 279.

52 Dussich, 'Decisions Not to Report Sexual Assault', p. 298.

53 Tsun-Yin Luo, '"Marrying My Rapist?!": The Cultural Trauma among Chinese Rape Survivors', *Gender and Society*, XIV/4 (August 2000), p. 588.

54 Jerome Kroll and Ahmed Ismail Yusuf, 'Psychiatric Issues in the Somali Refugee Population', *Psychiatric Times* (4 September 2013), n.p. Also see J. David Kinzie, 'A Model for Treating Refugees Traumatized by Violence', *Psychiatric Times* (10 July 2009), n.p.

55 Kimberley A. Ducey, 'Dilemmas of Teaching the "Great Silence": Rape-as-Genocide in Rwanda, Darfur, and Congo', *Genocide Studies and Prevention: An International Journal*, V/3 (December 2010), p. 311. Also see Anne-Marie de Brouwer and Sandra Chu, eds, *The Men Who Killed Me: Rwandan Survivors of Sexual Violence* (Vancouver, 2009), pp. 150–55.

56 Kelly Dawn Askin, 'Holding Leaders Accountable in the International Criminal Court (ICC) for Gender Crimes Committed in Darfur', *Genocide Studies and Prevention: An International Journal*, I/1 (July 2006), pp. 18–19; Pratiksha Baxi, Shirin M. Rai and Shaheen Sardar Ali, 'Legacies of Common Law: Crimes of Honour in India and Pakistan', *Third World Quarterly*, XXVII/7 (2006), p. 1241; Silvie Bovarnick, 'Universal Human Rights and Non-Western Normative Systems: A Comparative Analysis of Violence against Women in Mexico and Pakistan', *Review of International Studies*, 33 (2007), p. 67; 'War against Rape (WAR) Pakistan', *Reproductive Health Matters*, IV/7 (May 1996), p. 164.

57 Gregory L. Naarden, 'Nonprosecutorial Sanctions for Grave Violations of International Humanitarian Law: Wartime Conduct of Bosnian Police Officers', *American Journal of International Law*, XCVII/2 (April 2003), p. 343.

58 Ines Keygnaert, Nicole Vettenburg and Marleen Temmerman, 'Hidden Violence Is Silent Rape: Sexual and Gender-Based Violence in Refugees, Asylum Seekers, and Undocumented Migrants in Belgium and the Netherlands', *Culture, Health, and Society*, XIV/5 (May 2012), p. 510.

59 Karen Musalo, 'El Salvador – A Peace Worse Than War: Violence, Gender, and a Failed Legal Response', *Yale Journal of Law and Feminism*, XXX/1 (2018), p. 17.

60 Mariana Joffily, 'Sexual Violence in the Military Dictatorships of Latin America: Who Wants to Know?', *Sur International Journal on Human Rights*, 24 (2016), p. 172.

61 Amnesty International, 'Philippines. Fear, Shame, and Impunity: Rape and Sexual Abuse of Women in Custody' (London, 2001); Nicholas Haysom, 'Policing the Police: A Comparative Survey of Police Control Mechanisms in the U.S., South Africa, and the United Kingdom', *Acta Juridica* (1989), pp. 139–64; Patrick Kiage, 'Prosecutions: A Panacea for Kenya's Past Atrocities', *East African Journal of Human Rights and Democracy*, II/2 (June 2004), pp. 107–8.

62 Daniel E. Agbiboa, '"Policing Is Not Working: It Is Stealing by Force": Corrupt Policing and Related Abuses in Everyday Nigeria', *Africa Today*, LXII/2 (Winter 2015), p. 118.

63 Ibid.

64 Guitele J. Rahill, Manisha Joshi and Whitney Shadowens, 'Best Intentions Are Not Best Practices: Lessons Learned While Conducting Health Research in Trauma-Impacted Female Victims of Nonpartner Sexual Violence in Haiti', *Journal of Black Psychology*, XLIV/7 (2018), pp. 97–8. Also see Human Rights Watch, *'We'll Kill You If You Cry': Sexual Violence in the Sierra Leone Conflict* (Washington, DC, 2003), p. 48.

65 Human Rights Watch and National Coalition for Haitian Refugees, *Rape in Haiti: A Weapon of Terror*, VI/8 (1994), p. 11.

66 Michelle J. Anderson, 'Rape in South Africa', *Georgetown Journal of Gender and the Law*, I/3 (2000), p. 795; Hannah Britton, 'Organising against Gender Violence in South Africa', *Journal of Southern African Studies*, XXXII/1 (March 2006), p. 149.

67 Heather Reganass cited in Sue Armstrong, 'Rape in South Africa: An Invisible Part of Apartheid's Legacy', *Focus on Gender*, II/2 (June 1994), p. 36.

68 Anderson, 'Rape in South Africa', p. 806; Mervyn Dendy, 'When the Police Frolics: A South African History of State Liability', *Acta Juridica* (1989), pp. 39–41; Derek Fine, 'Kitskonstabels: A Case Study in Black on Black Policy', *Acta Juridica* (1989), pp. 61–2.

69 Britton, 'Organising against Gender Violence', p. 149, and Teckla Shikola, 'We Left Our Shoes Behind', in *What Women Do in Wartime: Gender and Conflict in Africa*, ed. Meredeth Turshen and Clotilde Twagiramariya (London, 1998), pp. 138–49.

70 Anderson, 'Rape in South Africa', p. 793.

71 Steven Robins, 'Sexual Rights and Sexual Cultures: Reflections on "The Zuma Affair" and "New Masculinities" in the New South Africa', *Horizontes Antropológicos*, XII/26 (July–December 2006), pp. 162–3.

72 Donna M. Goldstein, *Laughter Out of Place: Race, Class, Violence, and Sexuality in a Rio Shantytown* (Berkeley, CA, 2013).

73 Shalhoub-Kevorkian, 'Towards a Cultural Definition of Rape', p. 165.

74 Rebecca Kong et al., 'Sexual Offences in Canada', *Juristat. Canadian Centre for Justice Statistics*, XXIII/6 (July 2003), p. 6.

75 Eric R. Galton, 'Police Processing of Rape Complaints: A Case Study', *American Journal of Criminal Law*, 4 (1975–6), pp. 15–30.

76 Joanna Bourke, 'Police Surgeons and Victims of Rape: Cultures of Harm and Care', *Social History of Medicine*, XXXXI/4 (November 2018), pp. 679–87, t http:// doi.org/10.1093/shm/hky016; Jan Jordan, 'Beyond Belief? Police, Rape, and Women's Credibility', *Criminology and Criminal Justice*, IV/1 (2004), p. 51. Also see Joanna Jamel, 'Researching the Provision of Service to Rape Victims by Specially Trained Police Officers: The Influence of Gender – An Exploratory Study', *New Criminal Law Review*, 4 (Fall 2010), pp. 688–709; Teresa duBois, 'Police Investigation of Sexual Assault Complaints: How Far Have We Come Since *Jane Doe?*', in *Sexual Assault in Canada: Law, Legal Practice, and Women's Activism*, ed. Elizabeth A. Sheehy (Ottawa, 2012); Jennifer Temkin, '"And Always Keep A-Hold of Nurse, For Fear of Finding Something Worse": Challenging Rape Myths in the Courtroom', *New Criminal Law Review*, XIII/4 (Fall 2010), pp. 710–34.

77 Urvashi Butalia, 'Let's Ask How We Contribute to Rape', *The Hindu* (25 December 2012), at www.thehindu.com, accessed 3 April 2020.

78 Cited in Srimati Basu, 'Sexual Property: Staging Rape and Marriage in Indian Law and Feminist Theory', *Feminist Studies*, 371 (Spring 2011), p. 190.

79 Pablo Piccato, '"El Chalequero" or the Mexican Jack the Ripper: The Meanings of Sexual Violence in Turn-of-the-Century Mexico City', *Hispanic American Historical Review*, LXXXI/3–4 (August–November 2001), p. 637.

80 See my book for the British and U.S. contexts: *Rape: A History from the 1860s to the Present* (London, 2007). For an Indian context, see Shally Prasad, 'Medicolegal Responses to Violence against Women', *Violence against Women*, V/5 (May 1999), pp. 478–506.

81 Onesiphorus W. Bartley, *A Treatise on Forensic Medicine; or Medical Jurisprudence* (Bristol, 1815), p. 43.

82 'Todd Akin on Abortion', 19 August 2012, at www.huffingtonpost.com, accessed 28 December 2014.

83 'Rep. Trent Franks Claims "Very Low" Pregnancy Rate for Rape', *ABC News*, 12 June 2013, at http://abcnews.go.com.

84 Tanya Somanader, 'Angle: Rape Victims Should Use Their Pregnancies as a Way to Turn Lemons into Lemonade', *Think Progress*, 8 July 2010, at http:// thinkprogress.org, accessed 28 December 2014.

85 Jonathan A. Gottschall and Tiffani A. Gottschall, 'Are Per-Incident Rape-Pregnancy Rates Higher than Per-Incident Consensual Pregnancy Rates?', *Human Nature*, XIV/1 (2003), pp. 1–20.

86 Horatio R. Storer, 'The Law of Rape', *Quarterly Journal of Psychological Medicine and Medical Jurisprudence*, II (1868), p. 55.

87 Hans von Hentig, 'Interaction of Perpetrator and Victim', *Journal of Criminal Law and Criminal Behavior*, 31 (1940), p. 305.

88 George Devereux, 'The Awarding of a Penis as a Compensation for Rape: A Demonstration of the Clinical Relevance of the Psycho-Analytic Study of Cultural Data', *International Journal of Psycho-Analysis*, XXXVIII/4 (November–December 1957), p. 400.

89 Seymour Halleck, 'The Therapeutic Encounter', in *Sexual Behaviors: Social, Clinical, and Legal Aspects*, ed. H.L.P. Resnik and Marvin E. Wolfgang (Boston, MA, 1972), pp. 191–2. Also see Warren S. Wille, 'Case Study of a Rapist', *Journal of Social Therapy and Corrective Psychiatry*, VII/1 (1961), p. 19.

90 Muhammad Abdul Ghani, *Medical Jurisprudence: A Hand-Book for Police Officers and Students* (Vellore, 1911), p. 95. Some typos have been silently corrected.

91 Bejoy Kumar Sengupta, *Medical Jurisprudence and Texicology [sic]: With Post-Mortem Techniques and Management of Poisoning* (Calcutta, 1978), p. 335.

92 Ibid., p. 336.

93 B. Sardar Singh, *A Manual of Medical Jurisprudence for Police Officers*, 3rd edn (Moradabad, 1916), pp. 74–5.

94 Rames Chandra Ray, *Outlines of Medical Jurisprudence and the Treatment of Poisoning: For Students and Practitioners*, 6th edn (Calcutta, 1925), p. 362.

95 Ibid., p. 366.

96 Ibid., p. 365.

97 Joanne Fedler, 'Lawyering Domestic Violence through the Prevention of Family Violence Act 1993: An Evaluation after a Year in Operation', *South African Law Journal*, CXII/2 (1995), p. 237.

98 Ibid.

99 Iain McLean and Stephen L'Heureux, 'Sexual Assault Services in Japan and the UK', *Japan Forum*, XIX/2 (2007), p. 241.

100 Human Rights Watch, *'We'll Kill You If You Cry'*, p. 5.

101 For example, see Thomas W. McCahill, Linda C. Meyer and Arthur M. Fischman, *The Aftermath of Rape* (Lexington, MA, 1979), pp. 224–5, and 'The Victim in a Forcible Rape Case: A Feminist View', *American Criminal Law Review*, 11 (1973), p. 344.

102 Cited by Brett L. Shadle, 'Rape in the Courts of Guisiiland, Kenya', *African Studies Review*, LI/2 (September 2008), p. 33.

103 Ibid., p. 33.

104 *Congressional Record*, 2596 (1909), cited in Sarah Deer, 'Decolonizing Rape Law: A Native Feminist Synthesis of Safety and Sovereignty', *Wicazo Sa Review*, XXIV/2 (Fall 2009), p. 125.

105 Gray v. United States, 394 F. 2d 96, 101 (9th Cir. 1968), cited in Deer, 'Decolonizing Rape Law', p. 125.

106 Linda S. Parker, 'Statutory Change and Ethnicity in Sex Crimes in Four California Counties, 1880–1920', *Western Legal History*, 6 (1993), p. 85, and Deer, 'Decolonizing Rape Law', p. 151.

107 Dianne Hubbard, 'Should a Minimum Sentence for Rape Be Imposed in Namibia?', *Acta Juridica* (1994), p. 229.

108 Askin, 'Holding Leaders Accountable', p. 19.

109 Binaifer Nowrojee, '"Your Justice Is Too Slow": Will the ICTR Fail Rwanda's Rape Victims?', occasional paper no. 10 (Geneva, 2006), pp. v and 23–4.

110 Fa, 'Rape Myths', p. 82.

111 Nowrojee, '"Your Justice Is Too Slow"', pp. v and 23–4.

112 Swanee Hunt, *Rwandan Women Rising* (Durham, NC, 2017), p. 197.

113 Shadle, 'Rape in the Courts of Guisiiland, Kenya', p. 38.

114 Nguyen Thu Huong, 'Rape in Vietnam from Socio-Cultural and Historical Perspectives, *Journal of Asian History*, XL/2 (2006), p. 191. Also see Eileen J. Findlay, 'Courtroom Tales of Sex and Honor: *Rapto* and Rape in Late Nineteenth-Century Puerto Rico', in *Honor, Status, and Law in Modern Latin America*, ed. Sueann Caulfield, Sarah C. Chambers and Lara Putnam (Durham, NC, 2005), pp. 212–19.

115 Carla M. da Luz and Pamela C. Weckerly, 'Texas Condom-Rape Case: Caution Construed as Consent', *UCLA Women's Law Journal*, 3 (1993), pp. 95–6. See this article for cases where jurors were *not* convinced that requesting a condom signalled consent on the part of the rape victim.

116 Cited in da Luz and Weckerly, 'Texas Condom-Rape Case', p. 103.

117 Dorothy Q. Thomas and Regan E. Ralph, 'Rape in War: Challenging the Tradition of Impunity', *SAIS Review*, XIV/11 (Winter–Spring 1994), p. 90.

118 Human Rights Watch, *'We'll Kill You If You Cry'*, p. 52.

119 Shally Prasad, 'Medicolegal Responses to Violence against Women', *Violence against Women*, V/5 (May 1999), p. 479.

120 Calavita, 'Blue Jeans, Rape, and the De-Constitutive Power of Law', p. 89.

121 'Rapist Who Agreed to Use Condom Gets 40 Years', *New York Times* (15 May 1993), p. 6, at www.nytimes.com, accessed 1 September 2020.

3 GENDER TROUBLES

1 George Orwell, 'Politics and the English Language', in *George Orwell: A Collection of Essays* (New York, 1954), p. 167.

2 Judith Butler, 'Violence, Mourning, Politics', *Studies in Gender and Sexuality*, IV/1 (2003), p. 10.

3 Zara Nicholson, 'You Are Not a Man, Rapist Tells Lesbian', *Cape Argus* (4 April 2010), at www.iol.co.za, accessed 1 October 2020.

4 Jonah Hull, 'The South African Scourge', Al-Jazeera (20 February 2011), at www.aljazeera.com, accessed 1 September 2020.

5 See their website at www.luleki-sizwe.com.

6 Lea Mwambene and Maudri Wheal, 'Realisation or Oversight of the Constitutional Mandate: Corrective Rape of Black African Lesbians in South Africa', *African Human Rights Law Journal*, XV/1 (2015), p. 64.

7 Latashia Naidoo, 'Cape Town Lesbian Gets Justice', reporting for ENCA (27 November 2013), at www.youtube.com.

8 Action Aid, 'Hate Crimes: The Rise of "Corrective" Rape in South Africa' (7 May 2009), at www.actionaid.org.uk, accessed 14 June 2020.

9 For example, see Johanna Bond, 'Gender and Non-Normative Sex in Sub-Saharan Africa', *Michigan Journal of Gender and Law*, XXIII/1 (2016), p. 98.

10 'Advocacy', *Reproductive Health Matters*, XIX/37 (May 2011), p. 206.

11 Lorenzo Di Silvio, 'Correcting Corrective Rape: Charmichele and Developing South Africa's Affirmative Obligations to Prevent Violence against Women', *Georgetown Law Journal*, XCIX/5 (June 2011), p. 1471.

12 'Advocacy', p. 206.

13 Hannah Britton, 'Organising against Gender Violence in South Africa', *Journal of Southern African Studies*, XXXII/1 (March 2006), p. 146.

14 Michelle J. Anderson, 'Rape in South Africa', *Georgetown Journal of Gender and the Law*, I/3 (2000), p. 792.

15 'One in Four South African Men Admit Rape', Reuters (25 June 2000), at 'A Petition to Bring Suit against Defendants (Including the Pharmaceutical Manufacturers' Association and Members of the United States Government) on the Charge of Genocide against Individuals Living with HIV/AIDS' (29 July 2000), at www.fiar.us, accessed 1 October 2020. Anderson, 'Rape in South Africa', p. 792.

16 Nadia Sanger, '"The Real Problems Need to Be Fixed First": Public Discourses on Sexuality and Gender in South Africa', *Agenda: Empowering Women for Gender Equality*, 83 (2010), p. 116. Also see Lea Mwambene and Maudri Wheal, 'Realisation or Oversight of the Constitutional Mandate: Corrective Rape of Black African Lesbians in South Africa', *African Human Rights Law Journal*, XV/1 (2015), p. 67.

17 Zara Nicholson, 'You Are Not a Man, Rapist Tells Lesbian', *IOL* (4 April 2010), at www.iol.co.za, accessed 1 September 2020.

18 Zanele Muholi, 'Faces and Phases', *Transition*, 107 (2012), p. 121. She was writing in *The Telegraph* (March 2009).

19 Nkunzi Zandile Nkabinde, *Black Bull, Ancestors and Me: My Life as a Lesbian Sangoma* (Johannesburg, 2008), p. 146.

20 Interview with Duduzile on 17 February 2006, in Ashley Currier, *Out in Africa: LGBT Organizing in Namibia and South Africa* (Minneapolis, MN, 2012), p. 55.

21 Amanda Lock Swarr, 'Paradoxes of Butchness: Lesbian Masculinities and Sexual Violence in Contemporary South Africa', *Signs: Journal of Women in Culture and Society*, XXXVII/4 (Summer 2012), p. 981.

22 Zanele Muholi, 'Thinking through Lesbian Rape', *Agenda: Empowering Women for Gender Equity*, 61 (2004), p. 118.

23 Di Silvio, 'Correcting Corrective Rape', p. 1470.

24 Swarr, 'Paradoxes of Butchness', p. 962.

25 Cited in Roderick Brown, '"Corrective Rape" in South Africa: A Continuing Plight despite an International Human Rights Response', *Annual Survey of International and Comparative Law*, 18 (2012), p. 53.

26 For example, see Marc Epprecht, *Heterosexual Africa? The History of an Idea from the Age of Exploration to the Age of AIDS* (Athens, OH, 2008); Marc Epprecht, *Unspoken Facts: A History of Homosexualities in Africa* (Harare, 2008); Gilbert Herdt, 'Representations of Homosexuality: An Essay in Cultural Ontology and Historical Comparison. Parts I and II', *Journal of the History of Sexuality*, 1/3 and 1/4 (January and April 1991), pp. 481–504 and 603–32; Stephen O. Murray and Will Roscoe, eds, *Boy-Wives and Female Husbands: Studies of African Homosexualities* (Basingstoke, 1998); Boris de Rachewiltz, *Black Eros: Sexual Customs of Africa from Prehistory to the Present Day*, trans. Peter Whigham (London, 1964); Sylvia Tamale, 'Exploring the Contours of African Sexualities: Religion, Law, and Power', *African Human Rights Law Journal*, XIV/1 (2014), p. 166.

27 Brown, '"Corrective Rape" in South Africa', p. 51.

28 Yolanda Mufweba, 'Corrective Rape Makes You an African Woman', [South African] *Saturday Star* (8 November 2003).

29 Cited in Richard Lusimbo and Austin Bryan, '*Kuchu* Resilience and Resistance in Uganda: A History', in *Envisioning Global LGBT Human Rights: (Neo) Colonialism, Neoliberalism, Resistance, and Hope*, ed. Nancy Nicol et al. (London, 2018), p. 324.

30 Kapya Kaoma, *Globalizing the Culture Wars: U.S. Conservatives, African Churches, and Homophobia* (Somerville, MA, 2009), pp. 3 and 22, at www.arcusfoundation.org, accessed 5 April 2020.

31 For some discussions, seen Jessamym Bowling et al., 'Perceived Health Concerns among Sexual Minority Women in Mumbai, India: An Exploratory Qualitative Study', *Culture, Health, and Sexualities*, XVIII/7 (2016), p. 826; Joseph Gaskins, '"Buggers" and the Commonwealth Caribbean: A Comparative Examination of the Bahamas, Jamaica, and Trinidad and Tobago', in *Human Rights, Sexual Orientation, and Gender Identity in the Commonwealth*, ed. Corinne Lennox and Matthew Waites (London, 2013), p. 43; Sumia Basu Bandyopadhyay and Ranjita Biswas, *Vio-Mapping: Documenting and Mapping Violence and Rights Violation Taking Place in [the] Lives of Sexually Marginalized Women to Chart Out Effective Advocacy Strategies* (Kolkata, 2011); Carolyn Martin Shaw, *Women and Power in Zimbabwe* (Champaign, IL, 2015), p. 63.

32 Irene Caselli, 'Ecuador Clinics Said to "Cure" Homosexuality', *Christian Science Monitor* (10 February 2012), at www.csmonitor.com, accessed 6 April 2020.

33 'State v. Dutton, 450 N.W.2d (1990). State of Minnesota, Respondent, v. Robert Eugene Dutton, Appellant', pp. 191–2, at https://law.justia.com, accessed 4 April 2020.

34 Julie Decker quoted by Dominique Mosbergen, 'Battling Asexual Discrimination, Sexual Violence, and "Corrective" Rape', *Huffington Post* (20 June 2013), www.huffingtonpost.co.uk, accessed 5 April 2020.

35 Cited in Brown, '"Corrective" Rape in South Africa', p. 53.

36 People's Union for Civil Liberties, *Human Rights Violations against the Transgender Community* (Bangalore, 2003), at www.pucl.org, accessed 20 April 2020.

37 Gary W. Dowsett, 'HIV/AIDS and Homophobia: Subtle Hatreds, Severe Consequences, and the Question of Origins', *Culture, Health, and Sexuality*, v/2 (March–April 2003), p. 13.

38 People's Union for Civil Liberties Karnataka, *Human Rights Violations against the Transgender Community* (Karnataka, 2003), p. 40.

39 Venkatesan Chakrapani, Peter A. Newman and Murali Shunmugam. 'Secondary HIV Prevention among *Kothi*-Identified MSM in Chennai, India', *Culture, Health, and Sexuality*, x/4 (May 2008), p. 319.

40 Erin Wilson et al., 'Stigma and HIV Risk among *Metis* in Nepal', *Culture, Health, and Sexuality*, XIII/3 (March 2011), pp. 253 and 260.

41 J. M. Grant et al., *Injustice at Every Turn: A Report of the National Transgender Discrimination Survey* (Washington, DC, 2011).

42 L. Langenderfer-Magruder et al., 'Experiences of Intimate Partner Violence and Subsequent Police Reporting among Lesbian, Gay, Bisexual, Transgender, and Queer Adults in Colorado: Comparing Rates of Cisgender and Transgender Victimization', *Journal of Interpersonal Violence*, XXXI/5 (2014), pp. 1–17, and National Coalition of Anti-Violence Programs, 'Lesbian, Gay, Bisexual, Transgender, Queer, and HIV-Affected Intimate Partner Violence' (2012), at www.avp.org.

43 Morgan Tilleman, '(Trans)forming the Provocation Defence', *Journal of Criminal Law and Criminology*, C/4 (Fall 2010), p. 1671.

44 Bradford Bigler, 'Sexually Provoked: Recognizing Sexual Misrepresentation as Adequate Provocation', *UCLA Law Review*, LIII/3 (February 2006), pp. 800–801.

45 Tilleman, '(Trans)forming the Provocation Defence', p. 1683.

46 J. M. Grant et al., *Injustice at Every Turn*.

47 Jenna M. Calton, Lauren Bennett Cattaneo and Kris T. Gebhard, 'Barriers to Help Seeking for Lesbian, Gay, Bisexual, Transgender, and Queer Survivors of Intimate Partner Violence', *Trauma, Violence, and Abuse*, XVII/5 (December 2016), p. 591, and Michael J. Potocznick et al., 'Legal and Psychological Perspectives on Same-Sex Domestic Violence: A Multisystemic Approach', *Journal of Family Psychology*, XVII/2 (2003), p. 257.

48 Calton, Cattaneo and Gebhard, 'Barriers to Help Seeking', p. 587.

49 K. Fountain and A. A. Skolnik, *Lesbian, Gay, Bisexual, and Transgender Domestic Violence in the United States in 2006* (New York, 2007), p. 12.

50 Valerie Jennes et al., *Violence in California Correction Facilities: An Empirical Examination of Sexual Assault* (Irvine, CA, 2007), p. 43.

51 Ibid.

52 Sean Cahill, 'From "Don't Drop the Soap" to PREA Standards: Reducing Sexual Victimization of LGBT People in the Juvenile and Criminal Justice Systems', in *LGBTQ Politics: A Critical Reader*, ed. Marla Brettschneider, Susan Burgess and Christine Keating (New York, 2017), p. 142.

53 Valerie Jennes and Sarah Fenstermaker, 'Forty Years after Brownmiller: Prisons

for Men, Transgender Inmates, and the Rape of the Feminine', *Gender and Society*, XXX/1 (February 2016), p. 15.

54 Jennes et al., *Violence in California Correction Facilities*, pp. 50–51.

55 Doug Meyer, *Violence against Queer People: Race, Class, Gender, and the Persistence of Anti-LGBT Discrimination* (New Brunswick, NJ, 2015), p. 78.

56 Jennes and Fenstermaker, 'Forty Years after Brownmiller', p. 18.

57 James E. Robertson, 'A Clean Heart and an Empty Head: The Supreme Court and Sexual Terrorism in Prison', *North Carolina Law Review*, 81 (2003), p. 442; Christine A. Saum et al., 'Sex in Prison: Exploring Myths and Realities', *Prison Journal*, 75 (1995), pp. 413–30; David L. Struckman-Jones and Cynthia Struckman-Jones, 'Sexual Coercion Rates in Seven Midwestern Prison Facilities for Men', *Prison Journal*, 80 (2000).

58 Kristine Levan, Katherine Polzer and Steven Downing, 'Media and Prison Sexual Assault: How We Got to the "Don't Drop the Soap" Culture', *International Journal of Criminology and Sociological Theory*, IV/2 (December 2011), pp. 674–82.

59 U.S. Department of Justice, National Institute of Corrections, *Sexual Misconduct in Prisons: Law, Agency, Responses, and Prevention* (Longmont, CO, 1999), pp. 1–2.

60 Brenda V. Smith, 'Watching You, Watching Me', *Yale Journal of Law and Feminism*, XV/2 (2003), p. 232.

61 Christopher D. Man and John P. Cronan, 'Forecasting Sexual Abuse in Prison: The Prison Subculture of Masculinity as a Backdrop for "Deliberate Indifference"', *Journal of Criminal Law and Criminology*, XCII/1 (2001), pp. 127–85, and Christopher Hensley, Tammy Castle and Richard Tewksbury, 'Inmate-to-Inmate Sexual Coercion in a Prison for Women', *Journal of Offender Rehabilitation* (2003), p. 86.

62 Kristine Levan Miller, 'The Darkest Figure of Crime: Perceptions of Reasons for Male Inmates Not Reporting Sexual Assault', *Justice Quarterly*, XXVII/5 (October 2010), p. 694.

63 Cited in Man and Cronan, 'Forecasting Sexual Abuse in Prison', p. 146.

64 Miller, 'The Darkest Figure of Crime', p. 694.

65 Russell K. Robinson, 'Masculinity as Prison: Sexual Identity, Race, and Incarceration', *California Law Review*, XCIX/5 (October 2011), p. 310.

66 Cited in Man and Cronan, 'Forecasting Sexual Abuse in Prison', p. 144. Also see Miller, 'The Darkest Figure of Crime', p. 695.

67 Cited in Man and Cronan, 'Forecasting Sexual Abuse in Prison', p. 144.

68 Kim Shayo Buchanan, 'E-race-ing Gender: The Racial Construction of Prison Rape', in *Masculinities and the Law: A Multidimensional Approach*, ed. Frank Rudy Cooper and Ann C. McGinley (New York, 2012), p. 187.

69 Cahill, 'From "Don't Drop the Soap" to PREA Standards', p. 137, and Man and Cronan, 'Forecasting Sexual Abuse in Prison', p. 145.

70 Allen J. Beck and Candace Johnson, *Sexual Victimization Reported by Former State Prisoners, 2008* (Washington, DC, May 2012), p. 5, at www.bjs.gov, accessed 1 September 2020.

71 Ibid.

72 Jennes et al., *Violence in California Correction Facilities*, pp. 50–51.

73 '79 Countries where Homosexuality Is Illegal', at http://76crimes.com (16 October 2014), accessed on 18 December 2014.

74 Robert Mugabe, 'Homosexuals Are Worse Than Pigs and Dogs', *Zambian Watchdog* (27 November 2011), at www.zambiawatchdog.com, accessed on 20 March 2020.

75 Ashley Currier and Rashida A. Manuel, 'When Rape Goes Unnamed: Gay Malawian Men's Responses to Unwanted and Non-Consensual Sex', *Australian Feminist Studies*, XXIX/81 (2014), p. 293, and Michael J. Potocznick et al., 'Legal and Psychological Perspectives on Same-Sex Domestic Violence: A Multisystemic Approach', *Journal of Family Psychology*, XVII/2 (2003), p. 257.

76 Marietta Sze-Chie Fa, 'Rape Myths in American and Chinese Law and Legal Systems: Do Tradition and Culture Make the Difference?', *Maryland Series in Contemporary Asian Studies*, 4 (2007), p. 76.

77 D. A. Donnelly and S. Kenyon, '"Honey, We Don't Do Men": Gender Stereotypes and the Provision of Services to Sexually Assaulted Males', *Journal of Interpersonal Violence*, 11 (1996), pp. 441–8, and Pauline Oosterhoff, Prisca Zwanikken and Evert Ketting, 'Sexual Torture of Men in Croatia and Other Conflict Situations: An Open Secret', *Reproductive Health Matters*, XII/23 (May 2004), pp. 68–77.

78 Michael Peel et al., 'The Sexual Abuse of Men in Detention in Sri Lanka', *The Lancet*, XXXLV/9220 (10 June 2000), pp. 2069–70, at www.thelancet.com, accessed 1 August 2020.

79 Lara Temple cited by Will Storr, 'The Rape of Men: The Darkest Secret of War', *The Guardian* (16 July 2011), at www.theguardian.com, accessed 1 September 2020.

80 Cited in Storr, 'The Rape of Men'. See Chris Dolan, 'Letting Go of the Gender Binary: Charting New Pathways for Humanitarian Interventions on Gender-Based Violence', *International Review of the Red Cross*, XCVI/894 (2014), pp. 485–501.

81 Donnelly and Kenyon, '"Honey, We Don't Do Men"', pp. 444 and 446.

82 Ibid., p. 444.

83 National Coalition of Anti-Violence Programs, 'Lesbian, Gay, Bisexual, Transgender, Queer, and HIV-Affected Intimate Partner Violence' (New York, 2016), at https://avp.org, accessed 1 October 2020.

84 Sandesh Sivakumaran, 'Sexual Violence against Men in Armed Conflict', *European Journal of International Law*, XVIII/2 (2007), p. 256, and R. Charli Carpenter, 'Recognizing Gender-Based Violence against Civilian Men and Boys in Conflict Situations', *Security Dialogue*, XXXVII/1 (2006), p. 95.

85 Dara Kay Cohen, Amelia Hoover Green and Elisabeth Jean Wood, 'Wartime Sexual Violence: Misconceptions, Implications, and Ways Forward', *U.S. Institute of Peace Special Report*, 323 (February 2013), p. 10, at www.usip.org, accessed 1 October 2020.

86 Harry van Tienhoven, 'Sexual Torture of Male Victims', *Torture: Quarterly Journal on Rehabilitation of Torture Victims and Prevention of Torture*, III/4 (1993), p. 133.

87 R. J. McMullen, *Male Rape: Breaking the Silence on the Last Taboo* (London, 1990), p. 83; Eric Stener Carlson, 'Sexual Assault of Men in War', *The Lancet*, 349 (1997), p. 129; Sivakumaran, 'Sexual Violence against Men in Armed Conflict', pp. 253–76.

88 Eric Stener Carlson, 'The Hidden Prevalence of Male Sexual Assault during War: Observations on Blunt Trauma to the Male Genitals', *British Journal of Criminology*, XLVI/1 (January 2006), pp. 23 and 20.

89 M. C. Black et al., *The National Intimate Partner and Sexual Violence Survey. 2010 Summary Report* (Atlanta, GA, 2011), pp. 18–19, at www.cdc.gov, accessed 1 October 2020.

90 Ann M. Moore, Nyovani Madise and Kofi Awusabo-Asare, 'Unwanted Sexual Experiences among Young Men in Sub-Saharan African Countries', *Culture, Health, and Sexuality*, XIV/9–10 (October–November 2012), p. 1022.

91 Karen G. Weiss, 'Male Sexual Victimization: Examining Men's Experiences of Rape and Sexual Assault', *Men and Masculinity*, XII/3 (April 2010), pp. 280 and 284.

92 Ibid., pp. 284 and 286.

93 Barbara Krahé et al., 'Prevalence and Correlates of Young People's Sexual Aggression Perpetration and Victimisation in 10 European Countries: A Multi-Level Analysis', *Culture, Health and Sexuality: An International Journal for Research, Intervention, and Care*, XVII/6 (2015), pp. 682–99.

94 Moore, Madise and Awusabo-Asare, 'Unwanted Sexual Experiences', p. 1021.

95 Linda Halcón et al., 'Adolescent Health in the Caribbean: A Regional Perspective', *American Journal of Public Health*, XCIII/11 (November 2003), pp. 1851–7; R. Jewkes et al., 'Factors Associated with HIV-Sero-Positivity in Young, Rural South African Men', *International Journal of Epidemiology*, XXXV/6 (December 2006), pp. 1455–60; K. G. Santhya et al., 'Timing of First Sex before Marriage and Its Correlates: Evidence from India', *Culture, Health, and Sexuality*, XIII/3 (March 2011), p. 335.

96 Neil Andersson and Ari Ho-Foster, '13,915 Reasons for Equity in Sexual Offences Legislation: A National School-Based Survey in South Africa', *International Journal for Equity in Health*, 7 (2008), p. 1; Mburano Rwenge, 'Sexual Risk Behavior among Young People in Bamenda, Cameroon', *International Family Planning Perspectives*, 26 (2000), p. 118; Seth C. Kalichman et al., 'Gender Attitudes, Sexual Violence, and HIV/AIDS Risks among Men and Women in Cape Town, South Africa', *Journal of Sex Research*, XLII/4 (November 2005), p. 299.

97 For example, see Edward E. Baptist, '"Cuffy", "Fancy Maids", and "One-Eyed Men": Rape, Commodification, and the Domestic Slave Trade in the United States', *American Historical Review*, CVI/5 (December 2001), pp. 1619–50; Diana Ramey Berry, '*Swing the Sickle for the Harvest Is Ripe': Gender and Slavery in Antebellum Georgia* (Urbana, IL, 2007); Diana Ramey Berry and Leslie M. Harris, eds, *Sexuality and Slavery: Reclaiming Intimate Histories in the Americas* (Athens, GA, 2018); Crystal N. Feimster, '"What If I Am a Woman?" Black Women's Campaigns for Sexual Justice and Citizenship', in *The World the Civil War Made*, ed. Gregory P. Downs and Kate Masur (Durham, NC, 2015), pp. 249–68.

98 Isaac Williams in *A North-Side View of Slavery. The Refugee: or, the Narrative of Fugitive Slaves in Canada. Related by Themselves, with an Account of the History and Condition of the Colored Population of Upper Canada*, ed. Benjamin Drew (Boston, MA, 1856), pp. 56 and 60.

99 Theodore Dwight Weld, *American Slavery As It Is: Testimony of a Thousand Witnesses* (New York, 1839), p. 182.

100 William J. Anderson, *Life and Narrative of William J. Anderson, Twenty-Four Years a Slave; Sold Eight Times! In Jail Sixty Times!! Whipped Three-Hundred*

Times!!! Or The Dark Deeds of American Slavery Revealed (Chicago, IL, 1857), p. 24.

101 Thelma Jennings, '"Us Colored Women Had to Go through a Plenty": Sexual Exploitation of African-American Slave Women', *Journal of Women's History*, I/3 (1990), p. 50.

102 Thomas A. Foster, *Rethinking Rufus: Sexual Violations of Enslaved Men* (Athens, GA, 2019), p. 69.

103 Ibid., pp. 77 and 81–2.

104 A.W.R. Sipe, *Sex, Priests, and Power: Anatomy of a Crisis* (New York, 1995).

105 John Jay College of Criminal Justice at City University of New York, *The Nature and Scope of Sexual Abuse of Minors by Catholic Priests and Deacons in the United States, 1950–2002* (Washington, DC, June 2004), p. 68, at www.usccb.org, accessed 22 December 2014.

106 Mary Gail Frawley-O'Dea, 'Psychosocial Anatomy of the Catholic Sexual Abuse Scandal', *Studies in Gender and Sexuality*, V/2 (2004), p. 124.

107 Ibid., p. 134.

108 Ibid., p. 127.

109 Ibid.

110 Storr, 'The Rape of Men'.

111 Ibid.

112 Kirsten Johnson et al., 'Association of Combatant Status and Sexual Violence with Health and Mental Health Outcomes in Postconflict Liberia', *JAMA*, XXX/6 (2008), pp. 676–90.

113 Kirsten Johnson et al., 'Association of Sexual Violence and Human Rights Violations with Physical and Mental Health in Territories of the Eastern Democratic Republic of the Congo', *JAMA*, XXXIV/5 (2010), p. 560.

114 Richard Traumüller, Sara Kijewski and Markus Freitag, 'The Silent Victims of Wartime Sexual Violence: Evidence from a List Experiment in Sri Lanka', (2017), at https://papers.ssrn.com, accessed 1 October 2020.

115 Cherif Bassiouni, *Final Report of the United Nations Commission of Experts Established Pursuant to Security Council Resolution 780*, S/1994/674 (New York, 1994), p. 8.

116 Medical Center for Human Rights, *Report of Male Sexual Torturing as a Specific Way of War: Torturing of Males in the Territory of Republic of Croatia and Bosnia and Herzegovina* (Zagreb, 1995), p. 1.

117 Claire Bradford Di Caro, 'Call It What It Is: Genocide through Male Rape and Sexual Violence in the Former Yugoslavia and Rwanda', *Duke Journal of Comparative and International Law*, XXX/1 (2019), p. 81.

118 Christopher W. Mullins, '"He Would Kill Me with His Penis": Genocidal Rape in Rwanda as a State Crime', *Critical Criminology*, XVII/1 (2009), p. 26.

119 Di Caro, 'Call It What It Is', p. 82.

120 Donja De Ruiter, *Sexual Offenses in International Criminal Law* (The Hague, 2011), p. 10.

121 Amnesty International, 'Democratic Republic of Congo. Mass Rape – Time for Remedies' (25 October 2004), p. 19, at www.amnesty.org, accessed 1 September 2020.

122 Ibid.

123 For example, see I. Agger and S. Jensen, 'Tortura sexual de presos políticos de sexo masculino', in *Era de nieblas: Derechos humanos, terrorismo de estado y salud*

psicosocial en América Latina, ed. H. Riquelme (Caracas, 1990), pp. 63–4;
G. Daugaard et al., 'Sequelae to Genital Trauma in Torture Victims', *Archives of Andrology: Journal of Reproductive Systems*, x/3 (1983), p. 245; Medical Center for Human Rights, *Characteristics of Sexual Abuse of Men during the War in the Republic of Croatia and Bosnia and Herzegovina* (Zagreb, 1995), pp. 4–5.

124 G. Daugaard et al. 'Sequelae to Genital Trauma in Torture Victims', p. 245. They are citing the work of O. V. Rasmussen, A. M. Dam and I. L. Nielsen, 'Torture: An Investigation of Chileans and Greeks Who Had Previously Been Submitted [sic] to Torture', *Ugeskr Laeger*, CXXXIX/18 (2 May 1977), p. 1049.

125 Jorden Ortmann and Inge Lunde, 'Changing Identity, Low Self-Esteem, Depression, and Anxiety in 148 Torture Victims Treated at the RCT – Relation to Sexual Torture', paper presented at the WHO meeting of the Advisory Group on the Health Situation of Refugees and Victims of Organised Violence, Gothenburg (August 1988), cited by Inger Agger, 'Sexual Torture of Political Prisoners: An Overview', *Journal of Traumatic Stress*, II/3 (1989), p. 310.

126 Agger, 'Sexual Torture of Political Prisoners', p. 311.

127 Michael Peel et al., 'The Sexual Abuse of Men in Detention in Sri Lanka', *The Lancet*, XXXLV/9220 (10 June 2000), pp. 2069–70, at www.thelancet.com, accessed 1 August 2020.

128 Nayanika Mookherjee, 'The Absent Piece of Skin: Gendered, Racialized, and Territorial Inscriptions of Sexual Violence during the Bangladesh War', *Modern Asian Studies*, XLVI/6 (2012), p. 1584.

129 Ibid., p. 1598.

130 Donnelly and Kenyon, '"Honey, We Don't Do Men"', p. 446. Also see Human Rights Watch, *'We'll Kill You If You Cry': Sexual Violence in the Sierra Leone Conflict* (Washington, DC, 2003), p. 42.

131 Nicholas Groth and Ann W. Burgess, 'Male Rape: Offenders and Victims', *American Journal of Psychiatry*, 137 (1980).

132 For discussions, see Sandesh Sivakumaran, 'Male/Male Rape and the "Taint" of Homosexuality', *Human Rights Quarterly*, XXVII/4 (November 2005), pp. 1274–1306; Matt Seaton, 'The Unspeakable Crime', *The Guardian* [London] (18 November 2002); Gillian C. Mezey and Michael B. King, eds, *Male Victims of Sexual Assault* (Oxford, 2000).

133 For a discussion, see Kirsten Campbell, 'The Gender of Transitional Justice: Law, Sexual Violence and the International Criminal Tribunal for the Former Yugoslavia', *International Journal of Transitional Justice*, 1 (2007), pp. 411–32.

134 Moore, Madise and Awusabo-Asare, 'Unwanted Sexual Experiences', p. 1032.

135 Cited in Storr, 'The Rape of Men'.

136 Cited ibid.

137 Zanele Muholi, 'Faces and Phases', *Transition*, 107 (2012), p. 114.

4 CONJUGAL CRUELTY

1 Judy Gemmel, 'Into the Sun', in *Mother I'm Rooted: An Anthology of Australian Women Poets*, ed. Kate Jennings (Fitzroy, 1975), p. 186. Thanks to Catherine Kevin for bringing this poem to my attention in her 'Creative Work: Feminist Representations of Gendered and Domestic Violence in 1970s Australia', in *Everyday Revolutions: Remaking Gender, Sexuality, and Culture in 1970s Australia*, ed. Michelle Arrow and Angela Woollacott (Canberra, 2019), p. 216.

2 Konstantina Davaki, *The Policy on Gender Equality in Greece* (Brussels, 2013), p. 10.

3 NSW, 'Crimes (Sexual Assault) Bill and Cognate Bill (Second Reading)', *Parliamentary Debates Legislative Assembly* (8 April 1981), pp. 5479–80.

4 Mrs Beverley Cains, 'Nonsense Talked about Rape in Marriage', *Canberra Times* (2 November 1985), p. 7.

5 Jocelynne Scutt, *Even in the Best of Homes: Violence in the Family* (Melbourne, 1983), pp. 153–4, cited in Lisa Featherstone, 'Women's Rights, Men's Rights, Human Rights: Discourses of Rights and Rape in Marriage in 1970s and 1980s Australia', *Law and History*, v/2 (2018), p. 13.

6 Joyce Stevens, *A History of International Women's Day in Words and Images* (Sydney, 1985), p. 41.

7 Kevin, 'Creative Work', p. 203.

8 Catie Gilchrist, 'Forty Years of the Elsie Refuge for Women and Children', at https://dictionaryofsydney.org, accessed 1 December 2020.

9 Kevin, 'Creative Work', p. 204.

10 'MLC Calls for Change in Rape Laws', *Sydney Morning Herald* (5 November 1976), cited in Featherstone, 'Women's Rights, Men's Rights', p. 26.

11 Catherine Gander, 'The NSW Women's Refuge Movement', *Parity*, XIX/10 (2006), p. 28.

12 Sir Matthew Hale, *Pleas of the Crown* (London, 1678), pp. 628–9.

13 William Renwick Riddell, 'Sir Matthew Hale and Witchcraft', *Journal of the American Institute of Criminal Law and Criminology*, 17 (1926), pp. 5–12.

14 Sir William Blackstone, *Commentaries on the Laws of England. In Four Books*, 1st pub. 1765, vol. 1 (Philadelphia, PA, 1893), p. 441.

15 'Feminism and Film – A Roundtable Discussion with Curator Susan Charlton' (1 July 2017), at https://fourthreefilm.com, accessed 1 December 2020.

16 'Interview', *Filmnews* (1 December 1980), p. 9.

17 Ibid.

18 Jeni Thornley, 'Age before Beauty/Behind Closed Doors', *Filmnews* (1 December 1980), p. 8.

19 Gemmel, 'Into the Sun', p. 186.

20 'Feminism and Film – A Roundtable Discussion with Curator Susan Charlton'.

21 'On the Offensive', *Filmnews* (1 January 1981), p. 6.

22 Ibid.

23 'Australia', *Annual Human Rights Reports Submitted to Congress by the U.S. Department of State* (Washington, DC, 2010), p. 788.

24 'Interview', *Filmnews*, p. 9.

25 'Man and Wife Bill Sparks a Rumble', [Melbourne] *Herald* (23 October 1976).

26 *Parliamentary Debates, South Australian Legislative Council* (11 November 1976), p. 2097.

27 Wendy Larcombe and Mary Heath, 'Developing the Common Law and Rewriting the History of Rape in Marriage in Australia: PGA v the Queen', *Sydney Law Review*, XXXIV/1 (2012), p. 786.

28 Simon Bronitt, 'Is Criminal Law Reform a Lost Cause?', in *New Directions for Law in Australia: Essays in Contemporary Law Reform*, ed. Ron Levy (Canberra, 2017), p. 138.

29 Larcombe and Heath, 'Developing the Common Law', p. 804.

30 Aneta Michalska-Warias, 'Marital Rape in Poland from the Legal and Criminological Perspectives', *Prawo w Działaniu*, 26 (2016), pp. 63–4.

31 Davaki, *The Policy on Gender Equality in Greece*, p. 10.

32 Khethiwe Chelemu, 'Wife's Seven Year Wait for Justice', [Johannesburg] *Times* (19 January 2012), at www.timeslive.co.za, seen 1 December 2020.

33 Davaki, *The Policy on Gender Equality in Greece*, p. 10.

34 Amnesty International, 'Making Violence against Women Count: Facts and Figures – a Summary' (2004), p. 2, at www.amnesty.org.

35 Republic of South Africa, 'Act to Provide for the Granting of Interdicts with Regards to Family Violence', *Government Gazette* (1993), p. 4, at www.gov.za, accessed 1 December 2020.

36 Kristina Scurry Baehr, 'Mandatory Minimums Making Minimal Difference: Ten Years of Sentencing Sex Offenders in South Africa', *Yale Journal of Law and Feminism*, XX/1 (2008), p. 218.

37 Lisa Vetten and Kailash Bahan, *Violence, Vengeance, and Gender: A Preliminary Investigation into the Links between Violence against Women and HIV/AIDS in South Africa* (Johannesburg, 2001), pp. 8–9, cited in Baehr, 'Mandatory Minimums Making Minimal Difference', p. 218.

38 A. James Hammerton, *Cruelty and Companionship: Conflict in Nineteenth-Century Married Life* (London, 1992), p. 108.

39 Bipasha Ahmed, Paula Reavey and Anamika Majumdar, 'Cultural Transformations and Gender Violence: South Asian Women's Experiences of Sexual Violence and Familial Dynamics', in *Gender and Interpersonal Violence*, ed. Karen Thosby and Flora Alexander (London, 2008), p. 50.

40 Joanne Fedler, 'Lawyering Domestic Violence through the Prevention of Family Violence Act 1993: An Evaluation after a Year in Operation', *South African Law Journal*, CXII/2 (1995), p. 235.

41 Ahmed, Reavey and Majumdar, 'Cultural Transformations and Gender Violence', p. 51.

42 Ibid., p. 55.

43 Pragna Patel, 'Difficult Alliances: Treading the Minefield of Identity and Solidarity Politics', *Soundings*, 12 (Summer 1999), p. 120.

44 Ahmed, Reavey and Majumdar, 'Cultural Transformations and Gender Violence', p. 45.

45 Ibid., p. 58.

46 'Rape and Battery between Husband and Wife', *Stanford Law Review*, 6 (1953–4), pp. 719–28.

47 Jennie E. Burnet, 'Situating Sexual Violence in Rwanda (1990–2001): Sexual Agency, Sexual Consent, and the Political Economy of War', *African Studies Review*, LV/2 (September 2012), p. 100.

48 Corrine Williams, Laura Ann McCloskey and Ulla Larsen, 'Sexual Violence at First Intercourse against Women in Moshi, Northern Tanzania: Prevalence, Risk Factors, and Consequences', *Population Studies*, 62 (2008), p. 343.

49 Yoshihama Mieko, 'Domestic Violence: Japan's "Hidden Crime"', *Japan Quarterly*, XLVI/3 (July–September 1999), p. 79.

50 Ibid.

51 Sharmila Lodhia, 'Legal Frankensteins and Monstrous Women: Judicial Narratives of the "Family in Crisis"', *Meridians*, IX/2 (2009), p. 127.

52 Sally Cole and Lynne Phillips, 'The Violence against Women Campaigns in Latin America: New Feminist Alliances', *Feminist Criminology*, III/2 (2008), p. 149.

53 Press statement by David Phillips, Chairman of Festival of Light (26 November 1974), p. 4, cited in Duncan Chappell and Peter Sallmann, 'Rape in Marriage Legislation in South Australia: Anatomy of a Reform', *Australian Academy of Forensic Science*, 14 (1982), pp. 51 and 57.

54 S. Del Valle, *Catorce años a los culpables de violación conjugal* (Mexico DF, 1997), p. 1, quoted in Silvie Bovarnick, 'Universal Human Rights and Non-Western Normative Systems: A Comparative Analysis of Violence against Women in Mexico and Pakistan', *Review of International Studies*, 33 (2007), p. 65.

55 Sharmila Lodhia, 'Legal Frankensteins and Monstrous Women: Judicial Narratives of the "Family in Crisis"', *Meridians*, IX/2 (2009), p. 108.

56 Ibid., p. 127.

57 Marietta Sze-Chie Fa, 'Rape Myths in American and Chinese Law and Legal Systems: Do Tradition and Culture Make the Difference?', *Maryland Series in Contemporary Asian Studies*, 4 (2007), p. 93.

58 Glanville Williams, 'The Problem of Domestic Rape', *New Law Journal*, 141 (15 February 1991), p. 205, and 'The Problem of Domestic Rape', *New Law Journal*, 141 (22 February 1991), p. 246.

59 Ama Ata Aidoo, *Changes: A Love Story* (New York, 1991), p. 16.

60 Elizabeth Archampong and Fiona Sampson, 'Marital Rape in Ghana: Legal Options for Achieving State Accountability', *Canadian Journal of Women and the Law*, XXII/2 (2010), p. 513.

61 'Ray', cited in Phebemary Makafui Adodo-Samai, 'Criminalisation of Marital Rape in Ghana: The Perceptions of Married Men and Women in Accra', MA Dissertation in Sociology, University of Ghana (July 2015), p. 57.

62 Archampong and Sampson, 'Marital Rape in Ghana', pp. 512–13.

63 Nancy Kaymar Stafford, 'Permission for Domestic Violence: Marital Rape in Ghanaian Marriages', *Women's Rights Law Reporter*, 29 (2008), p. 63.

64 Edward Mahama, cited in Stafford, 'Permission for Domestic Violence', p. 63.

65 John Evans Atta Mills, cited in Stafford, ibid., p. 63.

66 Adodo-Samani, 'Criminalisation of Marital Rape in Ghana', p. 28.

67 Ibid., p. 1.

68 Ibid.

69 Michel Foucault, *Histoire de la sexualité* (Paris, 1976).

70 John Stuart Mill, 'The Subjection of Women', in *On Liberty. Representative Government. The Subjection of Women. Three Essays*, 1st pub. 1869 (London, 1912), pp. 463 and 522.

71 Elizabeth Cady Stanton, *History of Woman Suffrage* (New York, 1881), pp. 591 and 599.

72 Paulina Wright Davis, *A History of the National Women's Rights Movement* (New York, 1871), p. 66.

73 George Henry Napheys, *The Transmission of Life: Counsels on the Nature and Hygiene of the Masculine Functions* (Toronto, 1884), pp. 179–80.

74 Alice B. Stockham, *Tokology: A Book for Every Woman* (Chicago, IL, 1889), p. 154.

75 John Tosh, *A Man's Place: Masculinity and the Middle-Class Home in Victorian England* (New Haven, CT, 1999).

76 Diana H. Russell, *Rape in Marriage* (Indianapolis, IN, 1990). Also see Jana L. Jasinski and Linda M. Williams, with David Finklhor, *Partner Violence: A Comprehensive Review of 20 Years of Research* (Thousand Oaks, CA, 1998).

77 Liz Kelly, Jo Lovett and Linda Regan, *A Gap or a Chasm? Attrition in Reported Rape Cases*, Home Office Research Study 293 (London, February 2005), p. 15; R. Bergen, 'Surviving Wife Rape: How Women Define and Cope with the Violence', *Violence against Women*, 1/2 (1995), pp. 117–38; P. Esteal, 'Rape in Marriage: Has the License Lapsed?', in *Balancing the Scales: Rape, Law Reform, and Australian Culture*, ed. Patricia Weiser Easteal (Sydney, 1995); Patricia Weiser Easteal, 'Survivors of Sexual Assault: An Australian Survey', *International Journal of Sociology of Law*, 22 (1994), pp. 337–8; A. Myhill and J. Allen, *Rape and Sexual Assault of Women: The Extent and Nature of the Problem – Findings from the British Crime Survey*, Home Office Research Study 237 (London, 2002); Russell, *Rape in Marriage*, pp. 90 and 193.

78 Russell, *Rape in Marriage*, pp. 192–3 and 'To Have and to Hold: The Marital Rape Exemption and the Fourteenth Amendment', *Harvard Law Review*, 99 (1985–6), p. 1262.

79 R. v. R. [1991] 3 WLR 767. The text can be found at www.e-lawresources.co.uk, accessed 11 April 2020.

80 Rachel Browne, 'Historic Women's Refuge Elsie to Continue, New Management Promises' (23 June 2014), at www.smh.com.au, accessed 1 December 2020.

81 Carol Treloar, 'The Politics of Rape: A Politician's Perspective', in *Rape Law Reform: A Collection of Conference Papers*, ed. Jocelynne A. Scutt (Canberra, 1980), p. 193.

82 Hannah Britton and Lindsey Shook, '"I Need to Hurt You More": Namibia's Fight to End Gender-Based Violence', *Signs: Journal of Women in Culture and Society*, XL/1 (Autumn 2014), pp. 162–3.

5 MOTHERS AND MONSTERS

1 Catharine A. MacKinnon, 'Sexuality, Pornography, and Method: Pleasure under Patriarchy', *Ethics*, XCIX/2 (January 1989), pp. 326–7 and 335.

2 Sharon Marcus, 'Fighting Bodies, Fighting Words: A Theory and Politics of Rape Prevention', in *Feminists Theorize the Political*, ed. Judith Butler and Joan W. Scott (London, 1992), p. 391.

3 Michele Landsberg, 'Men behind Most Atrocities, but Women Are Singled Out', *Toronto Star* (21 September 2002), at http://freerepublic.com, accessed 1 September 2020.

4 See Lise Gotell and Emily Dutton, 'Sexual Violence in the "Manosphere": Antifeminist Men's Rights Discourses on Rape', *International Journal for Crime, Justice, and Social Democracy*, V/2 (2016), pp. 65–80. See the website of 'A Voice for Men', at https://avoiceformen.com.

5 Southern Poverty Law Center, 'Male Supremacy', at www.splcenter.org, accessed 1 October 2020.

6 U.S. Office of the Secretary of Defense, *Review of the Department of Defense Detention Operations and Detainee Interrogation Techniques (U)* (Washington, DC, 2005), pp. 181 and 183. A redacted version of the Church Report can be found at http://humanrights.ucdavis.edu, accessed 1 October 2020.

7 Erik Saar and V. Novak, *Inside the Wire: A Military Intelligence Soldier's Eyewitness Account of Life at Guantánamo* (New York, 2005), p. 222.

8 Kristine A. Huskey, 'The "Sex Interrogators" of Guantanamo', in *One of the Guys:*

Women as Aggressors and Torturers, ed. Tara McKelvey (New York, 2007), p. 176.

9 Ibid., p. 177.

10 Riva Khoshaba, 'Women in the Interrogation Room', in *One of the Guys*, ed. McKelvey, p. 179.

11 Carol Leonnig and Dana Priest, 'Detainees Accuse Female Interrogators: Pentagon Inquiry Is Said to Confirm Muslims' Accounts of Sexual Tactics at Guantánamo', *Washington Post* (10 February 2005), at www.washingtonpost.com, accessed 1 September 2020.

12 Luke Harding, 'The Other Prisoners', *The Guardian* (19 May 2004), at www.theguardian.com, accessed 1 September 2020.

13 Barbara Ehrenreich, 'Feminism's Assumptions Upended', in *Abu Ghraib: The Politics of Torture* (Berkeley, CA, 2004), pp. 65–70.

14 Coco Fusco makes this point in her introduction to the play: 'Artist's Statement', *TDR: The Drama Review*, LII/1 (Spring 2008), p. 139.

15 Bonnie Mann, 'How America Justifies Its War: A Modern/Postmodern Aesthetics of Masculinity and Sovereignty', *Hypatia*, XXI/4 (Fall 2006), p. 159.

16 U.S. Office of the Secretary of Defense, *Review of the Department of Defense Detention Operations*, pp. 181 and 183. Redacted version of the Church Report, at http://humanrights.ucdavis.edu.

17 Philip Gourevitch and Errol Morris, 'Exposure: The Woman behind the Camera', *New Yorker* (3 March 2008), at www.newyorker.com, accessed 1 September 2020.

18 Ibid.

19 Philip Gourevitch and Errol Morris, *Standard Operating Procedure* (New York, 2008), pp. 112–13.

20 Stone Phillips, 'Behind the Abu Ghraib Photos', *Dateline NBC* (2 October 2005), at www.nbcnews.com, accessed 1 October 2020.

21 Scheherezade Faramrzi, 'Former Iraqi Prisoner Says U.S. Jailers Humiliated Him', *Herald Net* (2 May 2004), at www.heraldnet.com, accessed 1 October 2020. Also see Natalja Zabeida, 'Not Making Excuses: Functions of Rape as a Tool in Ethno-Nationalist Wars', in *Women, War, and Violence – Personal Perspectives and Global Activism*, ed. R. M. Chandler, L. Wang and L. K. Fuller (New York, 2010).

22 Sheik Mohammed Bashir quoted in Mark Danner, *Torture and Truth: America, Abu Ghraib, and the War on Terror* (New York, 2004), p. 26.

23 For example, see my book *Rape: A History from the 1860s to the Present* (London, 2007); Ryan Ashley Caldwell, *Fallgirls: Gender and the Framing of Torture at Abu Ghraib* (London, 2016); Mark Danner, Barbara Ehrenreich and David Levi Strauss, eds, *Abu Ghraib: The Politics of Torture* (Berkeley, CA, 2005).

24 Fusco, 'Artist's Statement', pp. 142–3. Also see Coco Fusco, *A Field Guide for Female Interrogators* (New York, 2008).

25 Seymour M. Hersh, 'The Gray Zone: How a Secret Pentagon Program Came to Abu Ghraib', *New Yorker* (24 May 2004), at www.newyorker.com, accessed 1 October 2020.

26 Raphael Patai, *The Arab Mind* (New York, 1973).

27 Hersh, 'The Gray Zone'.

28 Fusco, 'Artist's Statement', p. 147.

29 Ibid.

30 Ibid., p. 152.

31 Ibid.

32 Bernadette Faedi Duramy, *Gender and Violence in Haiti: Women's Path from Victims to Agents* (New Brunswick, NJ, 2014).

33 Merima Husejnvic, 'Bosnian War's Wicked Women Get Off Lightly', *Balkan Insight* (7 February 2011), at https://balkaninsight.com, accessed 1 October 2020. Also see 'Bosnian Woman "Raped for 20 Days by Fighters"', *Balkan Insight* (4 July 2014), at https://balkaninsight.com, accessed 1 October 2020.

34 UN International Criminal Tribunal for the Former Yugoslavia, 'Prosecutor v. Biljana Plavšic: Trial Chamber Sentences the Accused to 11 Years' Imprisonment' (27 February 2003), at www.icty.org, accessed 1 October 2020.

35 Sabrina Gilani, 'Transforming the "Perpetrator" into "Victim": The Effect of Gendering Violence on the Legal and Practical Responses to Women's Political Violence', *Australian Journal of Gender and Law*, 1 (2010), at http://sro.sussex. ac.uk, accessed 1 December 2020.

36 Dara Kay Cohen, 'Female Combatants and the Perpetration of Violence: Wartime Rape in the Sierra Leone Civil War', *World Politics*, LXV/3 (July 2013), p. 385; Irma Specht, *Red Shoes: Experiences of Girl Combatants in Liberia* (Geneva, 2006); Dulce Foster et al., *A House with Two Rooms: Final Report of the Truth and Reconciliation Commission of Liberia Diaspora Project* (Saint Paul, MN, 2009), p. 245.

37 Lisa Sharlach, 'Gender and Genocide in Rwanda: Women as Agents and Objects of Genocide', *Journal of Genocide Research*, 1/3 (1999), p. 392.

38 Anne-Marie de Brouwer and Sandra K. Hon Chu, *The Men Who Killed Me* (Vancouver, 2009).

39 Reva N. Adler, Cyanne E. Loyle and Judith Globerman, 'A Calamity in the Neighborhood: Women's Participation in the Rwandan Genocide', *Genocide Studies and Prevention* (2007), p. 222, and African Rights, *Rwanda: Not So Innocent. Women as Killers* (London, 1995), p. 82.

40 Nicole Hogg, 'Women's Participation in the Rwandan Genocide: Mothers or Monsters?', *International Review of the Red Cross*, XCII/877 (March 2010), p. 78.

41 Alette Smeulers, 'Female Perpetrators: Ordinary and Extra-Ordinary Women', *International Criminal Law Review*, 15 (2015), p. 214.

42 Hogg, 'Women's Participation in the Rwandan Genocide', p. 79.

43 Lynn Lawry, Kirsten Johnson and Jana Asher, 'Evidence-Based Documentation of Gender-Based Violence', in *Sexual Violence as an International Crime: Interdisciplinary Approaches*, ed. A.L.M. Bouwer, C. de Ku, R. Römkens and L. van den Herik (Cambridge, 2013), p. 258.

44 Kirstin Johnson et al., 'Association of Sexual Violence and Human Rights Violations with Physical and Mental Health in Territories of the Eastern Democratic Republic of the Congo', *Journal of the American Medical Association*, CCCIV/5 (August 2010), p. 553. For a discussion, see Dunia Prince Zongwe, 'The New Sexual Violence Legislation in the Congo: Dressing Indelible Scars on Human Dignity', *African Studies Review*, LV/2 (September 2012), p. 44.

45 Cohen, 'Female Combatants and the Perpetration of Violence', p. 399.

46 Hilmi M. Zawati, 'Rethinking Rape Law', *Journal of International Law and International Relations*, 10 (2014), p. 42.

47 Cohen, 'Female Combatants and the Perpetration of Violence', p. 396.

48 Ibid., p. 399. Emphasis added.

49 Dora Apel, *War Culture and the Contest of Images* (New Brunswick, NJ, 2012), p. 86.

50 Johanna Bond, 'A Decade after Abu Ghraib: Lessons in Softening Up the Enemy and Sex-Based Humiliation', *Law and Inequality: Journal of Theory and Practice*, XXXI/1 (2012), p. 5.

51 Susan McKay, 'Girls as "Weapons of Terror" in Northern Uganda and Sierra Leonean Rebel Fighting Forces', *Studies in Conflict and Terrorism*, 28 (2005), p. 391.

52 Jeannie Annan et al., 'Civil War, Reintegration, and Gender in Northern Uganda', *Journal of Conflict Resolution*, LV/6 (December 2011), p. 884.

53 Chris Coulter, 'Female Fighters in the Sierra Leone War: Challenging the Assumptions', *Feminist Review*, 88 (2008), p. 60. Note that boy soldiers were also often required to rape girls and women, or risk being killed. In other words, this was not unique to female child-soldiers. See Amnesty International, 'Democratic Republic of Congo: Mass Rape – Time for Remedies' (25 October 2004), p. 15, at www.amnesty.org, accessed 1 October 2020.

54 Cohen, 'Female Combatants and the Perpetration of Violence', pp. 383–415.

55 Rachel Brett and Irma Specht, *Young Soldiers: Why They Choose to Fight* (Boulder, CO, 2004), p. 95.

56 McKay, 'Girls as "Weapons of Terror"', p. 393.

57 Coulter, 'Female Fighters in the Sierra Leone War', pp. 60–61.

58 McKay, 'Girls as "Weapons of Terror"', p. 393, and Megan MacKenzie, 'Securitization and Desecuritization: Female Soldiers and the Reconstruction of Women in Post-Conflict Sierra Leone', *Security Studies*, 18 (2009), pp. 244–5.

59 Primo Levi, *The Drowned and the Saved* (New York, 1989), p. 43.

60 Ibid., p. 59.

61 Claudia Card, 'Women, Evil, and Gray Zones', *Metaphilosophy*, XXXI/5 (October 2000), p. 509.

62 Ibid.

63 Ibid.

64 Laura Sjoberg and Caron E. Gentry, *Mothers, Monsters, Whores: Women's Violence in Global Politics* (London, 2007 and 2013), and Laura Sjoberg and Caron E. Gentry, *Beyond Mothers, Monsters, Whores: Thinking about Women's Violence in Global Politics* (London, 2015).

65 Sjoberg and Gentry, *Mothers, Monsters, Whores* (2007), p. 290.

66 Peter K. Landesman, 'A Woman's Work', *New York Times* (15 September 2002), at www.nytimes.com. See the case minutes of her trial at www.ictr.org. Also see Radhika Coomaraswamy, 'Report of the Mission to Rwanda' (United Nations Economic and Social Council, 4 February 1998), at www.unhchr.ch, and African Rights, *Rwanda: Not So Innocent*. Also Adam Jones, 'Gender and Genocide in Rwanda', *Journal of Genocide Research*, IV/1 (2002), pp. 65–94.

67 Landesman, 'A Woman's Work'.

68 Mark A. Drumbl, 'She Makes Me Ashamed to Be a Woman: The Genocide Conviction of Pauline Nyiramasuhuko', *Michigan Journal of International Law*, XXXIV/3 (2013), p. 566.

69 Landesman, 'A Woman's Work'.

70 'Updates from the International and Internationalized Criminal Tribunals', *Human Rights Brief*, XIX/1 (Fall 2011), p. 39.

71 Helen Trouille, 'How Far Has the International Criminal Tribunal for Rwanda

Really Come since Akayesu in the Prosecution and Investigation of Sexual Offences Committed against Women? An Analysis of Ndindiliyimana et al.', *International Criminal Law Review*, XIII/4 (2013), p. 781.

72 'Updates from the International and Internationalized Criminal Tribunals', *Human Rights Brief*, XIX/1 (Fall 2011), p. 39.

73 Drumbl, 'She Makes Me Ashamed to Be a Woman', p. 594, and Smeulers, 'Female Perpetrators', p. 214.

74 Donna Harman, 'A Woman on Trial for Rwanda's Massacre', *Christian Science Monitor* (7 March 2003), at www.csmonitor.com, accessed 5 April 2020.

75 Drumbl, 'She Makes Me Ashamed to Be a Woman', p. 592.

76 Landesman, 'A Woman's Work'.

77 Interviewed by Hogg, 'Women's Participation in the Rwandan Genocide', p. 93.

78 Chantal Mudahogora, 'When Women Become Killers', *Hamilton Spectator* (19 October 2002), p. M13.

79 Hogg, 'Women's Participation in the Rwandan Genocide', p. 93.

80 Drumbl, 'She Makes Me Ashamed to Be a Woman', p. 564.

81 Interview with Lindsay Hilsum, BBC, mid-August 1994, cited in African Rights, *Rwanda: Not So Innocent*, p. 106.

82 Landesman, 'A Woman's Work'.

83 Ibid.

84 Mark Kersten, 'If Simone Gbagbo Ends Up in the Hague, She Won't Be the First', *Justice in Conflict* (23 November 2012), at https://justiceinconflict.org, accessed 1 October 2020.

85 Judithe Kanakuze, interviewed by Hogg in 'Women's Participation in the Rwandan Genocide', p. 100.

86 Vincent Karangura, interviewed by Hogg, ibid., p. 100.

87 Alessandra Zaldivar-Giuffredi, 'Simone Gbagbo: First Lady of Cote d'Ivoire, First Woman Indicted by the International Criminal Court, One among Many Female Perpetrators of Crimes against Humanity', *ILSA Journal of International and Comparative Law*, XXV/1 (2018), p. 1.

88 Ibid., p. 6.

89 Ibid., p. 23.

90 'Ivory Coast's "Iron Lady" Jailed for 20 Years over Election Violence', *France24* (10 March 2015), www.france24.com, accessed 1 September 2020.

91 David Cloud, 'Psychologist Calls Private in Abu Ghraib Photographs "Overly Compliant"', *New York Times* (24 September 2005), p. 28.

92 Richard Goldstein, 'Bitch Bites Man!', in *Village Voice* (10 May 2004), at www.villagevoice.com, and Stone Phillips, 'Behind the Abu Ghraib Photos', *Dateline NBC* (2 October 2005), at www.nbcnews.com, accessed 1 October 2020.

93 Andrew Buncombe, 'The Sex Sadist of Baghdad', *The Star* (7 May 2004).

94 Evan G. Thomas, 'Explaining Lynndie England', *Newsweek* (14 May 2004), at www.newsweek.com.

95 Linda Chavez, 'Sexual Tension in the Military', *Townhall* (5 May 2004), at https://townhall.com, accessed 1 October 2020.

96 This argument is made by Laura Sjoberg, 'Agency, Militarized Femininity, and Enemy Others: Observations from the War in Iraq', *International Feminist Journal of Politics*, IX/1 (March 2007), p. 89.

97 Franca Cortoni, Kelly M. Babchishin and Clémence Rat, 'The Proportion of

Sexual Offenders Who Are Female Is Higher Than Thought: A Meta-Analysis', *Criminal Justice and Behavior*, XLIV/2 (February 2017), p. 149. See the original article for a full description of their intricate methodologies.

98 Ibid., p. 152.

99 Ibid., p. 155.

100 Ibid., p. 154.

101 Ibid., p. 156.

102 Ibid.

103 Judith Butler, *Gender Trouble* [1990] (Abingdon, 2010), p. 9.

6 RECKONINGS

1 Christopher Soto, 'In Support of Violence', *Tin House*, 70 (13 December 2016), at https://tinhouse.com, accessed 1 September 2020.

2 'Victims Turned Aggressors', *Economic and Political Weekly*, XXXIX/36 (4–10 September 2004), p. 3961, and Raekha Prasad, '"Arrest Us All": The 200 Women Who Killed a Rapist', *The Guardian* (16 September 2005), at www.theguardian.com, accessed 20 April 2020.

3 Prasad, '"Arrest Us All"'.

4 Ibid.

5 Ibid.

6 Srimati Basu, 'Sexual Property: Staging Rape and Marriage in Indian Law and Feminist Theory', *Feminist Studies*, XXXVII/1 (Spring 2011), p. 193.

7 Randeep Ramesh, 'Women's Revenge against Rapists', *The Guardian* (9 November 2004), at www.theguardian.com, accessed 20 April 2020.

8 Swati Mehta, *Killing Justice: Vigilantism in Nagpur* (New Delhi, 2005), p. 14, at https://humanrightsinitiative.org, accessed 10 January 2021.

9 Basu, 'Sexual Property', p. 193.

10 Prasad, '"Arrest Us All"' (16 September 2005), accessed 20 April 2020.

11 Ramesh, 'Women's Revenge against Rapists'.

12 Kalpana Kannabiran, *Tools of Justice: Non-Discrimination and the Indian Constitution* (London, 2012), p. 361. In 2000, Bhanwari's story was made into a film, directed by Jag Mundhra and entitled Bawander.

13 Anupama Rao, 'Understanding *Sirasgaon*: Notes towards Conceptualising the Role of Law, Caste, and Gender in the Case of "Atrocity"', in *Gender and Caste: Issues in Contemporary Feminism*, ed. Rajeswari Sunder Rajan (New Delhi, 2003), p. 281. Also see Anupama Rao, 'Violence and Humanity: Or, Vulnerability as Political Subjectivity', *Social Research*, LXXVIII/2 (Summer 2011), p. 624.

14 Vandana Peterson, 'Speeding Up Sexual Assault Trials: A Constructive Critique of India's Fast-Track Courts', *Yale Human Rights and Development Law Journal*, 1 (2016), p. 62.

15 Poulami Roychowdhury, 'Over the Law: Rape and the Seduction of Popular Politics', *Gender and Society*, XXX/1 (February 2016), p. 86.

16 Anu Ramdas, 'In Solidarity with All Rape Survivors', *Savari* (20 December 2012), at www.dalitweb.org.

17 Ibid. I am indebted to the discussion by Debolina Dutta and Oishik Sircar in 'India's Winter of Discontent: Some Feminist Dilemmas in the Wake of a Rape', *Feminist Studies*, XXXIX/1 (2013), p. 299.

18 Poulami Roychowdhury, 'The Delhi Gang Rape: The Making of International
   Causes', *Feminist Studies*, XXXIX/1 (2013), p. 284.

19 Ibid.

20 Ramesh, 'Women's Revenge against Rapists'.

21 Atreyee Sen, 'Women's Vigilantism in India: A Case Study of the Pink Sari
   Gang', at *Online Encyclopedia of Mass Violence* (20 December 2012), n.p., at
   www.sciencespo.fr, accessed 5 April 2020.

22 Ibid., and Amana Fontanella-Khan, *Pink Sari Revolution: A Tale of Women and
   Power in India* (New York, 2013).

23 Sen, 'Women's Vigilantism in India'.

24 Ibid.

25 'Chamania', cited in Sen, 'Women's Vigilantism in India'. Also see Partha
   Chatterjee, *The Politics of the Governed* (New York, 2004).

26 'The Westmorland Rape Case', *The Times* (29 August 1846), p. 6.

27 'At Clerkenwell', *The Times* (12 May 1886), p. 4.

28 Brett L. Shadle, 'Rape in the Courts of Guisiiland, Kenya', *African Studies
   Review*, LI/2 (September 2008), p. 42.

29 Sunday K. M. Anadi, 'Security and Crime Prevention in Under-Policed
   Societies: The Experiment of Community Vigilantism in Anambra State of
   Nigeria, West Africa', *Journal of Law, Policy, and Globalization*, 60 (2017), p. 122.

30 Daniel M. Goldstein, 'Flexible Justice: Neoliberal Violence and "Self-Help"
   Security in Bolivia', *Critique of Anthropology*, XXV/4 (2005), p. 400.

31 Angelina Snodgrass Godoy, 'Lynchings and the Democratization of Terror in
   Postwar Guatemala: Implications for Human Rights', *Human Rights Quarterly*,
   XXIV/3 (2002), p. 645.

32 Laurent Fourchard, 'The Politics of Mobilization for Security in South African
   Townships', *African Affairs*, CX/441 (October 2011), p. 624.

33 Paxton Quigley, *Armed and Female: 12 Million American Women Own Guns.
   Should You?* (New York, 1989); Quigley, *Armed and Female: 12 Million
   American Women Own Guns. Should You?* (New York, 1990); Quigley, *Not an
   Easy Target* (New York, 1995); Quigley, *Stayin' Alive: Armed and Female in an
   Unsafe World* (Bellevue, WA, 2005); Quigley, *Armed and Female: Taking Control*
   (Bellevue, WA, 2010). There is a huge overlap between all these books, with the
   same or similar stories recycled.

34 Quigley, *Stayin' Alive*, front flap.

35 Ibid., p. xvi. Also see George Flynn and Alan Gottlieb, *Guns for Women:
   The Complete Handgun Buying Guide for Women* (Bellevue, WA, 1988).

36 Quigley, *Armed and Female: Taking Control*, p. 5.

37 Quigley, *Armed and Female: 12 Million American Women Own Guns* (1989),
   p. 3.

38 Ibid., p. 40.

39 Ibid., p. 7. She does mention the race of victims, but not perpetrators.

40 Ibid., p. xiv.

41 Ibid., p. 7.

42 Quigley, *Stayin' Alive*, p. xv.

43 Quigley, *Armed and Female: 12 Million American Women Own Guns* (1989),
   pp. 47–8.

44 Joe Purshouse, '"Paedophile Hunters", Criminal Procedures, and Fundamental
   Human Rights', *Journal of Law and Society*, XLVII/3 (September 2020), p. 388.

45 Katerina Hadjimatheou, 'Citizen-Led Digital Policing and Democratic Norms: The Case of Self-Styled Paedophile Hunters', *Criminology and Criminal Justice*, XXI/4 (2019), p. 3.

46 Valerie Amos and Pratibha Parmar, 'Challenging Imperial Feminism', *Feminist Review*, 17 (Autumn 1984), p. 14.

47 Amy E. Nivette, 'Institutional Ineffectiveness, Illegitimacy, and Public Support for Vigilantism in Latin America', *Criminology*, LIV/1 (February 2016), p. 143.

48 Sen, 'Women's Vigilantism in India'.

49 Roychowdhury, 'Over the Law', p. 86.

50 Amrita Basu, 'The Dialectics of Hindu Nationalism', in *The Success of India's Democracy*, ed. Atul Kohli (New Delhi, 2001), pp. 163–89; Ratna Kapur and Brenda Crossman, '"Communalising Gender/Engendering Community": Women, Legal Discourse, Saffron Agenda', *Economic and Political Weekly*, XXVIII/17 (1993), pp. WS35–44; Patricia Jeffrey and Amrita Basu, *Appropriating Gender: Women's Activism and Politicized Religion in South Asia* (New York, 2012); Rajeswari Sunder Rojan, *Real and Imagined Women: Gender, Culture, and Postcolonialism* (London, 2003).

51 Roychowdhury, 'Over the Law', p. 87.

52 National Association for the Advancement of Colored People (NAACP), 'History of Lynchings', at www.naacp.org, accessed 1 December 2020.

53 Hortense Powdermaker, *After Freedom: A Cultural Study in the Deep South*, 1st pub. 1939 (New York, 1968), p. 389.

54 William Reynolds, 'The Remedy for Lynch Law', *Yale Law Journal*, VII/1 (October 1897), pp. 21–2.

55 Ibid., p. 20.

56 Luther Z. Rosser, 'Illegal Enforcement of Criminal Law', *American Bar Association Journal*, 7 (1921), pp. 519–24.

57 Jeffrey J. Pokorak, 'Rape as a Badge of Slavery: The Legal History of, and Remedies for, Prosecutorial Race-of-Victim Charging Disparities', *Nevada Law Journal*, VII/1 (Fall 2006), p. 25.

58 Lisa Lindquist Dorr, *White Women, Rape, and the Power of Race in Virginia, 1900–1960* (Chapel Hill, NC, 2004).

59 Diane Miller Sommerville, *Rape and Race in the Nineteenth-Century South* (Chapel Hill, NC, 2004), p. 126.

60 Ibid., p. 5.

61 Dorr, *White Women, Rape, and the Power of Race*.

62 Amirah Inglis, *The White Woman's Protection Ordinance: Sexual Anxiety and Politics in Papua* (London, 1975), and James A. Boutilier, 'European Women in the Solomon Islands, 1900–1942. Accommodation and Change on the Pacific Frontier', in *Rethinking Women's Roles: Perspectives from the Pacific*, ed. Denise O'Brien and Sharon W. Tiffany (Berkeley, CA, 1984), pp. 173–99.

63 *Natal Mercury* (19 February 1867), cited in Peter Spiller, 'Race and the Law in the District and Supreme Courts of Natal, 1846–1874', *South African Law Journal*, CI/3 (1984), p. 513. The judge was Justice Phillips.

64 Spiller, 'Race and the Law', p. 514.

65 *Rand Daily Mail* (19 September 1955), cited in B.V.D. van Diekerk, 'Hanged by the Neck until You Are Dead', *South African Law Journal*, LXXXVII/1 (1970), p. 60.

66 Van Diekerk, 'Hanged by the Neck', p. 60.

67 Richard von Krafft-Ebing, *Psychopathia Sexualis, with Especial Reference to Contrary Sexual Instinct: A Medico-Legal Study*, authorized trans. from German by Charles Gilbert Chaddock (Philadelphia, PA, 1892), p. 397.

68 Ibid., p. 378.

69 Ibid., p. 397.

70 Benjamin Karpman, *The Sexual Offender and His Offenses: Etiology, Pathology, Psychodynamics and Treatment* [1954], 9th edn (Washington, DC, 1964), p. 56.

71 Edward D. Hoedemaker, '"Irresistible Impulse" as a Defence in Criminal Law', *Washington Law Review*, XXIII/1 (February 1948), pp. 1–7, and Dwight D. Palmer, 'Conscious Motives in Psychopathic Behavior', *Proceedings of the American Academy of Forensic Sciences* (1954), pp. 146–9.

72 Albert Ellis, Ruth R. Doorbar and Robert Johnston III, 'Characteristics of Convicted Sex Offenders', *Journal of Social Psychology*, 40 (1954), pp. 10–11. Also see Ralph Brancale, Albert Ellis and Ruth R. Doorbar, 'Psychiatric and Psychological Investigations of Convicted Sex Offenders: A Summary Report', *American Journal of Psychiatry*, 109 (July 1952), p. 19.

73 George J. MacDonald and Robinson A. Williams, *Characteristics and Management of Committed Sexual Offenders in the State of Washington* (State of Washington, 1971), p. 9.

74 Miriam Ticktin, 'Sexual Violence as the Language of Border Control: Where French Feminist and Anti-Immigrant Rhetoric Meet', *Signs: Journal of Women in Culture and Society*, XXXIII/4 (Summer 2008), p. 871.

75 Christelle Hamel, '"Faire tourner les meufs". Les viols collectifs: Discours des médias et des agresseurs', *Gradhiva*, 33 (2003), pp. 85–92.

76 Quoting from *Midi Libre* on 11 September 2010; trans. and cited by Alice Debauche, '"They" Rape "Our" Women: When Racism and Sexism Intermingle', in *Violence against Women and Ethnicity: Commonalities and Differences across Europe*, ed. Ravi K. Thiara, Stephanie A. Condon and Monika Schröttle (Leverkusen, 2011), p. 344.

77 Homa Hoodfar, 'The Veil in Their Minds and on Our Heads: The Persistence of Colonial Images of Muslim Women', *Resources for Feminist Research*, XXII/3–4 (Fall 1992/Winter 1993), p. 7.

78 Jessica Harris and Sharon Grace, *A Question of Evidence? Investigating and Prosecuting Rape in the 1990s* (London, 1999), p. iii.

79 Haroon Siddique, '"We Are Facing the Decriminalisation of Rape", Warns Victims' Commissioner', *The Guardian* (14 July 2020), at www.theguardian. com, accessed 14 July 2020.

80 Roychowdhury, 'Over the Law'.

81 Audre Lorde, 'The Master's Tools Will Never Dismantle the Master's House', in *The Essential Feminist Reader*, ed. Estelle Freedman (New York, 2007), p. 332.

7 MILITARIZED RAPE

1 Hyanah Yang, 'Revisiting the Issue of Korean "Military Comfort Women": The Question of Truth and Positionality', *positions*, V/1 (1997), p. 60.

2 Gabriel Jonsson, 'Can the Japan-Korea Dispute on "Comfort Women" Be Resolved?', *Korea Observer*, XLVI/3 (Autumn 2015), p. 492.

3 David Andrew Schmidt, *Ianfu: The Comfort Women of the Japanese Imperial Army of the Pacific War* (Lewiston, NY, 2000), pp. 128–9.

4 Yuki Terazawa, 'The Transnational Campaigns for Redress for Wartime Rape by the Japanese Military: Cases for Survivors in Shanxi Province', *NWSA Journal*, XVIII/3 (Fall 2006), p. 133.

5 Yi Yŏngsuk, quoted in Keith Howard, ed., *True Stories of the Korean Comfort Women: Testimonies Compiled by the Korean Council for Women Drafted for Military Sexual Slavery by Japan and the Research Association on the Women Drafted for Military Sexual Slavery by Japan*, trans. Young Joo Lee (London, 1995), p. 56.

6 'Tetsuo Aso, Karyubyo no sekkyokuteki yoboho' ('Law for the Prevention of Sexually Transmitted Diseases') (1939), in Yeong-ae Yaamashita, 'Revisiting the "Comfort Women": Moving beyond Nationalism', trans. Malaya Ileto, in *Transforming Japan: How Feminism and Diversity Are Making a Difference*, ed. Kumiko Fujimura-Fanselow (New York, 2011), p. 368.

7 Tomo Shibata, 'Japan's Wartime Mass-Rape Camps and Continuing Sexual Human-Rights Violations', *U.S.-Japan Women's Journal. English Supplement*, 16 (1999), p. 57.

8 Yoshimi Yoshiaki, *Jugan Ianfu* (Tokyo, 1995), p. 2, cited in Shibata, 'Japan's Wartime Mass-Rape Camps', p. 58.

9 George Hicks, 'The Comfort Women Redress Movement', in *When Sorry Isn't Enough: The Controversy over Apologies and Reparations for Human Injustice*, ed. Roy L. Brooks (New York, 1999), p. 113.

10 Alice Yun Chai, 'Asian-Pacific Feminist Coalition Politics: The Chŏngshindae/Jūgunianfu ("Comfort Women") Movement', *Korean Studies*, 17 (1 January 1993), p. 74.

11 Vicki Sung-yeon Kwon, 'The Sonyŏsang Phenomenon: Nationalism and Feminism Surrounding the "Comfort Women"', *Korean Studies*, 43 (2019), p. 17.

12 Yang, 'Revisiting the Issue of Korean "Military Comfort Women"', p. 65.

13 Chai, 'Asian-Pacific Feminist Coalition Politics', p. 74, and Kwon, 'The Sonyŏsang Phenomenon', p. 14.

14 Yang, 'Revisiting the Issue of Korean "Military Comfort Women"', p. 56.

15 Hyeong-Jun Pak, 'News Reporting on Comfort Women: Framing, Frame Difference, and Frame Changing in Four South Korean and Japanese Newspapers, 1998–2013', *Journalism and Mass Communication Quarterly*, XCIII/4 (2016), p. 1007.

16 Cited in Hicks, 'The Comfort Women Redress Movement', p. 120.

17 Yoo Kyung Sung, 'Hearing the Voices of "Comfort Women": Confronting Historical Trauma in Korean Children's Literature', *Bookbird*, 1 (2012), p. 21.

18 Hyun Sook Kim, 'History and Memory: The "Comfort Women" Controversy', *positions*, V/1 (1997), p. 79.

19 Jordan Sand, 'Historians and Public Memory in Japan: The "Comfort Women" Controversy; Introduction', *History and Memory*, XI/2 (31 December 1995), p. 117.

20 Ibid.

21 Hicks, 'The Comfort Women Redress Movement', p. 115.

22 Cited in Chai, 'Asian-Pacific Feminist Coalition Politics', p. 79.

23 Cited in Kim, 'History and Memory', p. 98. This is from Korean Council, *Witness of the Victims of Military Sexual Slavery* (Seoul, 1992), p. 86, and can be found in Howard, ed., *True Stories of the Korean Comfort Women*.

24 Chai, 'Asian-Pacific Feminist Coalition Politics', p. 80.

25 See the exceptional website of international research group SVAC (Sexual Violence in Armed Conflicts), at www.warandgender.net, accessed 1 October 2020.

26 Ruth Harris, 'The "Child of the Barbarian": Rape, Race and Nationalism in France during the First World War', *Past and Present*, 141 (November 1993), p. 172.

27 Viscount James Bryce, *Report of the Committee on Alleged German Outrages* (London, 1915), at http://digital.slv.vic.gov.au, accessed 1 November 2020.

28 Harris, 'The "Child of the Barbarian"', p. 179.

29 J. Murray Allison, compiler, *Raemaekers' Cartoon History of the War*, vol. 1 (London, 1919), p. i.

30 Christopher Browning, *Remembering Survival: Inside a Nazi Slave-Labor Camp* (New York, 2010), pp. 185–91, and Steven T. Katz, 'Thoughts on the Intersection of Rape and *Rassenschande* during the Holocaust', *Modern Judaism*, XXXII/3 (October 2012), p. 295.

31 See my book, *Rape: A History from the 1860s to the Present* (London, 2007).

32 Miranda Alison, 'Wartime Sexual Violence: Women's Human Rights and Questions of Masculinity', *Review of International Studies*, XXXIII/1 (January 2007), p. 77.

33 Regina Mühlhäuser, 'Between "Racial Awareness" and Fantasies of Potency: Nazi Sexual Politics in the Occupied Territories of the Soviet Union, 1942–1945', in *Brutality and Desire: War and Sexuality in Europe's Twentieth Century*, ed. Dagmar Herzog (Basingstoke, 2009), p. 201.

34 Pascha Bueno-Hansen, *Feminism and Human Rights Struggles in Peru: Decolonizing Transitional Justice* (Urbana, IL, 2015), p. 125.

35 Veena Das, *Critical Events: An Anthropological Perspective on Contemporary India* (Delhi, 1995), p. 56.

36 Alison, 'Wartime Sexual Violence', p. 80.

37 Ruth Seifert, 'War and Rape: A Preliminary Analysis', in *Mass Rape: The War against Women in Bosnia-Herzegovina*, ed. Alexandra Stiglmayer (London, 1994), pp. 62–4.

38 Jan Perlin, 'The Guatemalan Historical Clarification Commission Finds Genocide', *ILSA Journal of International and Comparative Law*, VI/2 (2000), p. 408.

39 Megan H. MacKenzie, *Female Soldiers in Sierra Leone: Sex, Security, and Post-Conflict Development* (New York, 2012), p. 100.

40 Iris Chang, *The Rape of Nanking: The Forgotten Holocaust of World War II* (New York, 1997).

41 Schmidt, *Ianfu*, pp. 87–8.

42 For a discussion of rape committed by American soldiers, see my book, *Rape: A History from the 1860s to the Present*, and J. Robert Lilly, *La Face cachée des GI's: Les viols commis par des soldats américains en France, en Angleterre et en Allemagne pendant la Seconde Guerre mondiale* (Paris, 2003).

43 Robert Sommer, *Das KZ-Bordell: Sexuelle Zwangsarbeit in nationalsozialistischen Konzentrationslagern* (Paderborn, 2009), and Myrna Goldenberg, 'Sex, Rape, and Survival: Jewish Women and the Holocaust', at www.theverylongview.com, accessed 31 January 2015.

44 Krisztián Ungváry, *The Battle for Budapest: 100 Days in World War II*, trans. Ladislaus Löb (London, 2002), p. 289.

45 Richard W. McCormick, 'Rape and War, Gender and Nation, Victims and Victimizers: Helke Sander's *Befreir und Befreite*', *Camera Obscura*, XVI/1 (2001), p. 131.

46 Anonymous [Marta Hiller], *Eine Frau in Berlin: Tagebuchaufzeichnungen vom 20. April bis 22. Juni 1945,* 1st pub. 1959 (Frankfurt, 2003).

47 Boris Slutsky, *Things That Happened*, ed. G. S. Smith (Birmingham, 1998), pp. 147–8.

48 Madeline Morris, 'By Force of Arms: Rape, War, and Military Culture', *Duke Law Journal*, XLV/4 (February 1996), p. 170.

49 J. Robert Lilly, *Taken by Force: Rape and American GIs in Europe during World War II* (Basingstoke, 2007).

50 Veena Das, 'National Honour and Practical Kingship: Of Unwanted Women and Children', in *Critical Events*, ed. Veena Das (Delhi, 1995), pp. 345–98; Urvashi Butalia, 'Community, State, and Gender: On Women's Agency during Partition', *Economic and Political Weekly*, XXVIII/17 (24 April 1993), pp. WD12–WS24; Ritu Menon and Kamla Bhasin, 'Recovery, Rupture, Resistance: Indian State and Abduction of Women during Partition', *Economic and Political Weekly*, XXVIII/17 (24 April 1993), pp. WS2–11; Ritu Menon and Kamla Bhasin, *Borders and Boundaries: Women in India's Partition* (New Brunswick, NJ, 1998).

51 Sarmila Bose, 'Losing the Victims: Problems of Using Women as Weapons in Recounting the Bangladesh War', *Economic and Political Weekly*, XLII/38 (22–8 September 2007), p. 3864; S. Kamal, 'The 1971 Genocide in Bangladesh and Crimes Committed against Women', in *Common Grounds: Violence against Women in War and Armed Conflict Situations,* ed. I. L. Sajor (Quezon City, Philippines, 1998), pp. 268–81; S. U. Habiba, 'Mass Rape and Violence in the 1971 Armed Conflict of Bangladesh: Justice and Other Issues', in *Common Grounds*, ed. Sajor, pp. 257–67.

52 Bose, 'Losing the Victims', p. 3864.

53 Jean Franco, 'Rape and Human Rights', *PMLA*, CXXI/5 (October 2006), p. 1663.

54 Binaifer Nowrojee, *Shattered Lives: Sexual Violence during the Rwandan Genocide and Its Aftermath* (New York, 1996); Lisa Sharlach, 'Gender and Genocide in Rwanda: Women as Agents and Objects of Genocide', *Journal of Genocide Research*, 1 (1999), p. 393; Rachel Rinaldo, 'Women Survivors of the Rwandan Genocide Face Grim Realities', *IPS News* (6 April 2004), at www.ipsnews.net (accessed 31 January 2015); Patricia A. Weitsman, 'The Politics of Identity and Sexual Violence: A Review of Bosnia and Rwanda', *Human Rights Quarterly*, XXX/3 (August 2008), p. 573; Jennie E. Burnet, 'Situating Sexual Violence in Rwanda (1990–2001): Sexual Agency, Sexual Consent, and the Political Economy of War', *African Studies Review*, LV/2 (September 2012), p. 98.

55 Burnet, 'Situating Sexual Violence in Rwanda', p. 98, and Sharlach, 'Gender and Genocide in Rwanda', p. 387.

56 Dulce Foster et al., *A House with Two Rooms: Final Report of the Truth and Reconciliation Commission of Liberia Diaspora Project* (Saint Paul, MN, 2009), p. 236.

57 Sara Kuipers Cummings, 'Liberia's New War: Post-Conflict Strategies for Confronting Rape and Sexual Violence', *Arizona State Law Journal*, XLIII/1 (2011), pp. 234–5.

58 Mary H. Moran, *Liberia: The Violence of Democracy* (Philadelphia, PA, 2006), p. 162.

59 Rhonda Copelon, 'Surfacing Gender: Reconceptualizing Crimes against
   Women in Times of War', in *The Women and War Reader*, ed. Lois Ann
   Lorentzen and Jennifer Turpin (New York, 1988), p. 245.

60 Heather M. Turcotte, 'Contextualizing Petro-Sexual Politics', *Alternatives:
   Global, Local, Political*, XXXVI/3 (August 2011), p. 207.

61 Sara Meger, 'Rape in Contemporary Warfare: The Role of Globalization
   in Wartime Sexual Violence', *African Conflict and Peacebuilding Review*,
   I/1 (Spring 2011), p. 118.

62 Ola Olsson and Heather Congdon Fors, 'Congo: The Prize of Predation',
   Journal of Peace Research, XLI/3 (May 2004), p. 326.

63 Meger, 'Rape in Contemporary Warfare', p. 125.

64 For a discussion, see Dunia Prince Zongwe, 'The New Sexual Violence
   Legislation in the Congo: Dressing Indelible Scars on Human Dignity', *African
   Studies Review*, LV/2 (September 2012), pp. 37–57.

65 Amnesty International, *No End to War on Women and Children: North Kivu,
   Democratic Republic of the Congo* (29 September 2008), at www.amnesty.org.
   These statistics were based on 410 women who sought treatment for injuries
   sustained by rape in parts of Lubero (North Kivu).

66 Francis Lieber, *Instructions for the Government of Armies of the United States in
   the Field, General Orders no. 100* (24 April 1863), no. 44, at http://avalon.law.
   yale.edu.

67 Kelly D. Askin, 'Sexual Violence in Decisions and Indictments of the Yugoslav
   and Rwandan Tribunals: Current Status', *American Journal of International Law*,
   XCIII/1 (1999), p. 98.

68 Ibid., pp. 202–3.

69 Aryeh Neier and Laurel Fletcher, 'Rape as a Weapon of War in the Former
   Yugoslavia', *Hastings Women's Law Journal*, 5 (1994), pp. 69 and 77; Aryeh Neier,
   'Watching Rights: Rapes in Bosnia-Herzegovina', *The Nation* (1 March 1993),
   p. 259, and 'EC Investigative Mission into the Treatment of Muslim Women in
   the Former Yugoslavia: Report to EC Foreign Ministers', Warburton Mission
   Report (February 1993), at www.womenaid.org. For higher estimates, see
   Andrew Bell-Fialkoff, 'A Brief History of Ethnic Cleansing', *Foreign Affairs*,
   LXXII/3 (Summer 1993), pp. 110–19; Norma von Ragenfeld-Feldman, 'The
   Victimization of Women: Rape and Reporting in Bosnia-Herzegovina, 1992–
   1993', *Dialogue*, 21 (March 1997), at http://members.tripod.com, accessed 31
   January 2015; Todd A. Salzman, 'Rape Camps as a Means of Ethnic Cleansing:
   Religious, Cultural, and Ethnical Responses to Rape Victims in the Former
   Yugoslavia', *Human Rights Quarterly*, XX/2 (May 1998), p. 348.

70 Siobhán K. Fisher, 'Occupation of the Womb: Forced Impregnation as
   Genocide', *Duke Law Journal*, XLVII/1 (1996), p. 113, and Patricia A. Weitsman,
   'The Politics of Identity and Sexual Violence: A Review of Bosnia and Rwanda',
   Human Rights Quarterly, XXX/3 (August 2008), pp. 559–71.

71 Jill Benderly, 'Rape, Feminism, and Nationalism in the War in Yugoslav
   Successor States', in *Feminist Nationalism*, ed. Lois A. West (New York, 1997),
   p. 67.

72 *Globus* (11 December 1992), cited by Jelena Batinic, 'Feminism, Nationalism,
   and the War: The "Yugoslav Case" in Feminist Texts', *Journal of International
   Women's Studies*, III/1 (November 2001), p. 9, at http://vc.bridgew.edu, accessed
   1 November 2020.

73 Dubravka Zarkov, 'Gender, Orientalism and the History of Ethnic Hatred in the Former Yugoslavia,' in *Crossfires: Nationalism, Racism and Gender in Europe*, ed. Helma Lutz, Ann Phoenix and Nira Yuval-Davis (London, 1995), p. 114.

74 See www.women-war-memory.org.

75 Women in Black, 'Women in Black against War: A Letter to the Women's Meeting in Amsterdam on the 8th of March 1993', *Women Magazine* (December 1993), pp. 17–18.

76 Diane Conklin, 'Special Note', in Seada Vranic, *Breaking the Wall of Silence: The Voices of Raped Bosnia* (Zagreb, 1996), p. 20.

77 Beverly Allen, *Rape Warfare: The Hidden Genocide in Bosnia-Herzegovina and Croatia* (Minneapolis, MN, 1996), p. 316.

78 Miranda Alison, personal communication, 2014.

79 Kelly Dawn Askin, *War Crimes against Women: Prosecution in International War Crimes Tribunals* (The Hague, 1997), p. 263. Also see Catherine N. Niarchos, 'Women, War, and Rape: Challenges Facing the International Tribunal for the Former Yugoslavia', *Human Rights Quarterly*, 17 (1995).

80 ICTY, 'Celebici Case: The Judgement of the Trial Chamber' (16 November 1998), at www.icty.org, and ICTY, 'Furundzija', at www.icty.org.

81 Seifert, 'War and Rape', p. 54, and Fisher, 'Occupation of the Womb', pp. 91–133.

82 Karen Engle, 'Feminism and Its (Dis)contents: Criminalizing Wartime Rape in Bosnia and Herzegovina', *American Journal of International Law*, XCIX/4 (October 2005), p. 788.

83 Robyn Charli Carpenter, 'Surfacing Children: Limitations of Genocidal Rape Discourse', *Human Rights Quarterly*, XXII/2 (May 2000), p. 455.

84 Engle, 'Feminism and Its (Dis)contents', p. 808. Also see Tone Bringa, *Being Muslim the Bosnian Way: Identity and Community in a Central Bosnian Village* (Princeton, NJ, 1988), p. 151, and Weitsman, 'The Politics of Identity and Sexual Violence', p. 571.

85 For the best discussion, especially about the legal construction of memory, see Kirsten Campbell, 'Legal Memories: Sexual Assault, Memory, and International Humanitarian Law', *Signs: Journal of Women in Culture and Society*, XXVIII/1 (Autumn 2002), pp. 149–78.

86 Debra Bergoffen, 'February 22, 2001: Toward a Politics of the Vulnerable Body', *Hypatia*, XVIII/1 (Winter 2003), p. 117.

87 Dara Kay Cohen and Ragnhild Nordås, 'Sexual Violence in Armed Conflicts: Introducing the SVAC-Africa Dataset, 1989–2009', unpublished working paper (2012), cited in Dara Kay Cohen, Amelia Hoover Green and Elisabeth Jean Wood, 'Wartime Sexual Violence: Misconceptions, Implications, and Ways Forward', *United States Institute of Peace Special Report*, Report 323 (Washington, DC, February 2013), p. 3, at www.usip.org, accessed 1 October 2020.

88 Cohen, Green and Wood, 'Wartime Sexual Violence', p. 2. Also see Elisabeth Jean Wood, 'Variation in Sexual Violence during War', *Politics and Society*, XXXIV/3 (2006), pp. 307–42.

89 Cohen, Green and Wood, 'Wartime Sexual Violence', p. 3. Also see Amelia Hoover Green, Dara Cohen and Elisabeth Wood, 'Is Wartime Rape Declining on a Global Scale? We Don't Know – And It Doesn't Matter', *Political Violence at a Glance*, blog (1 November 2012), at www.politicalviolenceataglance.org, accessed 1 November 2020.

90 Cohen, Green and Wood, 'Wartime Sexual Violence', p. 3.

91 Ibid., p. 34.

92 Mark A. Drumbl, 'She Makes Me Ashamed to Be a Woman: The Genocide Conviction of Pauline Nyiramasuhuko', *Michigan Journal of International Law*, XXXIV/3 (2013), p. 588.

93 Régine Michelle Jean-Charles, *Conflict Bodies: The Politics of Rape Representation in the Francophone Imaginary* (Columbus, OH, 2014), p. 3.

94 Anne G. Sadler et al., 'Health-Related Consequences of Physical and Sexual Violence: Women in the Military', *Obstetrics and Gynecology*, XCVI/3 (September 2000), p. 473.

95 Megan MacKenzie, *Beyond the Band of Brothers: The U.S. Military and the Myth That Women Can't Fight* (Cambridge, 2015).

96 Heide Fehrenbach, *Race after Hitler: Occupation Children in Postwar Germany and America* (Princeton, NJ, 2018), p. 50.

97 Ibid., p. 51.

98 For a discussion, see James Mark, 'Remembering Rape: Divided Social Memory and the Red Army in Hungary, 1944–1945', *Past and Present*, 188 (August 2005), pp. 140–42.

99 Ibid., pp. 140–60.

100 Yasmin Saikia, *Women, War, and the Making of Bangladesh: Remembering 1971* (Durham, NC, 2011), p. 79.

101 Yuki Terazawa, 'The Transnational Campaigns for Redress for Wartime Rape by the Japanese Military: Cases for Survivors in Shanxi Province', *NWSA Journal*, XVIII/3 (Fall 2006), p. 139.

102 Ibid., p. 133.

103 Jennie E. Burnet, 'Situating Sexual Violence in Rwanda (1990–2001): Sexual Agency, Sexual Consent, and the Political Economy of War', *African Studies Review*, LV/2 (September 2012), p. 110.

104 Azad Essa, 'UN Peacekeepers Hit by New Allegations of Sex Abuse', *Al-Jazeera* (10 July 2017), at www.aljazeera.com, accessed 1 August 2020.

105 Bernd Beber et al., 'Peacekeeping, Compliance with International Norms, and Transitional Sex in Monrovia, Liberia', *International Organization*, LXXI/1 (Winter 2017), p. 11.

106 Cited in Pearl Karuhanga Atuhaire et al., *The Elusive Peace: Ending Sexual Violence during and after Conflict* (Washington, DC, 2018), p. 4.

107 Kwon, 'The Sonyŏsang Phenomenon', p. 8.

108 Ibid., pp. 11–12.

109 Hiroki Yamamoto, 'Socially Engaged Art in Postcolonial Japan: An Alternative View of Contemporary Japanese Art', *World Art*, XI/1 (2020), p. 13.

110 A photograph can be seen ibid., p. 12.

111 Kwon, 'The Sonyŏsang Phenomenon', p. 8.

112 Ibid., p. 23.

113 Ibid., p. 24.

114 Young-Hee Shim, 'Metamorphosis of the Korean "Comfort Women": How Did *Han* Turn into the Cosmopolitan Morality?', *Development and Society*, XLVI/2 (September 2017), p. 252.

115 Cited in Na-Young Lee, 'The Korean Women's Movement of Japanese Military "Comfort Women": Navigating between Nationalism and Feminism', *Review of Korean Studies*, XVII/1 (2014), p. 86.

116 Trans. Na-Young Lee, 'The Korean Women's Movement of Japanese Military "Comfort Women"', p. 85.

117 Cited in Chai, 'Asian-Pacific Feminist Coalition Politics', p. 85.

118 Purvi Mehta, 'Dalit Feminism in Tokyo: Analogy and Affiliation in Transnational Dalit Activism', *Feminist Review*, 121 (2019), p. 30.

119 Unnamed woman in Asian Women's Human Rights Council, *In the Court of Women II: Asia Tribunal on Women's Human Rights in Tokyo. Proceedings of the International Public Hearing on Traffic in Women and War Crimes against Women* (Kathmandu, 1994), p. 81.

8 TRAUMA

1 Laura S. Brown, 'Not Outside the Range: One Feminist Perspective on Psychic Trauma', in *Trauma: Explorations in Memory*, ed. Cathy Caruth (Baltimore, MD, 1995), p. 107.

2 'Extraordinary Case of Rape', *The Times* (28 October 1833), p. 4 and 'Extraordinary Case of Rape', *Globe* (28 October 1833), p. 3. Both claimed to be publishing an abridged version of the report in the *Manchester Chronicle*.

3 Ambroise Tardieu, *Étude médico-légale sur les attentats aux mœurs* (Paris, 1878).

4 Sigmund Freud, *Beyond the Pleasure Principle and Other Writings*, trans. John Reddick (London, 2003).

5 Sándor Ferenczi, *First Contributions to Psycho-Analysis*, trans. Ernest Jones (London, 2018); Pierre Maria Félix Janet, *État mental des hystériques* (Paris, 1894); Pierre Maria Félix Janet, *L'Automatisme psychologique* [1889] (Paris, 1930).

6 Charles R. Hayman et al., 'A Public Health Program for Sexually Assaulted Females', *Public Health Reports*, LXXXII/6 (June 1967), pp. 503–4. This wasn't through lack of demand, since when the District of Columbia Department of Public Health finally got around to initiating a follow-up service in 1965, 290 out of 322 assault women and girls eagerly accepted the help.

7 Joan Skirnick in Frederick P. Zuspan, 'Alleged Rape: An Invitational Symposium', *Journal of Reproductive Medicine*, XII/4 (April 1974), pp. 144–6.

8 Chaplain H. Rex Lewis in Zuspan, 'Alleged Rape', pp. 144–53.

9 L. Radzinowicz, *Sexual Offences: A Report of the Cambridge Department of Criminal Science* (London, 1957), p. 104.

10 Ann Wolbert Burgess, 'Putting Trauma on the Radar', in *Mapping Trauma and Its Wake: Autobiographical Essays by Pioneer Trauma Scholars*, ed. Charles R. Figley (New York, 2006), p. 19.

11 Ann Wolbert Burgess and Lynda Lytle Holmstrom, 'Rape Trauma Syndrome', *American Journal of Psychiatry*, 981 (1974), pp. 981–6.

12 Sandra Sutherland and Donald J. Scherl, 'Patterns of Response among Victims of Rape', *American Journal of Orthopsychiatry*, XL/3 (April 1970), pp. 503–11.

13 Debbie Hatmaker, 'Vital Signs: A SANE Approach to Sexual Violence', *American Journal of Nursing*, XCVII/8 (August 1997), p. 80.

14 May Duddle, 'The Need for Sexual Assault Centres in the United Kingdom', *British Medical Journal* (9 March 1985), p. 771.

15 Ian Blair, *Investigating Rape: A New Approach for Police* (London, 1985), pp. 30–31.

16 American Psychiatric Association, *Diagnostic and Statistical Manual of Mental Disorders*, 3rd edn (Washington, DC, 1980), p. 236.

17 Ibid.

18 Renato D. Alareón et al., 'Beyond the Funhouse Mirrors: Research Agenda on Culture and Psychiatric Diagnosis', in *A Research Agenda for DSM-V*, ed. David J. Kupfer, Michael B. First and Darrel A. Regier (Washington, DC, 2002), p. 241.

19 For a detailed, theoretical discussion, see my article 'Pain: Metaphor, Body, and Culture in Anglo-American Societies from the Eighteenth Century to the Present', *Rethinking History: The Journal of Theory and Practice*, XVIII/4 (October 2014), pp. 475–98.

20 For example, see Charlotte Blease, 'Scientific Progress and the Prospects for Culture-Bound Syndromes', *Studies in History and Philosophy of Biological and Biomedical Sciences*, 41 (2010), pp. 333–9; Havi Carel and Rachel Cooper, 'Introduction: Culture-Bound Syndromes', *Studies in History and Philosophy of Biological and Biomedical Sciences*, 41 (2010), pp. 307–8; Rachel Cooper, 'Are Culture-Bound Syndromes as Real as Universally-Occurring Disorders?', *Studies in History and Philosophy of Biological and Biomedical Sciences*, 41 (2010), pp. 325–32; Laurence J. Kirmayer, 'Cultural Variations in the Clinical Presentation of Depression and Anxiety: Implications for Diagnosis and Treatment', *Journal of Clinical Psychiatry*, 62 (2001), pp. 22–30; Anthony J. Marsella et al., eds, *Ethnocultural Aspects of Post-Traumatic Stress Disorder: Issues, Research, and Clinical Applications* (Washington, DC, 1996).

21 Pow Meng Yap, 'Words and Things in Comparative Psychiatry, with Special Reference to the Exotic Psychoses', *Acta Psychiatrica Scandinavica*, 38 (1962), pp. 163–9, and Pow Meng Yap, '"Koro" – A Culture-Bound Depersonalization Syndrome', *British Journal of Psychiatry*, 111 (1965), pp. 43–50. He had discussed cultural differences in responses to trauma a decade before using the term: see Pow Meng Yap, 'Mental Distress Peculiar to Certain Cultures: A Study of Comparative Psychiatry', *Journal of Mental Science*, 97 (1951), pp. 313–27.

22 Arthur Kleinman, 'Anthropology and Psychiatry: The Role of Culture in Cross-Cultural Research on Illness', *British Journal of Psychiatry*, 151 (1987), p. 452. Also see Patrick J. Bracken, Joan E. Giller and James K. Scekiwenuka, 'The Rehabilitation of Child Soldiers: Defining Needs and Appropriate Responses', *Medicine, Conflict, and Survival*, XII/2 (April–June 1996), p. 120.

23 Derek Summerfield, 'A Critique of Seven Assumptions behind the Psychological Trauma Programmes in War-Affected Areas', *Social Science and Medicine*, 48 (1999), p. 1449.

24 Ibid., p. 1454.

25 Brandon Kohrt and Daniel J. Hruschka, 'Nepali Concepts of Psychological Trauma: The Role of Idioms of Distress, Ethnopsychology, and Ethnophysiology in Alleviating Suffering and Preventing Stigma', *Culture, Medicine, and Psychiatry*, 34 (2010), p. 333.

26 Ibid., p. 334.

27 Katrin Fabian et al., '"My Heart Die In Me": Idioms of Distress and the Development of a Screening Tool for Mental Suffering in Southeast Liberia', *Culture, Medicine, and Psychiatry*, 42 (2018), p. 686.

28 Duncan Pedersen, Hanna Kienzler and Jeffrey Gamarra, '*Llaki* and *Ñakary*: Idioms of Distress and Suffering among Highland Quechua in the Peruvian Andes', *Culture, Medicine, and Psychiatry*, 34 (2010), pp. 279–300.

29 Bruce D. Smith et al., 'Ethnomedical Syndromes and Treatment-Seeking

Behavior among Mayan Refugees in Chiapas, Mexico', *Culture, Medicine, and Psychiatry*, 33 (2009), pp. 367–8.

30 Ibid., p. 368.

31 Ibid.

32 Howard Waitzkin and Holly Magaña, 'The Black Box in Somatization: Unexplained Physical Symptoms, Culture, and Narratives of Trauma', *Social Science and Medicine*, XLV/6 (1997), p. 818.

33 Fabian et al., '"My Heart Die In Me"', p. 697.

34 Waitzkin and Magaña, 'The Black Box in Somatization', p. 818.

35 Young-Hee Shim, 'Metamorphosis of the Korean "Comfort Women": How Did *Han* Turn into the Cosmopolitan Morality?', *Development and Society*, XLVI/2 (September 2017), p. 253.

36 Cited ibid., p. 257. He is quoting from Boo-wong Yoo, *Korean Pentecostalism: Its History and Theology* (New York, 1988), p. 221.

37 Shim, 'Metamorphosis of the Korean "Comfort Women"', p. 264.

38 Devon E. Hinton et al., '*Khyâl* Attacks: A Key Idiom of Distress among Traumatized Cambodian Refugees', *Culture, Medicine, and Psychiatry*, 34 (2010), p. 245.

39 Ibid., pp. 244–5.

40 For a discussion, see Arthur Kleinman, 'Anthropology and Psychiatry: The Role of Culture in Cross-Cultural Research on Illness', *British Journal of Psychiatry*, 151 (1987), p. 450.

41 Maggie Zraly and Laetilia Nyirazinyoye, 'Don't Let Suffering Make You Fade Away: An Ethnographic Study of Resilience among Survivors of Genocide-Rape in Southern Rwanda', *Social Science and Medicine*, 70 (2010), p. 1656.

42 Ibid., pp. 1659–60.

43 Smith et al., 'Ethnomedical Syndromes and Treatment-Seeking Behavior among Mayan Refugees', p. 374.

44 American Psychiatric Association, *Diagnostic and Statistical Manual of Mental Disorders*, 4th edn (Washington, DC, 1994), pp. 829–49 (Appendix I).

45 James Phillips, 'The Cultural Dimension of DSM-5: PTSD', *Psychiatric Times* (15 August 2010), n.p. Emphasis added.

46 Ibid.

47 Ethan Watters, *Crazy Like Us: The Globalization of the American Psyche* (New York, 2010).

48 Rachel Hall, '"It Can Happen to You": Rape Prevention in the Age of Risk Management', *Hypatia: A Journal of Feminist Philosophy*, XIX/3 (2004), p. 3.

49 Carine M. Mardorossian, 'Toward a New Feminist Theory of Rape', *Signs: Journal of Women in Culture and Society*, XXVII/3 (Spring 2002), p. 768.

50 Linda Alcoff and Laura Gray, 'Survivor Discourse: Transgression or Recuperation?', *Signs: Journal of Women in Culture and Society*, XVIII/2 (Winter 1993), p. 281.

51 Beth Goldblatt and Sheila Meintjes, 'Dealing with the Aftermath: Sexual Violence and the Truth and Reconciliation Commission', *Agenda: Empowering Women for Gender Equity*, 36 (1997), p. 11.

52 Jessica Duarte, in unpublished workshop proceedings, cited by Goldblatt and Meintjes, 'Dealing with the Aftermath', p. 11.

53 Alcoff and Gray, 'Survivor Discourse', p. 281.

54 Pablo Piccato, '"El Chalequero" or the Mexican Jack the Ripper: The Meanings

of Sexual Violence in Turn-of-the-Century Mexico City', *Hispanic American Historical Review*, LXXXI/3–4 (August–November 2001), p. 636.

55 Unnamed court interpreter speaking on 26 June 2006 to Jonneke Koomen, '"Without These Women, the Tribunal Cannot Do Anything": The Politics of Witness Testimony on Sexual Violence at the International Criminal Tribunal for Rwanda', *Signs: Journal of Women in Culture and Society*, XXXVIII/2 (Winter 2013), pp. 265–6.

56 Summerfield, 'A Critique of Seven Assumptions', p. 1455.

57 Smith et al., 'Ethnomedical Syndromes and Treatment-Seeking Behavior among Mayan Refugees', p. 376.

58 Theresa De Langis, 'Speaking Private Memory to Public Power: Oral History and Breaking the Silence on Sexual and Gender-Based Violence during the Khmer Rouge Genocide', in *Beyond Women's Words: Feminisms and the Practices of Oral History in the Twenty-First Century*, ed. Katrina Srigley, Stacey Zembrzycki and Franca Iacovetta (London, 2018), p. 166.

59 J. David Kinzie, 'A Model for Treating Refugees Traumatized by Violence', *Psychiatric Times* (10 July 2009), n.p.

60 Neil Boothby, 'Displaced Children: Psychological Theory and Practice from the Field', *Journal of Refugee Studies*, V/2 (1992), p. 107.

61 For an in-depth analysis, see John P. Wilson, 'Culture, Trauma, and the Treatment of Post-Traumatic Syndromes: A Global Perspective', in *Ethnocultural Perspectives on Disasters and Trauma: Foundations, Issues, and Applications*, ed. Anthony J. Marsella et al. (New York, 2008), pp. 351–75.

62 Nick Higginbotham and Anthony J. Marsella, 'International Consultation and the Homogenization of Psychiatry in Southeast Asia', *Social Science and Medicine*, XXVII/5 (1988), pp. 557–9.

63 Summerfield, 'A Critique of Seven Assumptions', p. 1449.

64 Joseph Breslau, 'Cultures of Trauma: Anthropological Views of Posttraumatic Stress Disorder in International Health', *Culture, Medicine, and Psychiatry*, XXVIII/2 (2004), pp. 113–26.

65 P. J. Bracken, J. E. Giller and D. Summerfield, 'Psychological Responses to War and Atrocity: The Limitations of Current Concepts', *Social Science and Medicine*, XL/8 (1995), pp. 1073–82; D. Silove, 'The Asylum Debacle in Australia: A Challenge for Psychiatry', *Australian and New Zealand Journal of Psychiatry*, XXXVI/3 (2002), pp. 290–96; M. C. Smith Fawzi et al., 'The Validity of Screening for Post-Traumatic Stress Disorder and Major Depression amongst Vietnamese Former Political Prisoners', *Acta Psychiatrica Scandinavica*, XCV/2 (1997), pp. 87–93.

9 A RAPE-FREE WORLD

1 The most notorious example is Randy Thornhill and Craig T. Palmer, *A Natural History of Rape: Biological Bases of Sexual Coercion* (Cambridge, MA, 2000).

2 For a detailed analysis, see Elisabeth J. Wood, 'Armed Groups and Sexual Violence: When Is Wartime Rape Rare?', *Politics and Society*, XXXVII/1 (March 2009), pp. 131–61.

3 For a discussion, see Robert M. Hayden, 'Rape and Rape Avoidance in Ethno-National Conflicts: Sexual Violence in Liminalized States', *American Anthropologist*, new series, CI/1 (March 2000), pp. 27–41.

4 Mary Kaldor, *New and Old Wars: Organized Violence in a Global Era* (Cambridge, 1999).

5 Elisabeth J. Wood, 'Variation in Sexual Violence during War', *Politics and Society*, XXXIV/3 (September 2006), pp. 307–41, and Wood, 'Armed Groups and Sexual Violence', pp. 131–61.

6 Peggy Reeves Sanday, 'The Socio-Cultural Context of Rape: A Cross-Cultural Study', *Journal of Social Issues*, 37 (1981), pp. 5–27, and Peggy Reeves Sanday, 'Rape-Free versus Rape-Prone: How Culture Makes a Difference', in *Evolution, Gender, and Rape*, ed. Cheryl Brown Travis (Cambridge, MA, 2003), pp. 337–62. Also see Gwen J. Broude and Sarah J. Greene, 'Cross-Cultural Codes on Twenty Sexual Attitudes and Practices', *Ethnology*, XV/4 (1976), pp. 409–30.

7 Maria-Barbara Watson-Franke, 'A World in Which Women Move Freely without Fear of Men: An Anthropological Perspective on Rape', *Women's Studies International Forum*, XXV/6 (2002), p. 601.

8 Christine Helliwell, '"It's Only a Penis": Rape, Feminism, and Difference', *Signs: Journal of Women in Culture and Society*, XXV/3 (Spring 2000), p. 795.

9 Ibid., p. 799.

10 Ibid., p. 800.

11 Ibid., pp. 800 and 804.

12 Ibid., p. 808.

13 Hollaback website, at www.ihollaback.org, accessed 1 December 2020.

14 Christopher Hensley, Tammy Castle and Richard Tewksbury, 'Inmate-on-Inmate Sexual Coercion in a Prison for Women', *Journal of Offender Rehabilitation*, XXXVII/2 (2003), pp. 77–87, and Christopher D. Man and John P. Cronan, 'Forecasting Sexual Abuse in Prison: The Prison Subculture of Masculinity as a Backdrop for Deliberate Indifference', *Journal of Criminal Law and Criminology*, XCII/1 (Fall 2001), pp. 127–85.

15 Lisa Sharlach, 'State Regulation of Rape Insurance and HIV Prevention in India and South Africa', a paper presented at the American Political Science Association meeting (3 September 2009), at https://ssrn.com, accessed 11 January 2021.

16 For a discussion, see Dunia Prince Zongwe, 'The New Sexual Violence Legislation in the Congo: Dressing Indelible Scars on Human Dignity', *African Studies Review*, LV/2 (September 2012), p. 40, and David Carey Jr, 'Forced and Forbidden Sex: Rape and Sexual Freedom in Dictatorial Guatemala', *The Americas*, LXIX/3 (January 2013), p. 362.

17 Kristin Bumiller, *In an Abusive State: How Neoliberalism Appropriated the Feminist Movement against Sexual Violence* (Durham, NC, 2008), and Rose Corrigan, *Up Against a Wall: Rape Reform and the Failure of Success* (New York, 2013). Also see Carine M. Mardorossian, 'Toward a New Feminist Theory of Rape', *Signs: Journal of Women in Culture and Society*, XXVII/3 (Spring 2002), pp. 743–75.

18 Donna Haraway, 'Situated Knowledges: The Science Question in Feminism and the Privilege of Partial Perspective', *Feminist Studies*, XIV/3 (Autumn 1988), p. 581.

19 Chandra Talpade Mohanty, '"Under Western Eyes" Revisited: Feminist Solidarity through Anticapitalist Struggles', *Signs: Journal of Women in Culture and Society*, XXVIII/2 (Winter 2003), p. 515.

20 Haraway, 'Situated Knowledges', p. 584.

21 Sally Cole and Lynne Phillips, 'The Violence against Women Campaigns in Latin America: New Feminist Alliances', *Feminist Criminology*, III/2 (2008), p. 161.

22 Ibid., p. 160. They cite N. Faria, 'Para a eradicação da violência doméstica e sexual', in *Feminismo e luta das mulheres: Analises e debates*, ed. A. Semprevivas (São Paulo, 2005), p. 28.

23 Ibid., pp. 160 and 163.

24 Ibid., p. 163.

25 Ibid., p. 164.

26 Mary Clark, 'Domestic Violence in the Haitian Culture and the American Legal Response: Fanm Ayisyen ki Gen Kouraj', *University of Miami Inter-American Law Review*, XXXVII/2 (Winter 2006), p. 308.

27 Lisa Davis, 'Still Trembling: State Obligation under International Law to End Post-Earthquake Rape in Haiti', *University of Miami Law Review*, LV/867 (2011), p. 869.

28 Sarah Deer, 'Toward an Indigenous Jurisprudence of Rape', *Kansas Journal of Law and Public Policy*, XIV/1 (2004), p. 135.

29 Ranjoo Seodu Herr, 'Reclaiming Third World Feminism: or Why Transnational Feminism Needs Third World Feminism', *Meridians: Feminism, Race, Transnationalism*, XII/1 (2014), p. 8. Her chief protagonists are Caren Kaplan and Inderpal Grewal, 'Transnational Practices and Interdisciplinary Feminist Scholarship: Refiguring Women's and Gender Studies', in *Women's Studies on Its Own*, ed. Robyn Wiegman (Durham, NC, 2002).

30 Maurice Eisenbruch, 'The Cultural Epigenesis of Gender-Based Violence in Cambodia: Local and Buddhist Perspectives', *Culture, Medicine, and Psychiatry*, 42 (2018), p. 317, and Alexandra Kent, 'Global Challenge and Moral Uncertainty: Why Do Cambodian Women See Refuge in Buddhism?', *Global Change, Peace, and Security*, XXIII/3 (2011), pp. 405–19.

31 Eisenbruch, 'The Cultural Epigenesis', p. 321.

32 Bruce D. Smith et al., 'Ethnomedical Syndromes and Treatment-Seeking Behavior among Mayan Refugees in Chiapas, Mexico', *Culture, Medicine, and Psychiatry*, 33 (2009), p. 371.

33 Clark, 'Domestic Violence', p. 309, and Shelley Wiley, 'A Grassroots Religious Response to Domestic Violence in Haiti', *Journal of Religion and Abuse*, V/1 (2003), pp. 23–33.

34 Adrienne Rich, 'Legislators of the World', *The Guardian* (18 November 2006), at www.theguardian.com, accessed 3 January 2014.

35 Anon. [Marta Hillers], *A Woman in Berlin: Eight Weeks in the Conquered City*, 1st pub. 1953, trans. Philip Boehm (London, 2005), p. 147.

36 Maurice Merleau-Ponty, cited in R.W.G. Gibbs, *Embodiment and Cognitive Science* (New York, 2006), p. 14.

37 For a discussion, see Lindsey Churchilll, 'Transnational Alliances: Radical U.S. Feminist Solidarity and Contention with Latin America, 1970–1989', *Latin American Perspectives*, XXXVI/6 (November 2009), pp. 10–26.

38 Patricia Hill Collins, *Black Feminist Thought: Knowledge, Consciousness, and the Politics of Empowerment*, 2nd edn (London, 2014), pp. 245–7.

39 Nira Yuval-Davis, 'Women, Ethnicity, and Empowerment', in *Shifting Identities, Shifting Racisms: A Feminist and Psychology Reader*, ed. Kum-Kum Bhavnani and Ann Phoenix (London, 1994), pp. 188–9.

40 Ibid., p. 193.
41 Nira Yuval-Davis, 'Dialogic Epistemology – An Intersectional Resistance to the "Oppression Olympics"', *Gender and Society*, XXVI/1 (February 2012), pp. 51–2. Also see Nira Yuval-Davis, *Gender and Nation* (London, 1997), pp. 130–31.
42 Hilary Charlesworth, 'Martha Nussbaum's Feminist Internationalism', *Ethics*, CXI/1 (October 2000), p. 75.
43 Françoise Lionnet and Shu-Mei Shih, 'Introduction: Thinking through the Minor, Transnationally', in *Minor Transnationalism*, ed. Françoise Lionnet and Shu-Mei Shih (Durham, NC, 2005), p. 11.
44 Haraway, 'Situated Knowledges', p. 586. Underlined emphasis added; italics in original.
45 Linnell Secomb, 'Fractured Community', *Hypatia*, XV/2 (2000), p. 134.
46 Iris Marion Young, *Inclusion and Democracy* (Oxford, 2000), pp. 6 and 8.

Bibliography

'79 Countries where Homosexuality Is Illegal', at http://76crimes.com
    (16 October 2014), accessed on 18 December 2014

Abu-Lughod, Lila, *Do Muslim Women Need Saving?* (Cambridge, MA, 2013)
Acquah, Kobena Eyi, *Music for a Dream Dance* (Accra, 1989)
Action Aid, 'Hate Crimes: The Rise of "Corrective" Rape in South Africa'
    (7 May 2009), at www.actionaid.org.uk, accessed 14 June 2020
Adler, Reva N., Cyanne E. Loyle and Judith Globerman, 'A Calamity in the
    Neighborhood: Women's Participation in the Rwandan Genocide', *Genocide
    Studies and Prevention* (2007)
Adodo-Samai, Phebemary Makafui, 'Criminalisation of Marital Rape in Ghana:
    The Perceptions of Married Men and Women in Accra', MA Dissertation in
    Sociology, University of Ghana (July 2015)
'Advocacy', *Reproductive Health Matters*, XIX/37 (May 2011)
African Rights, *Rwanda: Not So Innocent. Women as Killers* (London, 1995)
Agbiboa, Daniel E., '"Policing Is Not Working: It Is Stealing by Force": Corrupt
    Policing and Related Abuses in Everyday Nigeria', *Africa Today*, LXII/2
    (Winter 2015)
Agger, Inger, 'Sexual Torture of Political Prisoners: An Overview', *Journal
    of Traumatic Stress*, II/3 (1989)
—, and S. Jensen, 'Tortura sexual de presos políticos de sexo masculino', in *Era de
    nieblas: Derechos humanos, terrorismo de estado y salud psicosocial en Amíerica
    Latina*, ed. H. Riquelme (Caracas, 1990)
Ahmed, Bipasha, Paula Reavey and Anamika Majumdar, 'Cultural Transformations
    and Gender Violence: South Asian Women's Experiences of Sexual Violence
    and Familial Dynamics', in *Gender and Interpersonal Violence*, ed. Karen Thosby
    and Flora Alexander (London, 2008)
Ahmed, Sara, 'Who Knows? Knowing Strangers and Strangerness', *Australian
    Feminist Studies*, XV/31 (2000)
Aidoo, Ama Ata, *Changes: A Love Story* (New York, 1991)
Akinade, E. A., T.D.O. Adewuyi and A. A. Sulaiman, 'Socio-Legal Factors That
    Influence the Perpetration of Rape in Nigeria', *Procedia: Social and Behavioral
    Sciences*, 5 (2010)

Alareón, Renato D., et al., 'Beyond the Funhouse Mirrors: Research Agenda on Culture and Psychiatric Diagnosis', in *A Research Agenda for DSM-V*, ed. David J. Kupfer, Michael B. First and Darrel A. Regier (Washington, DC, 2002)

Alcoff, Linda and Laura Gray, 'Survivor Discourse: Transgression or Recuperation?', *Signs: Journal of Women in Culture and Society*, XVIII/2 (Winter 1993)

Alison, Miranda, 'Wartime Sexual Violence: Women's Human Rights and Questions of Masculinity', *Review of International Studies*, XXXIII/1 (January 2007)

Allen, Beverly, *Rape Warfare: The Hidden Genocide in Bosnia-Herzegovina and Croatia* (Minneapolis, MN, 1996)

Allison, J. Murray, compiler, *Raemaekers' Cartoon History of the War*, vol. 1 (London, 1919)

American Psychiatric Association, *Diagnostic and Statistical Manual of Mental Disorders*, 3rd edn (Washington, DC, 1980)

—, *Diagnostic and Statistical Manual of Mental Disorders*, 4th edn (Washington, DC, 1994)

Amnesty International, 'Democratic Republic of Congo: Mass Rape – Time for Remedies' (25 October 2004), at www.amnesty.org, accessed 1 September 2020

—, 'Making Violence against Women Count: Facts and Figures – a Summary' (2004), at www.amnesty.org

—, *No End to War on Women and Children: North Kivu, Democratic Republic of the Congo* (29 September 2008), at www.amnesty.org

—, 'Philippines. Fear, Shame, and Impunity: Rape and Sexual Abuse of Women in Custody' (London, 2001)

Amos, Valerie and Pratibha Parmar, 'Challenging Imperial Feminism', *Feminist Review*, 17 (Autumn 1984)

Anadi, Sunday K. M., 'Security and Crime Prevention in Under-Policed Societies: The Experiment of Community Vigilantism in Anambra State of Nigeria, West Africa', *Journal of Law, Policy, and Globalization*, 60 (2017)

Anderson, Michelle J., 'Rape in South Africa', *Georgetown Journal of Gender and the Law*, I/3 (2000)

Anderson, William J., *Life and Narrative of William J. Anderson, Twenty-Four Years a Slave; Sold Eight Times! In Jail Sixty Times!! Whipped Three-Hundred Times!!! Or The Dark Deeds of American Slavery Revealed* (Chicago, IL, 1857)

Andersson, Neil, and Ari Ho-Foster, '13,915 Reasons for Equity in Sexual Offences Legislation: A National School-Based Survey in South Africa', *International Journal for Equity in Health*, 7 (2008)

Annan, Jeannie, et al., 'Civil War, Reintegration, and Gender in Northern Uganda', *Journal of Conflict Resolution*, LV/6 (December 2011)

Anonymous [Marta Hiller], *Eine Frau in Berlin: Tagebuchaufzeichnungen vom 20. April bis 22. Juni 1945* [1959] (Frankfurt, 2003)

Anyidoho, Kofi, 'Poetry as Dramatic Performance: The Ghana Experience', *Research in African Literatures*, XXII/2 (Summer 1991)

Apel, Dora, *War Culture and the Contest of Images* (New Brunswick, NJ, 2012)

Archampong, Elizabeth, and Fiona Sampson, 'Marital Rape in Ghana: Legal Options for Achieving State Accountability', *Canadian Journal of Women and the Law*, XXII/2 (2010)

Armstrong, Sue, 'Rape in South Africa: An Invisible Part of Apartheid's Legacy', *Focus on Gender*, II/2 (June 1994)

Ashew, Kelly, [Review.] 'Umoja: No Men Allowed by Elizabeth Tadic', *African Studies Review*, LVII/3 (December 2014)

Asian Women's Human Rights Council, *In the Court of Women II: Asia Tribunal on Women's Human Rights in Tokyo. Proceedings of the International Public Hearing on Traffic in Women and War Crimes against Women* (Kathmandu, 1994)

Askin, Kelly Dawn, 'Holding Leaders Accountable in the International Criminal Court (ICC) for Gender Crimes Committed in Darfur', *Genocide Studies and Prevention: An International Journal*, I/I (July 2006)

—, 'Sexual Violence in Decisions and Indictments of the Yugoslav and Rwandan Tribunals: Current Status', *American Journal of International Law* (1999), XCIII/I

—, *War Crimes against Women: Prosecution in International War Crimes Tribunals* (The Hague, 1997)

'At Clerkenwell', *The Times* (12 May 1886)

Atuhaire, Pearl Karuhanga, et al., *The Elusive Peace: Ending Sexual Violence during and after Conflict* (Washington, DC, 2018)

'Australia', *Annual Human Rights Reports Submitted to Congress by the U.S. Department of State* (Washington, DC, 2010)

Baaz, Maria Eriksson, and Maria Stern, 'Why Do Soldiers Rape? Masculinity, Violence, and Sexuality in the Armed Forces in the Congo (DRC)', *International Studies Quarterly*, LIII/2 (June 2009)

Baehr, Kristina Scurry, 'Mandatory Minimums Making Minimal Difference: Ten Years of Sentencing Sex Offenders in South Africa', *Yale Journal of Law and Feminism*, XX/I (2008)

Bandyopadhyay, Sumia Basu, and Ranjita Biswas, *Vio-Mapping: Documenting and Mapping Violence and Rights Violation Taking Place in [the] Lives of Sexually Marginalized Women to Chart Out Effective Advocacy Strategies* (Kolkata, 2011)

Baptist, Edward E., '"Cuffy", "Fancy Maids", and "One-Eyed Men": Rape, Commodification, and the Domestic Slave Trade in the United States', *American Historical Review*, CVI/5 (December 2001)

Bardaglio, Peter W., 'Rape and the Law in the Old South: "Calculated to Excite Indignation in Every Heart"', *Journal of Southern History*, LX/4 (November 1994)

Bart, Pauline B., and Patricia H. O'Brien, *Stopping Rape: Successful Survival Strategies* (New York, 1985)

Bartley, Onesiphorus W., *A Treatise on Forensic Medicine; or Medical Jurisprudence* (Bristol, 1815)

Bassiouni, Cherif, *Final Report of the United Nations Commission of Experts Established Pursuant to Security Council Resolution 780*, S/1994/674 (New York, 1994)

Basu, Amrita, 'The Dialectics of Hindu Nationalism', in *The Success of India's Democracy*, ed. Atul Kohli (New Delhi, 2001)

Basu, Srimati, 'Sexual Property: Staging Rape and Marriage in Indian Law and Feminist Theory', *Feminist Studies*, XXXVII/I (Spring 2011)

Baxi, Pratiksha, Shirin M. Rai and Shaheen Sardar Ali, 'Legacies of Common Law: Crimes of Honour in India and Pakistan', *Third World Quarterly*, XXVII/7 (2006)

Beber, Bernd, et al., 'Peacekeeping, Compliance with International Norms, and Transitional Sex in Monrovia, Liberia', *International Organization*, LXXI/I (Winter 2017)

Beck, Allen J., and Candace Johnson, *Sexual Victimization Reported by Former State Prisoners, 2008* (Washington, DC, May 2012), at www.bjs.gov, accessed 1 September 2020

Bell, Diane, 'Dear Editors', *Women's Studies International Forum*, XIV/5 (1991)

——, 'A Reply to "The Politics of Representation"', *Anthropological Forum: A Journal of Social Anthropology and Comparative Sociology*, VI/2 (1990)

——, and Topsy Napurrula Nelson, 'Speaking about Rape Is Everyone's Business', *Women's Studies International Forum*, XII/4 (1989)

Bell-Fialkoff, Andrew, 'A Brief History of Ethnic Cleansing', *Foreign Affairs* (Summer 1993), LXXII/3

Benderly, Jill, 'Rape, Feminism, and Nationalism in the War in Yugoslav Successor States,' in *Feminist Nationalism*, ed. Lois A. West (New York, 1997)

Batinic, Jelena, 'Feminism, Nationalism, and the War: The "Yugoslav Case" in Feminist Texts', *Journal of International Women's Studies*, III/1 (November 2001), at http://vc.bridgew.edu, accessed 1 November 2020

Bergen, R., 'Surviving Wife Rape: How Women Define and Cope with the Violence', *Violence against Women*, I/2 (1995)

Bergoffen, Debra, 'February 22, 2001: Toward a Politics of the Vulnerable Body', *Hypatia*, XVIII/1 (Winter 2003)

Berry, Diana Ramey, '*Swing the Sickle for the Harvest Is Ripe': Gender and Slavery in Antebellum Georgia* (Urbana, IL, 2007)

——, and Leslie M. Harris, eds, *Sexuality and Slavery: Reclaiming Intimate Histories in the Americas* (Athens, GA, 2018)

Bigler, Bradford, 'Sexually Provoked: Recognizing Sexual Misrepresentation as Adequate Provocation', *UCLA Law Review*, LIII/3 (February 2006)

Black, M. C., et al., *The National Intimate Partner and Sexual Violence Survey: 2010 Summary Report* (Atlanta, GA, 2011), at www.cdc.gov, accessed 1 October 2020

Blackstone, William, *Commentaries on the Laws of England. In Four Books*, 1st pub. 1765, vol. 1 (Philadelphia, PA, 1893)

Blair, Ian, *Investigating Rape: A New Approach for Police* (London, 1985)

Blease, Charlotte, 'Scientific Progress and the Prospects for Culture-Bound Syndromes', *Studies in History and Philosophy of Biological and Biomedical Sciences*, 41 (2010)

Bond, Johanna, 'A Decade after Abu Ghraib: Lessons in Softening Up the Enemy and Sex-Based Humiliation', *Law and Inequality: Journal of Theory and Practice*, XXXI/1 (2012)

——, 'Gender and Non-Normative Sex in Sub-Saharan Africa', *Michigan Journal of Gender and Law*, XXIII/1 (2016)

Boose, Lynda E., 'Crossing the River Drina: Bosnian Rape Camps, Turkish Impalement, and Serbian Cultural Memory', *Signs: Journal of Women in Culture and Society*, XXVIII/1 (2008)

Boothby, Neil, 'Displaced Children: Psychological Theory and Practice from the Field', *Journal of Refugee Studies*, V/2 (1992)

Bose, Sarmila, 'Losing the Victims: Problems of Using Women as Weapons in Recounting the Bangladesh War', *Economic and Political Weekly*, XLII/38 (22–8 September 2007)

'Bosnian Woman "Raped for 20 Days by Fighters"', *Balkan Insight* (4 July 2014), at https://balkaninsight.com, accessed 1 October 2020

Bourke, Joanna, 'Discourses, Representations, Trauma: Reflections on Power', in
     SVAC, *Sexual Violence in Armed Conflicts* (Berlin, 2019)
—, 'A Global History of Sexual Violence from the Nineteenth Century to the
     Present', in *The Cambridge World History of Violence*, ed. Philip Dwyer and Joy
     Damousi (Cambridge, 2019)
—, 'The Mocking of Margaret and the Misfortune of Mary: Sexual Violence in Irish
     History, 1830s to the 1890s', *Canadian Journal of Irish Studies/Revue canadienne
     d'études irlandaises*, 43 (2021)
—, 'Neville Heath and the Politics of Sadism in Mid-Twentieth-Century Britain',
     in *New Interdisciplinary Landscapes in Morality and Emotion*, ed. Sara Graca da
     Silva (London, 2018)
—, 'Pain: Metaphor, Body, and Culture in Anglo-American Societies from the
     Eighteenth Century to the Present', *Rethinking History: The Journal of Theory
     and Practice*, XVIII/4 (October 2014)
—, 'Pandemics and Domestic Violence', in *Transform! Yearbook 2021. Capitalism's
     Deadly Threat*, ed. Walter Baier, Eric Canepa and Haris Golemis (London,
     2021)
—, 'Police Surgeons and Victims of Rape: Cultures of Harm and Care', *Social
     History of Medicine*, XXXI/4 (November 2018), free full text at http://doi.
     org/10.1093/shm/hky016
—, *Rape: A History from the 1860s to the Present* (London, 2007)
—, 'The Rise and Rise of Sexual Violence', in *On Violence in History*, ed. Philip
     Dwyer and Mark S. Micale (Oxford, 2021)
—, 'The Rise and Rise of Sexual Violence', *Historical Reflections. Réflexions
     Historiques*, XLIV/1 (Spring 2018)
—, 'Sadism: A History of Non-Consensual Sexual Cruelty', *International Journal of
     Forensic Psychotherapy*, 1/2 (2020)
Boutilier, James A., 'European Women in the Solomon Islands, 1900–1942:
     Accommodation and Change on the Pacific Frontier', in *Rethinking Women's
     Roles: Perspectives from the Pacific*, ed. Denise O'Brien and Sharon W. Tiffany
     (Berkeley, CA, 1984)
Bovarnick, Silvie, 'Universal Human Rights and Non-Western Normative Systems:
     A Comparative Analysis of Violence against Women in Mexico and Pakistan',
     Review of International Studies, 33 (2007)
Bowling, Jessamym, et al., 'Perceived Health Concerns among Sexual Minority
     Women in Mumbai, India: An Exploratory Qualitative Study', *Culture, Health,
     and Sexualities*, XVIII/7 (2016)
Bracken, P. J., J. E. Giller and D. Summerfield, 'Psychological Responses to War and
     Atrocity: The Limitations of Current Concepts', *Social Science and Medicine*,
     XL/8 (1995)
Bracken, Patrick J., Joan E. Giller and James K. Scekiwenuka, 'The Rehabilitation of
     Child Soldiers: Defining Needs and Appropriate Responses', *Medicine, Conflict,
     and Survival*, XII/2 (April–June 1996)
Brancale, Ralph, Albert Ellis and Ruth R. Doorbar, 'Psychiatric and Psychological
     Investigations of Convicted Sex Offenders: A Summary Report', *American
     Journal of Psychiatry*, 109 (July 1952)
Branson, Louise, 'Victims of War', *Chicago Tribune* (24 January 1993), at http://
     articles.chicagotribune.com
Breslau, Joseph, 'Cultures of Trauma: Anthropological Views of Posttraumatic Stress

Disorder in International Health', *Culture, Medicine, and Psychiatry*, XXVIII/2 (2004)

Brett, Rachel, and Irma Specht, *Young Soldiers: Why They Choose to Fight* (Boulder, CO, 2004)

Bringa, Tone, *Being Muslim the Bosnian Way: Identity and Community in a Central Bosnian Village* (Princeton, NJ, 1988)

Britton, Hannah, 'Organising against Gender Violence in South Africa', *Journal of Southern African Studies*, XXXII/1 (March 2006)

——, and Lindsey Shook, '"I Need To Hurt You More": Namibia's Fight to End Gender-Based Violence', *Signs: Journal of Women in Culture and Society*, XL/1 (Autumn 2014)

Bronitt, Simon, 'Is Criminal Law Reform a Lost Cause?', in *New Directions for Law in Australia: Essays in Contemporary Law Reform*, ed. Ron Levy (Canberra, 2017)

Broude, Gwen J., and Sarah J. Greene, 'Cross-Cultural Codes on Twenty Sexual Attitudes and Practices', *Ethnology*, XV/4 (1976)

Brown, Laura S., 'Not Outside the Range: One Feminist Perspective on Psychic Trauma', in *Trauma: Explorations in Memory*, ed. Cathy Caruth (Baltimore, MD, 1995)

Brown, Roderick, '"Corrective Rape" in South Africa: A Continuing Plight despite an International Human Rights Response', *Annual Survey of International and Comparative Law*, 18 (2012)

Browne, Rachel, 'Historic Women's Refuge Elsie to Continue, New Management Promises' (23 June 2014), at www.smh.com.au, accessed 1 December 2020

Browning, Christopher, *Remembering Survival: Inside a Nazi Slave-Labor Camp* (New York, 2010)

Bryce, Viscount James, *Report of the Committee on Alleged German Outrages* (London, 1915)

Brownmiller, Susan, *Against Our Will: Men, Women, and Rape* (New York, 1975)

Brysk, Alison, 'The Politics of Measurement: The Contested Count of the Disappeared in Argentina', *Human Rights Quarterly*, XVI/4 (November 1994)

Buchanan, Kim Shayo, 'E-race-ing Gender: The Racial Construction of Prison Rape', in *Masculinities and the Law: A Multidimensional Approach*, ed. Frank Rudy Cooper and Ann C. McGinley (New York, 2012)

Bueno-Hansen, Pascha, *Feminism and Human Rights Struggles in Peru: Decolonizing Transitional Justice* (Urbana, IL, 2015)

Bumiller, Kristin, *In an Abusive State: How Neoliberalism Appropriated the Feminist Movement against Sexual Violence* (Durham, NC, 2008)

Buncombe, Andrew, 'The Sex Sadist of Baghdad', *The Star* (7 May 2004)

Buramy, Benedetta Faedi, 'Rape, Blue Jeans, and Judicial Developments in Italy' (San Francisco, 2009), at http://digitalcommons.law.ggu.edu, accessed 1 September 2020

Burgess, Ann Wolbert, 'Putting Trauma on the Radar', in *Mapping Trauma and Its Wake: Autobiographical Essays by Pioneer Trauma Scholars*, ed. Charles R. Figley (New York, 2006)

——, and Lynda Lytle Holmstrom, 'Rape Trauma Syndrome', *American Journal of Psychiatry*, 981 (1974)

Burnet, Jennie E., 'Situating Sexual Violence in Rwanda (1990–2001): Sexual Agency, Sexual Consent, and the Political Economy of War', *African Studies Review*, LV/2 (September 2012)

Butalia, Urvashi, 'Community, State, and Gender: On Women's Agency during
    Partition', *Economic and Political Weekly*, XXVIII/17 (24 April 1993)
—, 'Let's Ask How We Contribute to Rape', *The Hindu* (25 December 2012),
    at www.thehindu.com, accessed 3 April 2020
Butler, Judith, *Gender Trouble* [1990] (Abingdon, 2010)
—, 'Violence, Mourning, Politics', *Studies in Gender and Sexuality*, IV/1 (2003)

Cahill, Sean, 'From "Don't Drop the Soap" to PREA Standards: Reducing Sexual
    Victimization of LGBT People in the Juvenile and Criminal Justice Systems', in
    LGBTQ Politics: A Critical Reader, ed. Marla Brettschneider, Susan Burgess and
    Christine Keating (New York, 2017)
Cains, Beverley, 'Nonsense Talked about Rape in Marriage', *Canberra Times*
    (2 November 1985)
Calavita, Kitty, 'Blue Jeans, Rape, and the De-Constitutive Power of Law', *Law
    and Society Review*, XXXV/1 (2001)
Caldwell, Ryan Ashley, *Fallgirls: Gender and the Framing of Torture at Abu Ghraib*
    (London, 2016)
Calton, Jenna M., Lauren Bennett Cattaneo and Kris T. Gebhard, 'Barriers to Help
    Seeking for Lesbian, Gay, Bisexual, Transgender, and Queer Survivors of Intimate
    Partner Violence', *Trauma, Violence, and Abuse*, XVII/5 (December 2016)
Campbell, Jamie, 'German Professor Rejects Indian Student Due to the Country's
    "Rape Problem"', *The Independent* (9 March 2015), at www.independent.co.uk,
    accessed 1 December 2020
Campbell, Kirsten, 'The Gender of Transitional Justice: Law, Sexual Violence and
    the International Criminal Tribunal for the Former Yugoslavia', *International
    Journal of Transitional Justice*, 1 (2007)
—, 'Legal Memories: Sexual Assault, Memory, and International Humanitarian
    Law', *Signs: Journal of Women in Culture and Society*, XXVIII/1 (Autumn 2002)
Card, Claudia, 'Women, Evil, and Gray Zones', *Metaphilosophy*, XXXI/5 (October
    2000)
Carel, Havi, and Rachel Cooper, 'Introduction: Culture-Bound Syndromes', *Studies
    in History and Philosophy of Biological and Biomedical Sciences*, 41 (2010)
Carey, David Jr, 'Forced and Forbidden Sex: Rape and Sexual Freedom in Dictatorial
    Guatemala', *The Americas*, LXIX/3 (January 2013)
Carlson, Eric Stener, 'The Hidden Prevalence of Male Sexual Assault during
    War: Observations on Blunt Trauma to the Male Genitals', *British Journal of
    Criminology*, XLVI/1 (January 2006)
—, 'Sexual Assault of Men in War', *The Lancet*, 349 (1997)
Carpenter, R. Charli, *Forgetting Children Born of War: Setting the Human Rights
    Agenda in Bosnia and Beyond* (New York, 2010)
—, 'Recognizing Gender-Based Violence against Civilian Men and Boys in Conflict
    Situations', *Security Dialogue*, XXXVII/1 (2006)
Carpenter, Robyn, 'Forced Maternity, Children's Rights, and the Genocide
    Convention: A Theoretical Analysis', *Journal of Genocide Research*, II/2 (2000)
—, 'Surfacing Children: Limitations of Genocidal Rape Discourse', *Human Rights
    Quarterly*, XXII/2 (May 2000)
Carroll, C. R., 'Woman', *Southern Literary Journal*, III (November 1836)
Caselli, Irene, 'Ecuador Clinics Said to "Cure" Homosexuality, *Christian Science
    Monitor* (10 February 2012), at www.csmonitor.com, accessed 6 April 2020

Chai, Alice Yun, 'Asian-Pacific Feminist Coalition Politics: The Chōngshindae/ Jūgunianfu ("Comfort Women") Movement', *Korean Studies*, 17 (1 January 1993)

Chakrapani, Venkatesan, Peter A. Newman and Murali Shunmugam, 'Secondary HIV Prevention among *Kothi*-Identified MSM in Chennai, India', *Culture, Health, and Sexuality*, X/4 (May 2008)

Chang, Iris, *The Rape of Nanking: The Forgotten Holocaust of World War II* (New York, 1997)

Chappell, Duncan, and Peter Sallmann, 'Rape in Marriage Legislation in South Australia: Anatomy of a Reform', *Australian Academy of Forensic Science*, 14 (1982)

Charlesworth, Hilary, 'Martha Nussbaum's Feminist Internationalism', *Ethics*, CXI/1 (October 2000)

Chatterjee, Partha, *The Politics of the Governed* (New York, 2004)

Chavez, Linda, 'Sexual Tension in the Military', *Townhall* (5 May 2004), at https://townhall.com, accessed 1 October 2020

Chelemu, Khethiwe, 'Wife's Seven Year Wait for Justice', [Johannesburg] *Times* (19 January 2012), at www.timeslive.co.za, seen 1 December 2020

Churchill, Lindsey, 'Transnational Alliances. Radical U.S. Feminist Solidarity and Contention with Latin America, 1970–1989', *Latin American Perspectives*, XXXVI/6 (November 2009)

Clark, Mary, 'Domestic Violence in the Haitian Culture and the American Legal Response: Fanm Ayisyen ki Gen Kouraj', *University of Miami Inter-American Law Review*, XXXVII/2 (Winter 2006)

Cloud, David, 'Psychologist Calls Private in Abu Ghraib Photographs "Overly Compliant"', *New York Times* (24 September 2005)

Cohen, Dara Kay, 'Female Combatants and the Perpetration of Violence: Wartime Rape in the Sierra Leone Civil War', *World Politics*, LXV/3 (July 2013)

——, Amelia Hoover Green and Elisabeth Jean Wood, 'Wartime Sexual Violence: Misconceptions, Implications, and Ways Forward', *United States Institute of Peace Special Report*, Report 323 (Washington, DC, February 2013), at www.usip.org, accessed 1 October 2020

Cole, Sally, and Lynne Phillips, 'The Violence against Women Campaigns in Latin America: New Feminist Alliances', *Feminist Criminology*, III/2 (2008)

Collins, Patricia Hill, *Black Feminist Thought: Knowledge, Consciousness, and the Politics of Empowerment*, 2nd edn (London, 2014)

'The Combahee River Collective Statement' (April 1977), at www.circuitous.org, accessed 1 October 2020

Comisión para el Esclarecimiento Histórico, *Guatemala, memoria del silenció*, vol. III (Guatemala, 1999)

Conklin, Diane, 'Special Note', in Seada Vranic, *Breaking the Wall of Silence: The Voices of Raped Bosnia* (Zagreb, 1996)

Coomaraswamy, Radhika, 'Report of the Special Rapporteur on Violence against Women, Its Causes and Consequences (Geneva, 1996), at https://digitallibrary. un.org, accessed 1 December 2020

Cooper, Rachel, 'Are Culture-Bound Syndromes as Real as Universally-Occurring Disorders?', *Studies in History and Philosophy of Biological and Biomedical Sciences*, 41 (2010)

Copelon, Rhonda, 'Surfacing Gender: Reconceptualizing Crimes against Women in Times of War', in *The Women and War Reader*, ed. Lois Ann Lorentzen and Jennifer Turpin (New York, 1988)

Corrigan, Rose, *Up Against a Wall: Rape Reform and the Failure of Success* (New York, 2013)

Cortoni, Franca, Kelly M. Babchishin and Clémence Rat, 'The Proportion of Sexual Offenders Who Are Female Is Higher Than Thought: A Meta-Analysis', *Criminal Justice and Behavior*, XLIV/2 (February 2017)

Coulter, Chris, 'Female Fighters in the Sierra Leone War: Challenging the Assumptions', *Feminist Review*, 88 (2008)

Crenshaw, Kimberlé, 'Demarginalizing the Intersection of Race and Sex: A Black Feminist Critique of Antidiscrimination Doctrine, Feminist Theory, and Antiracist Politics', *University of Chicago Legal Forum* (1989), no. 1

'Critics Say Berlusconi's Response to Rape Cases Flippant', *ABC News* (26 January 2009), cited at www.abc.net.au, accessed 1 September 2020

Cummings, Sara Kuipers, 'Liberia's New War: Post-Conflict Strategies for Confronting Rape and Sexual Violence', *Arizona State Law Journal*, XLIII/1 (2011)

Currier, Ashley, *Out in Africa: LGBT Organizing in Namibia and South Africa* (Minneapolis, MN, 2012)

——, and Rashida A. Manuel, 'When Rape Goes Unnamed: Gay Malawian Men's Responses to Unwanted and Non-Consensual Sex', *Australian Feminist Studies*, XXIX/81 (2014)

Cvetkovich, Ann, *An Archive of Feelings: Trauma, Sexuality, and Lesbian Public Cultures* (Durham, NC, 2004)

da Luz, Carla M., and Pamela C. Weckerly, 'Texas Condom-Rape Case: Caution Construed as Consent', *UCLA Women's Law Journal*, 3 (1993)

Danner, Mark, *Torture and Truth: America, Abu Ghraib, and the War on Terror* (New York, 2004)

——, Barbara Ehrenreich and David Levi Strauss, eds, *Abu Ghraib: The Politics of Torture* (Berkeley, CA, 2005)

Das, Veena, *Critical Events: An Anthropological Perspective on Contemporary India* (Delhi, 1995)

——, 'National Honour and Practical Kingship: Of Unwanted Women and Children', in *Critical Events*, ed. Veena Das (Delhi, 1995)

Daugaard, G., et al., 'Sequelae to Genital Trauma in Torture Victims', *Archives of Andrology: Journal of Reproductive Systems*, X/3 (1983)

Davaki, Konstantina, *The Policy on Gender Equality in Greece* (Brussels, 2013)

Davis, Angela, 'Joan Little: The Dialectics of Rape', *Ms. Magazine* (1975), at https://overthrowpalacehome.files.wordpress.com, accessed 1 October 2020

Davis, Lisa, 'Still Trembling: State Obligation under International Law to End Post-Earthquake Rape in Haiti', *University of Miami Law Review*, LV/867 (2011)

Davis, Paulina Wright, *A History of the National Women's Rights Movement* (New York, 1871)

Dawes, James, *That the World May Know: Bearing Witness to Atrocity* (Cambridge, MA, 2007)

Debauche, Alice, '"They" Rape "Our" Women: When Racism and Sexism Intermingle', in *Violence against Women and Ethnicity: Commonalities and Differences across Europe*, ed. Ravi K. Thiara, Stephanie A. Condon and Monika Schröttle (Leverkusen, 2011)

de Brouwer, Anne-Marie, and Sandra Chu, eds, *The Men Who Killed Me: Rwandan Survivors of Sexual Violence* (Vancouver, 2009)

Deer, Sarah, 'Decolonizing Rape Law: A Native Feminist Synthesis of Safety and Sovereignty', *Wicazo Sa Review*, XXIV/2 (Fall 2009)

—, 'Toward an Indigenous Jurisprudence of Rape', *Kansas Journal of Law and Public Policy*, XIV/1 (2004)

De Langis, Theresa, 'Speaking Private Memory to Public Power: Oral History and Breaking the Silence on Sexual and Gender-Based Violence during the Khmer Rouge Genocide', in *Beyond Women's Words: Feminisms and the Practices of Oral History in the Twenty-First Century*, ed. Katrina Srigley, Stacey Zembrzycki and Franca Iacovetta (London, 2018),

Del Valle, S., *Catorce años a los culpables de violación conjugal* (Mexico DF, 1997)

Dendy, Mervyn, 'When the Police Frolics: A South African History of State Liability', *Acta Juridica* (1989)

de Rachewiltz, Boris, *Black Eros: Sexual Customs of Africa from Prehistory to the Present Day*, trans. Peter Whigham (London, 1964)

De Ruiter, Donja, *Sexual Offenses in International Criminal Law* (The Hague, 2011)

Devereux, George, 'The Awarding of a Penis as a Compensation for Rape: A Demonstration of the Clinical Relevance of the Psycho-Analytic Study of Cultural Data', *International Journal of Psycho-Analysis*, XXXVIII/6 (November–December 1957)

Dew, Charles B., 'Speaking of Slavery', *Virginia Quarterly Review*, LIII/4 (Autumn 1977)

Di Caro, Claire Bradford, 'Call It What It Is: Genocide through Male Rape and Sexual Violence in the Former Yugoslavia and Rwanda', *Duke Journal of Comparative and International Law*, XXX/1 (2019)

Di Silvio, Lorenzo, 'Correcting Corrective Rape: Charmichele and Developing South Africa's Affirmative Obligations to Prevent Violence against Women', *Georgetown Law Journal*, XCIX/5 (June 2011)

Dolan, Chris, 'Letting Go of the Gender Binary: Charting New Pathways for Humanitarian Interventions on Gender-Based Violence', *International Review of the Red Cross*, XCVI/894 (2014)

Donnelly, D. A., and S. Kenyon, '"Honey, We Don't Do Men": Gender Stereotypes and the Provision of Services to Sexually Assaulted Males', *Journal of Interpersonal Violence*, 11 (1996)

Dorr, Lisa Lindquist, *White Women, Rape, and the Power of Race in Virginia, 1900–1960* (Chapel Hill, NC, 2004)

Dowsett, Gary W., 'HIV/AIDS and Homophobia: Subtle Hatreds, Severe Consequences, and the Question of Origins', *Culture, Health, and Sexuality*, V/2 (March–April 2003)

Drew, Benjamin, ed., *A North-Side View of Slavery. The Refugee: or, the Narrative of Fugitive Slaves in Canada. Related by Themselves, with an Account of the History and Condition of the Colored Population of Upper Canada* (Boston, MA, 1856)

Drumbl, Mark A., 'She Makes Me Ashamed to Be a Woman: The Genocide Conviction of Pauline Nyiramasuhuko', *Michigan Journal of International Law*, XXXIV/3 (2013)

duBois, Teresa, 'Police Investigation of Sexual Assault Complaints: How Far Have We Come Since *Jane Doe*?', in *Sexual Assault in Canada: Law, Legal Practice, and Women's Activism*, ed. Elizabeth A. Sheehy (Ottawa, 2012)

Ducey, Kimberley A., 'Dilemmas of Teaching the "Great Silence": Rape-as-Genocide in Rwanda, Darfur, and Congo', *Genocide Studies and Prevention: An International Journal*, V/3 (December 2010)

Duddle, May, 'The Need for Sexual Assault Centres in the United Kingdom', *British Medical Journal* (9 March 1985)

Duramy, Bernadette Faedi, *Gender and Violence in Haiti: Women's Path from Victims to Agents* (New Brunswick, 2014)

D'Urso, Giulio, et al., 'Risk Factors Related to Cognitive Distortions toward Women and Moral Disengagement: A Study on Sex Offenders', *Sexuality and Culture*, 23 (2019)

Dussich, John P. J., 'Decisions Not to Report Sexual Assault: A Comparative Study among Women Living in Japan Who Are Japanese, Korean, Chinese, and English-Speaking', *International Journal of Offender Therapy and Comparative Criminology*, XLV/3 (2001)

Dutta, Debolina, and Oishik Sircar, 'India's Winter of Discontent: Some Feminist Dilemmas in the Wake of a Rape', *Feminist Studies*, XXXIX/1 (2013)

Easteal, P., 'Rape in Marriage: Has the License Lapsed?', in *Balancing the Scales: Rape, Law Reform, and Australian Culture*, ed. Patricia Weiser Easteal (Sydney, 1995)

Easteal, Patricia Weiser, 'Survivors of Sexual Assault: An Australian Survey', *International Journal of Sociology of Law*, 22 (1994)

'EC Investigative Mission into the Treatment of Muslim Women in the Former Yugoslavia: Report to EC Foreign Ministers', Warburton Mission Report (February 1993), at www.womenaid.org

Edgar, J. Clifford, and Jas. C. Johnson, 'Medico-Legal Consideration of Rape', in *Medical Jurisprudence, Forensic Medicine and Toxiocology*, vol. II, ed. R. A. Witthaus and Tracy C. Becker (New York, 1894)

Ehrenreich, Barbara, 'Feminism's Assumptions Upended', in *Abu Ghraib: The Politics of Torture* (Berkeley, CA, 2004)

Eich, Thomas, 'A Tiny Membrane Defending "Us" against "Them": Arabic Internet Debate about Hymenorrhaphy in Sunni Islamic Law', *Culture, Health, and Sexuality*, XII/7 (October 2010)

Eisenbruch, Maurice, 'The Cultural Epigenesis of Gender-Based Violence in Cambodia: Local and Buddhist Perspectives', *Culture, Medicine, and Psychiatry*, XLII/2 (2018)

Ellis, Albert, Ruth R. Doorbar and Robert Johnston III, 'Characteristics of Convicted Sex Offenders', *Journal of Social Psychology*, 40 (1954)

Engle, Karen, 'Feminism and Its (Dis)contents: Criminalizing Wartime Rape in Bosnia and Herzegovina', *American Journal of International Law*, XCIX/4 (October 2005)

Epprecht, Marc, *Heterosexual Africa? The History of an Idea from the Age of Exploration to the Age of AIDS* (Athens, OH, 2008)

—, *Unspoken Facts: A History of Homosexualities in Africa* (Harare, 2008)

Essa, Azad, 'UN Peacekeepers Hit by New Allegations of Sex Abuse', *Al-Jazeera* (10 July 2017), at www.aljazeera.com, accessed 1 August 2020

Everhart, Amy Jo, 'Predicting the Effect of Italy's Long-Awaited Rape Law Reform in the Land of Machismo', *Vanderbilt Journal of Transnational Law*, XIII/3 (March 1998)

'Extraordinary Case of Rape', *Globe* (28 October 1833)

'Extraordinary Case of Rape', *The Times* (28 October 1833)

Fa, Marietta Sze-Chie, 'Rape Myths in American and Chinese Law and Legal Systems: Do Tradition and Culture Make the Difference?', *Maryland Series in Contemporary Asian Studies*, 4 (2007)

Fabian, Katrin, '"My Heart Die In Me": Idioms of Distress and the Development of a Screening Tool for Mental Suffering in Southeast Liberia', *Culture, Medicine, and Psychiatry*, 42 (2018)

Fanon, Frantz, *Black Skin, White Masks*, trans. Charles Lam Markmann (New York, 1967)

Faramrzi, Scheherezade, 'Former Iraqi Prisoner Says U.S. Jailers Humiliated Him', *Herald Net* (2 May 2004), at www.heraldnet.com, accessed 1 October 2020

Faria, N., 'Para a eradicação da violência doméstica e sexual', in *Feminismo e luta das mulheres: Analises e debates*, ed. A. Semprevivas (São Paulo, 2005)

Fawzi, M. C. Smith, et al., 'The Validity of Screening for Post-Traumatic Stress Disorder and Major Depression amongst Vietnamese Former Political Prisoners', *Acta Psychiatrica Scandinavica*, XCV/2 (1997)

Featherstone, Lisa, 'Women's Rights, Men's Rights, Human Rights: Discourses of Rights and Rape in Marriage in 1970s and 1980s Australia', *Law and History*, V/2 (2018)

Fedler, Joanne, 'Lawyering Domestic Violence through the Prevention of Family Violence Act 1993 – An Evaluation after a Year in Operation', *South African Law Journal*, CXII/2 (1995)

Fehrenbach, Heide, *Race after Hitler: Occupation Children in Postwar Germany and America* (Princeton, NJ, 2018)

Feimster, Crystal N., '"What If I Am a Woman?" Black Women's Campaigns for Sexual Justice and Citizenship', in *The World the Civil War Made*, ed. Gregory P. Downs and Kate Masur (Durham, NC, 2015)

'Feminism and Film – A Roundtable Discussion with Curator Susan Charlton' (1 July 2017), at https://fourthreefilm.com, accessed 1 December 2020

Ferenczi, Sándor, *First Contributions to Psycho-Analysis*, trans. Ernest Jones (London, 2018)

Findlay, Eileen J., 'Courtroom Tales of Sex and Honor: *Rapto* and Rape in Late Nineteenth-Century Puerto Rico', in *Honor, Status, and Law in Modern Latin America*, ed. Sueann Caulfield, Sarah C. Chambers and Lara Putnam (Durham, NC, 2005)

Fine, Derek, 'Kitskonstabels: A Case Study in Black on Black Policy', *Acta Juridica* (1989)

Fisher, Siobhán K., 'Occupation of the Womb: Forced Impregnation as Genocide', *Duke Law Journal*, XLVII/1 (1996)

Flaiano, Ennio, *Tempo di uccidere* [1947] (Milan, 1973)

Flynn, George, and Alan Gottlieb, *Guns for Women: The Complete Handgun Buying Guide for Women* (Bellevue, WA, 1988)

Fontanella-Khan, Amana, *Pink Sari Revolution: A Tale of Women and Power in India* (New York, 2013)

Foster, Dulce, et al., *A House with Two Rooms: Final Report of the Truth and Reconciliation Commission of Liberia Diaspora Project* (Saint Paul, MN, 2009)

Foster, Thomas A., *Rethinking Rufus: Sexual Violations of Enslaved Men* (Athens, GA, 2019)

Foucault, Michel, *Histoire de la sexualité* (Paris, 1976)

Fountain, K., and A. A. Skolnik, *Lesbian, Gay, Bisexual, and Transgender Domestic Violence in the United States in 2006* (New York, 2007)

Fourchard, Laurent, 'The Politics of Mobilization for Security in South African Townships', *African Affairs*, CX/441 (October 2011)

Franco, Jean, 'Rape and Human Rights', *PMLA*, CXXI/5 (October 2006)

Frawley-O'Dea, Mary Gail, 'Psychosocial Anatomy of the Catholic Sexual Abuse Scandal', *Studies in Gender and Sexuality*, V/2 (2004)

Freud, Sigmund, *Beyond the Pleasure Principle and Other Writings*, trans. John Reddick (London, 2003)

Fulu, E., et al., 'Prevalence of and Factors Associated with Male Perpetration of Intimate Partner Violence: Findings from the UN Multi-Country Cross-Sectional Study on Men and Violence in Asia and the Pacific', *The Lancet Global Health*, 1 (2013)

—, 'Why Do Some Men Use Violence against Women and How Can We Prevent It? Quantitative Findings from the United Nations Multi-Country Cross-Sectional Study on Men and Violence in Asia and the Pacific' (Bangkok, 2013)

Fusco, Coco 'Artist's Statement', *TDR: The Drama Review*, LII/1 (Spring 2008)

—, *A Field Guide for Female Interrogators* (New York, 2008)

Galton, Eric R., 'Police Processing of Rape Complaints: A Case Study', *American Journal of Criminal Law*, 4 (1975–6)

Gander, Catherine, 'The NSW Women's Refuge Movement', *Parity*, XIX/10 (2006)

Gaskins, Joseph, '"Buggers" and the Commonwealth Caribbean: A Comparative Examination of the Bahamas, Jamaica, and Trinidad and Tobago', in *Human Rights, Sexual Orientation, and Gender Identity in the Commonwealth*, ed. Corinne Lennox and Matthew Waites (London, 2013)

Gattrell, V.A.C., and T. B. Hadden, 'Criminal Statistics and Their Interpretation', in *Nineteenth-Century Society: Essays in the Use of Quantitative Methods for the Study of Social Data*, ed. E. A. Wrigley (London, 1972)

Gee, Dylan G., et al., 'Early Developmental Emergence of Human Amygdala-Prefrontal Connectivity after Maternal Deprivation', *Proceedings of the National Academy of Sciences of the United States of America*, CX/39 (24 September 2013)

Gemmel, Judy, 'Into the Sun', in *Mother I'm Rooted: An Anthology of Australian Women Poets*, ed. Kate Jennings (Fitzroy, 1975)

Ghani, Muhammad Abdul, *Medical Jurisprudence: A Hand-Book for Police Officers and Students* (Vellore, 1911)

Gibbs, R.W.G., *Embodiment and Cognitive Science* (New York, 2006)

Gilani, Sabrina, 'Transforming the "Perpetrator" into "Victim": The Effect of Gendering Violence on the Legal and Practical Responses to Women's Political Violence', *Australian Journal of Gender and Law*, 1 (2010), at http://sro.sussex.ac.uk, accessed 1 December 2020

Gilchrist, Catie, 'Forty Years of the Elsie Refuge for Women and Children', at https://dictionaryofsydney.org, accessed 1 December 2020

Gilmore, Leigh, 'Frames of Witness: The Kavanaugh Hearings, Survivor Testimony, and #MeToo', *Biography*, XLII/3 (2019)

Godoy, Angelina Snodgrass, 'Lynchings and the Democratization of Terror in Postwar Guatemala: Implications for Human Rights', *Human Rights Quarterly*, XXIV/3 (2002)

Goldblatt, Beth, and Sheila Meintjes, 'Dealing with the Aftermath: Sexual Violence and the Truth and Reconciliation Commission', *Agenda: Empowering Women for Gender Equity*, 36 (1997)

Goldenberg, Myrna, 'Sex, Rape, and Survival: Jewish Women and the Holocaust', at www.theverylongview.com, accessed 31 January 2015

Goldstein, Daniel M., 'Flexible Justice: Neoliberal Violence and "Self-Help" Security in Bolivia', *Critique of Anthropology*, XXV/4 (2005)

Goldstein, Donna M., *Laughter Out of Place: Race, Class, Violence, and Sexuality in a Rio Shantytown* (Berkeley, CA, 2013)

Goldstein, Richard, 'Bitch Bites Man!', in *Village Voice* (10 May 2004), at www.villagevoice.com

Gotell, Lise, and Emily Dutton, 'Sexual Violence in the "Manosphere": Antifeminist Men's Rights Discourses on Rape', *International Journal for Crime, Justice, and Social Democracy*, V/2 (2016)

Gottschall, Jonathan A., and Tiffani A. Gottschall, 'Are Per-Incident Rape-Pregnancy Rates Higher than Per-Incident Consensual Pregnancy Rates?', *Human Nature*, XIV/1 (2003)

Gourevitch, Philip, and Errol Morris, 'Exposure: The Woman behind the Camera', *New Yorker* (3 March 2008), at www.newyorker.com, accessed 1 September 2020

—, and —, *Standard Operating Procedure* (New York, 2008)

Grant, J. M., et al., *Injustice at Every Turn: A Report of the National Transgender Discrimination Survey* (Washington, DC, 2011)

Green, Amelia Hoover, Dara Cohen and Elisabeth Wood, 'Is Wartime Rape Declining on a Global Scale? We Don't Know – And It Doesn't Matter', *Political Violence at a Glance*, blog (1 November 2012), at www.politicalviolenceataglance. org, accessed 1 November 2020

Grewal, Inderpal, and Caren Kaplan, 'Introduction: Transnational Feminist Practices and Questions of Postmodernity', in *Scattered Hegemonies: Postmodernity and Transnational Feminist Practices*, ed. Inderpal Grewal and Caren Kaplan (Minneapolis, MN, 1994)

Grossmann, Atina, 'Remarks on Current Trends and Directions in German Women's History', *Women in German Yearbook*, 12 (1996)

Groth, Nicholas, and Ann W. Burgess, 'Male Rape: Offenders and Victims', *American Journal of Psychiatry*, 137 (1980)

Habiba, S. U., 'Mass Rape and Violence in the 1971 Armed Conflict of Bangladesh: Justice and Other Issues', in *Common Grounds: Violence against Women in War and Armed Conflict Situations*, ed. I. L. Sajor (Quezon City, Philippines, 1998)

Hadjimatheou, Katerina, 'Citizen-Led Digital Policing and Democratic Norms: The Case of Self-Styled Paedophile Hunters', *Criminology and Criminal Justice*, XXI/4 (2019)

Halcón, Linda, et al., 'Adolescent Health in the Caribbean: A Regional Perspective', *American Journal of Public Health*, XCIII/11 (November 2003)

Hale, Matthew, *Pleas of the Crown* (London, 1678)

Hall, Rachel, '"It Can Happen to You": Rape Prevention in the Age of Risk Management', *Hypatia: A Journal of Feminist Philosophy*, XIX/3 (2004)

Halleck, Seymour, 'The Therapeutic Encounter', in *Sexual Behaviors: Social, Clinical, and Legal Aspects*, ed. H.L.P. Resnik and Marvin E. Wolfgang (Boston, MA, 1972)

Hamel, Christelle, '"Faire tourner les meufs". Les viols collectifs: Discours des médias et des agresseurs', *Gradhiva*, 33 (2003)

Hammerton, A. James, *Cruelty and Companionship: Conflict in Nineteenth-Century Married Life* (London, 1992)

Haraway, Donna, 'Situated Knowledges: The Science Question in Feminism and the Privilege of Partial Perspective', *Feminist Studies*, XIV/3 (Autumn 1988)

Harding, Luke, 'The Other Prisoners', *The Guardian* (19 May 2004), at www.theguardian.com, accessed 1 September 2020.

Harman, Donna, 'A Woman on Trial for Rwanda's Massacre', *Christian Science Monitor* (7 March 2003), at www.csmonitor.com, accessed 5 April 2020

Harris, Jessica, and Sharon Grace, *A Question of Evidence? Investigating and Prosecuting Rape in the 1990s* (London, 1999)

Harris, Ruth, 'The "Child of the Barbarian": Rape, Race and Nationalism in France during the First World War', *Past and Present*, 141 (November 1993)

Hatmaker, Debbie, 'Vital Signs: A SANE Approach to Sexual Violence', *American Journal of Nursing*, XCVII/8 (August 1997)

Hayden, Robert M., 'Rape and Rape Avoidance in Ethno-National Conflicts: Sexual Violence in Liminalized States', *American Anthropologist*, new series, CI/1 (March 2000)

Hayman, Charles R., et al., 'A Public Health Program for Sexually Assaulted Females', *Public Health Reports*, LXXXII/6 (June 1967)

Haysom, Nicholas, 'Policing the Police: A Comparative Survey of Police Control Mechanisms in the U.S., South Africa, and the United Kingdom', *Acta Juridica* (1989)

Heineman, Elizabeth, 'The Hour of the Woman: Memories of Germany's "Crisis Years" and West German National Identity', *American Historical Review*, CI/3 (April 1996)

Helliwell, Christine, '"It's Only a Penis": Rape, Feminism, and Difference', *Signs: Journal of Women in Culture and Society*, XXV/3 (Spring 2000)

Hensley, Christopher, Tammy Castle and Richard Tewksbury, 'Inmate-to-Inmate Sexual Coercion in a Prison for Women', *Journal of Offender Rehabilitation* (2003)

Herdt, Gilbert, 'Representations of Homosexuality: An Essay in Cultural Ontology and Historical Comparison. Parts I and II', *Journal of the History of Sexuality*, I/3 and I/4 (January and April 1991)

Herr, Ranjoo Seodu, 'Reclaiming Third World Feminism: or Why Transnational Feminism Needs Third World Feminism', *Meridians: Feminism, Race, Transnationalism*, XII/1 (2014)

Hersh, Seymour M., 'The Gray Zone: How a Secret Pentagon Program Came to Abu Ghraib', *New Yorker* (24 May 2004), at www.newyorker.com, accessed 1 October 2020

Hesford, Wendy S., 'Documenting Violations: Rhetorical Witnessing and the Spectacle of Suffering', *Biography*, XXVII/1 (2004)

—, 'Reading Rape Stories: Material Rhetoric and the Trauma of Representation', *College English*, LXII/2 (November 2004)

Hicks, George, 'The Comfort Women Redress Movement', in *When Sorry Isn't Enough: The Controversy over Apologies and Reparations for Human Injustice*, ed. Roy L. Brooks (New York, 1999)

Higginbotham, Nick, and Anthony J. Marsella, 'International Consultation and the Homogenization of Psychiatry in Southeast Asia', *Social Science and Medicine*, XXVII/5 (1988)

Hintjens, Helen M., 'Explaining the 1994 Genocide in Rwanda', *Journal of Modern African Studies*, XXXVII/2 (June 1999)

Hinton, Devon E., et al., '*Khyâl* Attacks: A Key Idiom of Distress among
    Traumatized Cambodian Refugees', *Culture, Medicine, and Psychiatry*,
    34 (2010)
Hoedemaker, Edward D., '"Irresistible Impulse" as a Defence in Criminal Law',
    Washington Law Review, XXIII/1 (February 1948)
Hogg, Nicole, 'Women's Participation in the Rwandan Genocide: Mothers or
    Monsters?', *International Review of the Red Cross*, XCII/877 (March 2010)
Holmes, Amanda, 'That Which Cannot Be Shared: On the Politics of Shame',
    Journal of Speculative Philosophy, XXIX/3 (2015)
Hoodfar, Homa, 'The Veil in Their Minds and on Our Heads: The Persistence of
    Colonial Images of Muslim Women', *Resources for Feminist Research*, XXII/3–4
    (Fall 1992/Winter 1993)
Howard, Keith, ed., *True Stories of the Korean Comfort Women: Testimonies Compiled
    by the Korean Council for Women Drafted for Military Sexual Slavery by Japan
    and the Research Association on the Women Drafted for Military Sexual Slavery
    by Japan*, trans. Young Joo Lee (London, 1995)
Hubbard, Dianne, 'Should a Minimum Sentence for Rape Be Imposed in Namibia?',
    Acta Juridica (1994)
Huggins, Jackie, et al., 'Dear Editors', *Women's Studies International Forum*, XIV/5
    (1991)
Hull, Jonah, 'The South African Scourge', Al-Jazeera (20 February 2011), at
    www.aljazeera.com, accessed 1 September 2020
Human Rights Watch, *Shattered Lives: Sexual Violence during the Rwandan Genocide
    and Its Aftermath* (New York, 1996), at www.hrw.org
——, *'We'll Kill You If You Cry': Sexual Violence in the Sierra Leone Conflict*
    (Washington, DC, 2003)
Human Rights Watch and National Coalition for Haitian Refugees, *Rape in Haiti:
    A Weapon of Terror*, VI/8 (1994)
Hunt, Swanee, *Rwandan Women Rising* (Durham, NC, 2017)
Huong, Nguyen Thu, 'At the Intersection of Gender, Sexuality, and Politics: The
    Disposition of Rape Cases among Some Ethnic Minority Groups of Northern
    Vietnam', *Journal of Social Issues in Southeast Asia*, XXVIII/1 (March 2013)
——, 'Rape Disclosure: The Interplay of Gender, Culture, and Kinship in
    Contemporary Vietnam', *Culture, Health, and Sexuality*, 14.S1 (November 2012)
——, 'Rape in Vietnam from Socio-Cultural and Historical Perspectives', *Journal of
    Asian History*, XL/2 (2006)
Husejnvic, Merima, 'Bosnian War's Wicked Women Get Off Lightly', *Balkan Insight*
    (7 February 2011), at https://balkaninsight.com, accessed 1 October 2020
Huskey, Kristine A., 'The "Sex Interrogators" of Guantanamo', in *One of the Guys:
    Women as Aggressors and Torturers*, ed. Tara McKelvey (New York, 2007)

ICTY, 'Celebici Case: The Judgement of the Trial Chamber' (16 November 1998),
    at www.icty.org, and ICTY, 'Furundzija', at www.icty.org
Inglis, Amirah, *The White Woman's Protection Ordinance: Sexual Anxiety and Politics
    in Papua* (London, 1975)
'Interview', *Filmnews* (1 December 1980)
'Ivory Coast's "Iron Lady" Jailed for 20 Years over Election Violence', *France24*
    (10 March 2015), www.france24.com, accessed 1 September 2020

Jamel, Joanna, 'Researching the Provision of Service to Rape Victims by Specially
    Trained Police Officers. The Influence of Gender – An Exploratory Study', *New
    Criminal Law Review*, 4 (Fall 2010),
Janet, Pierre Maria Félix, *L'Automatisme psychologique* [1889] (Paris, 1930)
——, *État mental des hystériques* (Paris, 1894)
Jasinski, Jana L., and Linda M. Williams, with David Finklhor, *Partner Violence:
    A Comprehensive Review of 20 Years of Research* (Thousand Oaks, CA, 1998)
Jean-Charles, Régine Michelle, *Conflict Bodies: The Politics of Rape Representation
    in the Francophone Imaginary* (Columbus, OH, 2014)
Jeffrey, Patricia, and Amrita Basu, *Appropriating Gender: Women's Activism and
    Politicized Religion in South Asia* (New York, 2012)
Jennes, Valerie, and Sarah Fenstermaker, 'Forty Years after Brownmiller: Prisons for
    Men, Transgender Inmates, and the Rape of the Feminine', *Gender and Society*,
    XXX/1 (February 2016)
——, et al., *Violence in California Correction Facilities: An Empirical Examination
    of Sexual Assault* (Irvine, CA, 2007)
Jennings, Thelma, '"Us Colored Women Had to Go through a Plenty": Sexual
    Exploitation of African-American Slave Women', *Journal of Women's History*,
    1/3 (1990)
Jewkes, R., et al., 'Factors Associated with HIV-Sero-Positivity in Young, Rural South
    African Men', *International Journal of Epidemiology*, XXXV/6 (December 2006)
Joffily, Mariana, 'Sexual Violence in the Military Dictatorships of Latin America:
    Who Wants to Know?', *Sur International Journal on Human Rights*, 24 (2016)
John Jay College of Criminal Justice at City University of New York, *The Nature and
    Scope of Sexual Abuse of Minors by Catholic Priests and Deacons in the United
    States, 1950–2002* (Washington, DC, June 2004), at www.usccb org, accessed
    22 December 2014
Johnson, Kirsten, et al., 'Association of Combatant Status and Sexual Violence with
    Health and Mental Health Outcomes in Postconflict Libera', *JAMA (Journal of
    the American Medical Association)*, XXX/6 (2008)
——, 'Association of Sexual Violence and Human Rights Violations with Physical and
    Mental Health in Territories of the Eastern Democratic Republic of the Congo',
    JAMA, XXXIV/5 (2010)
Jones, Adam, 'Gender and Genocide in Rwanda', *Journal of Genocide Research*,
    IV/1 (2002)
Jonsson, Gabriel, 'Can the Japan-Korea Dispute on "Comfort Women" Be
    Resolved?', *Korea Observer*, XLVI/3 (Autumn 2015)
Jordan, Jan, 'Beyond Belief? Police, Rape, and Women's Credibility', *Criminology
    and Criminal Justice*, IV/1 (2004)
Joshi, Manisha, et al., 'Language of Sexual Violence in Haiti: Perceptions of Victims,
    Community-Level Workers, and Health Care Providers', *Journal of Health Care
    for the Poor and Underserved*, XXV/4 (November 2014)

Kabir, Ananya Jahanara, 'Double Violation? (Not) Talking about Sexual Violence
    in Contemporary South Asia', in *Feminism, Literature, and Rape Narratives:
    Violence and Violation*, ed. Sorcha Gunne and Zoë Brigley Thompson
    (New York, 2010)
Kaldor, Mary, *New and Old Wars: Organized Violence in a Global Era*
    (Cambridge, 1999)

Kalichman, Seth C., et al., 'Gender Attitudes, Sexual Violence, and HIV/AIDS Risks among Men and Women in Cape Town, South Africa', *Journal of Sex Research*, XLII/4 (November 2005)

Kamal, S., 'The 1971 Genocide in Bangladesh and Crimes Committed against Women', in *Common Grounds: Violence against Women in War and Armed Conflict Situations*, ed. I. L. Sajor (Quezon City, Philippines, 1998)

Kannabiran, Kalpana, *Tools of Justice: Non-Discrimination and the Indian Constitution* (London, 2012)

Kaoma, Kapya, *Globalizing the Culture Wars: U.S. Conservatives, African Churches, and Homophobia* (Somerville, MA, 2009), at www.arcusfoundation.org, accessed 5 April 2020

Kaplan, Caren, and Inderpal Grewal, 'Transnational Practices and Interdisciplinary Feminist Scholarship: Refiguring Women's and Gender Studies', in *Women's Studies on Its Own*, ed. Robyn Wiegman (Durham, NC, 2002)

Kapur, Ratna, and Brenda Crossman, '"Communalising Gender/Engendering Community": Women, Legal Discourse, Saffron Agenda', *Economic and Political Weekly*, XXVIII/17 (1993)

Karapinar, Christina, 'The Comfort Women's Activism through the Arts', *Dissenting Voices*, VIII/1 (Spring 2019)

Karmen, Erjaavee, and Zala Volčič, '"Target", "Cancer", and "Warrior": Exploring Painful Metaphors of Self-Presentation Used by Girls Born of War Rape', *Discourse and Society*, XXI/5 (September 2010)

Karpman, Benjamin, *The Sexual Offender and His Offenses: Etiology, Pathology, Psychodynamics and Treatment* [1954], 9th edn (Washington, DC, 1964)

Katz, Steven T., 'Thoughts on the Intersection of Rape and *Rassenschande* during the Holocaust', *Modern Judaism*, XXXII/3 (October 2012)

Kayitesi-Blewitt, Mary, 'Funding Development in Rwanda: The Survivors' Perspective', *Development in Practice*, XVI/3–4 (June 2006)

Kelly, Liz, Jo Lovett and Linda Regan, *A Gap or a Chasm? Attrition in Reported Rape Cases*, Home Office Research Study 293 (London, February 2005)

Kent, Alexandra, 'Global Challenge and Moral Uncertainty: Why Do Cambodian Women See Refuge in Buddhism?', *Global Change, Peace, and Security*, XXIII/3 (2011)

Kersten, Mark, 'If Simone Gbagbo Ends Up in the Hague, She Won't Be the First', *Justice in Conflict* (23 November 2012), at https://justiceinconflict.org, accessed 1 October 2020

Kevin, Catherine, 'Creative Work: Feminist Representations of Gendered and Domestic Violence in 1970s Australia', in *Everyday Revolutions: Remaking ender, Sexuality, and Culture in 1970s Australia*, ed. Michelle Arrow and Angela Woollacott (Canberra, 2019)

Keygnaert, Ines, Nicole Vettenburg and Marleen Temmerman, 'Hidden Violence Is Silent Rape: Sexual and Gender-Based Violence in Refugees, Asylum Seekers, and Undocumented Migrants in Belgium and the Netherlands', *Culture, Health, and Society*, XIV/5 (May 2012)

Khoshaba, Riva, 'Women in the Interrogation Room', in *One of the Guys: Women as Aggressors and Torturers*, ed. Tara McKelvey (New York, 2007)

Kiage, Patrick, 'Prosecutions: A Panacea for Kenya's Past Atrocities', *East African Journal of Human Rights and Democracy*, II/2 (June 2004)

Kim, Hyun Sook, 'History and Memory: The "Comfort Women" Controversy', *positions*, V/1 (1997)

Kinzie, J. David, 'A Model for Treating Refugees Traumatized by Violence', *Psychiatric Times* (10 July 2009)

Kirmayer, Laurence J., 'Cultural Variations in the Clinical Presentation of Depression and Anxiety: Implications for Diagnosis and Treatment', *Journal of Clinical Psychiatry*, 62 (2001)

Kleinman, Arthur, 'Anthropology and Psychiatry: The Role of Culture in Cross-Cultural Research on Illness', *British Journal of Psychiatry*, 151 (1987)

Klot, Jennifer F., Judith D. Auberbach and Miranda R. Berry, 'Sexual Violence and HIV Transmission: Summary Proceedings of a Scientific Research Planning Meeting', *American Journal of Reproductive Immunology*, LXIX/1 (February 2013)

Kohrt, Brandon, and Daniel J. Hruschka, 'Nepali Concepts of Psychological Trauma: The Role of Idioms of Distress, Ethnopsychology, and Ethnophysiology in Alleviating Suffering and Preventing Stigma', *Culture, Medicine, and Psychiatry*, 34 (2010)

Kong, Rebecca, et al., 'Sexual Offences in Canada', *Juristat. Canadian Centre for Justice Statistics*, XXIII/6 (July 2003)

Koomen, Jonneke, '"Without These Women, the Tribunal Cannot Do Anything": The Politics of Witness Testimony on Sexual Violence at the International Criminal Tribunal for Rwanda', *Signs: Journal of Women in Culture and Society*, XXXVIII/2 (Winter 2013)

Korean Council, *Witness of the Victims of Military Sexual Slavery* (Seoul, 1992)

Krafft-Ebing, Richard von, *Psychopathia Sexualis, with Especial Reference to Contrary Sexual Instinct: A Medico-Legal Study*, authorized trans. from German by Charles Gilbert Chaddock (Philadelphia, PA, 1892)

Krahé, Barbara Anja Berger, Ine Vanwesenbeeck et al., 'Prevalence and Correlates of Young People's Sexual Aggression Perpetration and Victimisation in 10 European Countries: A Multi-Level Analysis', *Culture, Health and Sexuality: An International Journal for Research, Intervention, and Care*, VIII/6 (January 2015)

Kroll, Jerome, and Ahmed Ismail Yusuf, 'Psychiatric Issues in the Somali Refugee Population', *Psychiatric Times* (4 September 2013)

Kwon, Vicki Sung-yeon, 'The Sonyŏsang Phenomenon: Nationalism and Feminism Surrounding the "Comfort Women"', *Korean Studies*, 43 (2019)

Landesman, Peter K., 'A Woman's Work', *New York Times Magazine* (15 September 2002), at www.nytimes.com

Landsberg, Michele, 'Men behind Most Atrocities, but Women Are Singled Out', *Toronto Star* (21 September 2002), at http://freerepublic.com, accessed 1 September 2020

Langenderfer-Magruder, Lisa, et al., 'Experiences of Intimate Partner Violence and Subsequent Police Reporting among Lesbian, Gay, Bisexual, Transgender, and Queer Adults in Colorado: Comparing Rates of Cisgender and Transgender Victimization', *Journal of Interpersonal Violence*, XXXI/5 (November 2014)

Larbalestier, Jan, 'The Politics of Representation: Australian Aboriginal Women and Feminism', *Anthropological Forum: A Journal of Social Anthropology and Comparative Sociology*, VI/2 (1990)

Larcombe, Wendy, and Mary Heath, 'Developing the Common Law and Rewriting the History of Rape in Marriage in Australia: PGA v the Queen', *Sydney Law Review*, XXXIV/1 (2012)

Lawry, Lynn, Kirsten Johnson and Jana Asher, 'Evidence-Based Documentation of Gender-Based Violence', in *Sexual Violence as an International Crime: Interdisciplinary Approaches*, ed. A.L.M. Bouwer, C. de Ku, R. Römkens and L. van den Herik (Cambridge, 2013)

Lee, Na-Young, 'The Korean Women's Movement of Japanese Military "Comfort Women": Navigating between Nationalism and Feminism', *Review of Korean Studies*, XVII/1 (2014)

Leonnig, Carol, and Dana Priest, 'Detainees Accuse Female Interrogators: Pentagon Inquiry Is Said to Confirm Muslims' Accounts of Sexual Tactics at Guantánamo', *Washington Post* (10 February 2005), at www.washingtonpost.com, accessed 1 September 2020

Levan, Kristine, Katherine Polzer and Steven Downing, 'Media and Prison Sexual Assault: How We Got to the "Don't Drop the Soap" Culture', *International Journal of Criminology and Sociological Theory*, IV/2 (December 2011)

Levi, Primo, *The Drowned and the Saved* (New York, 1989)

Lewis, Helen B., *Shame and Guilt in Neurosis* (New York, 1971)

Lieber, Francis, *Instructions for the Government of Armies of the United States in the Field, General Orders no. 100* (24 April 1863), no. 44, at http://avalon.law.yale.edu

Lilly, J. Robert, *La Face cachée des GI's: Les viols commis par des soldats américains en France, en Angleterre et en Allemagne pendant la Seconde Guerre mondiale* (Paris, 2003)

—, *Taken by Force: Rape and American GIs in Europe during World War II* (Basingstoke, 2007)

Lionnet, Françoise, and Shu-Mei Shih, 'Introduction: Thinking through the Minor, Transnationally', in *Minor Transnationalism*, ed. Françoise Lionnet and Shu-Mei Shih (Durham, NC, 2005)

Lipsett-Rivera, Sonya, 'The Intersection of Rape and Marriage in Late-Colonial and Early National Mexico', *Colonial Latin American Historical Review*, VI/4 (Fall 1997)

Lodhia, Sharmila, 'Legal Frankensteins and Monstrous Women: Judicial Narratives of the "Family in Crisis"', *Meridians*, IX/2 (2009)

Lorch, Dontella, 'Wave of Rape Adds New Horror to Rwanda's Trail of Brutality', *New York Times* (15 May 1995), at www.nytimes.com

Lorde, Audre, 'The Master's Tools Will Never Dismantle the Master's House', in *The Essential Feminist Reader*, ed. Estelle Freedman (New York, 2007)

Luo, Tsun-in, '"Marrying My Rapist?!": The Cultural Trauma among Chinese Rape Survivors', *Gender and Society*, XIV/4 (August 2000)

Lusimbo, Richard, and Austin Bryan, '*Kuchu* Resilience and Resistance in Uganda: A History', in *Envisioning Global LGBT Human Rights: (Neo)Colonialism, Neoliberalism, Resistance, and Hope*, ed. Nancy Nicol et al. (London, 2018)

McCahill, Thomas W., Linda C. Meyer and Arthur M. Fischman, *The Aftermath of Rape* (Lexington, MA, 1979)

McCormick, Richard W., 'Rape and War, Gender and Nation, Victims and Victimizers: Helke Sander's *Befreir und Befreite*', *Camera Obscura*, XVI/1 (2001)

MacDonald, George J., and Robinson A. Williams, *Characteristics and Management of Committed Sexual Offenders in the State of Washington* (State of Washington, 1971)

McKay, Susan, 'Girls as "Weapons of Terror" in Northern Uganda and Sierra Leonean Rebel Fighting Forces', *Studies in Conflict and Terrorism*, 28 (2005)

McKelvey, Robert S., *The Dust of Life: America's Children Abandoned in Vietnam* (Seattle, WA, 1999)

MacKenzie, Megan, *Beyond the Band of Brothers: The U.S. Military and the Myth That Women Can't Fight* (Cambridge, 2015)

—, 'Securitization and Desecuritization: Female Soldiers and the Reconstruction of Women in Post-Conflict Sierra Leone', *Security Studies*, 18 (2009)

MacKenzie, Megan H., *Female Soldiers in Sierra Leone: Sex, Security, and Post-Conflict Development* (New York, 2012)

McKinley, James C., Jr, 'Legacy of Rwanda Violence: The Thousands Born of Rape', *New York Times* (25 September 1996), at www.nytimes.com

MacKinnon, Catharine, 'Turning Rape into Pornography: Postmodern Genocide', *Ms.*, IV/1 (July/August 1993)

MacKinnon, Catharine A., 'Sexuality, Pornography, and Method: Pleasure under Patriarchy', *Ethics*, XCIX/2 (January 1989)

—, *Toward a Feminist Theory of the State* (Cambridge, 1989)

McLean, Iain, and Stephen L'Heureux, 'Sexual Assault Services in Japan and the UK', *Japan Forum*, XIX/2 (2007)

McMullen, R. J., *Male Rape: Breaking the Silence on the Last Taboo* (London, 1990)

Madigan, Lee, and Nancy C. Gamble, *The Second Rape: Society's Continued Betrayal of the Victim* (New York, 1991)

Man, Christopher D., and John P. Cronan, 'Forecasting Sexual Abuse in Prison: The Prison Subculture of Masculinity as a Backdrop for "Deliberate Indifference"', *Journal of Criminal Law and Criminology*, XCII/1 (Fall 2001)

'Man and Wife Bill Sparks a Rumble', [Melbourne] *Herald* (23 October 1976)

Mann, Bonnie, 'How America Justifies Its War: A Modern/Postmodern Aesthetics of Masculinity and Sovereignty', *Hypatia*, XXI/4 (Fall 2006)

Marcus, Sharon, 'Fighting Bodies, Fighting Words: A Theory and Politics of Rape Prevention', in *Feminists Theorize the Political*, ed. Judith Butler and Joan W. Scott (London, 1992)

Mardorossian, Carine M., 'Toward a New Feminist Theory of Rape', *Signs: Journal of Women in Culture and Society*, XXVII/3 (Spring 2002)

Mark, James, 'Remembering Rape: Divided Social Memory and the Red Army in Hungary 1944–1945', *Past and Present*, 188 (August 2005)

Marsella, Anthony J., et al., eds, *Ethnocultural Aspects of Post-Traumatic Stress Disorder: Issues, Research, and Clinical Applications* (Washington, DC, 1996)

Medical Center for Human Rights, *Characteristics of Sexual Abuse of Men during the War in the Republic of Croatia and Bosnia and Herzegovina* (Zagreb, 1995)

—, *Report of Male Sexual Torturing as a Specific Way of War: Torturing of Males in the Territory of Republic of Croatia and Bosnia and Herzegovina* (Zagreb, 1995)

Meger, Sara, 'Rape in Contemporary Warfare: The Role of Globalization in Wartime Sexual Violence', *African Conflict and Peacebuilding Review*, I/1 (Spring 2011)

Mehta, Purvi, 'Dalit Feminism in Tokyo: Analogy and Affiliation in Transnational Dalit Activism', *Feminist Review*, 121 (2019)

Mehta, Swati, *Killing Justice: Vigilantism in Nagpur* (New Delhi: Commonwealth

Human Rights Initiative, 2005), at https://humanrightsinitiative.org, accessed 10 January 2021

'Memphis Riots and Massacres', House of Representatives, 39th Congress, 1st session, Report No. 101 (25 July 1866)

Mendes, Kaitlynn, Jessica Ringrose and Jessalynn Keller, '#MeToo and the Promise and Pitfalls of Challenging Rape Culture through Digital Feminist Activism', *European Journal of Women's Studies*, XXV/2 (May 2018), at www.researchgate.net, accessed 1 October 2020

Menon, Nivedita, 'Harvard to the Rescue!', *Kafila* (16 February 2013), at https://kafila.online, accessed 11 April 2020

Menon, Ritu, and Kamla Bhasin, *Borders and Boundaries: Women in India's Partition* (New Brunswick, 1998)

—, 'Recovery, Rupture, Resistance: Indian State and Abduction of Women during Partition', *Economic and Political Weekly*, XXVIII/17 (24 April 1993)

Meyer, Doug, *Violence against Queer People: Race, Class, Gender, and the Persistence of Anti-LGBT Discrimination* (New Brunswick, NJ, 2015)

Mezey, Gillian C., and Michael B. King, eds, *Male Victims of Sexual Assault* (Oxford, 2000)

Michalska-Warias, Aneta, 'Marital Rape in Poland from the Legal and Criminological Perspectives', in *Prawo w Działaniu*, 26 (2016)

Mieko, Yoshihama, 'Domestic Violence: Japan's "Hidden Crime"', *Japan Quarterly*, XLVI/3 (July–September 1999)

Mill, John Stuart, 'The Subjection of Women', in *On Liberty. Representative Government. The Subjection of Women. Three Essays*, 1st pub. 1869 (London, 1912)

Miller, Kristine Levan, 'The Darkest Figure of Crime: Perceptions of Reasons for Male Inmates Not Reporting Sexual Assault', *Justice Quarterly*, XXVII/5 (October 2010)

Mkhize, Nonhlanhla, et al., *The Country We Want to Live In: Hate Crimes and Homophobia in the Lives of Black Lesbian South Africans* (Cape Town, 2010), at https://open.uct.ac.za, accessed 1 December 2020

'M. Night Shyamalan Foundation', at www.mnsfoundation.org, accessed 7 June 2020

Mohanty, Chandra Talpade, *Feminism without Borders: Decolonizing Theory, Practicing Solidarity* (Durham, NC, 2003)

—, 'Under Western Eyes: Feminist Scholarship and Colonial Discourses', *boundary*, XIII/2 (Spring–Autumn 1984)

—, '"Under Western Eyes" Revisited: Feminist Solidarity through Anticapitalist Struggles', *Signs: Journal of Women in Culture and Society*, XXVIII/2 (Winter 2003)

Mookherjee, Nayanika, 'The Absent Piece of Skin: Gendered, Racialized, and Territorial Inscriptions of Sexual Violence during the Bangladesh War', *Modern Asian Studies*, XLVI/6 (2012)

Moore, Ann M., Nyovani Madise and Kofi Awusabo-Asare, 'Unwanted Sexual Experiences among Young Men in Sub-Saharan African Countries', *Culture, Health, and Sexuality*, XIV/9–10 (October–November 2012)

Moran, Mary H., *Liberia: The Violence of Democracy* (Philadelphia, PA, 2006)

Morris, Madeline, 'By Force of Arms: Rape, War, and Military Culture', *Duke Law Journal*, XLV/4 (February 1996)

Mosbergen, Dominique, 'Battling Asexual Discrimination, Sexual Violence, and "Corrective" Rape', *Huffington Post* (20 June 2013), www.huffingtonpost.co.uk, accessed 5 April 2020

Mudahogora, Chantal, 'When Women Become Killers', *Hamilton Spectator* (19 October 2002)

Mufweba, Yolanda, 'Corrective Rape Makes You an African Woman', [South African] *Saturday Star* (8 November 2003)

Mugabe, Robert, 'Homosexuals Are Worse Than Pigs and Dogs', *Zambian Watchdog* (27 November 2011), at www.zambiawatchdog.com, accessed on 20 March 2020

Mühlhäuser, Regina, 'Between "Racial Awareness" and Fantasies of Potency: Nazi Sexual Politics in the Occupied Territories of the Soviet Union, 1942–1945', in *Brutality and Desire: War and Sexuality in Europe's Twentieth Century*, ed. Dagmar Herzog (Basingstoke, 2009)

Muholi, Zanele, 'Faces and Phases', *Transition*, 107 (2012)

—, 'Thinking Through Lesbian Rape', *Agenda: Empowering Women for Gender Equity*, 61 (2004)

Mullins, Christopher W., '"He Would Kill Me with His Penis": Genocidal Rape in Rwanda as a State Crime', *Critical Criminology*, XVII/1 (2009)

Murphy, Maureen, Mary Ellsberg and Manuel Contreras-Urbana, 'Nowhere to Go: Disclosure and Help-Seeking Behaviors for Survivors of Violence against Women and Girls in South Sudan', *Conflict and Health*, XIV/6 (2020)

Murray, Stephen O., and Will Roscoe, eds, *Boy-Wives and Female Husbands: Studies of African Homosexualities* (Basingstoke, 1998)

Musalo, Karen, 'El Salvador – A Peace Worse Than War: Violence, Gender, and a Failed Legal Response', *Yale Journal of Law and Feminism*, XXX/1 (2018)

Mwambene, Lea, and Maudri Wheal, 'Realisation or Oversight of the Constitutional Mandate: Corrective Rape of Black African Lesbians in South Africa', *African Human Rights Law Journal*, XV/1 (2015)

Myhill, A., and J. Allen, *Rape and Sexual Assault of Women: The Extent and Nature of the Problem – Findings from the British Crime Survey*, Home Office Research Study 237 (London, 2002)

Naarden, Gregory L., 'Nonprosecutorial Sanctions for Grave Violations of International Humanitarian Law: Wartime Conduct of Bosnian Police Officers', *American Journal of International Law*, XCVII/2 (April 2003)

Naidoo, Latashia, 'Cape Town Lesbian Gets Justice', reporting for eNCA (27 November 2013), at www.youtube.com

Napheys, George Henry, *The Transmission of Life: Counsels on the Nature and Hygiene of the Masculine Functions* (Toronto, 1884)

National Association for the Advancement of Colored People (NAACP), 'History of Lynchings', at www.naacp.org, accessed 1 December 2020

National Coalition of Anti-Violence Programs, 'Lesbian, Gay, Bisexual, Transgender, Queer, and HIV-Affected Intimate Partner Violence' (New York: NCAVP, 2012), at https://avp.org, accessed 1 October 2020

—, 'Lesbian, Gay, Bisexual, Transgender, Queer, and HIV-Affected Intimate Partner Violence' (New York: NCAVP, 2016), at https://avp.org, accessed 1 October 2020

Neier, Aryeh, 'Watching Rights: Rapes in Bosnia-Herzegovina', *The Nation* (1 March 1993)

—, and Laurel Fletcher, 'Rape as a Weapon of War in the Former Yugoslavia', *Hastings Women's Law Journal*, 5 (1994)

Nelson, Topsy Napurrula, 'Dear Editors', *Women's Studies International Forum*, XIV/5 (1991)

Niarchos, Catherine N., 'Women, War, and Rape: Challenges Facing the International
    Tribunal for the Former Yugoslavia', *Human Rights Quarterly*, 17 (1995)
Nicholson, Zara, 'You Are Not a Man, Rapist Tells Lesbian', *Cape Argus* (4 April
    2010), at www.iol.co.za, accessed 1 October 2020
Nivette, Amy E., 'Institutional Ineffectiveness, Illegitimacy, and Public Support for
    Vigilantism in Latin America', *Criminology*, LIV/1 (February 2016)
Nkabinde, Nkunzi Zandile, *Black Bull, Ancestors and Me: My Life as a Lesbian
    Sangoma* (Johannesburg, 2008)
Nowrojee, Binaifer, *Shattered Lives: Sexual Violence during the Rwandan Genocide
    and Its Aftermath* (New York, 1996)
——, '"Your Justice Is Too Slow": Will the ICTR Fail Rwanda's Rape Victims?',
    occasional paper no. 10 (Geneva, 2006)
NSW, 'Crimes (Sexual Assault) Bill and Cognate Bill (Second Reading)',
    Parliamentary Debates Legislative Assembly (8 April 1981)
Nyabola, Nanjala, 'Kenyan Feminisms in the Digital Age', *Women's Studies Quarterly*,
    XLVI/3–4 (Fall/Winter 2018)

Olsson, Ola, and Heather Congdon Fors, 'Congo: The Prize of Predation', *Journal
    of Peace Research*, XLI/3 (May 2004)
'One in Four South African Men Admit Rape', Reuters (25 June 2000), at 'A Petition
    to Bring Suit against Defendants (Including the Pharmaceutical Manufacturers'
    Association and Members of the United States Government) on the Charge
    of Genocide against Individuals Living with HIV/AIDS' (29 July 2000), at
    www.fiar.us, accessed 1 October 2020
'On the Offensive', *Filmnews* (1 January 1981)
Oosterhoff, Pauline, Prisca Zwanikken and Evert Ketting, 'Sexual Torture of Men in
    Croatia and Other Conflict Situations: An Open Secret', *Reproductive Health
    Matters*, XII/23 (May 2004)
Ortmann, Jorden, and Inge Lunde, 'Changing Identity, Low Self-Esteem,
    Depression, and Anxiety in 148 Torture Victims Treated at the RCT – Relation
    to Sexual Torture', paper presented at the WHO meeting of the Advisory Group
    on the Health Situation of Refugees and Victims of Organised Violence,
    Gothenburg (August 1988)
Orwell, George, 'Politics and the English Language', in *George Orwell: A Collection
    of Essays* (New York, 1954)

Pak, Hyeong-Jun, 'News Reporting on Comfort Women: Framing, Frame
    Difference, and Frame Changing in Four South Korean and Japanese
    Newspapers, 1998–2013', *Journalism and Mass Communication Quarterly*,
    XCIII/4 (2016)
Palmer, Dwight D., 'Conscious Motives in Psychopathic Behavior', *Proceedings
    of the American Academy of Forensic Sciences* (1954)
Parker, Linda S., 'Statutory Change and Ethnicity in Sex Crimes in Four California
    Counties, 1880–1920', *Western Legal History*, 6 (1993)
Parliamentary Debates, South Australian Legislative Council (11 November 1976)
Patai, Raphael, *The Arab Mind* (New York, 1973)
Patel, Pragna, 'Difficult Alliances: Treading the Minefield of Identity and Solidarity
    Politics', *Soundings*, 12 (Summer 1999)
Pedersen, Duncan, Hanna Kienzler and Jeffrey Gamarra, '*Llaki* and *Ñakary*: Idioms

of Distress and Suffering among Highland Quechua in the Peruvian Andes', *Culture, Medicine, and Psychiatry*, 34 (2010)

Peel, Michael, et al., 'The Sexual Abuse of Men in Detention in Sri Lanka', *The Lancet*, XXXLV/9220 (10 June 2000), at www.thelancet.com, accessed 1 August 2020

People's Union for Civil Liberties, *Human Rights Violations against the Transgender Community* (Bangalore, 2003), at www.pucl.org, accessed 20 April 2020

Perlin, Jan, 'The Guatemalan Historical Clarification Commission Finds Genocide', *ILSA Journal of International and Comparative Law*, VI/2 (2000)

Peterson, Vandana, 'Speeding Up Sexual Assault Trials: A Constructive Critique of India's Fast-Track Courts', *Yale Human Rights and Development Law Journal*, 1 (2016)

Phillips, James, 'The Cultural Dimension of DSM-5: PTSD', *Psychiatric Times* (15 August 2010)

Phillips, Stone, 'Behind the Abu Ghraib Photos', *Dateline NBC* (2 October 2005), at www.nbcnews.com, accessed 1 October 2020

Phipps, Alison, '"Every Woman Knows a Weinstein": Political Whiteness and White Woundedness in #MeToo and Public Feminisms around Sexual Violence', *Feminist Formations*, XXXI/2 (Summer 2019)

——, 'Whose Personal Is More Political? Experience in Contemporary Feminist Politics', *Feminist Theory*, XVII/3 (2016)

Piccato, Pablo, '"El Chalequero" or the Mexican Jack the Ripper: The Meanings of Sexual Violence in Turn-of-the-Century Mexico City', *Hispanic American Historical Review*, LXXXI/3–4 (August–November 2001)

Pokorak, Jeffrey J., 'Rape as a Badge of Slavery: The Legal History of, and Remedies for, Prosecutorial Race-of-Victim Charging Disparities', *Nevada Law Journal*, VII/1 (Fall 2006)

Polgreen, Lydia, 'Darfur's Babies of Rape are on Trial from Birth', *New York Times* (11 February 2005), at www.nytimes.com

Potocznick, Michael J., et al., 'Legal and Psychological Perspectives on Same-Sex Domestic Violence: A Multisystemic Approach', *Journal of Family Psychology*, XVII/2 (2003)

Powdermaker, Hortense, *After Freedom: A Cultural Study in the Deep South*, 1st pub. 1939 (New York, 1968)

Prasad, Raekha, '"Arrest Us All": The 200 Women Who Killed a Rapist', *The Guardian* (16 August 2005), at www.theguardian.com, accessed 20 April 2020

Prasad, Shally, 'Medicolegal Responses to Violence against Women', *Violence against Women*, V/5 (May 1999)

Price, Lisa S., 'Finding the Man in the Soldier-Rapist: Some Reflections on Comprehension and Accountability', *Women's Studies International Forum*, XXIV/2 (2001)

'The Problem of Domestic Rape', *New Law Journal*, 141 (15 February 1991)

Purshouse, Joe, '"Paedophile Hunters", Criminal Procedures, and Fundamental Human Rights', *Journal of Law and Society*, XLVII/3 (September 2020)

Quigley, Paxton, *Armed and Female: Taking Control* (Bellevue, WA, 2010)

——, *Armed and Female: 12 Million American Women Own Guns. Should You?* (New York, 1989)

——, *Armed and Female: 12 Million American Women Own Guns. Should You?* (New York, 1990)

——, *Not an Easy Target* (New York, 1995)
——, *Stayin' Alive: Armed and Female in an Unsafe World* (Bellevue, WA, 2005)

Radzinowicz, L., *Sexual Offences: A Report of the Cambridge Department of Criminal Science* (London, 1957)
Rahill, Guitele J., Manisha Joshi and Whitney Shadowens, 'Best Intentions Are Not Best Practices: Lessons Learned While Conducting Health Research with Trauma-Impacted Female Victims of Nonpartner Sexual Violence in Haiti', *Journal of Black Psychology*, XLIV/7 (22 November 2018)
Ramdas, Anu, 'In Solidarity with All Rape Survivors', *Savari* (20 December 2012), at www.dalitweb.org
Ramesh, Randeep, 'Women's Revenge against Rapists', *The Guardian* (9 November 2004), at www.theguardian.com, accessed 20 April 2020
Rao, Anupama, 'Understanding *Sirasgaon*: Notes towards Conceptualising the Role of Law, Caste, and Gender in the Case of "Atrocity"', in *Gender and Caste: Issues in Contemporary Feminism*, ed. Rajeswari Sunder Rajan (New Delhi, 2003)
——, 'Violence and Humanity: Or, Vulnerability as Political Subjectivity', *Social Research*, LXXVIII/2 (Summer 2011)
'Rape and Battery between Husband and Wife', *Stanford Law Review*, 6 (1953–4)
'Rapist Who Agreed to Use Condom Gets 40 Years', *New York Times* (15 May 1993), at www.nytimes.com, accessed 1 September 2020
Rasmussen, O. V., A. M. Dam and I. L. Nielsen, 'Torture: An Investigation of Chileans and Greeks Who Had Previously Been Submitted to Torture', *Ugeskr Laeger*, CXXXIX/18 (2 May 1977)
Ray, Rames Chandra, *Outlines of Medical Jurisprudence and the Treatment of Poisoning: For Students and Practitioners*, 6th edn (Calcutta, 1925)
Reid-Cunningham, Allison Ruby, 'Rape as a Weapon of Genocide', *Genocide Studies and Prevention*, III/3 (Winter 2008)
'Rep. Trent Franks Claims "Very Low" Pregnancy Rate for Rape', *ABC News*, 12 June 2013, at http://abcnews.go.com
Republic of South Africa, 'Act to Provide for the Granting of Interdicts with Regards to Family Violence', *Government Gazette* (1993), p. 4, at www.gov.za, accessed 1 December 2020
Reynold, William, 'The Remedy for Lynch Law', *Yale Law Journal*, VII/1 (October 1897)
Rich, Adrienne, 'Legislators of the World', *The Guardian* (18 November 2006), at www.theguardian.com, accessed 3 January 2014
Rich, Adrienne Cecile, 'Rape', in *Diving into the Wreck: Poems, 1971–72* (New York, 1973)
Riddell, William Renwick, 'Sir Matthew Hale and Witchcraft', *Journal of the American Institute of Criminal Law and Criminology*, 17 (1926)
Rinaldo, Rachel, 'Women Survivors of the Rwandan Genocide Face Grim Realities', *IPS News* (6 April 2004), at www.ipsnews.net (accessed 31 January 2015)
Robertson, James E., 'A Clean Heart and an Empty Head: The Supreme Court and Sexual Terrorism in Prison', *North Carolina Law Review*, LXXXI/2 (2003)
Robertson, Stephen, *Crimes against Children: Sexual Violence and Legal Culture in New York City, 1880–1960* (Chapel Hill, NC, 2005)
Robertson, Stephen, 'Seduction, Sexual Violence, and Marriage in New York City, 1886–1955', *Law and History Review*, XXIV/2 (Summer 2006)

——, 'Shifting the Scene of the Crime: Sodomy and the American History of Sexual Violence', *Journal of the History of Sexuality*, XIX/2 (May 2010)

Robins, Steven, 'Sexual Rights and Sexual Cultures: Reflections on "The Zuma Affair" and "New Masculinities" in the New South Africa', *Horizontes Antropológicos*, XII/26 (July–December 2006)

Robinson, Russell K., 'Masculinity as Prison: Sexual Identity, Race, and Incarceration', *California Law Review*, XCIX/5 (October 2011)

Rojan, Rajeswari Sunder, *Real and Imagined Women: Gender, Culture, and Postcolonialism* (London, 2003)

Rosser, Luther Z., 'Illegal Enforcement of Criminal Law', *American Bar Association Journal*, 7 (1921)

Roychowdhury, Poulami, 'The Delhi Gang Rape: The Making of International Causes', *Feminist Studies*, XXXIX/1 (2013)

——, 'Over the Law: Rape and the Seduction of Popular Politics', *Gender and Society*, XXX/1 (February 2016)

Ruicciardelli, Rosemary, and Mackenzie Moir, 'Stigmatized among the Stigmatized: Sex Offenders in Canadian Penitentiaries', *Canadian Journal of Criminology and Criminal Justice*, LV/3 (July 2013)

Russell, Diana H., *Rape in Marriage* (Indianapolis, IN, 1990)

Rwenge, Mburano, 'Sexual Risk Behavior among Young People in Bamenda, Cameroon', *International Family Planning Perspectives*, 26 (2000)

Saar, Erik, and V. Novak, *Inside the Wire: A Military Intelligence Soldier's Eyewitness Account of Life at Guantanamo* (New York, 2005)

Sadler, Anne G., et al., 'Health-Related Consequences of Physical and Sexual Violence: Women in the Military', *Obstetrics and Gynecology*, XCVI/3 (September 2000)

Saikia, Yasmin, *Women, War, and the Making of Bangladesh: Remembering 1971* (Durham, NC, 2011)

Salzman, Todd A., 'Rape Camps as a Means of Ethnic Cleansing: Religious, Cultural, and Ethnical Responses to Rape Victims in the Former Yugoslavia', *Human Rights Quarterly*, XX/2 (May 1998)

Sand, Jordan, 'Historians and Public Memory in Japan: The "Comfort Women" Controversy; Introduction', *History and Memory*, XI/2 (31 December 1995)

Sanday, Peggy Reeves, 'Rape-Free versus Rape-Prone: How Culture Makes a Difference', in *Evolution, Gender, and Rape*, ed. Cheryl Brown Travis (Cambridge, MA, 2003)

——, 'The Socio-Cultural Context of Rape: A Cross-Cultural Study', *Journal of Social Issues*, 37 (1981)

Sanger, Nadia, '"The Real Problems Need to be Fixed First": Public Discourses on Sexuality and Gender in South Africa', *Agenda: Empowering Women for Gender Equality*, 83 (2010)

Santhya, K. G., et al., 'Timing of First Sex before Marriage and Its Correlates: Evidence from India', *Culture, Health, and Sexuality*, XIII/3 (March 2011)

Saum, Christine A., et al., 'Sex in Prison: Exploring Myths and Realities', *Prison Journal*, 75 (1995)

Schmidt, David Andrew, *Ianfu: The Comfort Women of the Japanese Imperial Army of the Pacific War* (Lewiston, NY, 2000)

Scutt, Jocelynne, *Even in the Best of Homes: Violence in the Family* (Melbourne, 1983)

Seaton, Matt, 'The Unspeakable Crime', *The Guardian* [London] (18 November 2002)

Secomb, Linnell, 'Fractured Community', *Hypatia*, xv/2 (2000)
Seifert, Ruth, 'War and Rape: A Preliminary Analysis', in *Mass Rape: The War against Women in Bosnia-Herzegovina*, ed. Alexandra Stiglmayer (London, 1994)
Sen, Atreyee, 'Women's Vigilantism in India: A Case Study of the Pink Sari Gang', at *Online Encyclopedia of Mass Violence* (20 December 2012), at www.sciencespo.fr, accessed 5 April 2020
Sengupta, Bejoy Kumar, *Medical Jurisprudence and Texicology [sic]: With Post-Mortem Techniques and Management of Poisoning* (Calcutta, 1978)
Serisier, Tanya, *Speaking Out: Feminism, Rape, and Narrative Politics* (London, 2018)
Shadle, Brett L., 'Rape in the Courts of Gusiiland, Kenya, 1940s–1960s', *African Studies Review*, LI/2 (September 2008)
Shalhoub-Kevorkian, Nadera, 'Towards a Cultural Definition of Rape: Dilemmas in Dealing with Rape Victims in Palestinian Society', *Women's Studies International Forum*, XXII/2 (1999)
Sharlach, Lisa, 'Gender and Genocide in Rwanda: Women as Agents and Objects of Genocide', *Journal of Genocide Research*, I/3 (1999)
——, 'State Regulation of Rape Insurance and HIV Prevention in India and South Africa', a paper presented at the American Political Science Association meeting (3 September 2009), https://ssrn.com, accessed 11 January 2021
Shaw, Carolyn Martin, *Women and Power in Zimbabwe* (Champaign, IL, 2015)
Shibata, Toma, 'Japan's Wartime Mass-Rape Camps and Continuing Sexual Human-Rights Violations', *U.S.-Japan Women's Journal. English Supplement*, 16 (1999)
Shikola, Teckla, 'We Left Our Shoes Behind', in *What Women Do in Wartime: Gender and Conflict in Africa*, ed. Meredeth Turshen and Clotilde Twagiramariya (London, 1998)
Shim, Young-Hee, 'Metamorphosis of the Korean "Comfort Women": How Did *Han* Turn into the Cosmopolitan Morality?', *Development and Society*, XLVI/2 (September 2017)
Siddique, Haroon, '"We Are Facing the Decriminalisation of Rape", Warns Victims' Commissioner', *The Guardian* (14 July 2020), at www.theguardian.com, accessed 14 July 2020
Silove, D., 'The Asylum Debacle in Australia: A Challenge for Psychiatry', *Australian and New Zealand Journal of Psychiatry*, XXXVI/3 (2002)
Singh, B. Sardar, *A Manual of Medical Jurisprudence for Police Officers*, 3rd edn (Moradabad, 1916)
Sipe, A.W.R., *Sex, Priests, and Power: Anatomy of a Crisis* (New York, 1995)
Sivakumaran, Sandesh, 'Male/Male Rape and the "Taint" of Homosexuality', *Human Rights Quarterly*, XXVII/4 (November 2005)
——, 'Sexual Violence against Men in Armed Conflict', *European Journal of International Law*, XVIII/2 (2007)
Sjoberg, Laura, 'Agency, Militarized Femininity, and Enemy Others: Observations from the War in Iraq', *International Feminist Journal of Politics*, IX/1 (March 2007)
Sjoberg, Laura, and Caron E. Gentry, *Beyond Mothers, Monsters, Whores: Thinking about Women's Violence in Global Politics* (London, 2015)
——, *Mothers, Monsters, Whores: Women's Violence in Global Politics* (London, 2007 and 2013)
Slutsky, Boris, *Things That Happened*, ed. G. S. Smith (Birmingham, 1998)

Smeulers, Alette, 'Female Perpetrators: Ordinary and Extra-Ordinary Women',
    International Criminal Law Review, 15 (2015)
Smith, Brenda V., 'Watching You, Watching Me', *Yale Journal of Law and Feminism*,
    XV/2 (2003)
Smith, Bruce D., et al., 'Ethnomedical Syndromes and Treatment-Seeking Behavior
    among Mayan Refugees in Chiapas, Mexico', *Culture, Medicine, and Psychiatry*,
    33 (2009)
Smith, Helena, 'Revealed: The Cruel Fate of War's Rape Babies', *The Observer*
    [London] (16 April 2000)
Somanader, Tanya, 'Angle: Rape Victims Should Use Their Pregnancies as
    a Way to Turn Lemons into Lemonade', *Think Progress*, 8 July 2010, at
    http://thinkprogress.org, accessed 28 December 2014
Sommer, Robert, *Das kz-Bordell: Sexuelle Zwangsarbeit in nationalsozialistischen
    Konzentrationslagern* (Paderborn, 2009)
Sommerville, Diane Miller, *Rape and Race in the Nineteenth-Century South*
    (Chapel Hill, NC, 2004)
Soto, Christopher, 'In Support of Violence', *Tin House*, 70 (13 December 2016),
    at https://tinhouse.com, accessed 1 September 2020
Southern Poverty Law Center, 'Male Supremacy', at www.splcenter.org, accessed
    1 October 2020
Specht, Irma, *Red Shoes: Experiences of Girl Combatants in Liberia* (Geneva, 2006)
Spiller, Peter, 'Race and the Law in the District and Supreme Courts of Natal, 1846–
    1874', *South African Law Journal*, CI/3 (1984)
Stafford, Nancy Kaymar, 'Permission for Domestic Violence: Marital Rape in
    Ghanaian Marriages', *Women's Rights Law Reporter*, 29 (2008)
Stanton, Elizabeth Cady, *History of Woman Suffrage* (New York, 1881)
'State v. Dutton, 450 N.W.2d (1990). State of Minnesota, Respondent, v. Robert
    Eugene Dutton, Appellant', at https://law.justia.com, accessed 4 April 2020
Stefatos, Katherine, 'The Psyche and the Body: Political Persecution and Gender
    Violence against Women in the Greek Civil War', *Journal of Modern Greek
    Studies*, XXIX/2 (October 2011)
Stevens, Joyce, *A History of International Women's Day in Words and Images*
    (Sydney, 1985)
Stockham, Alice B., *Tokology: A Book for Every Woman* (Chicago, IL, 1889)
Stojsavljevic, Jovanka, 'Women, Conflict, and Culture in Former Yugoslavia', *Gender
    and Development*, III/1 (February 1995)
Storer, Horatio R., 'The Law of Rape', *Quarterly Journal of Psychological Medicine
    and Medical Jurisprudence*, II (1868)
Storr, Will, 'The Rape of Men: The Darkest Secret of War', *The Guardian*
    (16 July 2011), at www.theguardian.com, accessed 1 September 2020.
Struckman-Jones, David L., and Cynthia Struckman-Jones, 'Sexual Coercion
    Rates in Seven Midwestern Prison Facilities for Men', *Prison Journal*, 80
    (2000)
Stubbs-Richardson, Megan, Nicole E. Rader and Arthur G. Cosby, 'Tweeting Rape
    Cultures: Examining Portrayals of Victim Blaming in Discussions of Sexual
    Assault Cases on Twitter', *Feminism and Psychology*, XXVIII/1 (2018)
Summerfield, Derek, 'A Critique of Seven Assumptions behind the Psychological
    Trauma Programmes in War-Affected Areas', *Social Science and Medicine*, 48
    (1999)

Sung, Yoo Kyung, 'Hearing the Voices of "Comfort Women": Confronting
   Historical Trauma in Korean Children's Literature', *Bookbird*, 1 (2012)
Sutherland, Sandra, and Donald J. Scherl, 'Patterns of Response among Victims
   of Rape', *American Journal of Orthopsychiatry*, XL/3 (April 1970)
Swarr, Amanda Lock, 'Paradoxes of Butchness: Lesbian Masculinities and Sexual
   Violence in Contemporary South Africa', *Signs: Journal of Women in Culture
   and Society*, XXXVII/4 (Summer 2012)
Sze-Chie Fa, Marietta, 'Rape Myths in American and Chinese Law and Legal
   Systems: Do Tradition and Culture Make the Difference?', *Maryland Series
   in Contemporary Asian Studies*, 4 (2007)

Tamale, Sylvia, 'Exploring the Contours of African Sexualities: Religion, Law, and
   Power', *African Human Rights Law Journal*, XIV/1 (2014)
Tambe, Ashwini, 'Reckoning with the Silences of #MeToo', *Feminist Studies*, XLIV/1
   (2018)
Tardieu, Ambroise, *Étude médico-légale sur les attentats aux mœurs* (Paris, 1878)
Temkin, Jennifer, '"And Always Keep A-Hold of Nurse, For Fear of Finding
   Something Worse": Challenging Rape Myths in the Courtroom', *New Criminal
   Law Review*, XIII/4 (Fall 2010)
Terazawa, Yuki, 'The Transnational Campaigns for Redress for Wartime Rape by
   the Japanese Military: Cases for Survivors in Shanxi Province', *NWSA Journal*,
   XVIII/3 (Fall 2006)
Thapar-Björkert, Suruchi, and Madina Tlostanova, 'Identifying to Dis-Identify:
   Occidentalist Feminism, the Delhi Gang Rape Case, and Its Internal Others',
   Gender, Place, and Culture: A Journal of Feminist Geography, XXV/7 (2018)
Theidon, Kimberley, *Entre prójimos. El conflict armado interno y la política de la
   reconciliación en el Perú* (Lima, 2004)
Thomas, Dorothy Q., and Regan E. Ralph, 'Rape in War: Challenging the Tradition
   of Impunity', *SAIS Review*, XIV/11 (Winter–Spring 1994)
Thomas, Evan G., 'Explaining Lynndie England', *Newsweek* (May 2004), at https://
   www.newsweek.com/explaining-lynndie-england-128501
Thompson, Jessie, 'Pearl Mackie and Marai Larasi on Why UK Actresses and Activists
   are Saying Time's Up', *Evening Standard* (6 April 2018), at www.standard.co.uk,
   accessed 1 October 2020
Thornhill, Randy, and Craig T. Palmer, *A Natural History of Rape: Biological Bases
   of Sexual Coercion* (Cambridge, MA, 2000)
Thornley, Jeni, 'Age before Beauty/Behind Closed Doors', *Filmnews* (1 December 1980)
Thorpe, J. R., 'This Is How Many People Have Posted "Me Too" since October,
   According to New Data', *Bustle* (1 December 2017), at www.bustle.com, accessed
   1 October 2020
Ticktin, Miriam, 'Sexual Violence as the Language of Border Control: Where French
   Feminist and Anti-Immigrant Rhetoric Meet', *Signs: Journal of Women in
   Culture and Society*, XXXIII/4 (Summer 2008)
Tilleman, Morgan, '(Trans)forming the Provocation Defence', *Journal of Criminal
   Law and Criminology*, C/4 (Fall 2010)
'Todd Akin on Abortion', 19 August 2012, at www.huffingtonpost.com, accessed
   28 December 2014
'To Have and To Hold: The Marital Rape Exemption and the Fourteenth
   Amendment', *Harvard Law Review*, 99 (1985–6)

Tosh, John, *A Man's Place: Masculinity and the Middle-Class Home in Victorian England* (New Haven, CT, 1999)

Traumüller, Richard, Sara Kijewski and Markus Freitag, 'The Silent Victims of Wartime Sexual Violence: Evidence from a List Experiment in Sri Lanka' (2017), at https://papers.ssrn.com, accessed 1 October 2020

Treloar, Carol, 'The Politics of Rape: A Politician's Perspective', in *Rape Law Reform: A Collection of Conference Papers*, ed. Jocelynne A. Scutt (Canberra, 1980)

Trouille, Helen, 'How Far Has the International Criminal Tribunal for Rwanda Really Come since Akayesu in the Prosecution and Investigation of Sexual Offences Committed against Women? An Analysis of Ndindiliyimana et al.', *International Criminal Law Review*, XIII/4 (2013)

Turcotte, Heather M., 'Contextualizing Petro-Sexual Politics', *Alternatives: Global, Local, Political*, XXXVI/3 (August 2011)

Ungváry, Krisztián, *The Battle for Budapest: 100 Days in World War II*, trans. Ladislaus Löb (London, 2002)

UN International Criminal Tribunal for the Former Yugoslavia, 'Prosecutor v. Biljana Plavšic: Trial Chamber Sentences the Accused to 11 Years' Imprisonment' (27 February 2003), at www.icty.org, accessed 1 October 2020

'Updates from the International and Internationalized Criminal Tribunals', *Human Rights Brief*, XIX/1 (Fall 2011)

U.S. Department of Justice, National Institute of Corrections, *Sexual Misconduct in Prisons: Law, Agency, Responses, and Prevention* (Longmont, CO, 1999)

U.S. Office of the Secretary of Defense, *Review of the Department of Defense Detention Operations and Detainee Interrogation Techniques (U)* (Washington, DC, 2005)

Van Cleave, Rachel A., 'Renaissance Redux: Chastity and Punishment in Italian Rape Law', *Ohio State Journal of Criminal Law*, VI/1 (2008)

—, 'Sex, Lies, and Honor in Italian Rape Law', *Suffolk University Law Journal*, XXXVIII/2 (2005)

van Diekerk, B.V.D., 'Hanged by the Neck until You Are Dead', *South African Law Journal*, LXXXVII/1 (1970)

van Ijzendoorn, Marinus H., Maartji P. C. Luijk and Femmie Juffer, 'IQ of Children Growing Up in Children's Homes: A Meta-Analysis on IQ Delays in Orphanages', *Merrill-Palmer Quarterly*, LIV/3 (July 2008)

van Tienhoven, Harry, 'Sexual Torture of Male Victims', *Torture: Quarterly Journal on Rehabilitation of Torture Victims and Prevention of Torture*, III/4 (1993)

Vetten, Lisa, and Kailash Bahan, *Violence, Vengeance, and Gender: A Preliminary Investigation into the Links between Violence against Women and HIV/AIDS in South Africa* (Johannesburg, 2001)

'The Victim in a Forcible Rape Case: A Feminist View', *American Criminal Law Review*, 11 (1973)

'Victims Turned Aggressors', *Economic and Political Weekly*, XXXIX/36 (4–10 September 2004)

von Hentig, Hans, 'Interaction of Perpetrator and Victim', *Journal of Criminal Law and Criminal Behavior*, 31 (1940)

von Ragenfeld-Feldman, Norma, 'The Victimization of Women: Rape and Reporting in Bosnia-Herzegovina, 1992–1993', *Dialogue*, 21 (March 1997), at http://members.tripod.com, accessed 31 January 2015

Waitzkin, Howard, and Holly Magaña, 'The Black Box in Somatization: Unexplained Physical Symptoms, Culture, and Narratives of Trauma', *Social Science and Medicine*, XLV/6 (1997)

Walsh, Colleen, 'Me Too Founder Discusses Where We Go from Here', *Harvard Gazette* (21 February 2020), at https://news.harvard.edu, accessed 1 October 2020

'War against Rape (WAR) Pakistan', *Reproductive Health Matters*, IV/7 (May 1996)

Watson-Franke, Maria-Barbara, 'A World in Which Women Move Freely without Fear of Men: An Anthropological Perspective on Rape', *Women's Studies International Forum*, XXV/6 (2002)

Watters, Ethan, *Crazy Like Us: The Globalization of the American Psyche* (New York, 2010)

Wax, Emily, 'Rwandans Are Struggling to Love Children of Hate', *Washington Post* (28 March 2004), at www.genocidewatch.org

Weiss, Karen G., 'Male Sexual Victimization: Examining Men's Experiences of Rape and Sexual Assault', *Men and Masculinity*, XII/3 (April 2010)

Weitsman, Patricia A. 'The Politics of Identity and Sexual Violence: A Review of Bosnia and Rwanda', *Human Rights Quarterly*, XXX/3 (August 2008)

Weld, Theodore Dwight, *American Slavery As It Is: Testimony of a Thousand Witnesses* (New York, 1839)

West, A., ed., *Feminist Nationalism* (New York, 1997)

'The Westmorland Rape Case', *The Times* (29 August 1846)

Wiley, Shelley, 'A Grassroots Religious Response to Domestic Violence in Haiti', *Journal of Religion and Abuse*, V/1 (2003)

Wille, Warren S., 'Case Study of a Rapist', *Journal of Social Therapy and Corrective Psychiatry*, VII/1 (1961)

Williams, Carol J., 'Bosnia's Orphans of Rape: Innocent Legacy of Hatred', *LA Times* (24 July 1993), at http://articles.latimes.com

Williams, Corrine, Laura Ann McCloskey and Ulla Larsen, 'Sexual Violence at First Intercourse against Women in Moshi, Northern Tanzania: Prevalence, Risk Factors, and Consequences', *Population Studies*, 62 (2008)

Williams, Glanville, 'The Problem of Domestic Rape', *New Law Journal*, 141 (22 February 1991)

Wilson, Erin, et al., 'Stigma and HIV Risk among *Metis* in Nepal', *Culture, Health, and Sexuality*, XIII/3 (March 2011)

Wilson, John P., 'Culture, Trauma, and the Treatment of Post-Traumatic Syndromes: A Global Perspective', in *Ethnocultural Perspectives on Disasters and Trauma: Foundations, Issues, and Applications*, ed. Anthony J. Marsella et al. (New York, 2008)

Women in Black, 'Women in Black against War: A Letter to the Women's Meeting in Amsterdam on the 8th of March 1993', *Women Magazine* (December 1993)

Wood, Elisabeth J., 'Armed Groups and Sexual Violence: When Is Wartime Rape Rare?', *Politics and Society*, XXXVII/1 (March 2009)

——, 'Variation in Sexual Violence During War', *Politics and Society*, XXXIV/3 (September 2006)

Woodcock, Shannon, 'Gender as Catalyst for Violence against Roma in Contemporary Italy', *Patterns of Prejudice*, XLIV/5 (2010)

Yaamashita, Yeong-ae, 'Revisiting the "Comfort Women": Moving beyond Nationalism', trans. Malaya Ileto, in *Transforming Japan: How Feminism*

and Diversity Are Making a Difference, ed. Kumiko Fujimura-Fanselow
(New York, 2011)
Yamamoto, Hiroki, 'Socially Engaged Art in Postcolonial Japan: An Alternative
View of Contemporary Japanese Art', *World Art*, XI/1 (2020)
Yang, Hyanah, 'Revisiting the Issue of Korean "Military Comfort Women": The
Question of Truth and Positionality', *positions*, V/1 (1997)
Yap, Pow Meng, '"Koro" – A Culture-Bound Depersonalization Syndrome', *British
Journal of Psychiatry*, 111 (1965)
——, 'Mental Distress Peculiar to Certain Cultures: A Study of Comparative
Psychiatry', *Journal of Mental Science*, 97 (1951)
——, 'Words and Things in Comparative Psychiatry, with Special Reference to the
Exotic Psychoses', *Acta Psychiatrica Scandinavica*, 38 (1962)
Yasmin, Saikia, *Women, War, and the Making of Bangladesh: Remembering 1971*
(Durham, NC, 2011)
Yoo, Boo-wong, *Korean Pentecostalism: Its History and Theology* (New York, 1988)
Yoshiaki, Yoshimi, *Jugan Ianfu* (Tokyo, 1995)
Young, Iris Marion, *Inclusion and Democracy* (Oxford, 2000)
Yuval-Davis, Nira, 'Dialogic Epistemology – An Intersectional Resistance to the
"Oppression Olympics"', *Gender and Society*, XXVI/1 (February 2012)
——, *Gender and Nation* (London, 1997)
——, 'Women, Ethnicity, and Empowerment', in *Shifting Identities, Shifting Racisms:
A Feminist and Psychology Reader*, ed. Kum-Kum Bhavnani and Ann Phoenix
(London, 1994)

Zabeida, Natalja, 'Not Making Excuses: Functions of Rape as a Tool in Ethno-
Nationalist Wars', in *Women, War, and Violence – Personal Perspectives
and Global Activism*, ed. R. M. Chandler, L. Wang and L. K. Fuller
(New York, 2010)
Zaldivar-Giuffredi, Alessandra, 'Simone Gbagbo: First Lady of Cote d'Ivoire, First
Woman Indicted by the International Criminal Court, One among Many
Female Perpetrators of Crimes against Humanity', *ILSA Journal of International
and Comparative Law*, XXV/1 (2018)
Zarkov, Dubravka, 'Gender, Orientalism and the History of Ethnic Hatred in the
Former Yugoslavia', in *Crossfires: Nationalism, Racism and Gender in Europe*, ed.
Helma Lutz, Ann Phoenix and Nira Yuval-Davis (London, 1995)
Zawati, Hilmi M., 'Rethinking Rape Law', *Journal of International Law and
International Relations*, X (2014)
Zeng, Meg Jing, 'From #MeToo to #RiceBunny: How Social Media Users Are
Campaigning in China', *The Conversation* (6 February 2018), at https://
theconversation.com, accessed 1 October 2020
Zongwe, Dunia Prince, 'The New Sexual Violence Legislation in the Congo:
Dressing Indelible Scars on Human Dignity', *African Studies Review*, LV/2
(September 2012)
Zraly, Maggie, and Laetilia Nyirazinyoye, 'Don't Let Suffering Make You Fade Away:
An Ethnographic Study of Resilience among Survivors of Genocide-Rape in
Southern Rwanda', *Social Science and Medicine*, LXX (2010)
Zuspan, Frederick P., 'Alleged Rape: An Invitational Symposium', *Journal of
Reproductive Medicine*, XII/4 (April 1974)

Acknowledgements

Thanks to all the survivors of sexual harms who have shared your stories with me over the past decade. I have learnt so much from you. This book would not have been possible without your insights. *Disgrace* was written over many years, so there are too many people to list. Please know that your help and encouragement have been precious. Special mention must go to The Wellcome Trust, who provided financial, administrative and scholarly support for the SHaME (Sexual Harms and Medical Encounters: shame.bbk.ac.uk) project. As the Principal Investigator/Director of SHaME, I have been fortunate to work alongside some incredible people. Particular thanks must go to Rhea Sookdeosingh, whose imaginative thinking and tireless labour in directing the public engagement aspects of SHaME have transformed the project. The ideas shared by SHaME members and associates have had a major impact on my thinking: I am grateful to Louise Hide, Caitlin Cunningham, Ruth Beecher, Stephanie Wright, Rhian Keyse, George Severs, James Gray, Adeline Moussion, Emma Yapp, Allison McKibban, Charlie Jeffries, Julia Laite, Matt Cook and Marai Larasi. We have collaborated with many organizations dedicated to improving the lives of girls, women and minoritized people. I have enjoyed working with all the people at the WOW Foundation, directed by Jude Kelly. My family and friends in New Zealand, Australia, Switzerland, Britain and Greece have been invaluable in believing in the project and encouraging me. Throughout the journey of writing this book, I have been embedded within a community of colleagues, administrators and students at Birkbeck, University of London. Birkbeck is an inspiring place to work, because of not only its dazzling researchers but the Department of History, Classics and Archaeology's collegiate spirit and incomparable students. James Pullen of The Wylie Agency has supported me over the years. Reaktion Books is an incredible publisher. This book benefited from the enthusiastic labours of Michael Leaman, along with Martha Jay, Alex Ciobanu, Maria Kilcoyne and Fran Roberts. Finally, this book is dedicated to Costas Douzinas, feminist, intellectual, activist and my partner in everything.

Index